FROMMER'S
EasyGuide
TO

SEATTLE, PORTLAND &
THE OREGON COAST

By
Donald Olson

Easy Guides are ✦ Quick To Read ✦ Light To Carry
✦ For Expert Advice ✦ In All Price Ranges

FrommerMedia LLC

Published by
FROMMER MEDIA LLC

ISBN 978-1-62887-120-3 (paper), 978-1-62887-121-0 (e-book)

Editorial Director: Pauline Frommer
Editor: John Vorwald
Production Editor: Erin Geile
Cartographer: Elizabeth Puhl
Cover Design: Howard Grossman

For information on our other products or services, see www.frommers.com.

FrommerMedia LLC also publishes its books in a variety of electronic formats. Some content that appears
in print may not be available in electronic formats.

Manufactured in the United States of America

5 4 3 2 1

CONTENTS

ABOUT THE AUTHOR

Donald Olson is a travel writer, novelist, and playwright. His travel stories have appeared in *The New York Times*, *National Geographic*, and other national publications, and he is the author or of several major travel guides, including *Frommer's EasyGuide to Germany*, *Frommer's Germany Day by Day*, *Germany for Dummies* (aka *Deutschland für Dumköpke*), *Best Day Trips from London*, *England For Dummies*, *Frommer's Vancouver & Victoria*, and *Michelin Pacific Northwest Guide*. His three most recent novels were published under the pen name Swan Adamson. His new book, *Pacific Northwest Garden Tour* (Timber Press), is a full-color travel guide to the 60 best gardens in Oregon, Washington, and British Columbia. Donald lives, writes, and gardens in Manhattan and Portland, Oregon.

ABOUT THE FROMMER'S TRAVEL GUIDES

For most of the past 50 years, Frommer's has been the leading series of travel guides in North America, accounting for as many as 24% of all guidebooks sold. I think I know why.

Though we hope our books are entertaining, we nevertheless deal with travel in a serious fashion. Our guidebooks have never looked on such journeys as a mere recreation, but as a far more important human function, a time of learning and introspection, an essential part of a civilized life. We stress the culture, lifestyle, history, and beliefs of the destinations we cover, and urge our readers to seek out people and new ideas as the chief rewards of travel.

We have never shied from controversy. We have, from the beginning, encouraged our authors to be intensely judgmental, critical—both pro and con—in their comments, and wholly independent. Our only clients are our readers, and we have triggered the ire of countless prominent sorts, from a tourist newspaper we called "practically worthless" (it unsuccessfully sued us) to the many rip-offs we've condemned.

And because we believe that travel should be available to everyone regardless of their incomes, we have always been cost-conscious at every level of expenditure. Though we have broadened our recommendations beyond the budget category, we insist that every lodging we include be sensibly priced. We use every form of media to assist our readers, and are particularly proud of our feisty daily website, the award-winning Frommers.com.

I have high hopes for the future of Frommer's. May these guidebooks, in all the years ahead, continue to reflect the joy of travel and the freedom that travel represents. May they always pursue a cost-conscious path, so that people of all incomes can enjoy the rewards of travel. And may they create, for both the traveler and the persons among whom we travel, a community of friends, where all human beings live in harmony and peace.

Arthur Frommer

THE BEST OF SEATTLE, PORTLAND & THE OREGON COAST

There are a lot of "bests" in the Pacific Northwest. And three of the best of the Pacific Northwest bests are Seattle, Portland, and the Oregon coast. That's why the focus in this guide is on the region's two largest cities and its most spectacular stretch of coastline. The rest of Washington and Oregon are worth exploring too, of course, and you could spend days, weeks, or months doing just that. But Seattle and Portland are the best places to begin any exploration of this fascinating and fast-growing region, and on easy day trips from both cities you can get to an amazingly diverse array of scenic and historic highlights, including giant peaks in the Cascade Range, the Columbia River Gorge, and the Oregon Wine Country. As for the Oregon coast—well, it may leave you speechless, and not just because the wind on one of its towering headlands has sucked your breath away. These 364 miles (586 km) of coastline have a wild and dramatic splendor that is exciting, invigorating, and unforgettable. In the categories below, I've listed some of the highlights—the bests of the bests—to get you revved up and ready for your trip to the Pacific Northwest.

THE best AUTHENTIC EXPERIENCES

Seattle

o **Exploring Pike Place Market:** It's the oldest covered market in the country, and it's certainly one of the busiest, used by Seattle residents and restaurateurs looking for the freshest fish and produce. But the retail range of this world-unto-itself extends way beyond seafood, fruit, and vegetables and includes dozens of restaurants, intriguing shops, and stalls selling artisan products of all kinds. See p. 82.

o **Riding a ferry:** Seattle is one of the few cities where people live on islands and commute to work by ferry. An easy ferry ride to Bainbridge Island or Bremerton gets you out on Puget Sound and gives you a water's-eye view of the city's topography and skyline. See "Getting Around" in chapter 4, p. 52.

o **Strolling the waterfront:** Of course it's touristy—that's part of the fun. Presided over by the Seattle Great Wheel, a giant Ferris wheel, the waterfront is a wonderfully strollable area with fish and chips and fresh oysters along the way; bayside plazas with views of the Olympic Mountains; the Seattle Aquarium; piers for excursion boats and cruise ships; and lots of shops and restaurants. The area around the waterfront is being completely transformed now that the hideous elevated highway beside it is being demolished. See "The Waterfront" under "Neighborhoods in Brief" in chapter 4, p. 50.

o **Taking the Underground Tour:** For one of the most entertaining and authentic city tours you'll ever take, head underground with your witty guide to learn about Seattle's early days before and after the Great Fire and the Yukon Gold Rush, the two events that helped define the city as it is today. The commentary is frank and funny, and the warren of underground tunnels that were once streets is fascinating. See p. 85.

o **Fooling around in Fremont:** Downtown Seattle is exciting and full of attractions, but a stroll through the Fremont neighborhood will give you an up-close-and-personal glimpse of life in one of the funkiest and most interesting neighborhoods in the city, where a giant troll crouches under a bridge and the streets are lined with ethnic restaurants and eclectic shops. See "Fremont" under "Neighborhoods in Brief" in chapter 4, p. 51.

Portland

o **Walking around downtown:** Portland's downtown is compact and complex, with an attractive mixture of buildings, bridges, architectural styles, parks, and plazas that makes it wonderful for walking. From Tom McCall Waterfront Park right along the Willamette to Pioneer Square and the South Park Blocks, this is one of the most attractive, human-scale downtowns you'll ever see. See "Attractions in and Around Downtown Portland" in chapter 5, p. 137.

o **Sipping a latte at Caffe Umbria in the Pearl District.** It's the best latte in Portland, and the most attractive and congenial cafe in the upscale Pearl District. Order your coffee, a panini, a pastry, or a gelato, take a seat, and people watch. **Caffe Umbria** ★★★ is a good rest stop while you're exploring the rest of the Pearl. See p. 135.

o **Browsing through Powell's City of Books:** Even if you're totally committed to reading on your tablet, you shouldn't miss Powell's. One of the world's largest bookstores, Powell's is visited as a tourist attraction as well as by readers who love books and know they will be able to find a new or used copy of just about anything in one of Powell's color-coded rooms. But beware: Once you're inside and start browsing, it's difficult to tear yourself away. See p. 152.

o **Enjoying a microbrew in a brewpub:** Everyone in this metropolis of microbrews has their favorite brew and brewpub. In fact, as you've probably heard, there are more microbreweries in Portland that any other city in the world. Portland's numerous brewpubs are typically casual and super-friendly spots with good food (often but not always on the order of pizza and burgers) where Portlanders of all stripes congregate. See "Brewpubs" in chapter 5, p. 158.

Oregon & Washington

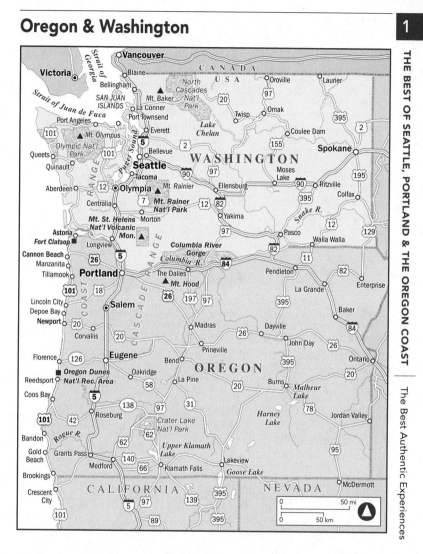

- **Hiking in Forest Park:** Few cities can claim, as Portland can, to have one of the largest urban forests in the world within its city limits. Giant Forest Park covers thousands of acres in Northwest and Southwest Portland and forms part of a wildlife corridor that stretches all the way to the Coast Range. Put on your hiking boots or a pair of comfortable walking shoes and hook up to one of the many trails that criss-cross this vast urban green space. See p. 146.

- **Sniffing the roses at the International Rose Test Garden:** The City of Roses loves its roses, and nowhere else in Portland is a rose more of a rose more of a rose than at the International Rose Test Garden. Visitors are wowed by the fragrant spectacle of tens of thousands of roses in all shapes and colors growing on terraces in beautiful Washington Park. Residents come for a hit of roses from late May through September, but especially during the annual June Rose Festival. See p. 144.

o **Riding the rails:** Take your pick: MAX, the light-rail train, or the Portland Streetcar. Buy a ticket, hop on, and go for a ride—it hardly matters where. Portland is way ahead of the curve when it comes to providing public transportation, and if you are coming from a place where you are a prisoner of your car, what could be more enjoyable than to let someone else do the driving? See "Getting Around" in chapter 5, p. 112.

o **Nosing around North Portland:** The transformation of North Portland over the last decade has been truly astonishing. North Mississippi, North Russell, and North Alberta have all become destination neighborhoods loaded with shops, galleries, and restaurants in neighborhoods (now branded as "districts") that were once off the grid but are now squarely in the center of what's happening in Portland. See "North Portland" under "Neighborhoods" in chapter 5, p. 106.

The Oregon Coast

o **Whale-watching:** Every year, about 18,000 giant gray whales migrate from the Bering Sea to Baja and back again, passing along the Oregon coast. From beaches, viewpoints, and headlands all up and down the coast you can often catch sight of a whale herd spouting its way north or south, and at Depoe Bay you can arrange for a whale-watching excursion to get even closer. See "Whale-Watching" under "Depoe Bay" in chapter 6, p. 209.

o **Walking on Cannon Beach:** On a clear sunny day, it's probably the busiest beach on the coast, but on a weekday or if the weather is gray and wet, you might have it all to yourself. Cannon Beach is one of the great beaches of Oregon, and the town of Cannon Beach, though touristy, is also the most charming. See p. 191.

o **Looping the Three Capes Scenic Loop:** For an eye-opening look at Oregon's dramatic North Coast, take this loop drive between Tillamook and Pacific City. Three spectacular headlands, a lighthouse, hiking trails, and eye-popping views of the thundering surf will wake up your senses. See p. 200.

o **Discovering Newport:** Though it relies on tourism and draws thousands of visitors to the acclaimed Oregon Coast Aquarium, Newport is also one of the most authentic and "real" working towns on the Oregon coast. Walk down the Bayfront and you'll have seafood restaurants on one side and the commercial fish warehouses on the other. And the old Nye Beach neighborhood is a charming throwback to a century ago when Newport became one of Oregon's first beach resort towns. See p. 209.

o **Alighting at Yaquina Bay Lighthouse:** You can (seasonally) visit seven of the nine historic lighthouses along the Oregon coast, but this lighthouse near Newport is perhaps the most easily accessible, and it happens to preside over Yaquina Head, designated an "Outstanding Natural Area." Before heading into the lighthouse, check out the visitor center to learn more about what life was like for the lighthouse keepers who manned these lonely lights and kept them burning through gales and ferocious storms. See p. 215.

o **Exploring the tide pools:** All up and down the Oregon coast, beautiful and amazing creatures cling to rocks near the shore and are nourished by the surging waters of the Pacific. Tentacled sea anemones, sea urchins, and starfish inhabit rocky tide pools that you can visit, including some at Cannon Beach. Whenever there is a good tide pool area, I mention it in the Oregon coast chapter. See chapter 6.

THE best HOTELS

Seattle

- o **The Arctic Club Hotel** (www.thearcticclubseattle.com; © **800/222-8733** or 206/340-0340): A former men's club founded by guys who'd struck it rich either in or because of the Yukon Gold Rush, the Arctic Club celebrates its history by giving its large, big-windowed rooms and public spaces the Art Deco look of the club's heyday. This Doubletree heritage property in the Pioneer Square area has restored the club's down-to-earth comfort and upgraded it to luxury standards. See p. 56.
- o **The Edgewater** (www.edgewaterhotel.com; © **800/624-0670** or 206/728-7000): Built atop a pier on the Seattle waterfront, this boutique hotel is the only hotel in Seattle to have rooms directly on the water. In fact, guests including the Beatles used to fish from their windows. The Edgewater is close to the Olympic Sculpture Park and cruise-ship terminals, and it has a very good restaurant with views across Elliott Bay to the Olympic Mountains. See p. 56.
- o **Executive Hotel Pacific** (www.executivehotels.net; © **888/388-3932** or 206/623-3900): It's not huge or luxurious; it's small and practical, and it has the lowest room rates of any downtown Seattle hotel. The Executive Hotel Pacific was built in the 1920s and has the compact rooms of that era to prove it, but they've all been upgraded to boutique hotel standards. See p. 61.
- o **Four Seasons Hotel** (www.fourseasons.com/seattle; © **206/749-7000**): In a choice spot just a block from Pike Street Market, the Four Seasons gives you big, luxurious rooms with views of Elliott Bay and spa-size bathrooms, plus a state-of-the-art fitness center with a heated, outdoor infinity pool and a spa, and fine dining. You can't help but feel pampered. See p. 57.
- o **Hotel Ändra** (www.hotelandra.com; © **877/448-8600** or 206/448-8600): Its design and furnishings are coolly Scandinavian, and its comfort level is Seattle all the way. Vibrant colors, natural fabrics, and beautiful materials and detailing make this boutique hotel in Belltown a real treat. See p. 59.
- o **Hotel Monaco** (www.monaco-seattle.com; © **800/715-6513** or 206/621-1770): With its lobby murals of leaping dolphins copied from the Palace of Knossos on Crete, its big, Southern-style restaurant, Sazerac, and its playfully eclectic rooms, you might never guess that this downtown Kimpton hotel was created from a former telephone-company office building. Bring your pet, or request a pet goldfish during your stay, and enjoy the complimentary wine tastings held every evening. See p. 59.
- o **Inn at the Market** (www.innatthemarket.com; © **800/446-4484**): For sheer romantic appeal, this cozy boutique hotel can't be beat. Its secretive little courtyard entrance makes it feel hidden from the world, and yet it's directly beside Pike Street Market, one of the busiest spots in Seattle. Some of the rooms have big views out over Elliott Bay to the Olympics. See p. 60.
- o **Inn at Virginia Mason & The Baroness Hotel** (www.innatvirginiamason.com; © **800/283-6453**): Up on First Hill, within easy walking distance of downtown and not far from the Frye Art Museum, the two buildings operated as hotels by Virginia Mason Hospital are heritage gems built as apartment buildings in the 1920s and 1930s. There's a wealth of authentic, unchanged period detail in both of these meticulously cared-for buildings, where you will stay in a former apartment for a fraction of the cost of a downtown hotel. See p. 63.

1 | Portland

o **Ace Hotel** (www.acehotel.com; ℂ **503/228-2277**): It was the second Ace Hotel after Seattle and, like that Ace, it is a creative and quirky re-use of a century-old building, emulating "European-style" hotels—which means that some of the rooms share a bathroom. With a good restaurant on one side and a good coffee bar on the other (and more-than-reasonable prices), this hotel has heritage appeal and captures something of Portland's creative spirit. See p. 120.

o **The Benson** (www.bensonhotel.com; ℂ **800/663-1144** or 503/228-2000): With its crystal chandeliers, walnut paneling, and ornate plasterwork ceiling in the lobby, this 1912 vintage hotel is Portland's most elegant lodging. The rooms are quiet and traditional, and the service is first-rate. See p. 115.

o **Embassy Suites** (www.embassyportland.com; ℂ **800/362-2779** or 503/279-9000): Unlike other Embassy Suites, this is a historic hotel, dating from 1912 with an unbelievably ornate lobby, but it still has those spacious suites that are great for families. Plus, there's a pool, complimentary cocktails at night, and a full hot breakfast in the morning. See p. 121.

o **Hotel deLuxe** (www.hoteldeluxe.com; ℂ **866/895-2094** or 503/219-2094): The deluxe takes its theme from the Golden Age of Hollywood and offers rooms with a pastel color scheme that makes them glow like southern California—even when the weather is in gray—and the fabulous, '50s-era Driftwood Room, where craft cocktails and small plates keep everyone happy. See p. 118.

o **Hotel Lucia** (www.hotellucia.com; ℂ **877/225-1717** or 503/225-1717): This downtown Portland hotel is sleek and stylish and loaded with original art and a fascinating collection of photographs by White House photographer David Hume Kennerly. The rooms are simple without being simplistic, and Imperial restaurant is a Portland haute spot. See p. 118.

o **Hotel Modera** (www.hotelmodera.com; ℂ **877/484-1084** or 503/484-1084): Whoever thought a 1950s-era downtown motor lodge could be turned into such a cool hotel? The makeover made Hotel Modera downtown's most sophisticated place to stay, with an outdoor lounge that draws guests and locals. See p. 119.

o **Inn @ Northrup Station** (www.northrupstation.com; ℂ **800/224-1180** or 503/224-0543): This fun-loving and comfortably cheerful hotel in Northwest Portland sets the tone with bright colors and retro-styling. The rooms are like little self-contained apartments with kitchens (or kitchenettes) and balconies. See p. 122.

o **McMenamins Kennedy School** (www.mcmenamins.com; ℂ **888/249-3983**): Only in Portland, and only because of the historical preservationists and brewmeister McMenamins, would a former elementary school be turned into a destination hotel where you can stay in former classrooms and walk halls that are now alive with restaurants, bars, and even a movie theater in the gym. See p. 123.

o **Portland Mayor's Mansion** (www.pdxmayorsmansion.com; ℂ **503/232-3588**): One of Portland's pre-eminent early-20th-century architects designed this brick mansion that sits right on gorgeous Laurelhurst Park. Now operated as a B&B, the house has most of its original fixtures and is a luxurious and comfortable place to stay with a park right in the backyard. See p. 123.

o **Sentinel** (www.sentinelhotel.com; ℂ **888/246-5631** or 503/224-3400): An ornate Elks Club and a distinctive hotel from the early 1900s were combined to create this new hotel that opened in 2014. On one side, you can book a room with a terrace overlooking downtown; on the other, a room loaded with heritage charm. The fitness area is the best of any downtown hotel, and you're right in the heart of downtown. See p. 120.

The Oregon Coast

This list runs from north to south along the coast.

○ **Cannery Pier Hotel** (Astoria; www.cannerypierhotel.com; ✆ **888/325-4996**): This luxurious hotel, built on the site of a former salmon cannery on the Columbia River, is a sign of Astoria's urban renewal. With big, glass-walled rooms directly on the river and a host of upscale amenities, Cannery Pier is the best catch in Astoria. See p. 184.

○ **The Ocean Lodge** (Cannon Beach; www.cannonbeachhotel.com; ✆ **800/238-4107**): The views are panoramic and the rooms are cozy and designed for contemporary comfort at this mid-sized inn. Step out on your balcony for a breath of fresh sea air, or step outside and you'll be right on one of the most famous beaches in Oregon. See p. 194.

○ **Stephanie Inn** (Cannon Beach; www.stephanie-inn.com; ✆ **800/633-3466**): The most traditional and upscale hotel in artsy, affluent Cannon Beach enjoys a beachfront setting, a fine-dining restaurant, and luxurious rooms with private balconies and oceanfront views. The Stephanie is a romantic, pampering retreat. See p. 195.

○ **Channel House** (Depoe Bay; www.channelhouse.com; ✆ **800/447-2140**): The in-your-face views from the rooms in this small inn—situated on a cliff directly above the ocean and to one side of the narrow channel into tiny Depoe Bay—are probably the most dramatic on the entire coast. You can soak in your outdoor hot tub and enjoy the spectacle. See p. 207.

○ **Sylvia Beach Hotel** (Newport; www.sylviabeachhotel.com; ✆ **888/795-8422**): One of the coast's earliest resort hotels, going way back to the early 1900s, this literary-minded hotel has a unique charm and character. Each room is dedicated to a writer with appropriate accoutrements, and there is a marvelous library upstairs. No phones or TVs, but you do get Wi-Fi. See p. 212.

○ **Heceta Head Lightstation** (near Yachats; www.hecetalighthouse.com; ✆ **866/547-3696**): A former lighthouse keeper's home, with the Heceta Head Lighthouse just down the path, this Victorian-era B&B is set high on a cliff with a truly spectacular outlook. You get breakfast, and maybe you'll even meet the ghost. See p. 217.

○ **Overleaf Lodge** (Yachats; www.overleaflodge.com; ✆ **800/338-0507**): This friendly resort hotel offers some pretty amazing views to go along with the comforts of its freshly refurbed oceanfront rooms. The coastal path right outside lets you enjoy a wonderful walk along a scenic section of the coast. See p. 218.

○ **Tu Tu' Tun Lodge** (Gold Beach; www.tututun.com; ✆ **800/864-6357** or 541/247-6664): A secluded setting on the lower Rogue River guarantees tranquility at this gorgeous-inside-and-out lodge. All the materials are real, and so are the people who greet you. It's the best around, and only 15 minutes from Gold Beach. See p. 233.

THE best RESTAURANTS

Seattle

○ **Poppy** (www.poppyseattle.com; ✆ **206/324-1108**): The fabulous food at Jerry Traunfeld's Capitol Hill restaurant is locally sourced and served Indian style, in multi-plate thalis. The assortment of tastes and textures in one of the daily thalis is exciting and delicious. Once you taste the sweet potato fries, you'll never be the same. See p. 69.

o **Lola** (© **206/441-1430**): The rich smells and savory tastes of Greece and the Mediterranean add up to memorable meals at this Tom Douglas restaurant in Belltown. Lamb is the specialty and what you should have—and maybe a big, fresh Greek salad to go with it. See p. 69.

o **Ray's Boathouse** (www.rays.com; © **206/789-3770**): Upstairs it's a casual bistro, downstairs it's a traditional fine-dining restaurant, and both up and down you will enjoy fresh seafood with eye-stretching views across Elliott Bay. Ray's is an institution in the old Scandinavian neighborhood of Ballard and will give you a taste of what's special about the neighborhood and the food. See p. 66.

o **Salty's on Alki Beach** (www.saltys.com; © **206/937-1600**): Hop in a water taxi and head over to Salty's on Alki Beach for a unique Seattle experience. The restaurant is huge and constantly hopping because of the amazing views looking back toward the Seattle skyline. And the food? That's surprisingly good, too. See p. 73.

o **Serious Pie** (www.tomdouglas.com; © **206/838-7388**): This Belltown pizzeria is seriously the best place to find a handcrafted pizza—but you have to find a seat first. It's not fancy, and the pies are delicious concoctions baked in a wood-fired oven. See p. 74.

o **Shiro's Sushi Restaurant** (www.shiros.com; © **206/441-9844**): Ask any Seattleite where to find the best sushi in town and they'll tell you Shiro's. The sushi and sashimi are so fresh you can taste the sea. See p. 68.

Portland

o **Andina** (www.andinarestaurant.com; © **503/621-9251**): Who knew Peruvian food could be so multifaceted and so loaded with flavor? Peruvians did, of course, and now Portland knows, too. This is a perennially popular scene restaurant at dinner time, so reserve a table and join the happy crowd. See p. 128.

o **Ava Gene's** (www.avagenes.com; © **971/229-0571**): If you want to see what's cooking over on SE Division, one of Portland's hottest new haute spots, pay a visit to this attractive trattoria, and order some food to share family-style with the whole table. Super-fresh local ingredients and sophisticatedly simple Italian cooking techniques make for a memorable meal on all fronts. See p. 131.

o **Grüner** (www.grunerpdx.com; © **503/241-7163**): The food, inspired by Germany and the Alsace, is both unusual and familiar at the same time. House-made charcuterie, sausages, sauerkraut, and spaetzle are elevated to gourmet status. See p. 129.

o **Le Pigeon** (www.lepigeon.com; © **503/546-8796**): Some people aren't entirely comfortable with the shared-table scheme, but most people find it part of the congenial and mouth-watering culinary experience found at this top-ranked Portland bistro. See p. 130.

o **St. Jack** (www.stjackpdx.com; © **503/360-1281**): They left their cozy old digs and moved across the river to a sleek new spot on NW 23rd, and thank goodness they brought their kitchen and cooking techniques with them, because St. Jack offers some of the best French food in Portland. See p. 133.

o **Tasty n Alder** (www.tastyntasty.com; © **503/621-9251**): It's a kind of casual steakhouse, albeit on the nontraditional side, where in addition to grilled meats you can get fresh grilled seafood and dishes that can be shared. See p. 133.

- **Toro Bravo** (www.torobravopdx.com; ✆ **503/281-4464**): Portland has many restaurants that serve small plates, but few that serve Spanish tapas of this superb quality. Every taste here is revelatory, which may account for the long lines. Any wait, however, is worth it. See p. 134.

The Oregon Coast

This list goes from north to south.

- **Clemente's** (Astoria; www.clementesrestaurant.com; ✆ **503/325-1067**): At lunchtime, stop in at this crisply attractive corner restaurant and enjoy a halibut or oyster sandwich, or fish and chips made from freshly caught halibut, salmon, cod, or oysters. Everything served here is locally sourced if possible, and you'll never go wrong with the seafood. See p. 186.

- **Roseanna's Cafe** (Oceanside; www.roseannascafe.com; ✆ **503/842-7351**): You can expect a long wait to get a table here on a summer weekend, but the view of the haystack rocks just offshore makes this place a must-stop stop on the scenic Three Capes Scenic Loop. See p. 202.

- **The Irish Table** (Canon Beach; ✆ **503/436-0708**): It's a small restaurant with a small menu, and it sits on the main road through Cannon Beach so it doesn't have a view, but diners flock to The Irish Table for filling delights like shepherd's pie, lamb chops, and a selection of fresh fish, simply prepared. See p. 196.

- **Newman's at 988** (Cannon Beach; www.newmansat988.com; ✆ **503/436-1151**): The menu is French- and Italian-inspired but relies exclusively on the freshest ingredients of the Pacific Northwest. The cooking is inventive, the dishes are beautifully presented, and there's a good wine list. See p. 196.

- **Stephanie Inn** (Cannon Beach; www.stephanie-inn.com; ✆ **503/436-2221**): The fine-dining restaurant at the Stephanie Inn is a lot more formal than most restaurants on the Oregon coast, but the seasonally changing menu presents diners with the freshest local products, and the cooking is creative without being overbearing. See p. 197.

- **Restaurant Beck** (Depoe Bay; www.restaurantbeck.com; ✆ **503/765-3220**): With windows that look out to Whale Cove, one of the prettiest little coves on the Oregon coast, this stylish, modern restaurant is a foodie's dream come true—highly creative cuisine and a view to match. Sunset dinners are unforgettable. See p. 208.

- **Tidal Raves** (Depoe Bay; ✆ **541/765-2995**): When the surf's up, you can practically forget about getting a table at this oceanfront restaurant. The windows overlook a rugged shoreline known for putting on some of the coast's best displays of crashing waves. See p. 208.

- **Local Ocean** (Newport; www.localocean.net; ✆ **541/574-7959**): The fish couldn't be any fresher—it comes from boats that unload their fresh-caught fish right across the street from this airy Bayfront restaurant. Get whatever is in season and maybe share a small plate or two. See p. 212.

- **Alloro Wine Bar** (Bandon; www.allorowinebar.com; ✆ **541/347-1850**): The ingredients are local, the cooking style is Italian, and the result is an unusually tasty and satisfying meal. Serving both locals and international visitors who've come to Bandon to play at the world-class Bandon Dunes Golf Resort, this little restaurant is surprisingly sophisticated and yet deliciously simple. Come for a glass of vino if not for dinner, and check out the crowd. See p. 228.

- **The Gallery** (Bandon Dunes Golf Resort; www.bandondunesgolf.com; ✆ **888/347-5737**): You don't have to be a golfer or even a guest to enjoy dining on the 18th hole at Bandon Dunes Golf Resort. The resort's fine-dining restaurant is just that—fine dining, with great service, great wine, and great food, all of it sourced locally and prepared with creative simplicity to bring out all the flavors. See p. 228.

THE best NATURAL WONDERS

Seattle

o **Alki Beach:** The closest Seattle comes to a L.A.-style "hang-out" beach, Alki Beach in West Seattle is where the first white settlers set up camp—and packed it up after one wet, miserable winter to move across the bay. Today's Seattleites don't let the weather keep them away from this stretch of rocky, sandy beach with its photo-op views of the Seattle skyline, the ever-popular Salty's on Alki Beach restaurant, and the paved walkway that lets you enjoy it all. You can reach Alki Beach by water taxi from Pier 55. See p. 52.

o **Elliott Bay:** If you're in Seattle, you're going to see Elliott Bay no matter what, because it forms the scenic backdrop to the entire downtown and west side of the city. Part of Puget Sound, a huge island-studded inlet of the Pacific Ocean, Elliott Bay provides a waterway from Seattle to the ocean and is one of the busiest ports in the U.S. You'll see ferries, sailboats, fishing trawlers, cruise ships, excursion boats, and pleasure craft of all kinds plying its waters. Taking a ferry over the Bainbridge Island is one of the easiest ways to get out on the bay yourself. See p. 52.

o **Lake Washington:** The main part of central Seattle is wedged between saltwater Elliott Bay to the west and freshwater Lake Washington to the east. The two are connected by the Lake Washington Ship Canal and the Hiram M. Chittenden Locks, a series of historic locks that provide a passing parade of boat traffic. Lake Washington is a major recreational area for Seattle, and its shoreline is dotted with lovely old parks and beaches. For details on the Hiram M. Chittenden Locks, see p. 78.

o **Mount Rainier National Park:** With its glaciers and easily accessible alpine meadows, Mount Rainier is Washington's favorite mountain. Sunrise and Paradise are the two best vantage points for viewing the massive bulk of Mount Rainier, and in these two areas of the park, you'll also find some of the best hiking trails. See "Mount Rainier National Park & Environs" under "Day Trips from Seattle," p. 100.

Portland

o **Columbia Gorge National Scenic Area:** Carved by ice-age floodwaters, the Columbia Gorge is a unique feature of the Oregon landscape and begins just a few miles east of Portland. The Historic Columbia Gorge Highway winds past waterfalls cascading down the basalt cliffs of the gorge, passes memorable viewpoints, and ends near Multnomah Falls, one of the tallest waterfalls in the country. See p. 172.

o **Mount Hood:** As Oregon's tallest mountain and the closest Cascade peak to Portland, Mount Hood is a recreational paradise 12 months a year. Hiking trails, alpine lakes, free-flowing rivers, and year-round skiing make this one of the most appealing natural attractions in the state. See p. 169.

The Oregon Coast

o **The Columbia River at Astoria:** The mighty Columbia is the second-longest river in the U.S. and the one most associated with Pacific Northwest history, since Lewis and Clark rafted down it to reach the Pacific in 1805. The river's mouth, near present-day Astoria, is some 14 miles wide, and its treacherous bar has been dubbed the "Graveyard of the Pacific." At Astoria, it's the Columbia that rules the waves. Take the Riverwalk along the old waterfront to get a feel for this legendary river, spanned by the giant Astoria-Megler Bridge. See "Astoria" in chapter 6, p. 183.

o **Three Capes Scenic Loop:** Really, the entire Oregon coast counts as a "best natural attraction," but for a dramatic introduction to the scenic splendors of the North Coast, this drive between Tillamook and Pacific City can't be beat. Giant headlands, sandy beaches, windswept vistas, dense forest, even a lighthouse—you'll see it all on this memorable drive. See p. 200.

o **Oregon Dunes National Recreation Area:** Towering sand dunes stretch for some 50 miles along the coast between Florence and Coos Bay, forming the Oregon Dunes National Recreation Area. This sand-seared area contains lakes where you can boat and swim and trails for hiking, horseback riding, and off-road vehicles. See p. 222.

o **Rogue River at Gold Beach:** Oregon's South Coast is called the Wild Rivers Coast because six free-flowing rivers hurtle down from the coastal mountain ranges to empty into the Pacific. None is more fabled and famous than the Rogue River, which pours into the ocean at Gold Beach. Zane Grey was one of the earliest to write about the salmon fishing on this river, and it has since become a mecca for white-water rafting trips and jet boats that roar up the Rogue from Gold Beach, as far as the wild and scenic section where the rapids begin. See p. 232.

THE best MUSEUMS & HISTORIC SITES

Seattle

o **Chihuly Garden and Glass:** Tacoma-born Dale Chihuly is perhaps the best-known glass artist in the world, and this exciting museum, which opened in 2012 beside the Space Needle, presents an outstanding retrospective of his work, from early pieces inspired by Indian baskets and pottery to the writhing, fluorescent colors of his famous chandeliers and marine environments. In the garden, pieces stand like giant glass flowers and plants. The virtuosity and vibrancy of the work will amaze you. See p. 76.

o **Seattle Art Museum (SAM):** Considered the best art museum north of San Francisco, SAM is particularly noteworthy for its outstanding collection of Northwest Native American art and artifacts. Another fascinating gallery is devoted to the history of Pacific Northwest painting, crafts, and sculpture. In addition, the museum has some intriguing contemporary pieces and often hosts major traveling exhibits. See p. 84.

o **Museum of History and Industry (MOHAI):** Newly relocated in 2013 to the former Naval Reserve building on Lake Union, MOHAI is a must for anyone interested in the story of Seattle and how it grew. The exhibits here are fun and fascinating, and they span the city's history from the Great Fire and Yukon Gold Rush to the founding of Microsoft, plus everything in between. Historic photographs and artifacts provide vivid glimpses into the city's boom-or-bust past. See p. 80.

o **Museum of Flight:** Seattle's aircraft industry began in 1916 and has grown over the years to become one of the largest in the world. The Museum of Flight at Boeing Field is dedicated to airplanes and spacecraft, from early biplanes to satellites and space stations launched by Russia and NASA. One giant wing displays an amazing collection of historic aircraft, and out on the field you can walk through a Concorde (remember sonic booms?) and the first Air Force One. Along the way, there are lots of hands-on exhibits and information about the rise and development of the aircraft industry in Seattle. See p. 80.

o **Olympic Sculpture Park:** An outstanding collection of outdoor sculpture has been assembled in this park at the north end of the waterfront overlooking Elliott Bay. Monumental pieces by Richard Serra, Alexander Calder, and Claes Oldenburg are interspersed with sculptures by lesser-known artists. Admission is free to this off-shoot of the Seattle Art Museum, and there's a pavilion where you can sit with a coffee or a glass of wine and enjoy the view. See p. 82.

Portland

o **Pittock Mansion:** Completed in 1914, this enormous French Renaissance Revival chateau, built for the owner of *The Oregonian* newspaper, occupies the highest point in Northwest Portland. Wander through rooms paneled with rare woods and sheathed in rare marbles, and enjoy the panoramic view of Portland from the gardens. See p. 147.

o **Portland Art Museum:** The collection of Native American art and artifacts is reason enough to visit Portland's art museum. It has a small collection of French Impressionists and galleries of contemporary Northwest art, and it hosts interesting but smaller-scale traveling shows. See p. 142.

The Oregon Coast

o **Columbia River Maritime Museum** (Astoria): The mighty Columbia River empties into the Pacific at Astoria, site of the oldest settlement west of the Mississippi. The collection of heritage boats, from Coast Guard rescue ships to fishing trawlers, and a docked light station that you can visit, highlight the many ways that the Columbia has been integral to Astoria's history. Nautical artifacts and memorabilia are scattered throughout this compact, well-designed museum, including rare maps, cannons washed up from shipwrecks, and exhibits explaining Astoria's once-thriving salmon canning industry. See p. 188.

o **Flavel House** (Astoria): Built in the 1880s for a wealthy sea captain, Flavel House is the grandest and most historic house in Astoria. On a self-guided tour, you can wander through the enormous rooms, furnished with original and period furniture, and see how the other half lived way back when. See p. 188.

o **Fort Clatsop–Lewis & Clark National Historic Park** (near Astoria): Of all the early explorers, Meriwether Lewis and William Clark are most ingrained in the consciousness of Pacific Northwesterners. On orders from President Thomas Jefferson, these two intrepid adventurers assembled the Corps of Discovery and traveled from St. Louis to the Pacific Ocean, traversing half the continent and going where no whites had ever gone before. When they reached the Pacific in 1805, they built a fort like the replica seen at this national historic park and spent a cold, wet winter there before heading back to civilization. See p. 190.

- **Yaquina Bay Lighthouse** (Newport): There are two lighthouses in Newport, but this one is in the town itself, and it happens to be the oldest lighthouse on the Oregon coast, dating from 1871. Even more unusual, it is built of wood and looks more like a house than a lighthouse. Now part of Yaquina Bay State Recreation Site, the lighthouse is open as a museum so you can go inside to visit the lighthouse keepers' quarters and gaze out over the same coast they kept watch over some 140 years ago. See p. 215.

THE best GARDENS

Seattle

- **Washington Park Arboretum:** One of the Northwest's great arboretums, this living museum was established in the 1930s and is planted with an extraordinary variety of specimen trees from the Pacific Northwest and around the world. In the springtime, Azalea Way—planted with thousands of azaleas and other flowering trees, plants, and shrubs—is an unforgettable sight. See p. 86.
- **Seattle Japanese Garden:** A traditional "strolling pond garden" designed around a lake in the Washington Park Arboretum, the Seattle Japanese Garden was one of the first Japanese gardens to be created in the U.S., and with its meticulous plantings, rocks, and stone lanterns, it is a highlight for any garden lover visiting Seattle. See p. 84.

Portland

- **International Rose Test Gardens:** You can't help but stop to sniff the roses at this enormous and enormously popular rose garden in Portland's Washington Park. Thousands of roses romance the eye and nose, blooming in fragrant profusion from late May into September. See p. 144.
- **Lan Su Chinese Garden:** The newest and most unusual (to Western eyes) of Portland's three major gardens, Lan Su was designed and constructed in Portland's Chinatown by a team from Suzhou, China, who created a classical Chinese scholar's garden of a type that was popular during the Ming dynasty. Winding paths with intricate stonework lead to ornate pavilions and colonnades around a lake, with sculpted rocks and carefully chosen plants to add even more interest along the way. See p. 140.
- **Portland Japanese Garden:** Situated in the hills above the rose gardens in Washington Park, the Portland Japanese Garden is considered the most authentic Japanese garden outside of Japan. With five different garden types based on Buddhist, Shinto, Taoist, and Zen principles, this exquisitely designed and maintained garden should be high on the list of anyone who loves gardens, no matter what time of year. See p. 145.

The Oregon Coast

- **Shore Acres State Park** (Charleston): It's rare to find roses blooming along the Oregon coast, but they are the summer stars at this formal garden, created decades ago on a bluff overlooking the Pacific. Once you've marveled at the flowers and strolled around the sunken lily pond, you can take a short walk down to a gorgeous little cove with a sandy beach. See p. 225.

THE best FAMILY ATTRACTIONS

Seattle

o **Argosy Cruises:** Head down to Pier 55 on the waterfront to catch one of the excursion cruises offered by this long-established tour-boat company. You can choose from a tour of Elliott Bay, a locks cruise over to lake Washington, or a trip to Tillicum Village, where Native American hosts put on a salmon bake and perform tradition dances. See p. 77.

o **Museum of Flight:** A fascinating collection of airplanes and spacecraft are on display in this enormous museum at Boeing Field, and you can walk through a Concorde, tour the first Air Force One, and steer a spaceship in one of the many interactive exhibits that appeal to kids. See p. 80.

o **Seattle Aquarium:** Seattle and western Washington are defined as much by their waters as by their land, so this aquarium on the Seattle waterfront is a great place to familiarize yourself with the sea life of the region. Get up close to giant Pacific octopuses, gently touch a sea anemone, watch the fish of Puget Sound in giant tanks, and enjoy the sea otters and harbor seals out on the pier. See p. 83.

o **Seattle Center:** Take the vintage monorail from downtown to the site of the 1962 World's Fair, where you can zoom up to the top of the Space Needle for an outstanding view of the entire city, then explore the interactive Pacific Science Center with its animatronic dinosaurs. See individual listings in chapter 4.

o **Seattle Great Wheel:** Up, up, and around. Opened on the waterfront in 2013, the Seattle Great Wheel is the largest Ferris wheel on the West Coast and takes you up in enclosed, non-shaky compartments for breathtaking views of Elliott Bay, the Olympic Mountains, and the Seattle skyline. See p. 84.

Portland

o **Oregon Museum of Science and Industry (OMSI):** With an OMNIMAX theater, a planetarium, a submarine, and loads of hands-on exhibits, this Portland museum is fun for kids and adults alike. See p. 148.

o **Oregon Zoo:** The state's top tourist attraction has elephants, apes, naked mole rats, bats, wolves, and hundreds of other animals in natural-looking habitats and enclosures. The zoo is a large one, and it can easily take up to 3 or 4 hours to see it all. See p. 145.

o **Washington Park:** There are two world-class gardens for you (and maybe the kids will enjoy them too), but there's also a big kids' playground, a miniature train that runs to the Oregon Zoo, and the World Forestry Discovery Museum—plus lots of walks and trails through this beautiful park near downtown Portland. See p. 142.

The Oregon Coast

o **Oregon Coast Aquarium** (Newport): This is the biggest attraction on the Oregon coast, and justly so. Tufted puffins and sea otters are always entertaining, while tide pools, jellyfish tanks, sharks, and a giant octopus also contribute to the appeal of this well-designed public aquarium. See p. 214.

o **Sea Lion Caves** (north of Florence): This massive cave, the largest sea cave in the country, is home to hundreds of Steller sea lions that lounge on the rocks beneath busy U.S. 101. An elevator takes you down to a viewing window where you can see the sea lions in their protected natural habitat. See p. 220.

o **Walking on an ocean beach:** It doesn't matter where or which one—all the beaches along the Oregon coast are free and open to the public (though you may have to pay a day-use fee at state parks), and most of them are flat and sandy. Just pick one wherever you are and go out for a walk beside the thundering surf. It's one of the best ways for an entire family to enjoy the natural spectacle of the Oregon coast. Explore tide pools, collect sand dollars, watch the sea birds and maybe the sea lions, and feel the giant power of the Pacific as it comes crashing onto the shore and offshore rocks. The coast's best beaches are described throughout chapter 6.

o **Whale-watching excursion** (Depoe Bay): There is nothing more exciting than catching sight of one of the giant gray whales that migrate up and down the Oregon coast. There are whale-watching viewpoints all up and down the coast, but Tradewind Charters in Depoe Bay offers excursions out into the open waters to get a closer look. Have your sea legs about you, because the waters can be choppy and the swells can, well, get to you. See "Whale-Watching" in the Depoe Bay section of chapter 6, p. 209.

SUGGESTED ITINERARIES

Are you going just to Seattle, or just to Portland, or just to the Oregon coast—or are you going to a combination or all of them? The Pacific Northwest covers a lot of ground and encompasses extremely varied terrain, yet it has a regional cohesion—at least, west of the Cascade Range it does. Seattleites love to weekend in Portland, and Portlanders love to weekend in Seattle. And everyone loves the Oregon coast. In addition, on day trips from both Seattle and Portland you can visit mountain peaks, volcanoes, river gorges, wine country, and the coast, too. It all depends on how much time you have and what you want to see. I've put together some suggested itineraries in this chapter to give you a few ideas of how you might want to allocate your time. I have provided you with all-Seattle, all-Portland, and all-Oregon coast itineraries, in case you want to concentrate on just one city or just the coast. But I have also created some overlapping itineraries that take in both Seattle and Portland, and a couple that include both cities and the coast as well. And finally, I've set up a 1-week itinerary for families visiting the region.

THE BEST OF SEATTLE IN 3 DAYS

This 3-day itinerary is perfect for those who want to spend a long weekend in Seattle. If you have more time, I've expanded it to 5 days so you can enjoy a couple of day trips and see the city and region in more depth.

Day 1

Spend your first day in Seattle getting a feel for the lay of the land and the spread of the sea. Start your exploration in the morning at **Pike Place Market ★★★** (p. 82), the oldest covered market in the country and the pulse of downtown Seattle. This is a "follow your nose" sort of place, and you can easily lose track of time as you browse the fish and produce stalls and explore the shops in the Down Under section. The market is a great place to stop for a cup of coffee or to have lunch at one of the many bistros and restaurants. From the market, head down to the Seattle **Waterfront** (p. 50). If you time it right, you can take a tour of Elliott Bay on an excursion boat operated by **Argosy Cruises** (p. 77) at Pier 55. Alternatively, or in addition to a cruise, stroll along the busy Waterfront, enjoying the piers, the people, and the various attractions, both tacky and tasteful. End your first day with a big dose of art at the **Olympic Sculpture Park ★★★** (p. 82) at the north end of the Waterfront, where you can gaze out over Elliott Bay while enjoying giant outdoor sculptures by a roster of renowned artists. You might want to choose a restaurant on or near the Waterfront for dinner. **Café Campagne ★★** (p. 71) is a good choice.

Day 2

Day 2 is your downtown and Seattle Center day. Start your morning with coffee and a baked treat at **Caffe Ladro Espresso Bar & Bakery ★★** (p. 74) or at the very first **Starbucks ★** (p. 75), down at Pike Place Market. When you're fueled, head over to the **Seattle Art Museum ★★★** (p. 84), the city's best place for viewing Pacific Northwest Native American art and contemporary international art; the museum also hosts traveling exhibitions. It's easy to dart back over to Pike Place Market (by now you understand its endless allure) for lunch, maybe a quick bowl of chowder at one of the market's hole-in-the-wall restaurants, or, for something a little fancier but still casual, **Purple Café and Wine Bar ★★** (p. 73). After lunch, head up to Westlake Center **★★** and catch the vintage 1962 **monorail** (p. 52) for the quick ride to **Seattle Center,** site of the 1962 World's Fair and still a major Seattle destination. You can take your pick of attractions at Seattle Center. Zoom up to the top of the **Space Needle ★★** (p. 85) for a 360° view of the city, and then visit **Chihuly Garden and Glass ★★★** (p. 76), right below the Space Needle, or the (to me, vastly overrated) **Experience Music Project.** Take the monorail back downtown for some afternoon retail. For dinner, choose a restaurant in one of Seattle's neighborhoods—**Poppy ★★★** (p. 69) on Capitol Hill is a good choice.

Day 3

You've seen the Waterfront and Seattle Center, now head back in time and have a look at the oldest part of Seattle, in and around the Pioneer Square neighborhood. Start with a coffee at **Caffe Umbria ★★★** (p. 75) or **Zeitgeist Coffee ★★** (p. 75). Then take the wonderfully entertaining **Underground Tour ★★★** (p. 85), where you'll wander through tunnels that were once streets and hear anecdotes about life in early Seattle. Afterward, explore the old streets around Pioneer Square. The Klondike Gold Rush National Historical Park will give you insight into one of the seminal events in Seattle's history. Then head over to the nearby **Chinatown/International District** for dim sum at **Jade Garden ★** (p. 76) and a look around the neighborhood, maybe visiting the **Wing Luke Asian Museum ★** (p. 87) or arranging for a walking tour. On your last evening in Seattle, have dinner at one of Seattle's many fine restaurants, perhaps **Lola ★★★** (p. 69) in Belltown or **Ray's Boathouse ★★★** (p. 66) in Ballard.

SEATTLE IN 5 DAYS

Day 4

Follow the itinerary above for your first 3 days in Seattle. On day 4, head down to Pier 52 and take a ferry over to Winslow on **Bainbridge Island.** There is regular ferry service throughout the day. The ferry ride will give you photo-op views of the Seattle skyline and is a fun way to get a feel for a very different sort of commuter experience. You can take your car on the ferry—a good idea if you want to explore a bit of Bainbridge Island—or you can walk on as a passenger. Either way, spend a little time exploring Winslow, and then drive or take the bus to **Bloedel Reserve ★★★** (p. 88), one of the great gardens of the Pacific Northwest. You can have a meal in Winslow before heading back to Seattle, but you will be back in plenty of time to arrange for dinner at a Seattle restaurant of your choice.

Day 5

You've seen the Waterfront, downtown, Pioneer Square, taken a ferry to Bainbridge Island—now it's time to visit a mountain. Mount Rainier, to be exact. This is a full-day day trip, so you'll need to get an early start. You will need a car or will have to arrange an escorted tour. There are many ways to explore **Mount Rainier National Park ★★★** (p. 100). You may want to do some hiking at Paradise or on one of the many easy trails. To see some enormous old-growth cedars, take the short **Patriarchs Trail ★★★**. Have a casual lunch or afternoon refreshments at the **National Park Inn ★** or **Paradise Inn ★★**, atmospheric alpine lodges, before heading back to Seattle.

PORTLAND IN 3 DAYS

You can see a lot of Portland in 3 days, which is what many Seattleites do when they come down for a long weekend. All the major city attractions are covered in this 3-day itinerary. If you have more time to spend in Portland, I've expanded the itinerary to 5 days so you can get out and see more of this wonderfully scenic region.

Day 1

Spend your first day in Portland getting oriented and discovering the downtown area. With its compact blocks and interesting mix of buildings, architectural styles, and parks, downtown Portland is easy to walk and a pleasure to explore. Start right in the heart of downtown at **Pioneer Courthouse Square ★★★** (p. 141), referred to as "Portland's living room." A big Starbucks on the southwest corner of the square has outdoor tables where you can sit in nice weather looking out over the waterfall fountain. This is downtown shopping central, with a Macy's on one side and a Nordstrom on the other and most of downtown's major malls and stores within a four-block radius. Head up to the **South Park Blocks** (p. 109) and have a look around the **Portland Art Museum ★** (p. 142), especially its Native American collection. Then walk south to have a look at the waterfall-like **Ira Keller Fountain ★** (p. 137). From there, head down Salmon Street to **Tom McCall Waterfront Park ★★★** (p. 142), where you can stroll along the esplanade with Portland's skyline on one side and the river with its historic bridges on the other. **Jake's Famous Crawfish ★★** (p. 130), Portland's oldest restaurant, is an atmospheric choice for happy hour or dinner.

Day 2

There are any number of downtown coffee bars where you can fuel up for today's activities. Head first to the **Oregon Historical Society Museum ★★** (p. 141) on the South Park Blocks, across from the Portland Art Museum, to get a sense of Oregon's and Portland's pioneer and more recent history. Then how about lunch at one of Portland's famous **food carts** (p. 136)? They are found at various locales around downtown and throughout the city. Now it's time to smell the roses. Take MAX (the light-rail), drive, or walk (it's about a half-hour steady walk from downtown) to **Washington Park** ★★★ (p. 142) in the southwest hills. Make your first stop the **International Rose Test Garden** ★★★ (p. 144), a dazzling display of tens of thousands of roses on a hillside overlooking downtown and Mount Hood. After you've sniffed and snapped (with a camera) your fill, head up to the **Portland Japanese Garden** ★★★ (p. 145), on the hillside directly above the rose gardens. This superlative garden will introduce you to an ancient and entirely different gardening style. There really aren't any places to eat right in the park, so make your way back downtown to enjoy happy hour at any one of Portland's restaurants, or a dinner at someplace casual but still special, like **Grüner** ★★ (p. 129) or **Tasty n Alder** ★★ (p. 133). And it's never too late to browse and shop at **Powell's City of Books** ★★★ (p. 152), which is open late every night of the week.

Day 3

It's time to explore a Portland neighborhood or two. How about starting the day at **Caffe Umbria** ★★★ (p. 135), the nicest coffee bar in the Pearl District. Afterward, explore the Pearl, stopping in galleries like **Bullseye Gallery** ★★★ (p. 152), just a block away, and heading west toward **Jamison Park,** named for William Jamison, a Portland gallery owner who had one of the first galleries in what is now the Pearl. The Pearl is a good spot to have lunch, too. There are microbreweries like **Deschutes Brewing** ★ (p. 159) where you can get a good lunch—and sit outside, if the weather's nice, all the better to people- and Pearl-watch. After strolling through the Pearl, catch the **Portland Streetcar**—or walk, it's only 15 minutes away by foot—to NW **23rd Avenue** and the **Nob Hill** neighborhood (see "Neighborhoods" in chapter 5, p. 106). NW 23rd between E Burnside and Thurman Street is one long promenade of boutiques, lifestyle stores, restaurants, and coffee shops. Wander into the streets west of NW 23rd, and you'll discover the fine old Portland Nob Hill neighborhood filled with attractive Victorian homes. **St. Honoré Boulangerie** ★★★ (p. 136) on Thurman Street is a great spot for afternoon coffee and a French pastry. Hop on the streetcar to return to downtown Portland, where you can catch MAX, the light-rail line, right over to **Lloyd Center** ★★ (p. 154) in Northeast Portland for some retail mall action, or head up into one of the hot new neighborhoods in **North Portland** (see "Neighborhoods" in chapter 5, p. 106). This would be a good area to find a restaurant and have dinner in one of Portland's newer, happening neighborhoods.

PORTLAND IN 5 DAYS

Day 4

Follow the suggestions for days 1 to 3 above, and then rent a car for your final 2 days in Portland. On day 4, have breakfast downtown at **Bijou Café** ★ (p. 134) before heading out of town on I-84. The spectacular **Columbia Gorge** ★★★ (p. 172) begins just a few miles east of downtown. For the most scenic drive, take the **Columbia Gorge Historic Highway**—we just call it "the Old Gorge Highway"—the first scenic road to be built in Oregon back in the 1920s, with bridges and walls constructed by Italian stonemasons. The old highway takes you up to Crown Point (p. 174), where the breathtaking view up and down the gorge extends for over 30 miles. Continue on the old highway and you will pass a handful of sparkling, rushing waterfalls until you come finally to the tallest and most dramatic waterfall of all—**Multnomah Falls ★★★** (p. 174). At this point you can jog back to I-84, the faster and newer highway that runs closer to the river. At this juncture you have several options. You can continue down I-84 to **Hood River** (p. 176), the windsurfing capital of the country, or you can head south and continue your expedition and continue up and over **Mount Hood ★★★** (p. 169). **Timberline Lodge ★★★** (p. 170) is one of the greatest alpine lodges ever built; inside and out it is a rugged yet sophisticated creation of the Works Progress Administration under Franklin D. Roosevelt in the 1930s. FDR came out for the opening. You can dinner at the lodge, or return to Portland, about 1½ hours away.

Day 5

Oregon is famous for the quality of its wines, particularly pinot noirs. You may have never tasted an Oregon wine, because it is produced in fairly small quantities that are snapped up locally by restaurants and Portland pinot-lovers. Vineyards are scattered throughout the western part of the state—west of the Cascades, that is—but the ones closest to Portland are in the North Willamette Valley. Have a look in chapter 5 at the day trip called **"The Wine Country"** (p. 163), and head into the rolling hills of the valley to visit and taste wine at some of the outstanding vineyards there. The vineyards in Oregon aren't, and hopefully never will be, the kind of big business operations found in Napa Valley, but on summer weekends especially, the wine country is hopping with wine-lovers. And you can reach it in about an hour or less.

SEATTLE & PORTLAND IN 1 WEEK

This itinerary is intended for urban explorers who plan to spend the majority of their time in Seattle and Portland. For this itinerary, you will need to plan out how you want to get from Seattle to Portland, or vice versa. You can make the 178-mile (286 km) trip easily by **car** in about 3 hours, depending on traffic (with an accident on the highway or slow-moving traffic, the trip can take up to 4 hr.). **Amtrak** has regular service between the two cities throughout the day, and **Bolt Bus** is a new, inexpensive bus service between the two cities; expect to spend about 3½ hours on either train or bus. There are also flights from **Sea-Tac International Airport** (p. 48) to **Portland International Airport** (p. 107) throughout the day, generally on smaller commuter aircraft; by air, the trip takes about 40 minutes. You will find information on all of these transportation options discussed in the "Getting There" sections in chapter 5 and chapter 6. If you don't want to backtrack to Seattle at the end of your Portland visit, see if you can fly into Seattle and out of Portland. There is often no great price difference in booking your flight itinerary this way.

Days 1–2: Seattle

To get a good dose of Seattle, follow the suggestions for days 1 and 2 in "The Best of Seattle in 3 Days," p. 16.

Day 3: Seattle/Day trip to LaConner & Skagit Valley

If it's tulip season, you definitely don't want to miss seeing the tulips fields in the Skagit Valley in and around the town of LaConner, 70 miles (113 km) north of Seattle. And if it's not tulip time, you'll enjoy exploring the charming town of LaConner and visiting its surprisingly good art museum devoted to the "Big Four" Northwest artists of the 1950s and '60s. You'll need a car for this trip, but it's an easy shot up I-5. The Skagit Valley is the prime tulip-growing area in the U.S., and the vast, colorful tulip fields rival and perhaps surpass those in Holland. Have lunch in LaConner and stroll its lovely old streets. You can easily be back in Seattle in time for a farewell dinner.

Days 4–5: Portland

For suggestions on how to spend your first 2 days in Portland, see "Day 1" and "Day 2" under "Portland in 3 Days," above.

Day 6: Portland/Columbia Gorge

Spend your last day in Portland by taking a day trip down the **Columbia Gorge** (p. 172), as outlined in "Day 4" under "Portland in 5 Days," above. I would suggest that you make this a full-day trip by going on from Multnomah Falls to Timberline Lodge on Mt. Hood. Doing this, you will be getting a grand look at the grandest scenery near Portland.

SEATTLE, PORTLAND & THE OREGON COAST IN 1 WEEK

Here's a suggested itinerary that gives you a couple of exciting days in Seattle and Portland and then continues on from Portland to take in some of the scenic grandeur of Oregon's North Coast. As with the "Seattle & Portland in 1 Week" itinerary above, you will need to plan out how you want to get from Seattle to Portland—by car, train, bus, or airplane—but once in Portland you will need to rent or use your own car for the Oregon coast part of this 1-week itinerary.

Days 1–2: Seattle

To get a good dose of Seattle, follow the suggestions in days 1 and 2 in "The Best of Seattle in 3 Days," p. 16.

Days 3–4: Portland

On day 3, if you're driving the 178 miles (286 km) down to Portland, head out of Seattle as early as you can to escape the morning rush hour. However you travel, you probably won't be settled in Portland until late morning or early afternoon. Spend your first afternoon in the City of Roses at the two magnificent gardens in Washington Park (p. 142), the **International Rose Test Garden ★★★** (p. 144) and the **Portland Japanese Garden ★★★** (p. 145). Afterward, depending on what you are in the mood for, you might want to have dinner at **St. Jack ★★** (French; p. 133), or **Bamboo Sushi ★★** (Japanese, sushi/sashimi; p. 134) on NW 23rd Avenue, or at **Caffe Mingo ★★** (Italian; p. 131) on NW 21st Avenue. All three restaurants are just minutes from Washington Park. From any of them you can easily get back downtown via the Portland streetcar.

On day 4, explore downtown Portland, visiting **Pioneer Courthouse Square** ★★★ (p. 141), the **South Park Blocks** (p. 109), and the Portland Art Museum ★ (p. 142) or the Oregon Historical Society Museum ★★ (p. 141). Have lunch at one of Portland's trend-setting food carts (p. 136) and then continue your downtown urban adventuring by strolling through **Chapman and Lownsdale squares** ★★ (p. 137) and **Tom McCall Waterfront Park** ★★★ (p. 142). Have dinner and a craft beer at one of Portland's many microbreweries (p. 158)—this is the microbrewery capital of the country, after all.

Day 5: Astoria/Cannon Beach

As mentioned above, you will need a car for the final 3 days of your whirlwind Pacific Northwest tour. Today you'll head west to the Pacific Ocean, but first you'll be able to marvel at the huge size of the Columbia River that empties into the ocean at **Astoria** ★★ (p. 183). The trip to Astoria, depending on your route, will take 1½ to 2 hours. Here, at the site of the oldest settlement west of the Mississippi, you can spend an enjoyable and enlightening hour visiting the compact and well-done **Columbia River Maritime Museum** ★★ (p. 188), which outlines the human history of the mighty Columbia with exhibits, artifacts, and heritage boats. Nearby, and also worth a few minutes of your time, is the **Flavel House** ★★ (p. 188), an ornate brick mansion built for a sea captain in the 1880s. Astoria is undergoing something of a renaissance just now and has several good restaurants where you can have lunch.

Save another hour to visit **Fort Clatsop—Lewis and Clark National Historic Park** ★★★ (p. 190), 5 miles (8 km) south of Astoria. Here, in a clearing in the woods, on a site thought to be just yards from the original fort, stands a replica of Fort Clatsop, the wooden fort built by Lewis and Clark and the Corps of Discovery when they finally reached the Pacific Ocean in 1805 after trekking for 18 months across a wilderness unknown to whites.

You'll get some wonderful ocean/beach time when you reach **Cannon Beach** ★★★ (p. 191), about 22 miles (35 km) south of Fort Clatsop on U.S. 101. Make this your overnight stop. With towering Haystack Rock jutting up from the shore, this flat, sandy beach is one of the best along the entire coast for long beach walks (no matter what the weather). The town is the most charming and affluent on the Oregon coast and offers lots of shopping and a handful of restaurants that are among the top dining spots anywhere along the coast. If you have time before the light fades, pay a visit to gorgeous **Ecola State Park** ★★★ (p. 198) at the north end of town, with miles of beach and forested hiking trails with panoramic ocean views.

Day 6: Three Capes Scenic Loop/Depoe Bay/Newport

Continuing south from Cannon Beach on U.S. 101, in about 40 miles (64 km) you'll come to Tillamook. Just south of Tillamook, watch for the turnoff for the **Three Capes Scenic Loop** ★★★ (p. 200), a scene-stealing byway on Oregon's North Coast. The 35-mile loop drive leaves U.S. 101 and winds past three windswept capes (one with a lighthouse) with viewpoints, beaches, picnic areas, and hiking trails. You might want to stop for lunch at **Roseanna's Cafe** (p. 202) in Oceanside. At Pacific City, the scenic byway rejoins U.S. 101, the main coast highway. It's another 22 miles (35 km) to **Lincoln City** ★ (p. 203), a good spot for lunch or a coffee. For a casual, fish-and-chips lunch in a restaurant with an ocean view, try **Kyllo's Seafood & Grill ★★** (p. 205) at the south end of Lincoln City. At Lincoln City, the Central Coast region begins. Continue on U.S. 101 to tiny **Depoe Bay ★★** (p. 207) with the world's smallest harbor. This is where you can sign up for a whale-watching expedition that will take you out onto the open waters of the bay, where a herd of giant gray whales spends part of every summer, and other gray whales pass back and forth on their annual migration.

In about 13 miles you'll reach **Newport ★★★** (p. 209), the most interesting town on the Oregon coast (you are now on the Central Coast). If you've taken the Three Capes Loop and done a whale-watching excursion in Depoe Bay, you probably won't be arriving in Newport until later in the afternoon. Spend the rest of the day relaxing in Newport. Stroll along the busy **Bayfront ★★** (p. 213), decide on a restaurant for dinner—if you want to stay on the Bayfront, **Local Ocean ★★★** (p. 212) offers the freshest seafood, and **Saffron Salmon ★★** (p. 213) will give you the best view. Also head over to the north part of Newport and enjoy an invigorating stroll on long, sandy Nye Beach. Afterward, explore the charming, artsy neighborhood of **Nye Beach ★★★** (p. 214). Looking for a good latte? **Panini ★** (p. 213) in Nye Beach is the place to find it. There are also some good restaurants in Nye Beach, including **April's at Nye Beach ★★** (p. 212).

Day 7: Newport/Portland

There's a lot more to enjoy in Newport before you head back to Portland. Start your explorations at the not-to-be-missed **Yaquina Head Outstanding Natural Area ★★★** (p. 216), site of **Yaquina Head Lighthouse,** one of the most photogenic and easily accessible lighthouses on the Oregon coast. With its unusual cobble beach and offshore rocks serving as resting and roosting spots for seals, sea lions, tufted puffins, and other sea birds, the area really lives up to its official designation as an "outstanding natural area." Have a look at the displays in the visitor center that tell about life in the lighthouses (a lonely occupation if ever there was one), and then go and visit the lighthouse itself. A stairway gets you down to the beach—not sand, this one, but cobblestones.

But Newport has two lighthouses, and your next stop is the oldest lighthouse on the Oregon coast, a two-story wood-frame house found at **Yaquina Bay State Recreation Site ★★★** (p. 215) on the north side of the Yaquina Bay Bridge in Newport. Here you can visit the living quarters of the lighthouse keepers who operated the light when the light cast its first beam in 1871.

Now head south across the beautiful green span of the Yaquina Bay Bridge, one of several bridges along the Oregon coast that were designed by Conde McCullough and built as WPA projects in the 1930s. On the south side of the bridge, make your way down to Newport's star attraction, the **Oregon Coast Aquarium ★★★** (p. 21). It's one of the great aquariums of the West Coast and a place you don't want to rush through—give yourself at least a couple of hours. The facility concentrates on local and West Coast marine life and has giant aquariums, a walk-through aquarium with sharks, and outdoor exhibits with tufted puffins, sea otters, and sea lions. It's both educational and fun, and a memorable way to end your Oregon coast experience.

Now it's time to head back up to U.S. 101 and start the drive back to Portland. It's about a 2½-hour drive via U.S. 20 and I-5.

THE OREGON COAST IN 1 WEEK

The Oregon coast stretches from Astoria in the north to Brookings in the south, a distance of about 364 miles (586 km). U.S. 101, the main artery, winds, climbs, twists, and curves along the entire coast, often but not always with the ocean in view. Staying on this (usually) two-lane highway, you could easily cover the entire coast in 2 or certainly 3 days. But why do that when there is so much to see? Spending a week exploring the Oregon coast will reinvigorate your senses, especially if you are an active traveler who likes to get out and go for a walk on the beach—even if it's rainy—or hike along a forest trail with stunning views of the Pacific below.

Bear in mind that the Oregon coast is not a bikini-and-surfboard playground. No, no, no. The water's too cold for swimming, and if you crashed your surfboard into one of the offshore rocks, you'd be a goner. The Oregon coast is wild, windy, rocky, forested, with a lot of towns and villages that almost look like afterthoughts. But this rugged seascape offers exciting sights and experiences like whale watching, surf-pounded white-sand beaches, giant headlands, lonely lighthouses, and scenic byways that leave the highway and take you to places of spectacular natural grandeur. So here's a week-long itinerary just for the Oregon coast. Of course, you will need a car. Bring a fleece, a hoodie, a hat, and some kind of rain gear, no matter what time of year you visit. I haven't focused on camping in this guide, but if you travel with a tent or RV, there are excellent campgrounds in state parks all along the coast. For a quick overview of campgrounds, visit **http://visittheoregoncoast.com/activities/camping**. Remember, too, that you will need a Forest Service–issued **Oregon Pacific Coast Passport** day-use pass to park or camp at the many state parks along the way. A 5-day pass costs $10; information on passes can be obtained at **www.fs.fed.us**.

Day 1: Astoria/Cannon Beach

Today, you'll head west from Portland to the Pacific Ocean, but before you actually meet up with the sea, you'll encounter the 14-mile-wide mouth of the Columbia River at **Astoria ★★** (p. 183). The trip to Astoria, depending on your route, will take 1½ to 2 hours. This historic river city, now sprucing itself up and home to a good maritime museum, historic house, and other sights, is worth a couple of hours, longer if you want to have lunch or stroll along the **Riverwalk ★★★** (p. 189). For ideas on how to spend your time in Astoria, see "Day 5" under "Seattle, Portland & the Oregon Coast in 1 Week," above.

From Astoria, head south about 5 miles (8 km) to visit **Fort Clatsop—Lewis and Clark National Historic Park ★★★** (p. 190), site of the 1805 winter headquarters of the trailblazing explorers Merimether Lewis and William Clark and their Corps of Discovery. Continue on to **Cannon Beach ★★★** (p. 191), about 22 miles (36 km) south of Astoria, for your first overnight stay along the Oregon coast. This is your first big Oregon beach experience, and it's a doozy, with scenic Haystack Rock rising out of the sea and miles of flat, sandy, surf-pounded beach to stroll on and enjoy. Try also to pay a visit to gorgeous **Ecola State Park ★★★** (p. 198) at the north end of town, with miles of beach and forested hiking trails with panoramic ocean views. Cannon Beach is perhaps the most charming and affluent town along the coast, and it has any number of fine ocean-view hotels and restaurants that are definitely a cut above the average. You'll find more information under "Day 5" in the "Portland, Seattle & the Oregon Coast" itinerary, above.

Day 2: Three Capes Scenic Loop/Depoe Bay

Continuing south from Cannon Beach on U.S. 101, in about 40 miles (64 km) you'll come to Tillamook, situated in an important dairy region of lush green fields. If you're a cheese-lover, you might want to stop at the **Tillamook Cheese Factory** (p. 200) to sample or buy some of Oregon's most famous cheese (you can also get an ice cream). Just south of Tillamook, watch for the turnoff for the **Three Capes Scenic Loop ★★★** (p. 200), a 35-mile loop drive that leaves U.S. 101 and takes you to three giant headlands where you can hike, camp, or just enjoy the spectacular scenery from viewpoints along the way. **Roseanna's Cafe** (p. 202) in Oceanside is one possible lunch-with-an-ocean-view stop along the route, or you can continue on through Pacific City, where the scenic loop rejoins U.S. 101.

Continue on U.S. 101 to **Depoe Bay ★★** (p. 207). Here, whale-watching excursion boats chug out from the nation's smallest harbor and into the open sea for possible sights of the 20-ton gray whales that pass along the Oregon coast during their annual migration. If you get sea sick, skip it; otherwise, this is one of your best opportunities to view gray whales from the water rather than shore. There's also a Whale Watching Center (p. 209) in Depoe Bay where you can learn more about these remarkable mammals that can reach almost 50 feet in length and 40 tons in weight at maturity. If you take a whale-watching trip, plan on spending at least 3 hours in Depoe Bay and on the water. You can push on to Newport, but I would recommend that you spend the night in Depoe Bay.

Day 3: Newport

The busy coast town of **Newport ★★★** (p. 209), with the largest commercial fishing fleet on the coast, is about 13 miles (21 km) south of Depoe Bay. There's a lot to see in Newport, so make it your day 3 overnight stop.

About 5 miles (8 km) north of Newport, follow the signs for **Yaquina Head Outstanding Natural Area ★★★** (p. 216), site of **Yaquina Head Lighthouse,** built in 1873 and open to visitors. The basalt headland here extends a mile out into the sea, with a series of dramatic offshore rocks that serve as wildlife sanctuaries for seabirds and seals. A staircase leads down to an unusual beach covered with cobbles, not sand, worn smooth by the sea. It's a remarkable and remarkably scenic area. Plan to spend at least an hour here, in the visitor center, the lighthouse, and exploring the beach.

From Yaquina Head, head south into Newport and get yourself checked into your hotel. Around lunch time, stop and find a place to eat along Newport's **Bayfront ★★** (p. 213), where tourists and fishermen from the city's fishing fleets share the street, and you can find seafood restaurants where your fish was caught just hours before.

After lunch, make your way to **Yaquina Bay State Recreation Site ★★★** (p. 215) on the north side of the Yaquina Bay Bridge. Here you'll find a very unusual lighthouse, the oldest one on the Oregon coast, dating from 1871. It is really a two-story wooden house with a light atop the roof. This lighthouse, one of the nine lighthouses on the Oregon coast, was decommissioned in 1873, when the Yaquina Head Lighthouse went into operation. You can tour the living quarters of the lighthouse keepers and enjoy a magnificent view over Yaquina Bay.

Newport has one of the most famous bridges on the Oregon coast, a long, graceful span designed by Conde McCullough in the 1930s. Cross the Yaquina

Bay Bridge and follow the signs to the **Oregon Coast Aquarium** ★★★ (p. 214), the top tourist attraction on the Oregon coast and unarguably one of the finest aquariums on the West Coast. You'll pass through an outdoor aviary with tufted puffins, and outdoor pools with sea otters, before reaching the fascinating tanks within. This is an excellent place to learn more about the sea creatures that inhabit the waters along the Oregon coast. Give yourself a minimum of 2 hours here.

It's been a full day, but what about a walk on a beach before dinner? Head to the **Nye Beach** ★★★ (p. 214) neighborhood, where you'll find access to a long, wonderfully strollable beach. Newport was one of the first resort towns on the Oregon coast, and many of the homes in Nye Beach date from the early 1900s. This is also a good spot to have dinner.

Day 4: Yachats/Cape Perpetua/Heceta Head

Let's be frank: from here to the California border, it's mostly about the scenery. There won't be any more big indoor tourist attractions such as the Oregon Coast Aquarium in Newport. But there will be areas of exceptional beauty, another lighthouse or two, and some interesting and at times charming coastal communities along the way. Like **Yachats** ★★★ (p. 215), 24 miles (39 km) south of Newport on—what else?—U.S. 101. This artsy and affluent village—it's pronounced *Yah*-hots, by the way—has no commercial development of any kind. But with an oceanfront like this, who wants commerce? If the magic of the place strikes your fancy, make it your overnight stop for day 4. Then all you need to do is enjoy the sea and the scenery. The beach here is marked by lots of rocky coves and tide pools, and you can beachcomb to your heart's content, because along this part of the Central Oregon coast, agates frequently wash ashore after storms. At its southern end, the town of 700 people is lorded over by the towering bulk of Cape Perpetua, a 600-foot-high headland that juts out into the Pacific and is the highest point on the Oregon coast. At some point during the day, drive south another 2½ miles to the **Cape Perpetua Scenic Area** ★★★ (p. 219). There is enough variety and natural splendor here to keep you occupied for hours. Pick up maps and detailed information on the area at the visitor center. Recreational possibilities here include breathtaking, headland-top vistas, hiking trails through old-growth forest areas, shoreline tide pools, and a natural formation called the Devil's Churn, where the force of incoming waves into a narrow fissure sends geysers of seawater high into the air. Back in Yachats, you'll be pleased to find that there are several top-quality restaurants, including **Ona** ★ (p. 219), **Heidi's Italian Dinners** ★★ (p. 218), and **Luna Sea Fish House** ★★ (p. 219).

Day 5: Florence/Oregon Dunes/Cape Arago Highway/Bandon

On the morning of day 5, head south again, up and over Cape Perpetua, and keep your eyes peeled for **Heceta Head Lighthouse State Scenic Viewpoint** ★★★ (p. 220). And have your camera ready. Heceta Head Lighthouse sits at the edge of a rocky promontory above the crashing waves of the Pacific. You can also, seasonally, park and head in for a closer look at the lighthouse and the Victorian-era lighthouse-keeper's house that is run as a B&B. and where yours truly had a possible run-in with the resident ghost. (The **Heceta Head Lightstation** ★★, p. 217, would be a good alternative to staying in Yachats.)

Just 1 mile south is one of the Oregon coast's most long-lived natural attractions, **Sea Lion Caves ★★** (p. 220). It's a wildlife-viewing area, but it's set up as a tourist attraction. An elevator takes you down to a viewing window that lets you peer into a giant sea cave that happens to be the largest sea lion rookery on the West Coast.

In another 6 miles (10 km) look for a highway sign marked **Darlingtonia State Natural Site ★** (p. 220). Although it's very small, this little marshy area beside U.S. 101 is one of my favorite natural areas along the entire coast. It's the home of the rare and endangered *Darlingtonia californica*, or cobra lily, a carnivorous (just insects, don't worry) plant that is found only in boggy coastal areas in southern Oregon and northern California. The mass of emerald-green plants rise up from the marshy ground like thousands of eyeless cobras. I have to report that on my last visit in April 2014, the area was parched because the entire southern coast of Oregon had received only a fraction of its usual winter rainfall, and the plants can only survive in ground that is permanently damp. I hope this gorgeous little patch of ancient nature is not going to disappear because of a changing climate.

Your lunch stop is the old river town of **Florence ★★** (p. 220), which got its start during the days of the California Gold Rush, when timber and provisions were floated down the Siuslaw River to be transported to San Francisco. The Siuslaw flows right through the heart of town, and the wooden storefront buildings along its riverside promenade give this small coastal community some real historical character. The most prominent building on Bay Street, a white false-fronted former general store, is now the **Bridgewater Fish House and Zebra Bar ★** (p. 221), a good lunch spot. After lunch, spend a few minutes strolling along Bay Street before heading south.

Although there's no official boundary line, the South Coast begins just south of Florence, and so does the **Oregon Dunes National Recreation Area ★★** (p. 222). If you like sand dunes, this 50-mile (80 kmz) swath of towering sand dunes between the shoreline and U.S. 101 is an area you will want to explore. Otherwise, continue south past Coos Bay, the largest town on the coast, and look for the turn-off for the **Cape Arago Highway ★★★** south of town. You may not want to stop at all of the three state parks on the Cape Arago Highway, but they are all worth visiting.

The first is **Sunset Bay State Park ★** (p. 225), a sheltered cove beneath high sandstone cliffs with such (relatively) placid waters that you can actually swim there—it's really the only place along the entire coast where swimming is possible. The second is **Shore Acres State Park ★★★** (p. 225), an extremely rare formal garden created almost a century ago by a shipping tycoon who lost his house and fortune but left behind his rose gardens and sunken pond garden to be rediscovered decades later and restored to their former glory. This is probably the only rose garden you'll ever visit where you'll hear seals barking in the distance. A trail leads down from the garden to a gorgeous little cove with a white-sand beach. The third spot is **Cape Arago State Park ★★** (p. 226), where offshore rocks, part of the Oregon Islands National Wildlife Refuge, harbor hundreds of seals and seabirds. Another natural treasure in the area, little visited but absolutely sublime, is the **South Slough National Estuarine Research Reserve ★★★** (p. 226), the first federally protected estuary in the U.S. (1971) with thousands of acres of unspoiled coastal habitat of the Coos river.

After you've visited one, or all, of the state parks, continue south on U.S. 101 to **Bandon** ★★★ (p. 226), your overnight stop for day 5. A stop is all the nicer because Bandon has some very good restaurants: **Alloro Wine Bar** ★★★ (p. 228), **The Loft Restaurant & Bar** ★★ (p. 228), **Lord Bennett's Restaurant and Lounge** ★ (p. 229), and **The Gallery** ★★★ (p. 228), the fine-dining restaurant at Bandon Dunes Golf Resort.

Day 6: Bandon/Gold Beach

If you're a golfer, Bandon may have been your destination all along. Golfers from all over the world descend on this small community to play at the five world-class links courses at **Bandon Dunes Golf Resort** ★★★ (p. 227). But this coastal community, located where the Coquille River spills into the Pacific, was popular with visitors long before the golf resort. At one point Bandon was called the "Playground of the Pacific" because, in the days before roads, passenger steamers would stop here on their trips between San Francisco and Seattle. The attractions of those days are gone, mostly wiped out in a 1936 fire. What remains is what was always here—a magnificent beach with a whole gallery of giant offshore rocks and monoliths that have been given fanciful names like Face Rock (it resembles a face staring up), Table Rock, the Sisters, and Cat and Kittens. You can see Bandon's famous rock formations—they are all part of the Oregon Islands National Wildlife Refuge—and walk on the beach, by taking Beach Loop Drive to **Bullards Beach State Park** ★★★ (p. 229). You'll also be able to visit the **Coquille River Lighthouse** ★★★ (p. 229), a sturdy, octagonal building with a light that cast its first beam in 1896.

As you head south from Bandon on U.S. 101 you will pass—surprise?—cranberry fields. This area is also known as the Cranberry Capital of Oregon. Look for **Misty Meadows** (p. 231), a store on the east side of the highway a few miles south of Bandon, and you can buy jams and jellies made with local cranberries and fruits.

Then it's another 59 miles (95 km) to **Gold Beach** ★★★, where the fabled Rogue River empties into the sea. At **Jerry's Rogue Jets** (p. 235) you can arrange for a jet-boat trip up the Rogue the next day. There are several fabulous hiking options in the Gold Beach area. The easily walkable **Frances Schrader Old Growth Trail** ★★★ (p. 235) takes you to a rare stand of giant trees; the **Rogue River Walk** ★★★ (p. 235) traverses a scenic area above the famous river. You have a few good choices for dinner: **Spinner's** ★★ (p. 234), **Nor'wester Seafood** ★ (p. 234), or the quirkier **Anna's by the Sea** ★★ (p. 234).

Day 7: Gold Beach/Brookings

Make the jet-boat trip up the Rogue your special experience of the day. Three different excursions cover three different lengths of the Rogue, but the best is the 104-mile (167 km) wilderness whitewater trip that takes you up to the wild and scenic part of the river. Along the way you will stop for lunch at one of the rustic fishing lodges along the river. It's an exciting and memorable trip, and it's suitable for all ages.

The 28 miles (45 km) between Gold Beach and Brookings is a scenic corridor with several pull-outs and state parks where you can stop to enjoy the view. Approaching Brookings, U.S. 101 moves down to skirt the ocean on a flat coastal plain. This area of the South Coast is referred to as the Banana Belt of Oregon because the climate and somewhat sheltered topography fosters the growth of semi-tropical plants. Most of the nation's Easter lilies are grown here.

To reach inland I-5 from Brookings, take U.S. 199 east to Grant's Pass. From there, it's a straight shot back up to Portland, a 246-mile (396-km) trip that takes about 5 hours.

SEATTLE, PORTLAND & THE OREGON COAST FOR FAMILIES

The Pacific Northwest is often cited for its "livability" and family-friendliness. I've noticed, in fact, that people who grow up in this neck of the woods often return, or want to return, or at least speak of it with fondness. If you are traveling with children, you will indeed find that there are many family-oriented things to see and do in Seattle, Portland, and along the Oregon coast. This is a great opportunity to introduce your kids to nature—perhaps as you learn more about it yourself. You can, without too much difficulty, go carless in Seattle and Portland, and you can get from one city to the other via train or bus if you don't want to drive. For the last 2 days, however, you will need a car. The following is a suggested 1-week itinerary with kids in mind.

Days 1–2: Seattle

Spend the first 2 days of your trip exploring the kid-friendly attractions of **Seattle** (chapter 4). A stroll on the Seattle Waterfront (p. 50) is a great way to start your visit. Here you'll find the **Seattle Aquarium ★★** (p. 83) and **Argosy Cruises** (p. 77), which offers boat tours of the harbor, Lake Washington, and the Hiram M. Chittenden Locks, and longer trips to Tillicum Village, where Native American tribes perform dances and have a salmon bake. The waterfront's newest attraction, the **Seattle Great Wheel ★★** (p. 84) is the tallest Ferris wheel on the West Coast. Instead of or in addition to a boat tour with Argosy, you can take a passenger ferry over to **Bainbridge Island** for a fun and easy excursion that gives kids the excitement of being on the water.

On day 2, get on the vintage **monorail** downtown at Westlake Center and whiz north to **Seattle Center.** At Seattle Center, you can zoom up to the observation deck of the **Space Needle ★★** (p. 85) for a 360° view of the city and surrounding area. Younger kids will find plenty of play activities at the **Pacific Science Center ★** (p. 82), which has some great animatronic dinosaurs and a lovely butterfly house, in addition to many other hands-on science-related exhibits. I personally find the **Experience Music Project** (p. 76) to be vastly over-rated and a yawn for kids unless they are avid, and I mean avid, budding rockers.

Days 3–4: Portland

On day 4, head down to Portland (chapter 5). If you're not driving the 178 miles (286 km), there are other transportation options including Amtrak, which makes the Seattle-Portland run several times a day and takes about 3½ to 4 hours. By car, without traffic snags, the trip takes about 2 hours and 45 minutes.

Explore the City of Roses via MAX, the light-rail train, and/or the Portland Streetcar—kids love both of them (so do I, and I'm not a kid). Spend a day at

Washington Park ★★★ (p. 142). They may not flip for the roses in the **International Rose Test Garden ★★★** (p. 144), but they will enjoy the little train that runs from the garden to the **Oregon Zoo ★★★** (p. 145), the state's top tourist attraction. Budding naturalists might enjoy the **World Forestry Center Discovery Museum ★** (p. 146), which focuses on trees, and smaller kids (up to about 10) will enjoy the **Portland Children's Museum ★** (p. 145). Another top family attraction is the Oregon Museum of Science and Industry (OMSI; p. 148) on the east side, which you can also reach by streetcar. If your kids like to hike—or even if they don't—the trails in **Forest Park ★★★** (p. 146) wind up through the West Hills and will provide a sense of adventure.

Day 5: Portland/Columbia Gorge National Scenic Area/Mount Hood

On day 5, head east out of Portland on I-84. The spectacular **Columbia Gorge National Scenic Area ★★★** (p. 172) begins just a few miles east of downtown. For maximum excitement, take the **Columbia Gorge Historic Highway,** the first scenic road to be built in Oregon back in the 1920s. The old highway takes you up to **Crown Point** (p. 174), where the breathtaking view up and down the gorge extends for over 30 miles. Continue on the old highway and you will pass a handful of gorgeous waterfalls until you come finally to the tallest and most dramatic waterfall of all—**Multnomah Falls ★★★** (p. 174). You can walk up an easy paved path to view the thundering falls from fairly close up. Just after Multnomah Falls, the old highway ends and returns you to I-84. Continue your expedition up and over **Mount Hood ★★★** (p. 169) to **Timberline Lodge ★★★** (p. 170), where you can hike or have lunch or dinner. Returning to Portland will take you about 1½ hours.

Day 6: Cannon Beach

Today, it's time to introduce the family to the Pacific Ocean. From Portland it takes about 1½ to 2 hours to get to **Cannon Beach ★★★** (p. 191) by car. Make this an overnight trip, and be sure to book your hotel well in advance if you are traveling in the summer. With towering Haystack Rock jutting up from the shore, this flat, sandy beach is one of the best along the entire coast for long beach walks. And I have never yet met a kid who didn't love running, walking, skipping, and digging on Cannon Beach. The town is the most charming on the coast and offers lots of shopping and good restaurants. In addition to getting all revved up on the beach, try to pay a visit to **Ecola State Park ★★★** (p. 198) at the north end of town, where you'll find miles of beach and forested hiking trails with stunning ocean views.

Day 7: Three Capes Scenic Loop/Depoe Bay/Newport

Continuing south from Cannon Beach on U.S. 101, in about 40 miles (64 km) you'll come to Tillamook. Just south of Tillamook, watch for the turnoff for the **Three Capes Scenic Loop ★★★** (p. 200), a 35-mile loop drive that winds past three giant headlands (one with a lighthouse) with viewpoints, beaches, picnic areas, and hiking trails. From Pacific City, where the loop drive ends, continue south on U.S. 101 for 34 miles (55 km) to tiny **Depoe Bay ★★** (p. 207), where you can take a whale-watching expedition out onto the open waters of the bay to view (hopefully) giant gray whales on their annual migration. Again, it's best to reserve a whale-watching trip in advance of your arrival. What could be more thrilling than to spot a spouting whale!

From Depoe Bay, continue on U.S. 101 for 13 miles (21 km) to **Newport** ★★★ (p. 209). If you've taken the Three Capes Loop and done a whale-watching excursion in Depoe Bay, you probably won't be arriving in Newport until later in the afternoon. Spend the rest of the day strolling along the busy **Bayfront** ★★ (p. 213) and the charming, artsy neighborhood of **Nye Beach** ★★★ (p. 214).

There's a lot more to enjoy in Newport before you head back to Portland. Start your explorations at the not-to-be-missed **Yaquina Head Outstanding Natural Area** ★★★ (p. 216), site of **Yaquina Head Lighthouse,** one of the most photogenic and easily accessible lighthouses on the Oregon coast. The off-shore monoliths here are wildlife refuges where you'll see seals and hundreds of sea birds.

Afterward, head south, back into Newport and across the Yaquina Bay Bridge. On the south side of the bridge, you'll find Newport's star attraction, the **Oregon Coast Aquarium** ★★★ (p. 214). It's one of the great aquariums of the West Coast and a place you don't want to rush through—give yourself at least a couple of hours. The facility concentrates on local and West Coast marine life and has giant aquariums, a walk-through aquarium with sharks and outdoor exhibits with tufted puffins, sea otters and sea lions. It will be a fun and memorable way to wind up your Pacific Northwest adventures.

SEATTLE, PORTLAND & THE OREGON COAST IN CONTEXT

3

H ere's the question I am most frequently asked by people who haven't been to the Pacific Northwest: "I've heard it's wonderful out there, and that the people are so nice, but what's it really like?" The simple answer, of course, is that it's pretty wonderful and that the people are, in fact, so nice that strangers will smile and say hello to you on the street. That's more likely to happen in Portland than Seattle, I must point out. The pace in both cities is fairly relaxed—again, more relaxed in Portland than Seattle. What it all boils down to is that most of the people who live in Seattle and Portland want to live there. More and more of them have moved there from somewhere else, and despite the urban travails that plague all of us, they tend to remain. It's called "livability," a nebulous but seductive word if there ever was one. Nature plays a big role, and mobility (Seattle traffic notwithstanding), good schools, safe neighborhoods, an arts and culture scene, good food, good beer, and good wine all play a part.

The Oregon coast is an entirely different kettle of fish, as it were, and people gravitate toward it not so much as a potential place to live (unless it's a second home) but as a place where the ocean is in charge and Nature ultimately calls the shots. You'll learn more about Seattle, Portland, and the Oregon coast in the chapters that follow. Here I want to give you, first of all, a general snapshot of Portland, Seattle, and the Oregon coast as they are today. After that, I've provided a short, general history of the region, followed by historic timelines for both Seattle and Portland. All this material is meant to give you a deeper understanding of the past and present of the Pacific Northwest.

SEATTLE TODAY

A quick 360-degree scan of the horizon on a sunny day in Seattle will present a mesmerizing view, over the shimmering waters of Puget Sound to the snow-covered peaks of the Olympic Mountains to the west and the massive mound of Mount Rainier to the east. In between, there's the iconic Space Needle and all the towers of downtown Seattle. With sights like these, it's easy to see why people would want to live here. The 1993 movie *Sleepless in Seattle* helped to romanticize a city that nobody saw as particularly romantic—until the tech boom brought Seattle into the national consciousness and gave the city and its residents a new edge of sophistication.

Although the weather in Seattle is notoriously drizzly, the residents for the most part don't let precipitation stand between them and the outdoors. The temptation is too great to head for the hills, the river, the beach, the Sound, or the San Juan Islands. Consequently, life in Seattle tends to revolve as much around parks, gardens, waterfronts, and other outdoor spaces and activities as it does around such traditional urban pastimes as shopping, the performing arts, and dining. And when the city's green spaces aren't wild enough to satisfy the craving for an outdoor adventure, there is something wilder close at hand. If you live in Seattle, you can be in a national park, national forest, or state park within an hour or two.

The region's outdoors aesthetic does not, however, preclude a strong support of the arts. The Seattle Opera is one of the finest companies in the country (well known for its stagings of Wagner's *Ring* cycle), as is the Seattle Symphony, which performs in downtown's Benaroya Hall. Seattle also has the best theater scene on the West Coast. (Seattle is where playwright August Wilson got his start and made his mark before Broadway.)

The visual arts aren't overlooked either. Seattle expanded its Seattle Art Museum back in 2007. Chihuly Garden and Glass, a stunning new museum dedicated to the work of internationally known glass-master Dale Chihuly, a Tacoma-native, opened next to the Space Needle in 2012.

Despite the collapse of the over-inflated real estate market, Microsoft co-founder Paul Allen's Vulcan company continued and continues with its ambitious redevelopment of Seattle's South Lake Union neighborhood, now home to the world headquarters of Amazon and attracting new biotech companies With the economy in better shape now, Seattle building and development is back in almost full swing. Cranes rise

SEATTLE DATELINE

1792 British Capt. George Vancouver explores and names Puget Sound.

1851 The Denny party makes land at Alki Point (now West Seattle) and endures a harsh first winter with the help of local Indian tribes.

1852 Denny and gang move their town to the more temperate east side of the Puget Sound; "Doc" Maynard names the town Seattle after Chief Sealth of the local Duwamish tribe.

1853 Henry Yesler opens the first of many sawmills to be built in the Puget Sound area.

1861 The University of Washington (then called Territorial University) opens its doors to students.

1863 *The Gazette*, later to become the *Seattle Post-Intelligencer*, publishes its first newspaper.

1878 Seattle gets its first telephones.

1885 Chinese immigrants are forced out of Seattle.

1889 Twenty-five blocks of Seattle burn to the ground in the Great Fire, prompting a frenzy of building—several feet higher than the original shops had been.

continues

up all over the South Lake Union area, which is quickly integrating with the rest of urban Seattle, and other building and rebuilding projects are advancing in downtown. Down on the waterfront, the new Seattle Great Wheel started spinning in 2013 and instantly became a new landmark.

The biggest building project in Seattle right now is not about construction but deconstruction. The horrible Alaskan Way Viaduct, put up in the 1950s directly next to the waterfront, effectively cutting off downtown from the harbor, is *finally* being dismantled, and a giant tunnel is being dug to funnel the traffic. The site of the viaduct will become a giant waterside park, transforming the city and bringing it back to the waterfront where it began. (Unfortunately, the huge boring machine used to create the tunnel was damaged in 2014, and work has been delayed for months.)

Despite its reputation for foot dragging when it comes to public transit, Seattle finally got a light-rail system up and running in 2009, and in 2010, service began between Seattle Tacoma International Airport and downtown Seattle. Seattle also has a new streetcar line that runs from downtown to South Lake Union. But Seattle also continues to have some of the worst traffic congestion outside of L.A. If you visit with a car, avoid driving at rush hour or, better yet, avoid driving altogether.

The economic news has been brighter for aerospace giant Boeing, the region's biggest employer, since the first of its new 787 Dreamliners finally took to the air in late 2009.

Like any big city in a global economy, Seattle has seen its share of boom and bust. That, in fact, is what Seattle is all about. Economy aside, however, Seattleites continue to share a common interest in the outdoors, and it is this interest that tends to dominate the character of the Puget Sound region. If winters are long, gray, and rainy, well, you just put on a colorful rain jacket, fill the travel mug with a double tall latte, and head for the hills anyway.

PORTLAND TODAY

Oregon's largest city sits at the north end of the Willamette Valley, straddling the Willamette River near its confluence with the Columbia, which acts as a natural dividing

1889	Washington becomes the nation's 42nd state.
1893	Transcontinental Great Northern Railway reaches Seattle.
1897–1899	Seattle booms as a stopping-off point for Klondike gold-seekers.
1907	Pike Place Market brings farmers and customers directly together.
1914	Smith Tower is completed in Seattle, becoming the tallest building west of Ohio.
1917	Construction is complete on the Lake Washington Ship Canal (Hiram M. Chittenden Locks).
1917	Boeing Airplane Co. is launched.
1919	Eddie Bauer's first store opens.
1921	The Alien Land Law is passed in Washington, restricting Asian immigrants' rights to own or lease property.
1924	Native Americans are made U.S. citizens.
1926	Seattle elects the first woman mayor of any major U.S. city.
1940	Lake Washington Floating Bridge becomes the first of its kind in the world.
1942	FDR signs order sending Japanese Americans from the West Coast to internment camps; thousands in the Seattle area are forced to abandon their homes and businesses.

line between Oregon and Washington. Like Seattle, 178 miles (286 km) to the north, Portland lies in an area of exceptional and easily accessible natural beauty, and this proximity to so many remarkable and varied landscapes adds to Portland's allure. On a clear day, Mount Hood—the city's alpine mascot—glows on the eastern horizon, about 90 minutes away. The Pacific Ocean is about 70 miles (113 km) to the west, just beyond the Coast Range. A drive through the Columbia River Gorge takes you, in about 1½ hours, through the Cascade Mountains to the high, dry, and much sunnier desert that covers almost two-thirds of the state. And the rolling hills of the fertile Willamette Valley's wine country begin right outside the city limits.

On some days, the air in Portland, cleansed by rain and scented with trees and earth, has a clean, sweet fragrance that goes right to your head. That's because there's green and greenery everywhere—in magnificent Washington Park, along the riverfront, in parks downtown and throughout the city, and in yards and gardens in Portland's many distinctive neighborhoods. The city counts some 200 parks, gardens, and wild spaces within the metropolitan area. Vast Forest Park, covering a huge swath of the city's West Hills, is one of the largest urban forests in the country.

The creation and protection of green spaces is a long-standing Portland tradition, and that includes farm and forest land outside the city. An urban growth boundary created in 1979 prevents urban sprawl—and has led to rapid development within the metro area. This new residential development, more than anything else, characterizes what's going on in Portland today. As demographics and lifestyles change, Portland is becoming more densely urban than it ever was. "Infill" is the developmental buzzword, as city lots get divided and multi-unit housing goes up everywhere. The old norm of "house and yard" has given way to "condo and balcony" and even "microapartment with shared kitchen facility." There are newly created neighborhoods like the affluent Pearl District and rediscovered old neighborhoods. One thing that urban infill hasn't changed is the Portland notion of living and participating in a neighborhood. The difference is one of self-consciousness; neighborhoods were once just neighborhoods, and now they are becoming "brands" and destinations. So today you say, "Let's go over and have dinner on SE Division" or "Let's go hang out on North

1942 Seattle native Jimi Hendrix is born.

1949 Sea-Tac International Airport is opened.

1951 Washington State Ferries begin service on Puget Sound.

1954 First successful passenger jet, Boeing 707, takes off.

1962 Seattle builds Space Needle and monorail for the Seattle World's Fair.

1966 Boeing builds 747 assembly plant.

1970s Boeing layoffs devastate the local economy.

1971 Starbucks opens its first shop.

1975 Microsoft is founded by Bill Gates and Paul Allen in Albuquerque; three years later it moves to Seattle area.

1979 The Seattle SuperSonics win the NBA Championship.

1999 A World Trade Organization conference in downtown Seattle prompts riots, property damage, and accusations of police misconduct.

2001 The Nisqually Earthquake causes extensive damage to many older Seattle buildings.

2004 Washington elects Christine Gregoire in tightest governor's race

continues

Mississippi" or "I know a great food cart on SE Hawthorne." This would have been unheard of even 15 years ago.

The result is that the city has more vitality as a city than it ever did—or maybe not since World War II, when it was hopping as a hub of shipbuilding. There is more going on now, and it's not dictated, as it once was, by "Old Portland" institutions and Old Portland money, or lack thereof. For, whether one wants to talk about it in polite society of not, that is one difference between Seattle and Portland—money, and how it's used, and how it's spent. Portland has never been as affluent or "showy" as Seattle, and at times it seems to strive to keep things that way. This is the only city where you will hear people say that something is "too spendy." (At least I've never heard that phrase used anywhere else.)

The so-called "creative class"—a definition given to people who move to Portland not because they have a job, but because they want to live there, and create a job for themselves after they arrive—has transformed the city in many ways. When you visit, you will notice a lot of younger people, and a fashion aesthetic that combines grunge and street fashion with sports paraphernalia. Glamor is not something Portland does well, or cares much about. Fashion is much more about comfort and weather conditions.

The TV show *Portlandia* embraces and satirizes Portland's new and sometimes quirky urban culture. This is a city where people keep chickens in their backyards (at least on the east side), and not because they are into Santeria. They also seem to spend hours in cafes, microbreweries, and hot new restaurants. Talking. Discussing. Arguing. Theorizing. Yes, it's kind of cerebral. In a way, it's nothing but a new version of the old, pot-smoking, countercultural Portland brought into the 21st century.

History is—or used to be—an important part of the Portland mind-set. "I'm a sixth-generation Oregonian" was not an unusual comment to hear. After all, the city was settled by pioneers who trekked thousands of miles by land or sailed around Cape Horn to get here, and their descendants were proud of their heritage. People from all over the country are still moving to Portland—it's one of the fastest-growing cities in the nation—but now they are not drawn by the rich farmland and forests sought by the

in U.S. history, giving Washington state three women in its powerful political positions—two U.S. senators and the governor.

2009 The Link light rail station opens at SeaTac Airport, providing rapid mass transportation from downtown Seattle to the airport.

2010 A new law makes it a primary offense to text message or hold a cellphone to your ear while driving.

2012 Washington State legalizes same-sex marriage and possession of small amounts of marijuana for recreational use; the two events are in no way related.

2013 Work begins on the demolition of Alaskan Way, a 1950s-era viaduct that blights the downtown waterfront; a new tunnel will carry traffic, and streets adjacent to Seattle's waterfront will eventually be transformed into a park.

2014 Seattle Seahawks beat the Denver Broncos and win the Super Bowl. An estimated 700,000 people celebrate the event at a downtown parade.

2014 Massive mudslide in Oso, 60 miles northeast of Seattle, kills 41 people, destroys dozens of homes, a highway, and a river.

pioneers of old. They come instead—well, why do they come? They've heard that Portland is great, that Portland is beautiful, that Portland is hip, and groovy, and cool, that Portland is where things are happening, that Portland is relatively inexpensive (there is no sales tax in Oregon). All of this is true. But you have to come to Portland yourself if you want to experience its new vibe.

I'm not casting aspersions when I say that Portland lacks Seattle's pulsing, pushing drive. It doesn't have the industries to support that kind of economic va-va-voom. But it keeps moving ahead, and so far it hasn't lost its human touch or the "old" traditions and charm that gave it character. It's always been a city where people loved to live, and where they often chose to stay even if a better offer came along. For all its newfound urban pizazz, Portland is still a city that likes to go to bed early and wake up to hear birds chirping—or chickens clucking—in the backyard.

THE OREGON COAST TODAY

Well, one thing that will never change is the relatively unspoiled beauty of the Oregon coast. Or will it? The biggest environmental controversy right now has to do with turning ports on the Oregon coast into shipping depots for the export of natural gas and coal to Asia. There is real reason for concern, and battle lines have been drawn between environmentalists and concerned citizens on one side, and eager developers and business interests on the other.

The two ports in question are Astoria and Coos Bay. Both cities came into prominence as processing centers (lumber and salmon) and shipping depots, and both have suffered great economic hardship since the decline of the timber and fishing industries.

Astoria is undergoing a minor renaissance right now, thanks in part to its proximity to Portland, the arrival of seasonal cruise ships (which means thousands of passengers disembark to spend a few hours in Astoria), and to the stock of fine old houses and buildings that are being rediscovered and restored. The ball got rolling with the restoration of the Liberty Theater—now a downtown performing arts

PORTLAND DATELINE

1805 Lewis and Clark camp along the Columbia Slough in what is now North Portland.

1830s The site of present-day Portland is a small clearing in the woods on the west side of the Willamette River, used by Chinookan Indian tribes, including the Multnomah and the Clackamas, and French-Canadian fur traders traveling between Oregon City and Fort Vancouver, the Hudson's Bay trading headquarters on the Columbia River.

1842 Opening of the Oregon Trail.

1843 Asa Lovejoy and William Overton file a joint land claim for the riverside clearing. Overton, who lacked the 25¢ filing fee, later sells his portion to Francis W. Pettygrove.

1845 Pettygrove wants the new townsite to be called Portland, after his hometown in Maine. Lovejoy wants it to be called Boston. The two New Englanders flip a coin and the site—today's downtown—becomes Portland.

continues

center—and the Union Hotel, and the establishment of a number of new restaurants and cafes.

Some of us remember the Oregon coast as it used to be, a place of simple, unpretentious, damp-smelling beach cottages, indifferent or nonexistent restaurants (even with all that seafood), and nothing but the roar of the surf and the crackle of a fire to keep you company. Those were the Days Before Casinos (DBC), when you went to the coast to dig for razor clams, look for Japanese glass floats, and walk on deserted beaches. You can still do all three, but you can also go to casinos in Lincoln City and Coos Bay, have meals of a caliber previously unknown, and watch the crashing waves from the warm, bubbling safety of a Jacuzzi.

Everything really started to change along the coast in the late 1980s and early 1990s, when people from elsewhere (read: with money) started to realize how incredibly magnificent this coastline is—a place where you could watch herds of 50-ton gray whales passing by on their annual migration from the Bering Sea to Baja Mexico. The amount of new building and development along the North Coast, the coast closest to Portland, has been enormous. But if you haven't been to the Oregon coast before, you probably won't notice it the way some of us do.

And let's shout hooray for the People's Coast. That's what the Oregon coast is called. Why? Because not an inch of it is privately owned. By which I mean *the entire shoreline*—with its clean, beautiful, white-sand beaches, towering headlands, dramatic offshore monoliths, secretive little coves, crashing waves, seals and seabirds. It's all there for you to enjoy.

The towns and communities on the coast are small and can no longer rely on commercial fishing and logging to keep them afloat. So tourism plays a major role in the coast economy. There's been an uptick in the number of upscale places to stay and the number of good restaurants to eat. When inlanders hear that a huge storm is due to hit the Oregon coast, with 100mph winds, they don't anticipate disaster—they get on the horn and make a reservation at their favorite oceanfront hotel.

The arrival of Bandon Dunes Golf Resort in 1999 put the small Central Coast town of Bandon on the map—for golfers, anyway. People arrive from all over the world to

1848 Congress establishes the Territorial Government of Oregon, and nearby Oregon City becomes its capital the following year.

1850 Under the Donation Land Act, males arriving in the Oregon Territory by Dec. 1, 1850 can claim 320 acres (twice that amount for married couples) if they agree to cultivate the land. As a result, land-hungry pioneers—about a quarter of them from New England and New York—pour into the Willamette Valley. In 1848, when Lovejoy and Pettygrove platted the first streets, Portland had a population of about 80. Two years later, an 1850 census counted just over 800 people. Stumps of fir trees cut down for the newly laid-out streets gave rise to the city's first nickname: Stumptown. Puddletown, another nickname, referred to the rain-filled tracks and ruts.

1851 The city officially incorporates, and the first plank road (part of today's Canyon Rd.) is laid, providing a trade route between Portland and the farmlands of the Tualatin Valley.

1850s–1880s Situated at the head of navigation on the Willamette, play at these 5 links courses that are modeled after the heritage courses in Scotland and Ireland. "Golf as it was meant to be played" is the resort's tag line. That means you walk the course and play in natural surroundings. It's really pretty great.

But playing in natural surroundings is, ultimately, what the Oregon coast is all about. A trip to the coast (or "the beach" as Oregonians say) is partly about being cozy despite the elements, and partly about reconnecting with those very elements. It's a powerful, unpredictable place, the Oregon coast, and if you give yourself up to it, and don't complain about the weather, you will enjoy a wonderful world of natural wonders.

WHEN TO GO
Seattle & Portland

In Portland and Seattle we like to say that summer begins on July 5th. It's mostly true—or as true as anything can be in an age of rapid climate change. So if you are planning to spend your holidays in either city, and want to maximize your chances for sunshine and warm weather, July 5 through September 15 are the best months to visit.

The summers truly are splendid, and life in both cities moves outdoors as much as possible. The parks are verdant, the gardens are glorious, there are outdoor festivals galore, and you can sit outside comfortably all evening, until it gets chilly enough for a sweater. That's the beauty of summer in Seattle and Portland—no matter how hot the day, the nights cool down (sometimes by 30 degrees) so that you need a blanket. And when it's hot, it's dry, not humid, because the hot air comes from the deserts east of the Cascades and flows down the Columbia Gorge and through the valleys to Portland and Seattle. The downside when it gets very warm and the winds stop blowing is inversion and air pollution. Ick.

Nobody but gardeners believe me when I tell them that Portland and Seattle actually have what is considered a Mediterranean climate. What this means is that it generally rains almost constantly in one form or another from mid-October through June, with plenty of clear days and periods of truly great weather along the way. From November

Portland quickly emerges as the region's best site for the development of a shipping port and trade center. Passengers and cargo from the East Coast come in ships sailing around Cape Horn; trade extends across the Pacific to China. The California Gold Rush and the rapid growth of San Francisco fuel the city's river-trade economy. The region's vast conifer forests provide lumber for ships and the new towns springing up throughout the West.

1860s A second wave of immigrants, this time from Ireland, Germany, China, Japan, England, Scandinavia, and Canada, starts to arrive in 1860. East Portland, where most of the city's newly arrived foreigners and transient workers live, is laid out in 1850–51 and incorporated in 1870; it remains a separate town until it being annexed by the City of Portland in 1891.

1872–1873 Disastrous fires destroy all of Portland's early wood-framed waterfront buildings and lead to the construction of brick buildings with cast-iron facades and structural supports. A significant number of late-19th-century

continues

through March, the temperature remains temperate, rarely dipping below freezing and usually hovering in the 40s. By April it starts warming up, though the precipitation persists, and by May and June temperatures rise to the mid-70s with (of late) sudden spikes into the 80s and even low 90s (all temperatures in Fahrenheit). Plants love this climate, and so do gardeners.

June is when Portland holds its famous Rose Festival, but I've often thought it should be called the Rain Festival because it always seems to rain during the two big parades. Why not celebrate what makes life out here so green?

But can I convince you to come earlier in the year? If you are a gardener, in love with the egregious excesses of spring, come to Seattle or Portland in late April through May. You will be dazzled by the exuberance of spring in the Northwest, as cherry trees burst into pink bloom; camellias open; rhododendrons, azaleas, magnolias, and dogwoods flower; and the tulip fields near Portland and Seattle rival—maybe surpass—those in Holland. Yes, the springtime weather is very changeable, and you will have rain, but you also won't miss the floral fecundity of these two cities when spring is at its freshest and richest.

The heavenly summer weather often stretches out through September, sometimes into early October. This, too, is a fabulous time to visit because of the bounty you'll find at the farmers markets and the cultural pleasures you'll enjoy as the performing arts venues swing into performance mode.

As for winter—well, if you're a skier or snowboarder, you know why winter would be a good time to come. The mountains (Mount Rainier and Mount Hood) are generally ready to chairlift skiers up their slopes by mid-November—though I hasten to add that in recent years the snow has been arriving later and staying longer.

Oregon Coast

The Oregon coast is entirely different. Expect rain and wind year-round, though less of it from June through September. Many visitors come to the Oregon coast in July and August expecting clear skies and windless days only to find the beaches enveloped in thick fog. That's because hot inland air draws a wet blanket of moisture from the

	cast-iron commercial buildings—more, in fact, than in any other city west of the Rockies—still remain in the Yamhill and Skidmore/Old Town districts along 1st, 2nd, and 3rd avenues.		West Portland are joined by the Morrison Bridge, the first span across the Willamette.
1880–1900	Major expansion continues as immigrants from around the world arrive, hoping to make their fortunes in shipping, farming, lumber, and gold.	1889	Downtown streets are illuminated by electric street lamps fueled by hydropower from Willamette Falls in Oregon City.
1883	Arrival of the first transcontinental railroad.	1890s	The business center gradually shifts to the west, away from the waterfront, as fashionable new buildings and public institutions begin to rise on downtown's Morrison Street in the 1890s.
1887	With the completion of the Portland-San Francisco rail line, the city's reliance on the river begins to diminish. East and	1900–1910	Portland's population doubles.
		1905	Lewis and Clark Exposition is held in northwest Portland. The city's growth is due, in large part, to

Pacific eastward and hangs it up on the coastal mountain ranges. The summer fogs, more common along the South Coast, don't dissipate until late afternoon, and then come back the next day. But you may be lucky, and certainly if you visit in the summer it will be warmer—but not warm enough to go without a fleece or sweatshirt. That's because of the winds blowing in off the Pacific.

My advice, if you can choose your date for visiting the Oregon coast, would be to come in early- to mid-September. But, as you will hear me pointing out throughout this guide, you don't visit the Oregon coast because of the weather, you visit it because of the nature. The best months for spotting migrating gray whales are mid-December to mid-January and March through June (some whales hang around all summer long). There are headlands where winter winds are clocked at 140mph, and storms so fierce that they reconfigure entire beaches. We love it. It's the Oregon coast.

A BRIEF HISTORY OF THE PACIFIC NORTHWEST

PREHISTORY Native American habitation in the Pacific Northwest dates back at least 10,000 years, perhaps 12,000 years. Before the arrival of Euro-Americans in the region that is today's Washington and Oregon, there were hundreds of distinct Northwest tribes speaking over 50 languages. Between the 1780s, when white explorers and traders first began frequenting the Northwest coast, and the 1830s, when the first settlers began arriving, the Native American population of the Northwest was reduced to perhaps a 10th of its historic numbers, wiped out by diseases such as smallpox, measles, malaria, and influenza. Native Americans had no resistance to these European diseases and entire tribes were decimated by fast-spreading epidemics.

Throughout the Puget Sound region, numerous small tribes subsisted primarily on salmon, halibut, shellfish, and whales. Seafood was a mainstay of the native diet. Cedar trees were the most important building material. Rot-resistant cedar wood and bark was used to build longhouses, large canoes, even clothing. The natural abundance

this well-planned exercise in city boosterism that introduced tens of thousands of visitors to the city. In 1903, to help prepare for the event, noted Boston landscape architect John Olmsted (stepson of Frederick Law Olmsted, who designed New York's Central Park) is hired to design a site plan for the exposition and to develop a citywide park plan.

1905–1929 Early land claims are subdivided as the city experiences two major real-estate booms, one from 1905 to 1913 and another from 1922 to 1928. Electric trolleys carry people throughout the downtown area and to new east-side flatland neighborhoods such as Sellwood, Ladd's Addition, and Irvington, Portland's first "streetcar suburbs." More affluent Portlanders built homes in the "highlands" of southwest and northwest Portland on streets that curve around and rise in sharp switchbacks up the hills.

Tall commercial buildings with steel frames and distinctive white terra-cotta facades with classical detailing were constructed along the major downtown streetcar lines.

continues

of the region allowed many of tribes to develop complex cultures. The Columbia River tribes became the richest of the Oregon tribes through their control of Celilo Falls, the richest salmon-fishing area in the Northwest. Today, Celilo Falls are gone, inundated by the water impounded behind The Dalles Dam, completed in 1957, and the enormous fish runs that were a mainstay of Native American life have been reduced to a trickle of what they once were.

THE AGE OF EXPLORATION   Though a Spanish ship reached what is now southern Oregon in 1542, the Spanish had no interest in the gray and rainy Northwest coast. Nor did famed British buccaneer Sir Francis Drake, who in 1579 sailed his ship the *Golden Hind* as far north as the mouth of Oregon's Rogue River. Drake called off his explorations in the face of what he described as "thicke and stinking fogges."

In 1775, Spanish explorers Bruno de Heceta and Juan Francisco de la Bodega y Quadra charted much of the Northwest coast, and though they found the mouth of the Columbia River, they did not enter it. Four of the Oregon coast's most scenic headlands—Cape Perpetua, Heceta Head, Cape Arago, and Cape Blanco—bear names from these early Spanish explorations.

Within a few years, Spanish claims to the region were challenged by English and Russian traders who found the native people eager to trade furs. The Chinese would pay astronomical prices for Northwest furs, especially sea otter pelts. By 1785, the fur trade between the Northwest and China was well underway, with the British asserting a claim to the Pacific Northwest. The Spanish and English teetered on the brink of war, but a settlement was reached in 1792 with Captain George Vancouver serving as English envoy. Vancouver (Vancouver, Washington; Vancouver, British Columbia; and Vancouver Island were all named for him) spent time exploring and mapping much of the Northwest. Though he passed off the Columbia River as unimportant, he sailed up the Strait of Juan de Fuca and discovered a large inland sea that he named Puget Sound, after one of his lieutenants.

A new player entered the Northwest arena of trade and exploration in the person of American trader Robert Gray. Risking a passage through treacherous sandbars, Gray sailed his ship, *Columbia Rediviva*, into the mouth of the long-speculated-upon Great

1929	Construction of the seawall on the Willamette River ends the floods that were a regular occurrence in downtown Portland since the city's founding.		metropolitan Portland counted some 140,000 defense workers. The city's population leapt from 501,000 to 661,000. A significant number of these workers were African-Americans who settled in North and Northeast Portland.
1930s	Construction in Portland comes to a virtual standstill.		
1941–1945	The demand for workers in Portland's shipyards creates a phenomenal war-time boom. Men and women are brought in by chartered trains from the East Coast and employed by the Kaiser shipbuilding yards in Vancouver, Washington and Portland. At the peak of wartime production in 1943–1944,	1942	FDR signs order sending Japanese Americans from the West Coast to internment camps; thousands in the Portland area are forced to abandon their homes and businesses.
		1948	A catastrophic flood completely destroys Vanport, a suburban Portland city built to house 17,500 war-time workers.

River of the West, which he named the Columbia River after his ship. Gray's discovery established the first American claim to the region.

Thomas Jefferson decided that the United States needed to find a better route overland to the Northwest and commissioned Meriwether Lewis and William Clark to lead an expedition up the Missouri River in hopes of finding a single easy portage that would lead to the Columbia River. Beginning in 1804, the members of the Lewis and Clark expedition (the Corps of Discovery) paddled up the Missouri, crossed the Rocky Mountains, and paddled down the Columbia River to its mouth. After spending the very dismal, wet winter of 1805 to 1806 at Fort Clatsop (p. 190), near today's Astoria, Oregon, the expedition headed back east. Discoveries made by the expedition added greatly to the scientific and geographical knowledge of the continent.

In 1819, the Spanish relinquished all claims north of the present California-Oregon state line, and the Russians gave up their claims to all lands south of Alaska. This left only the British and Americans dickering for control of the Northwest.

SETTLEMENT   Only 6 years after Lewis and Clark spent the winter at the mouth of the Columbia, employees of John Jacob Astor's Pacific Fur Company managed to establish themselves at the mouth of the Columbia River on the Oregon side at a site they called Fort Astoria. With the decline of the sea otter population, British fur traders turned to beaver and headed inland up the Columbia River. In 1824, the Hudson Bay Company (HBC) established its Northwest headquarters at Fort Vancouver, 100 miles up the Columbia near the mouth of the Willamette River (today's Vancouver, Washington). Between 1824 and 1846, when the 49th parallel was established as the boundary between British and American northwestern lands, Fort Vancouver was the most important settlement in the region. (Today, a replica of the fort has been built and is part of the Vancouver National Historic Reserve.)

By the 1830s, the future of the Northwest had arrived in the form of American missionaries, and in 1840, a slow trickle of American settlers began making the 2,000-mile journey across the continent. Their destination was the Oregon Country, which was promoted as a veritable Eden with wide expanses of land just waiting to be claimed. The small population of retired trappers, missionaries, and HBC employees living at

SEATTLE, PORTLAND & THE OREGON COAST IN CONTEXT | A Brief History of the Pacific Northwest

1950s–1960s   As streetcars vanish and a car culture takes over, many of Portland's oldest buildings and west-side neighborhoods are demolished to make way for highways and parking lots. The city's first high-rise towers appear on the downtown skyline in the late 1960s.

1970s   Portland's reputation as one of the country's best-planned cities dates back to 1972 when the Downtown Plan was approved by the city council. This detailed agenda, which set forth new strategies for land use, commercial development, architecture, and public transportation, resulted in a series of urban renewal projects that effectively reclaimed the downtown area for pedestrians. In the following years, a new light-rail system was built; a transit mall was constructed; a parking lot in the center of the downtown was refashioned into a public piazza; and the highway that ran along the downtown waterfront was replaced by Tom McCall Waterfront Park. Historic structures were preserved, and ordinances limited the height of new buildings, protecting views of the mountains.

continues

Fort Vancouver and nearby Oregon City formed a provisional government in anticipation of the land-claim problems that would arise with the influx of settlers to the region. The losers in the land grab that ensued were, of course, the Native Americans who had lived, fished, and hunted the land for untold generations.

In 1844, Oregon City became the first incorporated town west of the Rocky Mountains. This outpost in the wilderness, a gateway to the fertile lands of the Willamette Valley, was the destination of the wagon trains that began traveling the Oregon Trail, and which each year brought more and more settlers to the region. When all the land in the Willamette Valley was claimed, settlers began fanning out to different regions of the Northwest, and during the late 1840s and early 1850s many new towns, including Seattle and Portland, were founded.

Subsequent demand for territorial status and U.S. military protection brought about the establishment of the first U.S. territory west of the Rockies. Although the line between American and British land in the Northwest had been established in 1846 at the 49th parallel (the current U.S.-Canada border), it was not until 1848 that Oregon was finally given U.S. territorial status. Washington had to wait until 1853 to officially become a territory. Oregon became a state in 1859, Washington in 1889.

In 1881, the first transcontinental railroad reached Spokane, in eastern Washington, and finally linked the Northwest with the eastern United States. In 1893, trains reached Seattle. The arrival of the railroads (and, earlier, steam ships) led to a great leap forward for the development of Washington and Oregon No longer a remote wilderness, the Pacific Northwest began to attract industry.

INDUSTRIALIZATION & THE 20TH CENTURY   From the very beginning of Euro-American settlement in the Northwest, the region based its growth on a short-sighted, resource-extractive economy. The early fur traders completely wiped out Washington's and Oregon's sea otter population (which has since been reestablished, with otters from Alaska, off the Olympic Peninsula) and the beaver population after that. Lumber and salmon, the two natural resources that Washington and Oregon had in the greatest abundance, were both exploited relentlessly, and the history of the timber and salmon-fishing industries ran parallel to one another for more than a century.

1971   Nike founded. Oregon becomes the first state to pass a bottle bill mandating a refundable deposit on beer and soft-drink cans and bottles.

1980   Mt. St. Helens erupts, coating the city with volcanic ash but otherwise doing no damage.

1980s   Portland's Urban Growth Boundary is designed to preserve neighboring farmlands and open spaces from unchecked commercial development.

1980s–1990s   The city is roiled by several virulent and costly anti-gay rights battles fomented by a homophobic right-wing "Christian" group called the Oregon Citizens Alliance (OCA).

1993   Soon after a geologic study verifies the existence of two earthquake faults under the city, a quake measuring 5.6 on the Richter scale rocks the entire region. Its epicenter is located about 30 miles south of Portland. Since that time, city seismic codes have been updated to make buildings more earthquake-resistant.

1996   A flood causes considerable damage in low-lying areas north

3

SEATTLE, PORTLAND & THE OREGON COAST IN CONTEXT   A Brief History of the Pacific Northwest

At the close of the 20th century, both industries had arrived at similar situations—severely depleted wild resources that required government intervention to preserve the remaining old-growth forests and wild salmon populations.

The 1897 gold rush in Alaska and the Klondike brought great prosperity to Seattle. However, trees were still the foundation of the state's economy. Nurtured on steady rains, Douglas fir, Sitka spruce, western red cedar, and hemlock grew as much as 300 feet tall. Washington's first sawmill began operation near present-day Vancouver, Washington in 1828, and between the 1850s and 1870s, Washington sawmills supplied the growing California market as well as a limited foreign market. When the transcontinental railroads arrived in the 1880s, mills began shipping to the eastern states. Oregon, too, cut down its trees and overfished its rivers, exporting both by ship to San Francisco during the gold rush years and to worldwide markets for more than 100 years.

At the outbreak of World War I, more than 20% of the forestlands in the Northwest were owned and being clear-cut by three companies—Weyerhaeuser, the Northern Pacific Railroad, and the Southern Pacific Railroad—and more than 50% of the workforce labored in the timber industry.

The timber industry has always been extremely susceptible to fluctuations in the economy and experienced a roller-coaster ride of boom and bust throughout the 20th century. Boom times in the 1970s brought on record-breaking production that came to a screeching halt in the 1980s and 1990s, first with a nationwide recession, and then with the listing of the northern spotted owl as a threatened species. By the 1980s, environmentalists, shocked by vast clear-cuts on public lands, began trying to save the last old-growth trees. Today the battle between the timber industry and environmentalists continues.

Just as trees in the Northwest were huge and plentiful, so too were the salmon. These fish, which spend their adult lives in the ocean before returning to fresh water to spawn, were the dietary mainstay of Northwest Native Americans for thousands of years before the first whites arrived in the region. However, within 10 years of the opening of the first salmon cannery in the Northwest, the fish population was severely

and south of downtown. The same year, rapid snowmelt and above-average rainfall combined with tree-cutting and erosion results in mudslides and property damage in residential sections of the West Hills.

1998 Oregon is the first state to legalize euthanasia with the Death with Dignity Act.

2004 With no advance warning, Multnomah County (Portland) issues marriage licenses for same-sex couples. Over 3,000 couples rush to get married.

2005 After a court challenge and public referendum, Multnomah County rescinds same-sex marriage ruling and sends all married same-sex couples refund checks for their license fees.

2008 Oregon Legislature passes the Oregon Family Fairness Act, which makes it possible for same-sex couples to legally establish a domestic partnership.

2008–2013 Nationwide recession results in unemployment figures in Portland that are among the highest in the nation. It doesn't matter. People keep moving to Portland anyway.

depleted. In 1877, the first fish hatchery was developed to replenish dwindling runs of salmon. Salmon canning reached a peak on the Columbia River in Astoria in 1895 and on Puget Sound in 1913. Later in the 20th century, salmon runs would be further reduced by the construction of numerous dams on the Columbia and Snake rivers. Although fish ladders help adult salmon make their journeys upstream, the young salmon heading downstream have no such help, and a large percentage are killed by the turbines of hydroelectric dams. One solution to this problem has been the barging and trucking of young salmon downriver. Today the salmon populations of the Northwest are so diminished that entire runs of salmon have been listed as threatened or endangered.

In 1916, William Boeing launched a small seaplane from the waters of Seattle's Lake Union and laid down the foundation for what would become the Seattle area's single largest employer: Boeing. The company became a major employer in Seattle when it began manufacturing B-17s and B-29s during World War II and today continues to be one of the largest employers in Washington state. However, this has had its drawbacks for Seattle. The city's fortunes were for many years so closely linked to the aircraft manufacturer that any cutback in production at Boeing had a devastating ripple effect on the local economy. And Boeing, because of its power, holds Seattle hostage in terms of tax breaks, threatening to move elsewhere if their demands are not met. However, with the global ascendancy of Bill Gates's software giant Microsoft (based just outside Seattle), the Seattle economy has begun to diversify.

In Portland, Kaiser Steel played a major role in the shipbuilding boom of World War II. The war brought over 100,000 workers to the Portland shipyards—including the city's first African-Americans—and many of the new arrivals stayed after the war was over. Portland's economy never had a Boeing to keep it afloat. Today, the Portland economy is a mixture of high-tech, advertising, health care, and sports apparel and equipment. The sportswear giant Nike was founded in Portland in 1971.

SEATTLE

I f you distilled Seattle's history into five points, it would read something like this: a great fire (1889), a frenzied gold rush (1897), a World's Fair (1962), the formation of an airplane company called Boeing (1917), and the emergence of a game-changing computer company named Microsoft (1975). Of course, the city's location on Puget Sound didn't hurt, either, because that gave Seattle access to the Pacific Ocean. For much of its relatively brief existence, Seattle was the wettest, wildest city in the Pacific Northwest, a gritty maritime depot that became the jumping-off point for tens of thousands of Alaska-bound gold-seekers. Puget Sound was Seattle's gateway to the rest of the world until the railroad arrived, at which point it became a major freight terminus by land and a port by sea. Then Boeing and the aerospace industry came along, and Seattle took to the air, too. A wartime boom in shipbuilding and plane manufacturing bumped the city's fortunes up another notch. The Seattle World's Fair of 1962 was another turning point, an event that introduced this unique and atmospheric city on Elliott Bay to a new generation of visitors. Then came computers and software, personified by Bill Gates and Paul Allen of Microsoft, and Seattle was again "discovered" by the rest of the world. The city experienced phenomenal growth in the 1980s, and turned into a Big City where people raced around with a Starbucks cup in one hand and a cellphone in the other. And during the real-estate bubble it did more than bubble—it frothed.

So it's safe to say that when Seattle sees an opportunity, it takes it and runs. This opportunistic nature is what makes for its highs and lows, its booms and busts, and gives it the big city edge and push that Portland looks at half-longingly yet doesn't quite covet.

Seattle's location amid great natural splendor and its up-to-the-minute trendoid consciousness adds to the pleasures and excitement of a visit. Yes, it does rain a lot, but it's *supposed* to. That's what this northerly Pacific Northwest maritime climate west of the Cascades does: It precipitates. Without those gray, misty days with the smell of saltwater in the air, it wouldn't be Seattle—and you might not appreciate the clear days, when the Olympic Mountains glow far across the water to the west and Mount Rainier appears majestically to the east. Nor, without the precip, would you see as much green. If you look around at the green coniferous forests that are another characteristic of this moist, temperate climate, you'll understand why Seattle's nickname is The Emerald City. The name has nothing to do with Oz, but there is a natural and self-made magic to the place. It's casual and caffeinated, definitely into good food, arts, and recreation, and offers visitors plenty to see and do, along with a great big dose of fresh sea air.

ESSENTIALS

Arriving

BY PLANE   **Seattle-Tacoma International Airport (Sea-Tac),** 17801 International Blvd. (www.portseattle.org/sea-tac; ℂ 206/787-5388), is located about 14 miles south of downtown Seattle.

By far the most convenient way to get to downtown Seattle from the airport is by taking Sound Transit's (www.soundtransit.org) **Link Light Rail** service, which runs from 5am to 1am Monday through Saturday and 6am to midnight on Sundays. Trains arrive and depart every 7½ to 15 minutes, depending on the time of day. The SeaTac Airport Station, reached by a covered walkway, is located on the fourth floor of the airport garage (follow signs from the terminals). The adult fare from the airport to one of the downtown stops is $2.75; buy your ticket from a vending machine on the platform before you board. The trip takes approximately 35 minutes.

It's slower and far less convenient, but you can also take a bus operated by **King County Metro Transit** (http://metro.kingcounty.gov) into the city. Sound Transit Metro bus stops are located on International Boulevard (State Hwy. 99) and South 176th Street by the Link Light Rail Station. To reach them, take the walkway through the north end of the fourth floor of the Airport Parking Garage to the Sound Transit Link Light Rail Station and exit to International Boulevard. Departure times are shown on information signs at the bus stop. You also can pick up printed bus timetables at the Ground Transportation Information Booth on the Baggage Claim level near door number 16 (across from baggage carousel 12).

By car, the trip to downtown Seattle takes about 30 minutes, depending on traffic. All major rental car agencies have counters in the lower, baggage claim area of the airport.

A metered taxi ride from the airport to downtown Seattle costs approximately $45 to $50. However, many companies now charge a lower fixed rate. **Yellow Cab** (www.yellowtaxi.net; ℂ 206/ 622-6500), available outside the baggage claim area, and **Horizon Car Service** (www.seattleairport-taxi.com; ℂ 206/306-2000) both charge a flat rate of $40 to downtown Seattle.

BY TRAIN   Seattle is served by **Amtrak** trains (www.amtrak.com) running north from Los Angeles, south from Vancouver, British Columbia, and points east. Trains arrive and depart from the newly revamped **King Street Station,** 303 South Jackson St., near the Pioneer Square area of downtown Seattle.

BY BUS   Greyhound (www.greyhound.com; ℂ 800/345-3109) provides long-distance bus service to Seattle from cities around the U.S. The Seattle Greyhound Station is located in downtown Seattle at 811 Stewart St. If you're traveling between Portland and Seattle, **Bolt Bus** (www.boltbus.com; ℂ 877/265-8287) offers super-cheap rates and free onboard Wi-Fi.

BY CAR   Seattle is 110 miles from Vancouver, British Columbia, 175 miles from Portland, 810 miles from San Francisco, 1,190 miles from Los Angeles, 835 miles from Salt Lake City, and 285 miles from Spokane. I-5 is the main north–south artery, running south to Portland and north to the Canadian border. I-405 is Seattle's eastside bypass and accesses Bellevue, Redmond, and Kirkland on the east side of Lake

Seattle & Environs

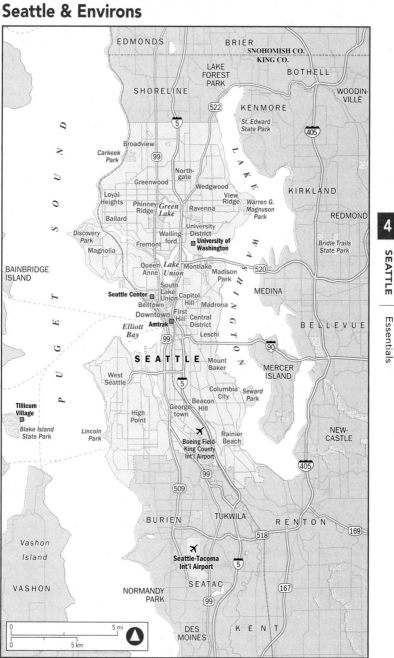

Washington. I-90, which ends at I-5, connects Seattle to Spokane in the eastern part of Washington. Wash. 520 connects I-405 with Seattle just north of downtown and also ends at I-5. Wash. 99, the Alaskan Way Viaduct, is another major north–south highway through downtown Seattle, but it's slated to be removed by 2017 and replaced by a tunnel. All the major car-rental agencies have offices in Seattle and at or near Sea-Tac International Airport.

Visitor Information

For more information about Seattle, contact **Seattle's Convention and Visitors Bureau,** 701 Pike St., Suite 800, Seattle, WA 98101 (www.visitseattle.org; ✆ **866/732-2695** or 206/461-5800). This organization operates the **Seattle Visitor Center** inside the Washington State Convention and Trade Center, Seventh Avenue and Pike Street (✆ **206/461-5840**); and the **Market Information Center**, Southwest Corner of 1st Avenue and Pike Street in the Pike Place Market (✆ **206/461-5840**). For additional information on other parts of Washington, contact **Washington State Tourism** (www.experiencewa.com; ✆ **800/544-1800**).

Neighborhoods in Brief

Seattle is a maritime city wedged between Elliott Bay in Puget Sound to the west, and giant, freshwater Lake Washington to the east. The freshwater lake is connected to the saltwater Sound by the Chittenden Locks and Lake Union at the north end of downtown. Puget Sound is dotted with islands that are not part of Seattle proper but are bedroom communities served by commuter ferries; the most prominent and populous are Bainbridge Island, Vashon Island, and Whidbey Island.

Downtown This is Seattle's main business district and can be defined roughly as the area from Pioneer Square in the south to around Pike Place Market in the north, and from First Avenue to Eighth Avenue. It's characterized by steep streets, high-rise office buildings, luxury hotels, and a high density of department stores, shopping malls, and shops. This is also where you'll find the Seattle Art Museum and Benaroya Hall, home to the Seattle Symphony. Hotels in this area are convenient to Pioneer Square, Pike Place Market, and the Convention Center.

The Waterfront The Seattle waterfront stretches along Alaskan Way from roughly Washington Street in the south to Broad Street and Myrtle Edwards Park in the north. This is the most touristy neighborhood in Seattle, presided over by the Seattle Great Wheel. In addition to the many tacky gift shops, fish-and-chips windows, and tour-boat docks, you'll also find the city's only waterfront hotel (The Edgewater), the Seattle Aquarium, and a few excellent seafood restaurants.

Belltown This neighborhood, stretching north from Pike Place Market to Seattle Center, is home to the city's liveliest restaurant and club scene and is constantly expanding and redefining itself. There are some good, out-of-downtown shops and a couple of good hotels, including the Warwick and The Ace.

Pioneer Square The Pioneer Square Historic District, known for its restored 1890s buildings, is centered on the corner of First Avenue and Yesler Way. This is the oldest settled part of Seattle, and its tree-lined streets and cobblestone plazas make it the most atmospheric neighborhood downtown. Pioneer Square (which refers to the neighborhood, not a specific square) is full of antiques shops, art galleries, restaurants, bars, and nightclubs; it's also where you'll find the wonderfully entertaining Underground Tour.

South Lake Union At the north end of downtown, extending east of Seattle Center to the southern and western shores of Lake Union, this is Seattle's newest and still developing neighborhood. Most of it is owned and has been developed by Microsoft gazil-lionaire Paul Allen and his Vulcan company. Formerly a low-rise warehouse and industrial area, South Lake Union has been trans-formed over the last decade into a residen-tial and business neighborhood that is home to Amazon and other high-tech and biotech companies. A new streetcar line connects the area to downtown. The Pan Pacific Hotel serves the high-end business side of the neighborhood. In 2013, the fascinating Museum of History and Industry (MOHAI) moves to the former Naval Reserve building on Lake Union.

Chinatown/International District Known to locals as the I.D., this small but distinctive neighborhood is home to a large Asian population. Here you'll find the Wing Luke Asian Museum, Hing Hay Park (a small park with an ornate pagoda), Uwajimaya (an Asian supermarket), and many small shops and restaurants. The Chinatown/Inter-national District begins around Fifth Avenue South and South Jackson Street.

First Hill Because it is home to several large hospitals, this hilly neighborhood just east of downtown and across I-5 is called "Pill Hill" by Seattleites. First Hill is home to the Frye Art Museum and a couple of good hotels. It is an old Seattle residential neighborhood, too; once grand, now not so but with some nice strollable streets.

Capitol Hill To the northeast of downtown, centered along Broadway near Volunteer Park, Capitol Hill is Seattle's main gay neigh-borhood and has long been a popular youth-culture shopping and entertainment district. Broadway sidewalks are often crowded, and it is nearly impossible to find a parking space. In recent years, the area has been undergoing a big spruce-up. New condominiums have been built on Broad-way, and along 12th Avenue, near the inter-section with Pike Street and there are now some good restaurants. Outside its commer-cial area, parts of Capitol Hill are undeniably attractive, with fine old homes and man-sions; Volunteer Park is one of Seattle's great parks and contains a wonderful plant conser-vatory and the Seattle Asian Museum.

University District This neighborhood in the northeast section of the city surrounding the University of Washington is called the U District for short. Because it's a college neighborhood, it's a good place to find inex-pensive ethnic restaurants, pubs, clubs, espresso bars, and music stores. Visitors come to this area to visit the great Washing-ton Park Arboretum and the gorgeous Seat-tle Japanese Garden.

Queen Anne Hill With its great city and water views, affluent Queen Anne, just northwest of Seattle Center, has long been one of the most prestigious residential areas in Seattle and features some of Seattle's old-est homes. The neighborhood is divided into the Upper Queen Anne and Lower Queen Anne. Upper Queen Anne is very peaceful and abounds in moderately priced restaurants. Lower Queen Anne, adjacent to theaters and Marion Oliver McCaw Hall at Seattle Center, is something of a theater district and has a more urban character.

Fremont If you have time to visit only one neighborhood outside of downtown, make it Fremont. North of the Lake Washington Ship Canal between Wallingford and Ballard, Fre-mont is home to Seattle's best-loved piece of public art—*Waiting for the Interurban*—as well as the famous *Fremont Troll* sculpture. This is Seattle's most independent neighbor-hood, filled with eclectic shops and ethnic restaurants. During the summer, there's a Sunday flea market. The neighborhood cel-ebrates its left-leaning vitality with a yearly street fair—watch for the nude bicyclists!

Ballard In northwest Seattle, bordering the Lake Washington Ship Canal and Puget Sound, Ballard is a former (hard-)working-class Scandinavian community that prides itself in its past (the Nordic History Museum is here) and is rediscovering its old urban charms and character. One of Seattle's most enjoyable neighborhoods, Ballard is a great place to discover off-the-beaten-path shops and restaurants. Art galleries and interesting boutiques and shops are set along the tree-shaded streets of the neighborhood's old commercial center, also the site of Ballard's famous Sunday Farmers Market. Ray's

Boathouse is probably the best-known of Ballard's restaurants.

The Eastside Home to Bill Gates, Microsoft, countless high-tech spinoff companies, and seemingly endless suburbs, the Eastside lies across Lake Washington from Seattle proper and comprises the cities of Kirkland, Bellevue, Redmond, and a few other smaller communities. As the presence of Bill Gates's mansion attests, there are some pretty wealthy neighborhoods here; but except for Bellevue this isn't an area that draws tourists.

West Seattle West Seattle, across from the downtown port facility, is not just the site of the terminal for ferries to Vashon Island and the Kitsap Peninsula. It's also the site of Seattle's favorite beach, Alki, which is as close to a Southern California beach experience as you'll find in the Northwest. Here, too, is the waterfront restaurant with the best view of Seattle: Salty's on Alki Beach. Seattle's very first white settlers landed on Alki Point, but after a miserably wet winter moved east to the area that would become Pioneer Square.

GETTING AROUND

Seattle is a sprawling city with lots of neighborhoods to explore, a lively downtown core, and a half-carny waterfront that attracts the sea-lion's share of tourist attention. Seattle is notorious for its traffic jams, but that doesn't seem to prevent anyone from driving.

By Public Transportation

BY BUS Seattle's **Metro** (http://metro.kingcounty.gov; ✆ **800/542-7876** in Washington or 206/553-3000) bus and electric trolley system covers all of greater Seattle. Fares are based on zones and travel time. Off-peak fares for all zones are $2.25 for adults, 75¢ for seniors, and $1.25 for ages 6–18. During peak commuter hours, adult fares go up to $2.50 for 1 zone, $3.00 for 2 zones; senior and children fares remain the same. Use exact change and pay on the bus.

BY STREETCAR The new **Seattle Streetcar** (www.seattlestreetcar.org) runs from downtown to Lake Union and will eventually have another line up First Hill and along Broadway. Fares are $2.50 for adults.

BY LIGHT RAIL The **Central Link Light Rail** (www.soundtransit.org) runs beneath 3rd Avenue from Westlake Station to Sea-Tac airport, making key downtown stops along the way. Adult fares range from $2 to $2.75 depending on distance traveled.

BY MONORAIL The fastest way to get between downtown and Seattle Center is the **Seattle Monorail** (www.seattlemonorail.com; ✆ **206/905-2620**), an elevated train built for the 1962 Seattle World's Fair. It leaves every 10 minutes from Westlake Center shopping mall (Fifth Ave. and Pine St.) and covers the 1¼ miles in 2 minutes, dropping you off near the Space Needle. The monorail operates daily from 9am to 11pm (in winter, Sun–Thurs 8am–8pm; Fri and Sat 9am–11pm). Departures are every 10 minutes. A one-way fare is $2 for adults, $1 for seniors, and 75¢ for ages 5 to 12.

BY WATER TAXI A water taxi runs between Pier 55 on the downtown Seattle waterfront to Seacrest Park in West Seattle, providing access to West Seattle's popular Alki Beach and adjacent paved path. For schedules, check with Metro (http://metro.kingcounty.gov). The one-way fare is $4.75 for adults and ages 6 to 18, $2 for seniors.

BY FERRY **Washington State Ferries** (www.wsdot.wa.gov/ferries; ✆ **800/843-3779** or 888/808-7977 in Washington or 206/464-6400) is the most extensive ferry system in the United States. These big passenger and car ferries, used primarily by commuters, won't help you get around Seattle itself, but they offer great options for scenic trips from downtown Seattle to Bremerton (1-hr. crossing) and Bainbridge Island (35-min. crossing), among other destinations. One-way walk-on (no car) fares between Seattle and Bainbridge Island are $7.85 for adults, $3.90 for seniors and ages 6 to 18. You'll pay more, of course, if you take your car.

By Car

Keep in mind that Seattle traffic congestion is bad, parking is limited (and expensive), and streets are almost all one-way. You'll avoid frustration by leaving your car in your hotel parking garage. You might not need a car at all. The city center is well served by public transportation. Plus, Seattle is very walkable. It's more difficult, without a car, if you want to explore beyond Seattle proper—that is, north of Seattle Center, east of Lake Washington, south of the sports stadiums, or to any of the islands in Puget Sound (Bainbridge, Vashon, Whidbey)—or take day trips farther afield, to Mount Rainier, La Conner, or Leavenworth. You could certainly have a very fun trip to Seattle without renting a car.

PARKING   On-street parking in downtown Seattle is expensive and extremely limited. Most downtown parking lots charge $20 to $25 per day, though many offer early-bird specials. Some lots near the Space Needle charge less, and you can leave your car there, then take the monorail downtown. Some restaurants and Pike Place Market merchants validate parking permits. Expect to pay about $40 a day for valet parking at downtown hotels.

DRIVING RULES & TIPS   You can make a right turn at a red light after coming to a full stop. A left turn at a red light is permissible from a one-way street onto another one-way street after coming to a full stop.

If you park your car on a sloping street, be sure to turn your wheels to the curb. When parking on the street, check the time limit on your parking meter. During rush hour, be sure to check whether or not your street parking space is restricted.

By Taxi

Taxis can be difficult to hail on the street in Seattle, so it's best to call or wait at the taxi stands at major hotels. Two reliable companies are **Yellow Cab** (www.yellowtaxi .net; ✆ **206/622-6500**) or **Farwest Taxi** (www.farwesttaxi.net; ✆ **206/622-1717**). The flag-drop charge is $2.50; after that, it's $2.50 per mile. A maximum of four passengers can share a cab; the third and fourth passengers will each incur a surcharge of 50¢.

On Foot

Seattle is a surprisingly compact city. Following north-south avenues, you can easily walk from Pioneer Square to downtown Seattle, Pike Place Market, the waterfront, and Seattle Center. Walking from west to east is another story. When you head east from the waterfront, you will be climbing some steep hills or stairways.

WHERE TO STAY

Seattle offers a wide range of hotel choices. If your time is limited, I'd suggest that you opt for a hotel in downtown or in adjacent Belltown or Pioneer Square areas. From those locations, you can walk or easily access public transportation to all of the major attractions and feel close to the city's urban, bayside heartbeat. I've selected and spread

Where to Stay in Seattle

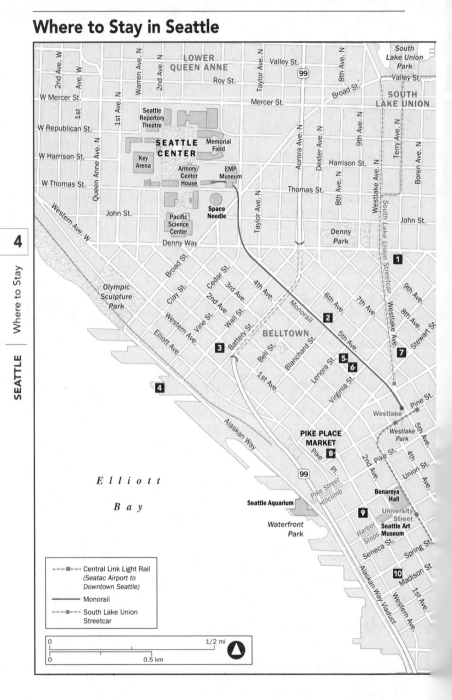

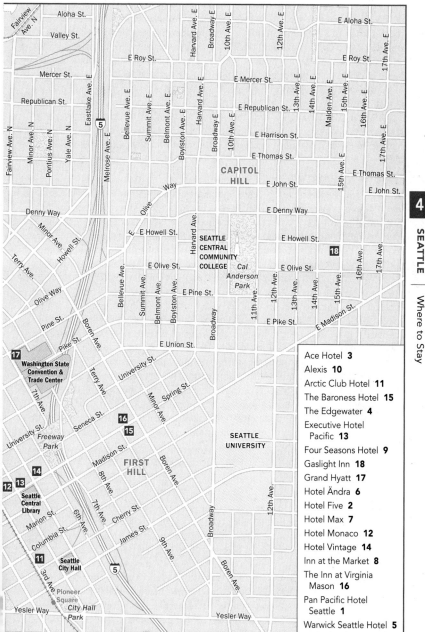

Ace Hotel **3**

Alexis **10**

Arctic Club Hotel **11**

The Baroness Hotel **15**

The Edgewater **4**

Executive Hotel
Pacific **13**

Four Seasons Hotel **9**

Gaslight Inn **18**

Grand Hyatt **17**

Hotel Ändra **6**

Hotel Five **2**

Hotel Max **7**

Hotel Monaco **12**

Hotel Vintage **14**

Inn at the Market **8**

The Inn at Virginia
Mason **16**

Pan Pacific Hotel
Seattle **1**

Warwick Seattle Hotel **5**

my hotel choices over a wide range of hotel types and prices, the goal being to present you with the best and most interesting options in all price ranges within the central part of the city. Keep in mind that the prices listed here are undiscounted rack rates—that is, the undiscounted rate you would pay if you walked in without an advance reservation—for a double room from winter low season to summer high season. Book in advance, and online, and you'll usually pay far less. In the winter, especially, it's not so difficult really to get the price of a luxury hotel down to a more affordable mid-range level. The rates quoted here don't include taxes (around 16%). If you are driving to Seattle, expect to pay anywhere from $25 to $42 dollars per night for valet parking at your hotel.

Although I wouldn't recommend that anyone arrive at a destination without a hotel reservation, if you do, check out www.hoteltonight.com. This is a site that lists last-minute hotel deals for that night only. The savings can amount to hundreds of dollars.

VERY EXPENSIVE

Arctic Club Hotel ★★★   There's nothing quite like the Arctic Club in Seattle, and if you're a fan of historic hotels, you'll love this restored relic of the post–gold rush days. Back in 1917, when the Arctic Club was built as an exclusive gentlemen's club for lucky prospectors who struck it rich in the Yukon gold fields, rooms were roomy and forthright, with beamed ceilings, wood baseboards and crown moldings, and beds were big and solid and covered with woolen blankets. That's how it is today, too, only with updated amenities of all kinds and furniture that evokes the Art Deco era when the club was in its heyday. The exterior of this period gem (on the Seattle Register of Historic Places) is still decorated with the sculpted terra-cotta walrus masks that recalled Alaska to those who had prospected there. The lobby, with its fireplace, ornate Polar Bar, ceiling carvings, and billiard table, instantly transports you back to earlier decades of travel and adventure. (Photographs of the stern-faced men who funded the all-male club line the walls of the reception area.) The bathrooms in this Doubletree boutique property are comfortably man-sized, with marble sink stands and patterned wallpaper. The rooms, with their big windows, king-sized beds and Art Deco–style armchairs, also have a sturdy, period look. The Arctic Club has a great location for exploring the oldest and most architecturally interesting part of Seattle (Pioneer Square), and you can easily walk to downtown, the waterfront, and Pike Place Market.

700 3rd Ave. (entrance on Cherry). www.thearcticclubseattle.com. ℂ **800/222-8733** or 206/340-0340. 120 units. $349–$429 double. Valet parking $33. **Amenities:** Restaurant; lounge; exercise room; Wi-Fi ($10/day).

The Edgewater ★★   It may seem odd in maritime Seattle, but there is no other hotel in Seattle that sits, as this one does, on a pier facing Elliott Bay and Puget Sound. Open the windows of one of the water-view rooms and you'll hear the waves lapping, the gulls crying, and the sounds of harbor craft plying the waters. To be honest, it doesn't make sense to stay here unless you *do* book a water-view room or suite; the outlook from the city-view rooms is not what you'd call memorable. The Edgewater is basically a relic from the 1962 Seattle World's Fair, when it was built to house workers and afterward turned into a hotel with the novel tag line "Fish from every window." Guests could buy bait and tackle at what is now the gift shop and literally drop a line from their rooms—which is what the Beatles were photographed doing when they stayed at The Edgewater during their 1964 world tour (if you're a fan of the Fab Four, you can book the suite they stayed in). The hotel has been steadily upgrading itself over the decades and is now a triple-diamond property with rooms that were completely refurbished in 2013. Its utilitarian, motel-like facade has been disguised, but something of its quirky, freewheeling spirit still survives in the lobby, where columns are disguised as tree trunks, and in the rooms, where footstools are disguised as shaggy dogs. Some rooms have gas fireplaces, walk-in showers, and modern clawfoot tubs; you can slide open the bathroom wall to enjoy the view and the fireplace while you soak. The Edgewater's **Six-Seven** (as in Pier 67) restaurant (see p. 70) is one of Seattle's best waterfront dining spots. But its on-the-waterfront location is ultimately The Edgewater's biggest selling point. The lively Seattle waterfront begins right outside the hotel's door; the *Victoria Clipper,* a high-speed catamaran that travels daily to Victoria, British Columbia, departs from the adjacent pier; and other cruise-ship and excursion boat tours are all within walking distance. The Olympic Sculpture Park is a 5-minute walk north.

Pier 67, 2411 Alaskan Way. www.edgewaterhotel.com. ✆ **800/624-0670** or 206/728-7000. 223 units. $189–$749 double. Valet parking $40. Pets accepted (free). **Amenities:** Restaurant; lounge; exercise room and access to nearby health club; free Wi-Fi.

Four Seasons Hotel ★★★ Seattle has plenty of funky and quirky boutique hotels, and lots of corporate cookie-cutter hotels, but it has only one Four Seasons, and if you're seeking calm, refined luxury in the heart of the Pike Place Market area, this hotel can't be beat. Opened in 2008, the Four Seasons occupies the first 10 floors of a 21-story residential tower overlooking Elliott Bay and the Olympic Mountains. It has a sleek Northwest look, with a long, low lobby fireplace set in a wall of textured basalt, and art from the Seattle Art Museum (located right across the street). The rooms and suites are unusually generous in size and comfort, with a quiet, cocooning quality that invites you to relax and linger. Instead of the dark tones and mixed patterns found in so many of Seattle's trendier boutique hotels, the color scheme here is almost no color—it's white offset by the warm glow of ash wood desks and cabinetry; the muted palette maximizes the light from floor-to-ceiling windows. Luxurious marble-clad bathrooms feature soaker tubs, walk-in rain showers; and L'Occitane toiletries. This full-service hotel offers a full roster of amenities, including Seattle's only heated, outdoor infinity pool with vistas of the bay and mountain; a truly state-of-the-art fitness center; and, a 6,000-square-foot spa that offers a full menu of skin-care treatments and therapies. At ART, the hotel's artful, fine-dining restaurant, Chef Kerry Sear sources local organic ingredients from the Pike Place Market to create seasonal, Northwest-inspired meals. And the bar—what a wonderfully sophisticated spot to sip a cocktail as the sun goes down over Puget Sound.

99 Union St.. www.fourseasons.com/seattle. ✆ **206/749-7000.** 147 units. $275–$545 double; $745–$5,000 suite. Valet parking $41. **Amenities:** Restaurant; lounge; large fitness center; Jacuzzi; year-round outdoor pool; full-service spa; free Wi-Fi.

Pan Pacific Hotel Seattle ★★★ The only hotel located in the South Lake Union neighborhood, the Pan Pacific is ideal for visitors who want to be close to the city's downtown attractions and also explore Seattle's newest neighborhood, created over the last decade by Microsoft co-founder Paul Allen. The lobby, aglow with big windows; travertine floors; a long, low fireplace; and tigerwood accents on the walls, sets the hotel's overall tone of minimalist Northwest and Japanese fusion style. You'll find the same cool, uncluttered elegance and attention to detail in the rooms and suites, where light-colored stone tile, carpets, and fabric wall coverings serve as calm backdrops for the few well-chosen and well-designed pieces of furniture. (One thing to note is that none of the rooms have twin beds.) The wood-and-stone bathrooms have both a walk-in shower and a deep soaking tub. In-suite dining is a special amenity offered to guests staying in the suites. The table is set with flowers and candles, you order from a special menu from Seastar, the hotel's well-regarded restaurant, and the meal is served in your room by a waiter. For some added oomph, request a room with a view of the iconic Space Needle. A large gym with state-of-the-art equipment, dry saunas, and a hydropool is located in a separate building across the cobblestoned front plaza. Adjacent to it is a Vida spa offering soothing massages and ayurvedic skincare treatments. A Whole Foods anchors the bottom level of the hotel, and there's a Starbuck's right next door. And by the way, the new Amazon corporate headquarters is right across the street.

2125 Terry Ave. www.panpacific.com/seattle. ✆ **877/324-4856** or 206/264-8111. 206 units. Double $285–$375. Valet parking $39. **Amenities:** Restaurant, lounge, fitness room, spa, free Wi-Fi.

EXPENSIVE

Alexis ★★   The two early-20th-century buildings that have been combined to make this hotel are on Seattle's Historic Register, but the interior decor is anything but old fashioned. A youthful and surprising design aesthetic mixes patterns, colors, styles, and accessories in a way that's both bold and comfortable. Works by local, national, and international artists hang in the lobby and in the gallery-like corridor that connects the two buildings. Darker shades of taupe and brown are used as a background in the rooms, where paintings, ornate headboards, and one-of-a-kind accessories like a desk lamp with a sculpted head as its base add personality of the space. There are dozens of different room configurations, including some enormous suites with wood-burning fireplaces, media rooms, and Elliott Bay views. There's a complimentary evening wine hour, a happy hour with local oysters for a dollar, and complimentary morning and afternoon coffee. A new bar-restaurant called **The Bookstore** serves breakfast, lunch, and dinner. For a relaxing treat, reserve the private sauna (free) on the fourth floor. This is a rare Seattle hotel where you can actually open the windows, but unfortunately you'll probably keep them closed because of the traffic on First Avenue. The last time I stayed at the Alexis, the elevator doors in the lobby opened and a young woman wearing a white bridal gown got out of one car, and an older guest with a giant poodle got in the other. That, to me, is the Alexis.

1007 First Ave. (at Madison St.). www.alexishotel.com. ✆ **888/850-1155** or 206/624-4844. 121 units. $175–$485 double. Rates include evening wine reception. Valet parking $42. Pets accepted (free). **Amenities:** Restaurant; lounge; small exercise room, Aveda day spa; Wi-Fi ($10/day).

Grand Hyatt ★★   What I like about the Grand Hyatt, besides its reasonable rates, is that it is solid and exceptionally well-built. Opened in 2001, it's a high-rise, business-oriented hotel next to the Seattle Convention Center. Although the enormous lobby isn't particularly noteworthy, and even seems a bit bare, the rooms at the Grand go beyond the bland, cookie-cutter sterility found in so many large corporate hotels. The doors are solid and heavy, and the comfortable, clean-lined furniture includes a sizeable work desk. But it's the bathrooms that really stand out here and give the Grand a sense of luxury: Wonderfully roomy, with marble floors and countertops, each bathroom has a great soaking tub and a walk-in shower. The corner suites are your best bet for size and views (water views are of course the most popular, though you're looking at it through a forest of downtown buildings). The thing to remember is that you can upgrade to a Corner King Suite for only $30 (based on availability), or to one of the 850-square-feet Emerald Suites for an additional $150. The large health Club is well-equipped with cardio and weight machines, as well as free weights. A Ruth's Chris

Steak House is accessed from the lobby, and there's also a Starbucks, a NY Deli, and a Blue Sushi for on-site noshes. Step out the front door and you're smack-dab in the center of Pine Street, one of downtown's busiest shopping streets.

721 Pine St.. www.grandseattle.hyatt.com. © **800/233-1234** or 206/774-6120. 425 units. $179–$369 double. Valet parking $42. **Amenities:** Restaurants, health club.

Hotel Ändra ★★★   The word *ändra* in Swedish means "change," and change is what Hotel Ändra is about. The building dates from 1926, but the owner completely renovated the interior so that when it opened in 2003, it had a brand-new look and life. The neighborhood where it's located is also undergoing change as Amazon and other corporate giants move their headquarters into the nearby South Lake Union area. As an homage to Seattle's Nordic heritage, nearly everything in this trendsetting boutique hotel—furniture, fabrics, even bathroom fixtures—comes from Sweden or Scandinavia and reflects a sophisticated and richly textured European aesthetic geared toward comfort and casual elegance. The tone is set in the lobby with its distressed plank floors, thick wool carpets, stone-mantled fireplace, and a chic-casual bar on the mezzanine. The rooms have a warm, rich look augmented by soft alpaca-covered headboards, crisp white linens with striped chenille coverlets, patterned drapery, and minimalist wood furniture. All the rooms have walk-in closets, vanity areas, and small but well-designed bathrooms with green tiled showers with glass half-walls, sloping white sinks, grey slate flooring, lighted mirrors, fluffy Turkish towels, and FACE Stockholm bath products. The hotel's fitness center is small and basic, as is the business center. The Ändra's central location makes it easy to walk to all of Seattle's downtown and waterfront attractions, shopping, and restaurants. Within a two-block area, foodies can dine at four of Seattle super-chef Tom Douglas's restaurants (Lola, Serious Pie, and Etta's), all reviewed under "Where to Eat."

2000 Fourth Ave. www.hotelandra.com. © **877/448-8600** or 206/448-8600. 119 units. $229–$299 double. Valet parking $41 Pets accepted (free). **Amenities:** Restaurant, lounge; small exercise room and access to nearby health club; Wi-Fi ($10/day).

Hotel Monaco ★★   You know you're in for something out of the ordinary when you enter the lobby, look up, and see frescoes of leaping dolphins copied from the Palace of Knossos on Crete. Those playful mammals are indicative of the sophisticated but playful nature of this Kimpton hotel created in 1997 from a rather undistinguished office building in downtown Seattle. Patterned wallpapers, lush colors, quirky art, and an unpredictable mix of comfy sofas and chairs add pizazz to the rooms and suites (former offices); in the suites, curtains rather than doors separate the living and bedroom areas. (Unless you are using the room only to sleep, you might want to steer clear of the smaller rooms that face the grim FBI building next door.) At 5pm, head down to the light, airy, high-ceilinged lobby and curl up next to the fireplace with a glass of complimentary wine. You can also dine on spicy New Orleans–style food at Sazerac, the hotel's restaurant (reviewed on p. 74). Kids are very welcome at the Monaco, where you can request a pet goldfish for your room or bring your own pet with you. The staff at this unstuffy luxury boutique hotel are super-friendly and helpful.

1101 Fourth Ave. www.monaco-seattle.com. © **888/454-8397** or 206/621-1770. 189 units. $179–$319 double. Rates include evening wine tasting. Valet parking $40. Pets accepted (free). **Amenities:** Restaurant; lounge; small exercise room; free Wi-Fi.

Hotel Vintage ★★   This pleasant, wine-themed boutique hotel underwent a complete renovation in 2014 and is now nicer than ever. Occupying a quietly dignified 11-story brick building from the 1920s, the Hotel Vintage is friendly, low-key, and romantic in an under- rather than overstated way. Wine is the beverage and brand of choice here. All the rooms are named for Washington state wineries, and at the complimentary wine hour between 5 and 6pm you can sample excellent West Coast vintages. The newly refurbed rooms are calm and quiet, with patterned carpets, earth-tone walls, and a mix of traditional and contemporary furnishings, including big sofas and sizeable work desks. Bathrooms have nice finishes but are fairly small and straightforward in their layout. Service at this hotel is exceptionally personable, and you can dine on-site at one of Seattle's finest Italian restaurants, Tulio (p. 70). The hotel sits right across the street from the striking Seattle Public Library designed by Dutch architect Rem Koolhass.

1100 Fifth Ave. www.hotelvintage-seattle.com. © **800/853-3914** or 206/624-8000. 124 units. $139–$394 double. Valet parking $34. **Amenities:** Restaurant; lounge; small exercise room; complimentary wine hour and morning coffee; Wi-Fi ($10/day).

Inn at the Market ★★★ Connoisseurs of Seattle hotels have been enjoying Inn at the Market since it opened in 1986. One of the best small hotels in the Pacific Northwest, this charming hotel overlooking the Pike Place Market is one of the most romantic small hotels in the city. Built on a steeply sloping street between First Avenue and the market, Inn at the Market is close to the buzz and bustle of Seattle's number one tourist destination (the Pike Place Market) and the busy downtown core. But step into the hotel's quiet inner courtyard and you're in another world. The small lobby, with its cheery fireplace and quietly traditional decor, is what comfort is all about. There are several different room categories, but basically there are two room types: those with a city view (facing First Avenue) and those with a water view (facing Elliott Bay and the Olympic Mountains). Whatever the view, the rooms are large and uncluttered with a nod to relaxed comfort rather than fussy formality. Colors are muted and calm, furnishings sturdily modern, bathrooms roomy, and the amenities include Gilchrist & Soames toiletries. If your room doesn't have a water view, you can still enjoy one from the roof deck overlooking Elliott Bay and the market, a perfect spot for enjoying a morning coffee or a Seattle sunset. In the rooms, you can open the windows for a breath of fresh air, but be advised that this can be a noisy area, with street life and, in the water-facing rooms, the hum of traffic on the elevated Alaskan Way highway. When they're closed, the hotel's double-paned windows and doors block out all the noise, and by 2016 the Alaskan Way will be demolished. All the rooms and bathrooms in this personable, five-story hotel were refurbished in 2013 and 2014. If you want to spring for something really special, book Beecher's Loft, a second-floor open-plan apartment in the building next door. A former architect's studio, it's been completely redone in a Seattle-chic way with a wrap-around balcony that's right above the Pike Place Market.

86 Pine St. www.innatthemarket.com. © **800/446-4484** or 206/443-3600. 70 units. $215–$350 double. Valet parking $39. **Amenities:** Restaurant; lounge; access to nearby health club; free Wi-Fi.

MODERATE

Ace Hotel ★ There are now Ace Hotels in several U.S. cities and London, but back in 1999 there was only one, and this was it. The idea and aesthetic behind Ace is an appealing one: Convert old(er) buildings into cool new hotels using reclaimed materials and architectural details; have some of the rooms share bathrooms, European style; and charge a reasonable rate. So this is not a hotel with frills and frou-frou, but it is a hotel that is something of an adventure to stay in. In the century-old building in Belltown, Ace made use of the original brick walls and wood floors but painted them white. Bathrooms were created from scratch, using white tile and small stainless steel sinks as accents. Half the rooms share (immaculate) bathrooms, the others have private bathrooms with showers. Each room is unique. Two of them have wall art by famed graffiti artist Shepard Fairey. Others are decorated with nostalgic photos of Washington scenes. The furnishings are simple and minimal—no more than a 1960s-era sculpted plastic chair in some, a vinyl sofa in others. They all have work desks, but the lighting in some rooms could be better. Green plants add a nice living touch to this minimalist urban aesthetic. This is the kind of intriguing small hotel you might find in Europe, and it draws people of all ages from around the globe. There are several good restaurants within easy walking distance, the fabulous Macrina Bakery (p. 75) is right across the street, and you can get to Pike Place Market on foot in about 10 minutes. The reception area is up a fairly steep flight of stairs and there's no elevator, so if mobility is an issue, you probably don't want to stay here.

2423 First Ave. www.acehotel.com. © **206/448-4721.** 28 units, 14 with shared bathroom. $99–109 double with shared bathroom; $165–$195 double with private bathroom. Rates include continental breakfast. Parking $22 (secure lot, two blocks away). Pets accepted (free). **Amenities:** Lounge; free Wi-Fi.

Executive Hotel Pacific ★★ I'm giving this downtown hotel two stars not because it's luxurious and stuffed with amenities but because it is relatively small and simple—and has the lowest room rates of any hotel in downtown Seattle. I really like this place. It's in a brick building built in 1928, and it's so unobtrusive that you can walk by and hardly be aware of its presence. It started life as a hotel but went through many subsequent incarnations and name changes before a Canadian firm bought and started refurbishing it in 2009. There's nothing glamorous or showy here, but that's part of its charm. The hotel is built on one of Seattle's steep hills, so from the mid-level reception area you walk up to the lounge and elevators or down to the cafe facing Fourth Avenue. The rooms are typical of older hotels in that you can actually open the windows—a feature I always appreciate—and the layout is economical and straight-forward. But there's a spark in the decorating, so the beds have high wood headboards and snaps of red on white comforters. There are desks in the king rooms but not in the smaller queen rooms. Bathrooms are small but have been completely retiled and renovated—tubs are too small for bathing, but each one has a rainshower. Head down to the lounge in the evening for the complimentary wine hour—chances are you'll notice that many of the hotel's guests are from Europe, Canada, and Asia, travelers who recognize a good deal when they find it.

400 Spring St. www.executivehotels.net. © **888/388-3932** or 206/623-3900. 156 units. $109–$239 double. Valet parking $35. Pets accepted (free). **Amenities:** Cafe; lounge; complimentary evening wine; small exercise room; free Wi-Fi.

Hotel Max ★★ Hotel Max is sexy and arty and has a loose-fitting European sensibility that suits Seattle and may suit you, too, especially if you're under 40 and aren't traveling with kids. Refashioned in 2005 from a 1927 hotel just a couple of blocks north of all the major downtown action. Works by contemporary Pacific Northwest artists add a sophisticated punch to the rooms and the small lobby with its fireplace, low-slung furniture, and fiery red reception desk. Designed to be cozy, efficient, and attractive, the rooms have dark gray walls and carpeting with bright orange and red accent colors on the beds. The eye-popping red is also used in the bathrooms with their stainless-steel vanities and, in many rooms, separate toilet and tiled shower areas. Fans of Seattle's pop/grunge music scene may want to book a room on the Sub Pop floor, decorated with photos and memorabilia by Charles Peterson, who followed and photographed the bands Nirvana, Pearl Jam, and Sound Garden. The rooms on this floor come with a selection of vintage LPs that you can play on an honest-to-garsh turntable. The only potential drawback in this hotel is that heat and air conditioning come from window-mounted units; on the plus side, this is one of the few hotels where you can open the windows to catch those sweet summertime breezes. This is also the only hotel in Seattle that hosts a complimentary craft beer tasting every evening, and I think it's safe to say that the sexy amenities that come with the romance package aren't offered anywhere else. The hotel's partner restaurant, Miller's Guild ★★ (p. 73), serves outstanding cocktails and grilled meats.

620 Stewart St. www.hotelmaxseattle.com. ✆ **866/986-8087** or 206/728-6299. 163 units. $149–$389 double. Rate includes complimentary beer hour. Valet parking $40. **Amenities:** Restaurant; lounge; fitness center; Wi-Fi ($10/day).

Warwick Seattle Hotel ★★   Built in 1981, this French-owned mid-sized hotel in Belltown was ahead of its time in terms of boutique-style amenities, offering an indoor heated pool and floor-to-ceiling angled windows that open up to create an in-room balcony. From 2010 to 2013, the rooms were refurbished with an eclectic mix of patterns and furnishings that are both stylish and comfortable. The beechwood work desks are actually big enough to work on and have convenient outlets on the top of the desk. The unique window-balconies let in lots of light and provide a glimpse of Elliott Bay, and, if you're in a higher-floor north-facing room, give you a view of the Space Needle. (But with Amazon and other corporate giants building towers in the nearby South Lake Union area, the urban landscape around here seems to change by the day.) The bathrooms are small but have a nicely luxe feel to them. Additional upscale touches include evening turn-down service, Gilchrist & Soames toiletries, and an on-site restaurant, **Margaux,** which serves delicious French-inspired Northwest cuisine. If you're traveling with kids, they'll love the pool.

401 Lenora St. www.warwickwa.com. ✆ **206/443-4300.** 231 units. $159–$499 double. Valet parking $35. **Amenities:** Restaurant; lounge; heated indoor pool; small exercise room; business center; free Wi-Fi in Executive and Premiere rooms, $11 in other rooms.

INEXPENSIVE

Gaslight Inn ★   B&Bs are not for everyone, but the best of them always provide insight into the personality of a neighborhood and the special architectural style of a once-private residence. At the Gaslight Inn, the style is not Victorian, as the name implies, but Craftsman, a handsome and once-ubiquitous early-20th-century Northwest Arts and Crafts style characterized by wide porches, overhanging eaves, a low pitched roofline, and handcrafted stone and woodwork. Inside this charming Capitol Hill bungalow, the doors and windows are trimmed with oak and decorated with Stickley furniture and art glass from the same era. There are eight guest bedrooms, some on the first, some of the second floor, some sharing a bathroom, others with private bathrooms, some with decks, some with fireplaces. What they all have in common is a calm, comfortable period ambience and a reasonable price. A heated outdoor pool (summer use only) adds a touch of non-Craftsman luxury.

1727 15th Ave. www.gaslight-inn.com. ✆ **206/325-3654.** 8 units, 3 with shared bathroom. $128–$138 double with shared bathroom; $138–$178 double with private bathroom. Rates include continental breakfast. No children allowed. **Amenities:** Seasonal Jacuzzi; small seasonal heated outdoor pool; free Wi-Fi.

Hotel Five ★   A former Ramada Inn with completely reimagined decor, Hotel Five is a reasonably priced and conveniently located choice. Although the hotel is not right in the downtown shopping core, you can easily walk there or to Seattle Center within a few minutes, and the cafes and restaurants of Belltown are all around the neighborhood. (The iconic Seattle Monorail runs from Westlake Center to Seattle Center, passing directly in front of the hotel, but it does not make stops along the way.) Now about that room decor: It uses a lot of red (with dark comforters), and it seems to have taken its inspiration from urban graffiti and semi-psychedelic swirl-art paintings. It's not what you'd call serene; however the rooms are surprisingly nice and have a bedroom-at-home feel to them, with hardwood floors and good bathrooms. Down in the more retro-70s-looking lobby, Max's Café serves breakfast and lunch.

2200 Fifth Ave. (at Blanchard St.). www.hotelfiveseattle.com. (C) **206/441-9785.** 120 units. $120–$235 double. Self-park $15. **Amenities:** Cafe (breakfast/lunch only); free Wi-Fi.

The Inn at Virginia Mason & The Baroness Hotel ★★★
Three stars for a pair of hotels that are among the least expensive in Seattle? Can it be true? Yes, I'm happy to report that it can be and is. I'm not awarding this coveted three-star rating because these hotels offer luxurious rooms and heated pools. I'm awarding them because of their surprising charm and personality. Both of them are managed as nonprofits by Virginia Mason Hospital up on First Hill. That's why they are so inexpensive. Both the Inn and the Baroness are often used by family members of patients in one of the area's three hospitals (this area is called Pill hill for a reason). But there is nothing medicinal about a stay in either property—in fact, I can almost guarantee that you will end up telling your friends about what a great find they are. The guest rooms in both are actually former apartments, and because the Inn dates from 1928 and the Baroness from the 1930 Art Deco era, both of the buildings are loaded with period details that you simply will not find in any other Seattle hotels. At the Inn, you enter your room through a little hallway with an arched doorway that opens into the roomy bedroom area. It's even nicer in the Baroness across the street. This Art Deco gem, complete with curving walls and untampered-with period details, is completely charming. A suite here is, again, a former apartment (with a doorbell), but comes with a separate kitchen, a bedroom, and a sitting area—decorated with tasteful traditional furniture and full of original details, like the former phone nook now used as a little library shelf and the small dining table and Art Deco chairs in the kitchen. In both buildings the rooms have flatscreen TVs but not much in the way of fancy bathroom amenities. However, you'll get lots of hot water and plenty of towels. And, unbelievably, you can order room service at the Inn and get a meal delivered to your door for under $15. These two hotels are faves with Europeans, older travelers who appreciate the architectural details, and budget travelers who are looking for something authentic and inexpensive. But really, they are ideal for anybody who is looking for a unique hotel experience in Seattle. And, by the way, you can walk downtown (downhill) from here, and find plenty of spots for breakfast in the intriguing First Hill neighborhood.

1006 Spring St. www.innatvirginiamason.com. (C) **800/283-6453** or 206/583-6453. Inn: 79 units; Baroness: 57 units. Inn: $119–$234 double; Baroness $129–$244 double. **Amenities:** Restaurant; free Wi-Fi.

WHERE TO EAT

Over the last 25 years or so, Seattle's reputation as one of the great restaurant cities in the U.S. has grown steadily. Before that time, there were some good ethnic Asian and Italian restaurants, and always one or two classic French eateries, but eating out in Seattle was mostly about seafood and steak. And the seafood was usually wonderful,

Downtown & Capitol Hill Restaurants

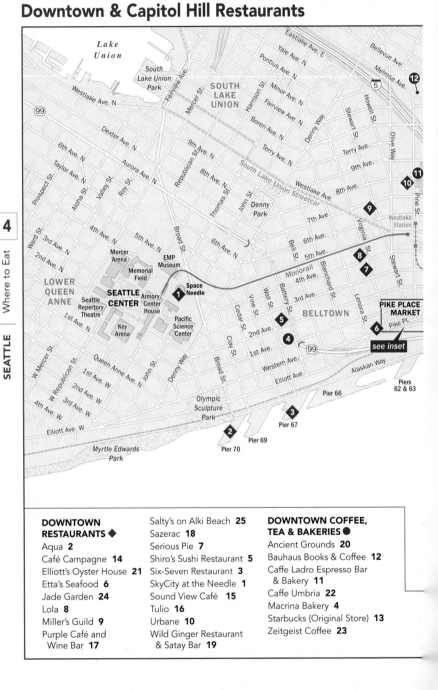

DOWNTOWN RESTAURANTS ◆

Aqua **2**
Café Campagne **14**
Elliott's Oyster House **21**
Etta's Seafood **6**
Jade Garden **24**
Lola **8**
Miller's Guild **9**
Purple Café and Wine Bar **17**

Salty's on Alki Beach **25**
Sazerac **18**
Serious Pie **7**
Shiro's Sushi Restaurant **5**
Six-Seven Restaurant **3**
SkyCity at the Needle **1**
Sound View Café **15**
Tulio **16**
Urbane **10**
Wild Ginger Restaurant & Satay Bar **19**

DOWNTOWN COFFEE, TEA & BAKERIES ●

Ancient Grounds **20**
Bauhaus Books & Coffee **12**
Caffe Ladro Espresso Bar & Bakery **11**
Caffe Umbria **22**
Macrina Bakery **4**
Starbucks (Original Store) **13**
Zeitgeist Coffee **23**

Pike Place Market

14
13
15

1st Ave.
Pike St.
Pine St.
Post Alley
Pike Place
Western Ave.
Stewart St.

SEATTLE
UNIVERSITY
Broadway
Boylston Ave.

E Pine St.
E Belmont Ave.
E Union St.
Summit Ave.

Minor Ave.

Boren Ave.
University St.
Seneca St.

FIRST
HILL

Terry Ave.
Cherry St.
9th Ave.
Yesler Way
12th Ave. S

Wash. State
Convention
& Trade
Center
Hubbell Pl.
Madison St.
Spring St.
8th Ave.
James St.

Freeway
Park
University St.
7th Ave.

S King St.
S Dearborn St.

6th Ave.
16
5th Ave.
Columbia St.
4th Ave.

Seattle
Central
Library

Seattle
City Hall
City Hall
Park

INTERNATIONAL
DISTRICT
International
District/
Chinatown
8th Ave. S
7th Ave. S
Maynard Ave. S

24

Pike St.
Westlake
Park
Union St.
University St.
17
18
University St.
3rd Ave.
Pioneer
Square

Washington St.
Way
6th Ave. S
5th Ave. S
Seattle Blvd. S
Airport Way S
6th Ave. S

Central Link Light Rail
2nd Ave.
S Main St.
S Jackson St.

19
Benaroya
Hall
Seneca St.
Spring St.

Seattle Art
Museum
20
1st Ave.
Marion St.

PIONEER
SQUARE

King St.
Station
(Amtrak)
4th Ave. S

Western Ave.
Occidental
Park
22
23
CenturyLink
Field

Alaskan Way Viaduct
1st Ave. S
S King St.

21
Pier 56
Pier 54
Pier 52

Seattle
Aquarium
Pier 59

25

Pier 46

E Roy St.
Harvard E
10th Ave. E
26
E Mercer St.
0   1/5 mi
0   0.2 km

E Republican St.

15th Ave. E
16th Ave. E
E Harrison St.

E Thomas St.

E John St.

E Denny Way

Cal
Anderson
Park
12th Ave.
E Howell St.

15th Ave.
16th Ave.
E Olive St.

11th Ave.
E Pine St.

Broadway
E Pike St.

E Union St.
E Madison St.
13th Ave.
14th Ave.
15th Ave.
16th Ave.
27

SEATTLE
UNIVERSITY
Capitol Hill

*Elliott
Bay*

**CAPITOL HILL
RESTAURANTS**

Lark **27**
Poppy **26**

0   1/4 mi
0   0.5 km

because it's hard to ruin a slab of salmon or a fresh Dungeness crab. Creamy clam or oyster chowder, or tomato-based seafood chowders, were on just about every menu. The incredible bounty of the region was on display every day at the Pike Street Market. Then the food scene exploded. It was like a complete change of food consciousness, or awareness. Cooking became an art and the materials needed to create that art were close at hand, where they'd always been, but perhaps not appreciated. The "buy fresh, eat local" food philosophy now pervades the Seattle food scene, which now places a premium on sustainable fishing and organic farming practices. The ethnic restaurants are as plentiful and popular as ever, but "Pacific Northwest cuisine" is the general code term for locally sourced ingredients. The big difference now is that many different styles of cooking and flavoring are used to turn those ingredients, no matter how humble, into edible adventures. I've covered a wide range of dining choices for you, some of them old favorites that have lost none of their appeal, some that are special destination restaurants where Seattleites go for good food and fabulous views, and others that showily showcase the "new" style of Pacific Northwest cuisine. Many of Seattle's best downtown restaurants are independent kitchens attached to hotels, others are neighborhood spots outside the downtown core. Wherever you choose to eat, I think you will be impressed with the quality of the food and the professional friendliness of the service.

VERY EXPENSIVE

Canlis ★★★ FREMONT *CONTEMPORARY NORTHWEST* There aren't many formal restaurants left anymore—I mean the kind where guys must wear ties, and gals can put on their dressiest duds—but this is one of them. By formal, however, I don't mean stiff or stuffy. It's Canlis's special-occasion atmosphere and impeccable service that are formal, not the food. That's wonderfully fresh and creative. A Seattle fine-dining destination for over 6 decades, dinner-only Canlis has kept up with the times without losing any of the ingredients that have contributed to its remarkable longevity. This culinary standout in the Queen Anne neighborhood was the first restaurant in Seattle to serve what is now referred to as "contemporary Northwest cuisine." It likes to call its cooking "Comfort Geek," meaning that it combines modern technique with a comfortable, approachable style suitable to the tech-savvy but culinarily challenged techies that rule Seattle. The quietly stylish dining room, in a two-story bluff-top building, uses Asian antiques as focal pieces and provides soft piano music to accompany your meal. Though you'll find an array of fabulous menu choices, steaks from the copper grill, the Canlis salad, and Peter Canlis's prawns are perennial favorites that have been on the menu since 1950. There's a comprehensive wine list, including delicious Northwest vintages. Reserve as far in advance as you can, because formality has lost none of its popularity here.

2576 Aurora Ave. N. www.canlis.com. ℂ **206/283-3313.** Reservations essential. Main courses $36–$78; chef's tasting menu $85–$115. Mon–Thurs 5:30–9pm; Fri 5:30–10pm; Sat 5–10pm.

Ray's Boathouse/Ray's Café ★★★ BALLARD *PACIFIC NORTHWEST/ SEAFOOD* You'll enhance your meal at Ray's if you arrive when it's still light enough to take in the stunning views. Located in the Ballard neighborhood, Ray's sits right on the water's edge overlooking Shilshole Bay, Bainbridge Island, and the Olympic Mountains. As you might expect from a bayside restaurant that started life as a boathouse, seafood reigns supreme at Ray's. As a starter, try the rich seafood chowder with razor clams, smoked salmon, rhyme fingerling potatoes and fennel layered in a bowl with fresh cream added at the table. For your main course, you can't go wrong

North Seattle Restaurants

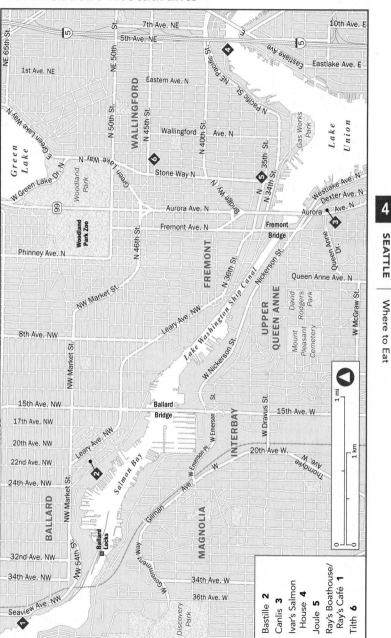

Bastille **2**
Canlis **3**
Ivar's Salmon House **4**
Joule **5**
Ray's Boathouse/ Ray's Café **1**
Tilth **6**

with the sumptuous slab of grilled Pacific Northwest king salmon served medium-rare with grilled Manila clams, fregola sarda, and black kale; or with the sablefish (smoked or cooked with sake). The main floor restaurant, open for dinner only, is a casually elegant, low-ceilinged room with a central bar and giant windows all around. The second floor café, with its high, exposed-beam ceiling, is a more casual dining area with a huge, heated deck that's a beloved spot for outdoor, family-friendly dining from spring through fall. Many of the same dishes are served in both dining rooms, but the restaurant is where you'll want to dine if you're in a romantic mood. Great local and international wines are available to accompany the succulent seafood that makes Ray's such a standout. It would be worth dining here even if it didn't have one of the best outlooks in Seattle. In the end, I like Ray's because it represents the best of what Seattle seafood restaurants used to be, with fairly straightforward preparation that concentrates on the basic flavors of the fish.

6049 Seaview Ave. NW. www.rays.com. ✆ **206/789-3770** for Boathouse or 782-0094 for Café. Reservations recommended. Main courses $24–$50 at Boathouse, $11–$25 at Café. Boathouse daily 5–9pm; Café Sun–Thurs 11:30am–9pm; Fri–Sat 11:30am–10pm.

Shiro's Sushi Restaurant ★★★ BELLTOWN *SUSHI/JAPANESE*   Sushi lovers, whether they're locals or businessmen from Tokyo, flock to Shiro's in Belltown because, quite simply, it has the best sushi in Seattle. Sushi master and local legend Shiro Kashiba serves only the finest, freshest fish to his customers, so you will never taste anything but the best here. For a sumptuous repast, order the chef's selection of omakase sushi or sashimi. Tempura and other traditional Japanese favorites are also available. One of Shiro's signature dishes is broiled black cod kasuzuke.

2401 Second Ave. www.shiros.com. ✆ **206/441-9844.** Sushi and sashimi $17.50–$65, main courses $6.50–$15. Daily 5:30–10:30pm.

SkyCity at the Needle ★ SEATTLE CENTER *NORTHWEST*   Where else in Seattle would you pay $27 for a burger and fries? They couldn't get away with those prices even in New York! But, before you bust a gasket and turn away with a disgusted harrumph from the idea of dining at SkyCity, consider that the price of that pricey burger includes admission to the observation deck atop the Space Needle (which is close to $20 for adults). That should lessen the pain and make the idea more palatable. I happen to have fond memories of this restaurant because I was taken here as a child and was thrilled by the view and horrified that frog legs were on the menu ("they taste just like chicken"). The restaurant, which sits atop the observation deck, has been revolving and serving overpriced food since 1962. But I'm including it because eating here is a classic Seattle experience. The kitchen has to cater to a huge variety of customers, and it does pretty well, offering lots of local seafood choices prepared in different ways, from salmon fritters to poached wild king salmon and Pacific halibut and fresh oysters and Dungeness crab. The dinner menu offers something for everyone, including Kobe steak and beef shortribs. But, let's be honest, the real main course is the view. You'll see Seattle from every angle as SkyCity slowly revolves.

Space Needle, 400 Broad St. www.spaceneedle.com. ✆ **206/905-2100.** Main courses $27–$59. Mon–Fri 11:30am–2pm, Sun–Thurs 5–9:45pm, Fri–Sat 5–10:45pm, Sat–Sun brunch,10am–2:45pm.

EXPENSIVE

Aqua ★★ WATERFRONT *SEAFOOD*   From a seasonal variety of local oysters to crispy-skinned salmon and Alaskan king crab legs in truffle aioli, Chef Wesley Hood's seafood is always fresh and delicious, but landlubbers can enjoy with one of the 28-day dry aged steaks from Niman Ranch or custom-aged Angus beef prepared on an open-air charcoal grill. One signature side dish you might want to try: lobster mashed potatoes.

2801 Alaskan Way, Pier 70. www.waterfrontpier70.com. ℭ **206/956-9171.** Main courses $28–$89. Daily 4–11pm.

Ivar's Salmon House ★ LAKE UNION *SEAFOOD*   Ivar's on Lake Union is one of Seattle's most iconic restaurants, and made its name with the fish most closely identified with the Pacific Northwest (although nowadays the salmon often comes from Alaska). For centuries, salmon was a mainstay of the Native American tribes in this region, and it was they who developed the alder-smoked cooking method that is the signature salmon style at Ivar's. Although the restaurant keeps up with the times and serves other "upscale" dishes, it's the salmon—grilled or roasted—that defines the place. Ivar's is meant to resemble a Native American longhouse, only one with great views across Lake Union with Seattle in the distance, and it celebrates Native American heritage with artifacts and photographs. As you dine here you'll be able watch a lot of boat traffic on Lake Union, which adds to the ambience. You can't be in a hurry, though, because the restaurant is large and the service can be slow.

401 NE Northlake Way. www.ivars.net. ℭ **206/632-0767.** Main courses $15–$30. Mon–Thurs 11am–9pm; Fri–Sat 11am–10pm; Sun 9:30am–2pm and 3:30–9pm.

Lola ★★★ BELLTOWN *GREEK/MEDITERRANEAN*   Lamb is Lola's specialty, and it is delectable, whether you order the *monti* (lamb ravioli with yogurt, Aleppo, and pine nuts); the kebabs (with caramelized garlic and red wine); the slow-roasted lamb seasoned with oregano, mint, rosemary, and jus; or the lamb burger. This narrow, high-ceilinged, all-booth restaurant was started by Tom and Jackie Douglas over 10 years ago and has never waned in popularity. Start with some pita bread and one of the Lola spreads—my favorite is the *kopanisti* made with feta and blue cheese, pistachio, and garlic. Then share a *meze* (small plate)—the traditional Greek salad is excellent; so is the lamb ravioli. Order a kebab (three skewers of lamb, beef, chicken, squid, or pork) and a main course, and you're set. Another recommendation: the Northwest seafood extravaganza with scallops, Dungeness crab, black cod, gulf shrimp, clams, mussels, potatoes, bacon, and ouzo broth. For a light, delicious dessert try the Greek yogurt–semolina pudding. You won't find better Greek-inspired food in Seattle. Lola also serves a wonderful weekend breakfast and lunch.

2000 Fourth Ave. ℭ **206/441-1430.** Main courses $17–$37. Mon–Thurs 6am–midnight, Fri 6am–2am, Sat 7am–2am, Sun 7am–1am.

Poppy ★★★ CAPITOL HILL *PACIFIC NORTHWEST*   If there is one Seattle restaurant that I would recommend to anyone interested in the art of food, it would be Poppy. In 2012, *Seattle Magazine* named Poppy Seattle's best Northwest cuisine restaurant, a well-deserved accolade for this bright, assured, and consistently inventive dining mecca in the Capitol Hill neighborhood. Created by chef Jerry Traunfeld, Poppy presents a fresh take on the Indian *thali*, a compartmentalized platter holding various dishes with many different tastes. Traunfeld, who spent 17 years as executive chef at The Herbfarm restaurant in Woodinville, uses local, seasonal, fresh (never dried) herbs and products to create his daily thalis. These are, quite simply, works of edible art. Before you order your thali, though, you must try the eggplant fries with sea salt and honey—there's a reason why they are one of Poppy's signature appetizers and always on the menu. You might want one of the herby-fresh craft cocktails to go with them. Now the thali. On my last trip, my thali came with miso-roasted black cod with carrot vinaigrette and cucumber shiso salad. The little side dishes included cauliflower-almond soup with harissa; black rice with yams and scallion; kohlrabi with coconut milk, tamarind, and dill; rhubarb and fennel pickle; and a nigella-poppy naan. The medley of textures, herbs, and spices was surprising and delightful. You can dine in Poppy's high-ceilinged dining room or, in summer, out on the sidewalk or in the back herb garden.

622 Broadway E. www.poppyseattle.com. *C* **206/324-1108.** Thalis $24–$28. Daily 5:30–10pm.

Six-Seven Restaurant ★★ WATERFRONT *PACIFIC NORTHWEST*   The restaurant at The Edgewater hotel on Pier 67 always had a great view, and now, under the guidance of Chef John Roberts, it has fine dining as well. The glass-walled room opens out to a narrow patio overlooking Elliott Bay and the Olympic Mountains. This is definitely the place to dine in warm summer months. The food is locally sourced and usually organic. Menus change with the seasons, but you can never go wrong with the chef's signature crab- and shrimp cake, a delicious appetizer made with an egg binder instead of breadcrumbs. Order whatever fish is fresh that day. The cedar plank salmon, baked in a traditional Native American way but served with rich additions of truffle cream, blackberry honey, and bacon, is another melt-in-the-mouth specialty. All the entrees can be ordered in half-portions, or you can choose from a selection of small plates featuring unadorned fish and meat selections. Six-Seven is a destination restaurant and great for a romantic dining experience, but because this is Seattle, it is relaxed and casual in its approach.

The Edgewater, Pier 67, 2411 Alaskan Way. *C* **206/269-4575.** Main courses $29–$42. Mon–Fri 6:30am–9pm, Sat–Sun 7am–9:30pm.

Tilth ★★★ WALLINGFORD *NEW AMERICAN*   This cozy restaurant in a Craftsman bungalow in North Seattle's Wallingford neighborhood showcases the organic and wild bounty of the region. Renowned chef and owner Maria Hines whips up a mouthwatering and ever-changing menu of organic seasonal delicacies—and when I say organic, I mean organic, because this is one of the few restaurants in the U.S. to receive an organic certification. What I would recommend here is to try one of the many tasting menus. There is one for every appetite, preference, and allergy: 5 course, 8 course, 5-course vegan, 5- and 8-course vegetarian, and 5-course gluten-free. Has anyone been left out? I don't think so. The 5-courser might begin with a scrumptious savory apple soup with caramelized onion and friend shallot, go on to an escarole salad with sprouted almond vinaigrette, Alaskan king crab with sunchoke and kale, a Dakota beef hangar steak with sauerkraut, and finish with olive oil cake with fennel ice cream. But you can also mix and match various dishes, because all the dinner entrees are available as appetizers or main courses. If you've never had a duck burger, this is the place to try one. The desserts are so good that's there's a dessert tasting menu.

1411 N. 45th St. www.tilthrestaurant.com. *C* **206/633-0801.** Main courses $16–$33, tasting menus $70–$95. Mon–Fri 5–10pm; Sat–Sun 10am–2pm and 5–10pm.

Tulio ★★ DOWNTOWN *TUSCAN/ITALIAN*   Tulio started Tulio about a quarter-century ago, before the Hotel Vintage appeared on the scene. The Kimpton Group liked his Tuscan-influenced cooking so much that Tulio became the Hotel Vintage's signature restaurant. Today it's run by Tulio's son. Tulio's endeavors to have a hands-on, family feel to it. All of the pasta—gnocchi, tortellini, tagliatelle, ravioli, linguine, orecchiette—is handmade every morning by Maria, who's been making it for years. One of her standouts is the sweet potato gnocchi with sage butter and mascarpone; it practically melts in your mouth. For your main course, try the fresh fish of the day—tuna, salmon, or halibut depending on the season. The semolina scallops served on squash puree and topped with pork belly are noteworthy, and so is the succulent braised Kurobuta pork shank served with ricotta whipped potatoes. The restaurant is strong on Italian wines, of course (particularly Barberas and Chiantis), and otherwise limits itself to West Coast vintages.

1100 Fifth Ave. (in Hotel Vintage). *☎* **206/624-5500.** Main courses: $16–$33. Mon–Thurs 7am–10pm, Fri 7am–11pm, Sat 8am–11pm, Sun 8am–10pm.

Urbane ★★ DOWNTOWN *PACIFIC NORTHWEST*   Head Chef Audrey Spence likes her food fresh and local whenever possible. An advocate of the farm to table philosophy, she personally selects everything on the menu, including produce and fish, and she'll even visit ranches to check out the quality of their beef. All of this is then cooked up at Urbane, a casual but culinarily sophisticated restaurant at the Hyatt @ Olive, Seattle's only LEED-certified hotel. Because everything's so fresh, the menu changes daily. If a half a hog becomes available in the morning, a delicious head cheese (pork pâté) will show up on the menu that evening. Seafood lovers will want to try whatever fish is on the menu—the wild king salmon and black cod are both tender and delectable, the cod served (on my last visit) with garlicky bok choi and carrots. The cool, unfussy restaurant, on a corner with big windows, doubles as a bar-lounge, or vice versa, so you can sit at high tables next to the windows or low ones in the center of the room, or a banquette. Service is friendly and efficient.

1639 Eighth Ave. (in Hyatt @ Olive). www.urbaneseattle.com. *☎* **206/676-4600.** Main courses $18–$38. Mon–Fri 6:30am–2:30pm and 5–10pm, Sat–Sun 6:30am–2:30pm and 5–10pm.

MODERATE

Bastille ★ BALLARD *FRENCH*   The best choices at this fashionable Parisian-style brasserie are the *plats du jour,* such as tender-crisp boneless quail, but the *plats principaux* won't disappoint you, either—they are French classics like cassoulet, roasted chicken, mussels in white wine sauce, and steak frites. This is a great place to come for Sunday brunch when the Ballard Farmers Market adds in spice to the scene and you can people-watch from the enclosed patio while enjoying a fluffy omelet.

5307 Ballard Ave. NW. www.bastilleseattle.com. *☎* **206/453-5014.** Main courses $15–$25. Sun–Thurs 5:30–10pm, Fri–Sat 5:30–11pm, Sun brunch 10am–3pm.

Café Campagne ★★ PIKE PLACE MARKET *COUNTRY FRENCH*   Tucked away in the secret little courtyard of Inn at the Market, this charming, romantic café-bistro overlooks the crowds and noise of Pike Place Market with a kind of Gallic nonchalance. You're here for food, not sightseeing, but the sightseeing—or market-watching, anyway—is part of the atmosphere. Now that its more formal French parent has closed, Café Campagne has become the Pike Place place for casual and delicious French bistro food. Try one of the pâtés as an appetizer, then consider the mussels in wine—so very French, and always on the menu—or the roast chicken. Other dishes change with the seasons, but the cooking here is always reliable and satisfying.

1600 Post Alley. www.campagnerestaurant.com. *☎* **206/728-2233.** Main courses $13–$23 lunch, $15–$23. Mon–Thurs 11am–10pm; Fri 11am–5pm and 5:30–11pm; Sat 8am–4pm and 5:30–11pm; Sun 8am–4pm and 5–10pm.

Elliott's Oyster House ★★ WATERFRONT *SEAFOOD*   It's right on the waterfront, but it's the oysters and seafood that will grab your attention here more than the view (which actually isn't all that great). Elliott's is one of the most trustworthy lunch and dinner dining spots along Seattle's fish-and-chips-oriented waterfront. I happen to love fresh Northwest oysters, and I love the vast selection available at Elliott's oyster bar. Sample them the way you might sample wine—each variety has a different size, shape, texture, and taste. If you're an oystermaniac, come during Elliott's oyster happy hour (Mon–Fri 3–6pm) to sample these briny bivalves at a more than reasonable price. Other Northwest staples like salmon and Dungeness crab are on the menu, but it's really the oysters that shine at Elliott's.

Pier 56, 1201 Alaskan Way. www.elliottsoysterhouse.com. ⓒ **206/623-4340.** Main courses $11–$50. Sun–Thurs 11am–10pm; Fri–Sat 11am–11pm.

Etta's Seafood ★★ PIKE PLACE MARKET *SEAFOOD* Singers are often associated with a certain song, and famous chefs with a signature dish. In Tom Douglas's case, it's Dungeness crab cakes, which he perfected right here, when the restaurant belonged to someone else and he was an employee rather than the owner. Seattle's most prominent chef-entrepreneur made his name with these crunchy-on-the-outside, creamy-on-the-inside delights, and when you taste one, you'll understand why. But there's more to Etta's than crab cakes. Located in the perpetually busy Pike Place Market neighborhood, with big windows that let you people-watch as you dine, Etta's roster of seafood dishes includes seafood chowders, really good fish and chips, razor clams, and other seasonal specialties. But this casual and comfortable restaurant goes beyond the standard seafood staples to include dishes like the tuna sashimi salad with green onion pancakes.

2020 Western Ave. www.tomdouglas.com. ⓒ **206/443-6000.** Main courses $16–$36. Mon–Thurs 11:30am–9:30pm; Fri 11:30am–10pm; Sat 9am–3pm and 4–10pm; Sun 9am–3pm and 4–9pm.

Joule ★★★ WALLINGFORD *KOREAN/FRENCH FUSION* Though Asian influence is common in the Seattle culinary world, there is nothing common about the cuisine at Joule. The owner-chefs blend French, Korean, and American flavors for delightful results. The names of the dishes are exotic—black bean and squid pancake, kabocha rice grits, octopus and smoked pork belly salad—and the tastes divine. On a chilly day, what could be more comforting than a cup of roasted apple bisque with curry? The weekend brunch is wonderful, too, with dishes like spicy salted cod, wintergreen, and boiled egg on toast; potato hash with smoked mackerel; and maitake mushroom omelet with Chinese celery and truffle oil. The restaurant is in the Wallingford neighborhood, about 15 minutes from downtown Seattle by car.

3506 Stone Way N. www.joulerestaurant.com. ⓒ **206/632-5685.** Entrees $17–$30. Daily 5pm–10pm, Sat–Sun brunch 10am–2pm.

Lark ★★ CAPITOL HILL *PACIFIC NORTHWEST* This delightful neighborhood restaurant on Capitol Hill is the lovechild of Chef Johnathan Sundstrom, who fled the showy downtown food scene to open his own bistro. This is a restaurant that encourages family-style sharing, serving exclusively small- to medium-sized plates featuring locally produced and organic grains, cheese, vegetables, fish, charcuterie, and meats. The fresh fish plates might include Kusshi oysters on the half shell, Penn Cove blue mussels with ginger, and yellowtail tuna carpaccio with preserved lemon and green olives. Vegetables and grains selections, depending on the season, could be raw artichoke salad with lemon and anchovy, sunchoke soup, or semolina gnocchi with pinenuts. In each category you'll find about a half-dozen choices. But whatever you do, don't miss the cheeses here. These artisanal delights offer an array of tastes and textures that will delight your taste buds.

926 12th Ave. www.larkseattle.com. ⓒ **206/323-5275.** Main courses $8–$20. Tues–Sun 5–10:30pm.

Miller's Guild ★★ DOWNTOWN *PACIFIC NORTHWEST* Applause for the short ribs, please—which are actually quite long, off the bone, and so melt-in-your-mouth delicious that you won't believe your taste buds. Above all, this is a place for meat. A giant mesquite-burning stove in the open kitchen grills ribs, steaks, chops (and seafood) to perfection. Before your main course, whet your appetite with a craft cocktail and an appetizer of coal-roasted beets with dill, mint, caraway salt and horseradish; or the charred radicchio salad with house-cured bacon, creamy Parmesan, and marrow beans. Then go for the meat, and especially those huge short ribs from Niman Ranch in California, one of the top purveyors of choice cuts of beef on the West Coast (the juicy rib-eye and New York steaks also come from there). Order a couple of sides, like creamy mashed potatoes and crispy Brussels sprouts, and a glass of Oregon pinot noir, and you're set. Miller's Guild opened in late 2013, adjacent to Hotel Max, and if they keep cooking like this, they will be around for a long time to come. The scene here is casual but sophisticated.

612 Stewart St. www.millersguild.com. ℂ **206/443-3663.** Main courses $26–$63. Daily 7am–10pm.

Purple Café and Wine Bar ★★ DOWNTOWN *NORTHWEST/INTERNATIONAL FUSION* Diners at Purple are somewhat dwarfed by the enormous room, with its huge glass windows and floor-to-ceiling wine storage tower, but no one seems to mind. Nor should they, since the food is always good and the atmosphere is relaxed in a "smart-casual" sort of way. Wine is a big feature at Purple, and wine pairings with your various plates are surprisingly inexpensive compared to other Seattle restaurants. The menu at Purple gives a nod to international influences but makes abundant use of the bounty of the Pacific Northwest in dishes like Dungeness crab and chanterelle mushroom pasta. You can also order crispy-crust pizzas and a burger made from free-range, Painted Hills beef. You can share small plates or order larger ones. You can't be shy or retiring here; you'll have to speak up if you want to be heard over the lively hub-bub in this downtown hotspot. Lunch is less expensive but just as noisy.

1225 Fourth Ave. www.purplecafe.com. ℂ **206/829-2280.** Main courses $8–$35. Mon–Thurs 11am–10pm, Fri 11am–midnight, Sat noon–midnight, Sun noon–11pm.

Salty's on Alki Beach ★★ WEST SEATTLE *SEAFOOD* For a fun Seattle adventure, hop in the water taxi on the waterfront, take the 10-minute ride over to Alki Beach in West Seattle, and have lunch, dinner, or weekend brunch at Salty's. This is a big and perennially popular restaurant because it has one of the eye-poppingest views in the city. From the giant dining room or deck overlooking Elliot Bay, you look back and see the downtown towers of The Emerald City gleaming in the sunshine (or peeking through the mist and rain, this being Seattle). Salty's is especially famous for its weekend brunch buffet, laden with fresh seafood (basics along with inventive dishes like Vietnamese catfish with red pepper sauce), pasta (such as lobster-filled ravioli), omelets to order, meats, and more. The gingerbread pancakes are addictive, and the dessert buffet, starring a chocolate fountain, will leave you reeling with a sugar high. The other time-honored tradition here is a sunset dinner—hopefully on a clear summer evening. But if you do have sunny summer weather, I'd suggest you make Salty's part of a day trip. Have lunch on one of the giant decks, then take the local jitney for a ride from the beach up into the hills.

1936 Harbor Ave. SW. www.saltys.com. ℂ **206/937-1600.** Main courses $14–$23 lunch, $15–$56 dinner. Mon–Fri 11:15am–3pm and 5–9:30pm; Sat 9:30–1:30pm and 5–10pm; Sun 8:45am–1:30pm and 4:30–9pm.

"I HEARD THEY HAVE GOOD coffee IN SEATTLE"

You heard right, my friend. Good bakeries, too. Seattle is full of cafes where you can order your favorite forms of caffeine and sugar. These congenial spots are a way of life in the city where the first Starbucks opened in 1971 and is now pointed out as a tourist attraction. Here's a brief list of coffees and cafes of special merit.

o **Ancient Grounds ★** For an unusual Seattle espresso experience, stop in at Ancient Grounds not far from Pike Place Market. It's both a cafe and an intimate art gallery, loaded with intriguing treasures including Native American and Asian masks and netsuke. The espresso is strong, the ambience pure Seattle. Just don't expect smiling or overly friendly service. 1227 1st Ave. 𝒞 **206/749-0747.** Tues–Wed 7:30am–4pm; Thurs–Fri 7:30am–4pm and 6–10pm; Sat noon–10pm.

o **Bauhaus Books & Coffee**
★ This cozy spot in a diverse Capitol Hill neighborhood is stacked with books and great for people watching. The view of the Space Needle is impressive, too. Best of all, caffeine vampires can suck up coffee every night until 1 am. 414 E. Pine St. www.bauhaus coffee.net. 𝒞 **206/625-1600.** Mon–Fri 6am–1am, Sat 7am–1am, Sun 8am–1am.

o **Caffe Ladro Espresso Bar & Bakery ★★** Serving only organic, fair-trade, shade-grown coffee, Caffe Ladro serves a good latte and a small selection of baked goodies. They have locations elsewhere, but this one is convenient if you're downtown near Pike Place Market or the Seattle Art Museum. 801 Pine St. www.caffeladro.com. 𝒞 **206/405-1950.** Mon–Thurs 5:30am–7pm; Fri

Sazerac ★★ DOWNTOWN *NEW ORLEANS/NORTHWEST* The spicy South meets salty Seattle at Sazerac, a big, casual, family-friendly restaurant with an open kitchen and wood-fired oven at the Hotel Monaco. All their fiery barbecue sauces, crunchy slaws, dill pickles, salad dressings, ice creams, and cornbreads are made in-house. Start with something like the brick oven Gulf prawns served with chorizo and lots of garlic, or the Medjool dates stuffed with smoked bacon, goat cheese, and balsamic vinegar. One of the specialties here is crispy catfish, deep-fried and served with jalapeño-lime brown butter and creamy whipped potatoes with lemon. I love the super-spicy, melt-in-your-mouth, cider-chile-glazed St. Louis–style pork ribs that come with cheddar baked grits. After your main course, ice creams like the chocolate-root beer or buttermilk are not-too-sweet ways to cool down your overheated palate.

1101 Fourth Ave. (in Hotel Monaco). 𝒞 **206/624-7755.** Main courses $14–$28. Mon–Fri 6:30am–10pm; Sat 8am–10pm.

Serious Pie ★★ DOWNTOWN *PIZZA* Chef Tom Douglas is serious about food, and that includes pizza. His applewood-burning oven turns out artisan-quality pies with crispy, chewy crusts and mouth-wateringly delicious toppings. Two of my favorites are the Yukon gold potato pizza with rosemary and pecorino, and the sweet fennel sausage pizza with roasted peppers and provolone. These pies are perfectly sized for sharing, although I have been known to eat one all by myself. Serious Pie is located in

5:30am–8pm; Sat 6am–8pm; Sun 6am–6pm.

o **Caffe Umbria ★★★** The Bizzarri family has been roasting beans since grandfather Ornello opened his first shop in Perugia, Italy. Five blends are available, including fair-trade beans. Enjoy a heavenly extra-foamy cappuccino at their cafe in in Pioneer Square. 320 Occidental Ave. S. www.caffeumbria.com. ⓒ **206/624-5847.** Mon–Fri 6am–6pm; Sat 7am–6pm; Sun 8am–5pm.

o **Macrina Bakery ★★★** This Belltown café is justly famous for its baked goods—their morning bun is the best I've ever had—and for their excellent breakfasts and lunch specials. Get one of their great lattes to go with your nosh and you're set. 2408 1st Ave. www.macrina bakery.com. ⓒ **206/448-4032.** Daily 7am–6pm.

o **Starbucks ★** Seattle's coffee culture began at this little shop at Pike Place Market back in 1971. The very first Starbucks still features the chain's original brand image of the topless mermaid with a double fish tail, an image that was toned down over the years as the Starbucks brand became ubiquitous and they didn't want to offend anyone. 1912 Pike Pl. ⓒ **206/448-8762.** Mon–Fri 6am–9pm; Sat–Sun 6:30am–9pm.

o **Zeitgeist Coffee ★★** This spacious European-style coffeehouse in Pioneer Square is an urban oasis and cultural hub that serves up film screenings and rotating exhibits by local artists along with its popular Italian beans, illy Caffe. 171 S. Jackson St. www.zeitgeistcoffee.com. ⓒ **206/583-0497.** Mon–Fri 6am–7pm; Sat 7am–7pm; Sun 8am–6pm.

the "Tom Douglas District" around 4th and Virginia, near his other landmark restaurants (Dahlia Lounge, Lola, and Etta's). This is a low-ceilinged room that's reminiscent of a pub, very casual, where you wait for a table. There's beer on tap, a limited wine list, some excellent ciders, and a refreshing array of non-alcoholic concoctions that are as good as any cocktail: try the house-made Seville orange and pink peppercorn on tap.

316 Virginia St. www.tomdouglas.com. ⓒ **206/838-7388.** Reservations not accepted. Main courses $15–$18. Sun–Wed 11am–10pm; Thurs–Sat 11am–10pm.

Wild Ginger Asian Restaurant & Satay Bar ★★ DOWNTOWN *ASIAN* This Pan-Asian restaurant across from Benaroya Hall and above the Triple Door jazz club in downtown Seattle has been a favorite with Seattleites for some time, and for good reason. The location is great, the ambience is bright and lively without being a noisy scene, and the cooking is always good. Skewers of chicken, prawns, lamb, and salmon arrive hot from the satay bar accompanied by sticky rice and pickled cucumber. You can also order deliciously pungent dishes like panang beef, a curry made with prime rib-eye beef in a sauce of cardamom, coconut milk, basil, and peanuts. A vegan menu is also available.

1401 Third Ave. www.wildginger.net. ⓒ **206/623-4450.** Satays $5–$13; main courses $9–$30. Mon–Sat 11:30am–3pm; Mon–Fri 5pm–11pm; Sat 4:30pm–11pm; Sun 4–9pm.

INEXPENSIVE

Jade Garden ★ INTERNATIONAL DISTRICT *CHINESE*   In a town blessed with a number of good dim sum spots, this is one of the best for variety and freshness, though the ambience is practical rather than fancy. *Dim sum* is small plates of steamed or fried food that are hustled around the restaurant on carts. When you want something from a particular cart, you motion to the waiter and tell him how many plates of that particular dish you want (dim sum is about sharing). If you're new to dim sum, start with some basics like *humbow* (steamed buns stuffed with sweet barbecued pork), *ha gao* (shrimp dumpling) and sticky rice wrapped in lotus leaves. Don't faint if a cart of steamed chicken feet rolls past: In China they are a delicacy.

424 Seventh Ave. S. (C) **206/622-8181.** Main courses $5–$13. Daily 9am–midnight.

EXPLORING SEATTLE

Chihuly Garden and Glass ★★★ ART MUSEUM   Not many living artists are given their own museum, and especially not glass artists, but Dale Chihuly is an exception. By now, this Pacific Northwest phenomenon is almost a household name, primarily because of his enormous and enormously intricate glass chandeliers, which hang in museums and public spaces around the world. I personally found Chihuly's work—what I knew of it—a little overwrought and even somewhat vulgar. But a visit to this new museum, which opened right below the Space Needle in 2012, changed my mind. Perhaps it was the eye-searing colors of the pieces in contrast to the gray Seattle day, or perhaps it was seeing the almost unbelievable intricacy of the large installations. Some hang from the ceiling, others rise like giant neon-colored underwater seascapes with twisting, nestling, writhing organic shapes that look soft and hard at the same time. The museum presents an overview of this Tacoma-born artist's 40-year career, including marvelous early works, such as flattened glass vessels influenced by Native American basketry and pottery. Outside, in the museum's garden, Chihuly's vibrant glass pieces rise up like plants and trees among the natural vegetation. Every piece you see in this dynamic museum—which is half funhouse, half shrine—explores, reimagines, and ultimately transcends the traditional boundaries and limitations of glass art. And, by the way, there's an excellent gift shop.

305 Harrison St. (below Space Needle). www.chihulygardenandglass.com. (C) **206/753-4940.** $19 adults, $17 senior, $12 ages 4–12. Sun–Thurs 11am–8pm; Fri–Sat 10am–8pm.

Experience Music Project (EMP) MUSEUM   This is one of those museums you feel obligated to include in a guidebook because it is something people have heard

---

Save Cash with a Seattle CityPass

A CityPass (www.citypass.com) is one of the best deals is town. You can visit five popular Seattle destinations for half price (if you take them all in). Better yet, you don't have to wait in line—this is especially helpful at the Space Needle. The passes will get you into the Space Needle (where general admission is $26 for adults), Seattle Aquarium (general admission $22 for adults), Pacific Science Center, Experience Music Project, an Argosy Cruises harbor tour of Elliott Bay, and the option of either the Museum of Flight or Woodland Park Zoo. A CityPass costs $74 for adults and $49 for kids ages 4 to 12. You can buy them at any of the included attractions, or order them from the website.

boat **TOURS**

If you want to experience something of the maritime character that makes Seattle unique, consider taking one of the family-friendly tours offered daily, year-round, by **Argosy Cruises** (www.argosy cruises.com), departing from Pier 55 on the waterfront. Argosy offers a 1-hour harbor cruise that shows off the sights of the Seattle skyline ($24 adults, $21 seniors, $12 kids 4-12); a 2½-hour locks tour that takes you through the century-old Chittenden Locks connecting salt-water Puget Sound to freshwater Lake Union ($41 adults, $37 seniors, $20 kids 4-12); and a 4-hour trip to Tillicum Village on Blake Island, where you can enjoy a meal of plank-baked salmon and enjoy storytelling and native dances performed by the Coast Salish tribe in a re-created longhouse ($79 adults, $72 seniors, $25 kids 4–12). Check the website for departure times and special Internet discounts for prebooking.

From May through September, **Let's Go Sailing** (www.sailingseattle.com; ℂ **206/624-3931**) at Pier 54 offers daily 90-minute excursions on a 70-foot sail-boat ($33 per passenger), and 2½-hour sunset cruises ($49 per passenger). There is no commentary per se, but the captain is right there to answer any questions. This is an open boat, so if it rains you'll get wet.

For another take on maritime Seattle, where many people commute to the city by ferry, hop on a commuter ferry operated by **Washington State Ferries** (www.wsdot.wa.gov/ferries) and enjoy a ride, with a scenic skyline view, between downtown and Bainbridge Island. A round-trip ferry ticket to Bainbridge Island costs $16 adults, $7.80 for seniors and children 6 to 18.

about and are curious to see—but I have to tell you, unless you are an ardent fan of Jimi Hendricks or Kurt Cobain, save your money and skip it entirely. EMP is over-rated, overly expensive, and badly curated. Many of the people milling around inside seem to be scratching their heads and wondering why they're there. The museum is basically a personal collection of rock-'n'-roll memorabilia assembled by Microsoft gazillionaire Paul Allen with the help of architect Frank Gehry, who designed a bloated, purple building to house it. From the air, it's supposed to look like one of Jimi Hendrix's smashed guitars, but who cares (and who looks at a museum from the air)? Hendrix and Cobain are two Seattle rock-'n'-roll legends, and the rooms devoted to their short, drug-addled lives and careers are the main exhibitions here—but the kids wandering through don't have a clue who these musicians were or why they were important. There are some interactive exhibits that let you record your own music, and there is a collection of electric guitars—wowee. Even the new feature, a Science Fiction and Horror Museum, is dull, full of text panels and boring video commentary that sheds light on nothing. I hate to sound like a grump, and one can say that EMP is unusual, but I would caution you to think twice before shelling out the admission price.

Seattle Center, 325 Fifth Ave. N. www.empsfm.org. ℂ **877/367-7361** or 206/770-2700. Admission $20 adults, $17 seniors, $14 ages 5–17; free 1st Thurs of each month 5–8pm. Daily 10am–5pm (until 8pm 1st Thurs of each month). Closed Thanksgiving and Christmas.

Frye Art Museum ★★ ART MUSEUM   Located on First Hill, just north of downtown, the Frye was Seattle's first free art museum, thanks to the legacy of Charles and Emma Frye. A child of German immigrants, Charles Frye made a fortune by start-ing a meatpacking plant during the 1890s gold-rush days (if you take the highly enter-taining Underground Tour, described below, you'll see where the meat lockers were).

Downtown Attractions

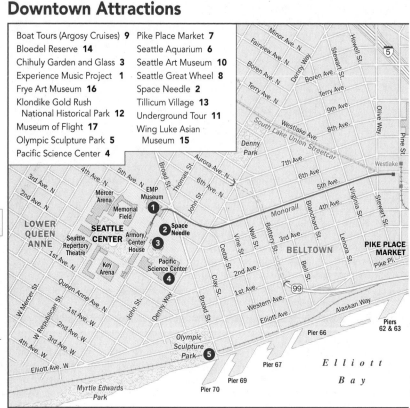

Boat Tours (Argosy Cruises) **9**
Bloedel Reserve **14**
Chihuly Garden and Glass **3**
Experience Music Project **1**
Frye Art Museum **16**
Klondike Gold Rush
  National Historical Park **12**
Museum of Flight **17**
Olympic Sculpture Park **5**
Pacific Science Center **4**

Pike Place Market **7**
Seattle Aquarium **6**
Seattle Art Museum **10**
Seattle Great Wheel **8**
Space Needle **2**
Tillicum Village **13**
Underground Tour **11**
Wing Luke Asian
  Museum **15**

With their wealth, the Fryes began to collect paintings and bequeathed their enormous collection to the city with the stipulation that the works be displayed free to the public in one location. The original collection of portraits, still lifes, and landscapes by late-19th- and early-20th-century French, German, and American painters is actually the least interesting part of the museum today, though the hundreds of paintings are dramatically exhibited in one enormous room (this layout, which recreates the way the paintings were originally exhibited, changes periodically). In recent years, the museum has re-invented itself, adding modern and abstract art to the collection and exhibiting an interesting array of works by artists active in the Pacific Northwest or with ties to it. The galleries are serene, the shows interesting, and there's a lovely little cafe and garden.

704 Terry Ave. (at Cherry St.). www.fryemuseum.org. © **206/622-9250.** Free admission. Tues–Wed and Fri–Sat 10am–5pm; Thurs 10am–8pm; Sun noon–5pm. Closed New Year's Day, July 4th, Thanksgiving, and Christmas.

Hiram M. Chittenden Locks/Lake Washington Ship Canal ★★ LAND-
MARK/PARK/GARDEN   Seattleites love boats—even when they're not theirs. The yearly Seafair is a major event and features hydroplane races and all manner of maritime and boating-related activities. So it's not really surprising that this set of historic

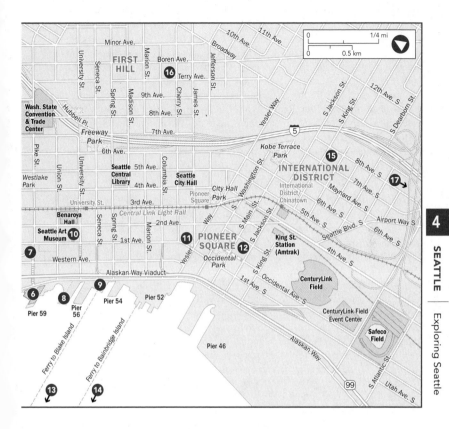

locks in Ballard is one of the city's top attractions. Created in 1917 by the Army Corps of Engineers, the locks link saltwater Puget Sound with freshwater Lake Union and Lake Washington. All day, every day, a passing parade of yachts, barges, fishing trawlers, and other vessels make their way from one body of water to the other. And people line the shore to watch, wave, and maybe wish they had a boat of their own. Exhibits in the Visitor Center explain how this engineering feat came about and was executed (water levels in the lakes dropped about 17 feet as a result). On the hill above the locks you'll find the **Carl S. English Botanical Garden,** well worth a stroll. Over a 43-year period a botanist named Carl S. English, Jr. transformed the once barren grounds into, in his words, "a garden worthy of serious study." The garden is filled with unusual trees and shrubs; there are more traditional flower gardens down behind the Visitor Center.

3015 N.W. 54th Street (Ballard). www.corpslakes.us/lakewashingtonshipcanal. Visitor Center ✆ **206/783-7059.** Admission free. Daily year-round dawn–dusk.

Klondike Gold Rush National Historical Park ★ MUSEUM   It's not a park; it's a museum dedicated to a pivotal event in Seattle's history and housed in a historic building in the city's most historic neighborhood (Pioneer Square). In 1897, when word got out that gold had been discovered in Alaska, tens of thousands of wannabe prospectors from around the world, both men and women, descended on Seattle to outfit themselves for the arduous trip north to the Klondike gold fields. A few made their fortunes, but most did not. Seattle had burnt to the ground just a few years earlier, but the gold rush put it on the map and filled the city's coffers. As the closest departure point where prospectors could buy all the provisions and equipment necessary to dig for gold, Seattle had the market cornered. This museum recounts the city's gold-rush rush in an entertaining and informative way, focusing on individuals, their preparations for the journey, and the rough-and-tumble adventures and living conditions they encountered. At 10am and 3pm daily, park rangers give demonstrations of mining techniques, and on Friday, Saturday, and Sunday they offer a free walking tour of the historic Pioneer Square neighborhood that dates from the gold rush days (check website for seasonal departure times).

319 2nd Ave. S. www.nps.gov/klse. ℂ **206/220-4240.** Free admission. Daily 9am–5pm. Closed New Year's Day, Thanksgiving, and Christmas.

Museum of Flight ★★★ MUSEUM   The history of aviation in Seattle goes back almost as far back as the Wright Brothers. Since it was founded in 1916, Boeing has been the most important player in Seattle's aerospace industry, and the city's economic health and vitality is closely linked to Boeing's. This top-flight museum located at Boeing Field (and sponsored by them) is a paean to every form of flight, flying, and aircraft. The historic Red Barn (Boeing's first manufacturing building), houses exhibits on early aviation, including the mail bag carried by William E. Boeing and Eddie Hubbard on the first international U.S. Air Mail flight from Vancouver, BC to Seattle in 1919. The exhibit ends with the Boeing 707, which ushered in the jet age. The cavernous Great Gallery features dozens of historic aircraft, many of them hanging from the ceiling as though in flight. Visitors can climb into the cockpit of a real Blackbird, the fastest jet ever made. The Personal Courage Wing tells the stories of fighter aviators in World Wars I and II. And at the Airpark, you can walk through legendary aircraft including the Concorde and the first jet Air Force One, used by presidents Kennedy, Johnson, and Reagan. The simulator exhibit lets you try virtual flight and hang-gliding. The museum's Space Gallery displays NASA and Russian spacecraft (and mock-ups).

9404 E. Marginal Way S. www.museumofflight.org. ℂ **206/764-5720.** $19 adults, $16 seniors, $11 ages 5–17; free 5–9pm 1st Thurs of every month. Daily 10am–5pm. Closed Thanksgiving and Christmas. Bus: 124. Take exit 158 off I-5.

Museum of History and Industry (MOHAI) ★★ MUSEUM   It may not have the most exciting name, but there is nothing dull about this museum. It's a great way to learn about Northwest and Seattle history through fascinating, often hands-on exhibits, historic photos and films, and some wonderful artifacts. Every aspect of Seattle's cultural, scientific, and industrial history is covered, from pre-Great Fire Seattle (in 1889 the city was reduced to ashes), through the Klondike Gold Rush of 1897, the founding of Boeing and the aerospace industry, right up to the arrival of Microsoft. This is a large museum, and not everything here will interest you, but it's not just a granny's attic of dusty memorabilia by any stretch. Look up and you'll see one of the first hydroplanes used in the yearly Seafair boat races (these boats can reach speeds of 200mph), look over and you'll encounter one of the earliest computers. It's engaging and engrossing. In 2013, MOHAI moved to the historic Naval Reserve Building on the shores of Lake Union.

820 Terry Ave. N. www.mohai.org. ℂ **206/324-1126.** $14 adults, $12 seniors, free ages 14 and under. Also, free first Thursday of each month. Daily 10am–5pm, Thurs until 8pm.

North Seattle Attractions

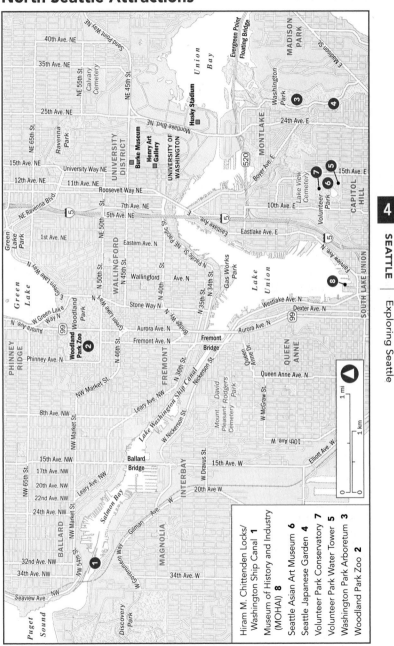

Hiram M. Chittenden Locks/
Washington Ship Canal **1**
Museum of History and Industry
(MOHAI) **8**
Seattle Asian Art Museum **6**
Seattle Japanese Garden **4**
Volunteer Park Conservatory **7**
Volunteer Park Water Tower **5**
Washington Park Arboretum **3**
Woodland Park Zoo **2**

Olympic Sculpture Park ★★★ MUSEUM/PARK/GARDEN/VIEW   One of the city's must-see attractions opened in 2007 on a 9-acre site overlooking Puget Sound at the north end of the Seattle waterfront. Free to the public and open every day, the Olympic Sculpture Park is an alfresco offshoot of the Seattle Art Museum with a stellar collection of outdoor sculptures by the likes of Alexander Calder, Richard Serra, Claes Oldenburg, and Roxy Paine. The panoramic view of the Sound, the Olympic Mountains and, when the weather cooperates, the snow-white peak of Mount Rainier, adds to the pleasure. An indoor cafe in the PACCAR Pavilion serves homemade soups, panini sandwiches, and a full menu of lattes and desserts.

2901 Western Ave. www.seattleartmuseum.org. © **206/654-3100.** Free admission. Sculpture Park daily sunrise-sunset; PACCAR Pavilion Nov–Feb Sat–Sun 10am–4pm, Mar–Oct Tues–Sun 10am–5pm.

Pacific Science Center ★ MUSEUM   If you have kids in tow, this is one museum where everyone will find something to enjoy. Older kids will love the interactive exhibits, such as Adventures in 3Dimensions, which shows how 3-D technology involves our brains to create special effects. Younger kids will enjoy the crawl-and-climb area, which includes a treehouse and a table-height "stream" for water play. At the Insect Village, kids of all ages will thrill and chill to the giant robotic insects and live animal displays. And then there are the animatronic dinosaurs—life-size replicas that move their heads and tails and grunt and bellow. All in all, the museum, housed in a building from the 1962 Seattle World's Fair, is like a giant playhouse dedicated to science and technology. In addition to all the hands-on exhibits, there's a great planetarium with evening laser shows and an IMAX theater that shows wonderfully entertaining and educational films, some in 3D. My personal favorite here is the Butterfly House, a humid greenhouse where colorful butterflies flit and fly freely.

Seattle Center, 200 2nd Ave. N. www.pacificsciencecenter.org. ©**800/664-8775** or 206/443-2001, 206/443-4629 for IMAX information, or 206/443-2850 for laser-show information. Admission $18 adults, $16 seniors, $13 ages 6–15, $10 ages 3–5. IMAX $9–$14 adults, $8–$12 seniors, $7–$10.50 ages 6–15, $6–$9 ages 3–5,. Laser show $5–$9. Various discounted combination tickets available. Mon and Wed–Fri 10am–5pm; Sat–Sun 10am–6pm. Closed Thanksgiving and Christmas.

Pike Place Market ★★★ LANDMARK/ICON/SPECIALTY SHOPPING/FOOD SPECIALTIES   Seattle's number one tourist attraction is a world unto itself—a big, sprawling farmers' market overlooking Elliott Bay and the waterfront where you'll find stalls selling gorgeous produce, fish, seafood, jams and honey, handmade crafts, specialty foods and spices, baked goods, tourist trinkets, and everything in between. Don't miss the Gum Wall (only in Seattle), a wall where parked wads of gum have become (at least in the eyes of some) a work of masticated art, and Rachel the Pig, the bronze porcine sculpture that greets visitors near the Pike Street entrance (drop a coin in her to help support local charities). There are a couple of venerable restaurants, like Lowell's, and the Sound View Cafe, where you can get a good basic meal, including breakfast. The fun here is simply to wander up and down the ramps and stairways and poke around in the market's different levels. It's usually jammed (at least in the summer and on weekends) by 10am and pretty much closes down by 6pm. Some of the vendors have become performers, like the fishmongers who draw crowds by tossing huge salmon back and forth, but the market is still used by Seattleites looking for top-quality comestibles of all kinds. There's nothing upscale or high-end about Pike Place Market, except for the quality and price of its fish and produce—it's as close as an American city can come to having a bazaar. It also happens to be the oldest such public

Market Munching

It's impossible to list all the food vendors at Pike Place Market, but here a few to look for as you cruise through the corridors and various levels. If you're planning a picnic, **DeLaurenti ★**, 1435 First Ave. (www.delaurenti.com; **℡ 800/873-6685** or 206/622-0141), near the market's brass pig, is the perfect spot to get your pâté, sandwiches, and wine. Sausage lovers will love the sausage sandwiches at **Uli's Famous Sausage,** 1511 Pike Place (www.ulis famoussausage.com; **℡ 206/839-1000**). **Piroshky Piroshky,** 1908 Pike Place (www.piroshkybakery.com; **℡ 206/441-6068**), sells sweet or savory stuffed rolls. At **Beecher's Handmade Cheese,** 1600 Pike Place (www.beecherscheese

.com; **℡ 206/956-1964**), you can watch cheese being made and sample some of the products or get some of their macaroni and cheese to go. **The Spanish Table,** 1426 Western Ave. (www.spanish table.com; **℡ 206/682-2827**), a specialty food shop on the lower level, offers Spanish-style sandwiches and great soups. For something sweet, cold, and creamy, try the much-lauded gelato at **Bottega Italiana,** 1425 First Ave. (www.bottegaitaliana.com; **℡ 206/343-0200**), or the conveniently located **Procopio,** 1501 Western Ave. (www.procopiogelateria.com; **℡ 206/622-4280**), which is on the Pike Street Hillclimb that links the waterfront with Pike Place Market.

market in the country, having opened in 1907. Back in the "let's tear everything down and put in a freeway" 1960s, Seattleites banded together to save this beloved institution from the wrecking ball. The market extends along Western Avenue, the street in front, where you'll find still more specialty and ethnic food shops, and if you follow the staircases behind the market (called the Hillclimb), you can get down to the waterfront.

Btw. Pike and Pine sts., at First Ave. www.pikeplacemarket.org. **℡ 206/682-7453.** General business hours Mon–Sat 10am–6pm, Sun 11am–5pm; restaurant hours vary. Closed New Year's Day, Thanksgiving, and Christmas.

Seattle Aquarium ★★ AQUARIUM/MUSEUM   The sounds and exclamations of wonder that you hear as you walk through Seattle's waterfront aquarium are not all from kids, although there are plenty of children squealing, "Look! Look! Look!" as they excitedly point to an octopus, a sea otter, or a tiny seahorse shyly fluttering in its tank. And look you should, because many of the creatures on view here are inhabitants of Puget Sound or the large Pacific region. You'll get your first glimpse at the giant "Window on Washington Waters" tank, just inside the entrance, where salmon, rockfish, lingcod, and wolf eels swim among gently swaying kelp beds; and sea anemone, sea urchins, sea stars and corals cling to large rock formations. Three times a day (10am, 11:30am, 12:15pm) divers wearing special masks enter the tanks and answer questions from the audience. In "Life on the Edge," you can reach in to gently stroke the sea urchins and sea cucumbers that are typically found in Pacific tide pools. The male and female Giant Pacific Octopus are kept in separate tanks with a watery corridor between them until it's time for them to mate, at which point the doors are removed and the two quickly find one another; they are fed at 2 and 4pm daily. In addition to the many other tanks filled with rare and beautiful fish, the aquarium has outdoor marine mammal pools where adorable (but mean) sea otters float on their backs while eating, and harbor seals dive and bark. You can watch them from the underwater dome or out on the deck. The staff here goes out of its way to answer any questions you or your kids may have.

Pier 59, 1483 Alaskan Way. www.seattleaquarium.org. ✆ **206/386-4300.** Admission $22 adults, $15 children 4–12. Daily 9:30am–5pm.

Seattle Art Museum (SAM) ★★★ ART MUSEUM   The postmodern facade by Robert Venturi is dated, but the once-cramped gallery spaces have been redesigned, expanded, and reconfigured, making a visit to the Seattle Art Museum a real pleasure. Outside, Jonathan Borofsky's giant kinetic sculpture *Hammering Man* pays homage to Seattle's manual-labor workforce. The entrance lobby showcases a big, eye-catching, but rather intellectually shallow installation called *Inopportune: Stage One* by Chinese artist Cai Quo-Qiang with several full-size cars suspended in a topsy-turvy sequence across the ceiling with colored lights shooting out of their sides. There is usually a first-rate exhibition or traveling show to be seen here, but the permanent collections are definitely worth your time. One is devoted to painting, furniture, sculpture, and decorative arts from the Pacific Northwest, with historic gems like the mid–19th-century painting *Astoria Harbor,* its ships bathed in golden light, by Cleveland Rockwell. Even more impressive is the sizeable collection of Northwest Coast Native American art, which includes totem poles, masks, wood carvings, and many other treasures. Also worthwhile is the African Art collection and the Northwest Contemporary Art Collection, featuring works by the so-called Big Four artists (Guy Anderson, Kenneth Callahan, Morris Graves, Mark Tobey) active in and around Seattle and La Conner, Washington.

1300 First Ave. www.seattleartmuseum.org. ✆ **206/854-3100.** $20 adults, $18 seniors, $13 students/teens, free 12 and under. Wed–Sun 10am–5pm (Thurs until 9pm).

Seattle Great Wheel ★★ VIEW/LANDMARK   Located on a pier on the Seattle waterfront, the 175-foot-high Seattle Great Wheel opened in 2012 and is the largest observation wheel on the West Coast. Even if you hate Ferris wheels, this is an enjoyable way to get your bearings while taking in an incomparable view of the city and its surroundings. The observation pods are completely enclosed, seat four, move slowly and silently, and don't sway. On a clear day you'll see across Puget Sound to the Olympic Mountains to the west, and Mount Rainier to the east. On a gray, wet day, you'll have to be content with the Seattle skyline and Elliott Bay. If you want a longer-lasting, high-rise-view experience, opt for a trip up to the top of the Space Needle instead.

1301 Alaskan Way. www.seattlegreatwheel.com. ✆ **206/263-8600.** $13 adults, $11 seniors, $8.50 kids 4–11. Mon–Thurs 11am–10pm, Fri 11am–midnight, Sat 10am–midnight, Sun 10am–10pm.

Seattle Japanese Garden ★★★ GARDEN/PARK   The Japanese influence on Pacific Northwest garden design and plant material has been enormous, and luckily, thanks to the region's cultural ties to Japan, Seattle (and Portland, see p. 145) have the best examples of Japanese gardens outside of Japan. This garden is lovely any time of year, but it is absolutely gorgeous in the springtime months of April and May, when the cherry trees are in bloom, or in the fall, when then bright orange and red tints of the Japanese maples add a burnished luster to the scene. The Seattle Japanese Garden, designed and constructed under the supervision of Japanese garden designer Juki Iida, fits like a jewel into its 3½-acre setting within the University of Washington Arboretum. Opened in 1960, the garden has now had over 60 years to mature and is the oldest formal Japanese garden in the Pacific Northwest. This is a "strolling garden" with several meticulously created miniaturized landscapes within it. It is meant to be seen one landscape at a time, like a scroll of painted landscapes that unrolls and reveals new vistas as you follow the winding path around the central lake from one viewpoint to the next. Take your time—that's the point. In addition to a gorgeous selection of trees and shrubs, you'll encounter all the elements used in formal Japanese garden design— water, rocks and sand, bridges, stone lanterns, and water basins. Blue herons often fly over from Lake Washington and help keep the *koi* (Japanese carp) population in check. You may see them along the shores and on the rocks in the lake.

Washington Park Arboretum, 1075 Lake Washington Blvd. E. (north of E. Madison St.). http://www.seattle.gov/parks/parkspaces/japanesegarden.htm. ℂ **206/684-4725.** Admission $6 adults; $4 seniors/students/ages 6–17. Mid-Feb to Apr Tues–Sat 10am–4pm; May to mid-Sept daily 10am–7pm; mid-Sept to Oct daily 10am–5pm; Nov Tues–Sun 10am–4pm.

Space Needle ★★ LANDMARK/VIEW This is one of those iconic structures that architecturally epitomize an era—in this case, the early 1960s—and come to symbolize a city. So you could say that the Space Needle is Seattle's Eiffel Tower. I'm quite fond of the old Space Needle and have never forgotten the scary thrill of being taken up to the top of it as a kid. From a distance, it looks like a flying saucer on a tripod, and when it was built for the 1962 World's Fair, the 605-foot-tall Space Needle was meant to suggest "the future" (today it definitely looks retro). Once you finally get into the glass elevator, you'll zoom up 520 feet to an observation deck that provides superb and unobstructed views of the entire city and its surroundings. More than 60 sites are identified on wall panels, and high-powered telescopes let you zoom in on them. You'll also find a pricey restaurant, SkyCity ★ (reviewed on p. 68), atop the observation deck (the price of admission to the Space Needle is included if you dine there). The lines in summer and on weekends can be really long, so it's wise to get there early; the admission price allows you to return in the evening to see Seattle at night. (If you purchased a Seattle CityPass described under "Save Cash with a Seattle CityPass," p. 76, you get to skip the long line.)

Seattle Center, 400 Broad St. www.spaceneedle.com. ℂ **206/905-2100.** Admission $26 adults, $24 seniors, $17 ages 4–13, Mon–Thurs 10am–9pm; Fri–Sat 9:30am–10:30pm; Sun 9:30am–9:30pm.

Tillicum Village ★★★ TOUR/CRUISE You can only get there by boat, and the entire trip takes about 4 hours, but a journey to Tillicum Village on Blake Island is a unique way to learn something more about the Seattle area and the Native American tribes that called this region home for thousands of years. At Tillicum Village, a number of local tribes cooperatively present a salmon bake in a re-created longhouse, then perform traditional dances illustrating creation stories. Skilled tribal artists carve masks and other items that can be purchased. The setting is forested Blake Island, believed to be an ancient campground of the Duwamish and Suquamish tribes, and the likely birthplace of Chief Seattle. You can enjoy a walk on the beach or a short hike after the meal. There's a playground for children, and you'll likely spot a few deer.

Tillicum Village, Blake Island State Park. Accessible by Argosy Cruises, Pier 55, Seattle Waterfront. www.tillicumvillage.com. ℂ **206/933-8600.** Price with lunch and cruise: $79 adults, $72 seniors, $30 ages 5–12. Daily May–Labor Day, Fri–Sat only Mar–Apr and Oct; times vary by month; see website for details.

Underground Tour ★★★ TOUR It's both funny and fascinating, and it's one of the very best ways to learn about Seattle's past. Wonderfully entertaining guides lead you into a warren of underground tunnels below Pioneer Square, pointing out businesses that were once at street level until the great fire of 1889 wiped out the city and led to a massive regarding of Seattle. The anecdotes are hilarious and sometimes a bit

visiting VOLUNTEER PARK

Capitol Hill's century-old Volunteer Park, designed by the Olmsted Brothers (see below), is one of the gems of Seattle's park system and has several interesting attractions. Chief among them is the **Volunteer Park Conservatory** (1402 E. Galer St.; www.volunteerparkconserva-tory.org; admission by donation; Tues–Sun 10am–4pm), one of only three Victorian-style glasshouse conservatories on the West Coast. You'd never guess from looking at this elegant building that it was shipped as a prefab kit from Brookline, Massachusetts, and assem-bled on site in 1912. In addition to its many species of palm trees, the central Palm House showcases a collection of tropical orchids, and the Seasonal Dis-play House presents an ever-changing show of color and fragrance (in the spring, it's loaded with blooming bulbs, lilies, cyclamen, azaleas, and hydran-geas). Beyond it is the Cactus House, where the variety of shapes, thorns, and growing habits is amazing, as are the flowers the cacti produce in the spring. Other rooms showcase ferns and bromeliads.

After visiting the Conservatory, take some time to wander through the rest of Volunteer Park. In the early 1900s, the

Olmsted Brothers, America's pre-eminent landscape design firm (their father, Fred-erick Law Olmsted, designed New York's Central Park), were hired to draw up a plan that set aside portions of Seattle's uniquely beautiful terrain as places for relaxation and recreation. Climb the stairway in the Romanesque-style brick **water tower** (open daily 11am–dusk) located in the southeast corner of the park near the reservoir, where the free **Olmsted Interpretive Exhibit** on the observation deck chronicles the Olmsted legacy in creating Seattle's parks and offers great views of Seattle and Puget Sound. Another highlight of Volunteer Park is the **Seattle Asian Art Museum** (1400 E. Prospect St.; www.seattleart museum.org; (*) **206/654-3100;** $7 adults, $5 seniors/students/ages 13–17; Wed–Sun 10am–5pm), housed in a clas-sic 1933 Art Moderne building near the Conservatory. This small museum fea-tures rotating exhibits and a permanent collection of ancient and contemporary art treasures from a variety of Asian cul-tures. Across from it stands Isamo Nogu-chi's 1968 outdoor sculpture called *Black Sun,* a circular form created from Brazil-ian granite; look through the center hole and you'll see the Space Needle.

off-color, but Seattle's history is anything but genteel. You'll learn about exploding toilets, "seamstresses" who never sewed a stitch (and sometimes didn't wear one), city rogues, city fathers and mothers, early businesses, and how the city infrastructure and rebuilding required people to climb ladders to get from one street to the next. Go with a sense of humor and you'll have a great time. There's an intriguing little gift shop at the end of the tour.

Pioneer Building, 610 1st Ave. #200. www.undergroundtour.com. (*) **206/682-4646.** $17 adults, $14 seniors, $9 ages 7–12. Tours daily throughout the day. Closed Thanksgiving and Christmas Day.

Washington Park Arboretum ★★ PARK/GARDEN   Since its official found-ing in 1935, the arboretum has weathered funding crises, neighborhood controversies, and storms that have toppled trees and frozen shrubs. But it has survived and survived beautifully. Walking trails crisscross the varied terrain of woodland, wetland, and gar-dens, taking visitors to acclaimed collections of azaleas, rhododendrons, oaks, coni-fers, camellias, magnolias, Japanese maples, and hollies. The Seattle Japanese

Seattle is one of the few cities in the United States where floatplanes are a regular sight in the skies and on the lakes. If you want to see what it's like to take off and land from the water, contact **Seattle Seaplanes ★★,** 1325 Fairview Ave. E. (www.seattle seaplanes.com; ℂ **800/637-5553** or 206/329-9638). Their floatplanes take off from Lake Union for 20-minute scenic flights over the city at a cost of $98.

Garden (p. 84) occupies the southwestern portion of arboretum but is separate from it. The arboretum is full of seasonal highlights, and there is always something of special interest to discover (pick up a map in the Graham Visitors Center). But the arboretum's must-see springtime spectacle is, without a doubt, **Azalea Way**, bordered by hundreds of Japanese cherry trees, eastern dogwoods, and an undergrowth of azaleas. It required over 10,000 hours of hand labor by WPA workmen to complete. For a refreshing waterside stroll in any season, walk north along Arboretum Drive East, cross the road, and follow the gravel trail along the shoreline to the large wetlands area that's a favorite spot for birders. But all this only hints at the riches you'll find in this wonderfully explorable urban treasure trove.

2300 Arboretum Drive E. www.arboretumfoundation.org. ℂ **206/325-4510.** Free admission. Arboretum daily dawn–dusk; Graham Visitors Center daily 10am–4pm, closed holidays.

Wing Luke Asian Museum ★ MUSEUM   Asians and Pacific Islanders have contributed to the growth and culture of Seattle almost from its inception, and this small, interesting museum in Chinatown/International District tells their stories. The main exhibit, "Honoring Our Journey," explains how they came to Seattle and why and what they did, in an age of rampant racism, once they were here. One exhibit, called "Camp Harmony D-4-44," focuses on the internment of Japanese-American citizens during World War II, re-creating one of the livestock stalls converted into a family holding cell, barbed wire and all; filmed interviews with internees add a human dimension to this episode in U.S. history. The museum is housed in the historic Freeman Hotel, where many early Asian immigrants lived while working in the region's canneries and lumber mills. Tours of the hotel add still more insight into the Asian experience in Seattle, and the museum also offers walking tours of the Chinatown and Japan Town neighborhoods, pointing out locations in the bestselling novel *Hotel on the Corner of Bitter and Sweet* (Ballantine Books, 2009), a Chinese-Japanese love story set in this area. The museum is named for Wing Luke, the first Asian-American to hold public office in the Northwest.

719 S. King St. www.wingluke.org. ℂ **206/623-5124.** $13 adults, $10 seniors and students, $9 ages 5–12; admission price includes tour of historic hotel. Free admission 1st Thurs and 3rd Sat of each month. Tues–Sun 10am–5pm (until 8pm 1st Thurs and 3rd Sat of each month). Closed New Year's Day, July 4th, Thanksgiving, Christmas Eve, and Christmas.

Woodland Park Zoo & Rose Garden ★ ZOO/PARKGARDEN   Woodland Park Zoo has won awards for several exhibits, including the primate area with gorillas and orangutans and the African Savanna with giraffes and zebras. The newest exhibits are the Humboldt penguin habitat, where an underwater viewing area gives you a close-up view of frolicking penguins from Peru, and the fun-loving meerkats' area. Other exhibits focus on Alaska, with a popular brown-bear habitat, and the tropical

bloedel reserve: A GREAT GARDEN OF THE NORTHWEST

If you have an interest in gardens and gardening, don't miss an opportunity to visit **Bloedel Reserve ★★★,** 6 miles north of the Winslow ferry terminal off Wash. 305 (turn right on Agate Point Rd.) on Bainbridge Island (frequent all-day ferry service runs from Seattle to Winslow). This is not the kind of garden with showy flowerbeds, but one in which Northwest native and non-native plants, shrubs, and trees have been skillfully combined to create a series of gardens that are artfully woven into a forested, maritime landscape. In the spring, the woods and meadows are lushly carpeted with naturalized bulbs, and rhododendrons and camellias put on a spectacular show. In the summer and fall, you'll find other plant treasures along the sun-dappled paths. The garden was created by Prentice Bloedel, son of a timber baron. Bloedel and his wife, Virginia, lived on the property from 1951 to 1986, in a French

chateau-style house built by the previous owner in 1931. About 70 acres of the estate were left as undisturbed forest, and the remaining 80 acres were shaped into a remarkable, elegant series of gardens Pick up a map at the gatehouse when you arrive because there is no signage along the winding trails, and, if you're able, follow the route that gives you the full tour (you'll need about 1½ hours).

At the end of your visit, I can almost guarantee that you'll agree with Prentice Bloedel, who said "The Bloedel Reserve is a place where people find refreshment and tranquility in the presence of natural beauty." 7571 NE Dolphin Dr., 6 miles north of Winslow ferry terminal (turn right on Agate Rd.) www.bloedelreserve.org. (℡ **206/842-7631.** $15 adults, $10 seniors/students, $8 ages 13–18, $5 ages 5–12. Tues–Sun 10am–4pm. The #90 bus from the Winslow ferry terminal stops 1 mile from the reserve.

rainforest. At the Zoomazium, an indoor play area, kids 8 and under can explore nature, listen to stories, and generally burn off energy. The zoo also has a beautiful 1918 carousel. The 2½-acre **Woodland Park Rose Garden** adjacent to the zoo showcases the genus *Rosa* in all its myriad forms—floribunda, grandiflora, hybrid tea, hybrid musk, miniature, polyantha, rugosa, David Austen, climber, shrub, tree—they're all here. A circular fountain bubbles at the center and a semi-circular bas-relief wall fountain burbles at the north end. A rectangular lily pond sits between the two fountains, with a gazebo anchoring the east end and a pergola at the south end. This elegant and enjoyable rose garden is unique in that it is 100% organic and pesticide-free. Late May through June is the best time to see and smell the roses, but some remain in bloom throughout the summer.

750 N. 50th St. www.zoo.org. (℡ **206/684-4800.** Zoo: May–Sept $19 ages 13–64, $12 ages 3–12; Oct–Apr: $13 ages 13–64, $8.75 ages 3–12. May–Sept daily 9:30am–6pm; Oct–Apr daily 9:30am–4pm. Rose Garden: Admission free; daily year-round dawn–dusk.

ORGANIZED TOURS

Within its downtown core, Seattle is an easy walking city—but because of its maritime topography, the layout of the streets doesn't always follow an easily understandable

World War II amphibious vehicles called Ducks are used for fun and intriguing tours that combine both land and water. **Seattle Duck Tours ★★★** at 516 Broad St. (www.ridetheducksof seattle.com) ☎ **800/817-1116** or 206/441-3825; show off the standard Seattle sights, but then plunge right into Lake Union for a tour of the Portage Bay waterfront, with its many houseboats and great views. The 90-minute tours leave from a parking lot across from the Space Needle and cost $28 for adults and $17 for kids.

grid. It is also a large, sprawling city. To take in more of the Seattle, and to understand it better, you may want to sign up for an organized tour. For boat tours, see the box "Boat Tours" (p. 77) under "Exploring Seattle"; the highly entertaining and highly recommended Underground Tour (p. 85) is listed in that section as well.

Walking Tours

See Seattle Walking Tours (www.see-seattle.com; ☎ **425/226-7641**) offers guided walking tours of downtown Seattle with a knowledgeable guide, visiting Pike Place Market, the waterfront, and the Pioneer Square area. Tours cost $20.

You'll learn a lot about local history and discover hidden corners of the city on the 2-hour tours offered year-round by **Duse McLean/Seattle Walking Tours** (www.seattlewalkingtours.com; ☎ **425/885-3173**). These tours wind their way from the International District to Pike Place Market, taking in historic buildings, public art, and scenic vistas. Tour price is $15 per person.

For an insider's glimpse of life in Seattle's Chinatown/International District, hook up with **Chinatown Discovery** (www.seattlechinatowntour.com; ☎ **206/623-5124**). They offer tours of the neighborhood and specialized tours based on locales used in the best-selling novel *The Hotel on the Corner of Bitter and Sweet*, set in Seattle's Chinatown.

Food-focused tours of Pike Place Market are offered by **Savor Seattle** (www.savor seattletours.com; ☎ **888/987-2867**), which charges $38 for a 2-hour tour, and **Seattle Food Tours** (www.seattlefoodtours.com; ☎ **206/725-4483**), which charges $39 for a 2½-hour tour.

SHOPPING

Downtown Seattle is the home of retail giants like **Nordstrom, Eddie Bauer** and **REI,** all of which were founded here. High-end shops abound, and you can find every top designer name in a downtown location. But to find local treasures and unique Seattle specialties, leave downtown and explore the shops in Ballard, Fremont, and other neighborhoods.

ANTIQUES & COLLECTIBLES

If antiques are your passion, you won't want to miss the opportunity to spend a day browsing the many antiques stores in the historic farm town of **Snohomish,** located roughly 30 miles north of Seattle. The town has hundreds of antiques dealers and is, without a doubt, the antiques capital of the Northwest. There are also plenty of antiques stores right in Seattle.

Ballard Sunday Farmers Market

Pike Place Market is the best and biggest public market, and open daily, but it is not Seattle's only market. Stretching for two blocks along Ballard Avenue, between NW 20th and NW 22nd avenues in the picturesque heart of the old Ballard neighborhood, the year-round **Sunday Farmers Market** in Ballard is a destination for locals and market-lovers throughout the city. Open from 10am to 3pm, the stalls sell fresh organic produce, cheeses, meats, mushrooms, fish, bread and baked goods, wine, and artisan crafts. There are also ethnic food stalls. Many of Ballard's most delightful shops are open as well, and so are restaurants and places to stop for a coffee and some people-watching.

Antiques at Pike Place ★ ANTIQUES   Located in the Pike Place Market area, this antiques and collectibles mall hosts more than 80 dealers. 92 Stewart St. www.antiques atpikeplace.com. ✆ **206/441-9643.**

Laguna ★ VINTAGE POTTERY   Twentieth-century art pottery is the specialty of this Pioneer Square shop, with pieces from such mid-century pottery factories as Fiesta, Roseville, Bauer, Weller, and Franciscan. 116 S. Washington St. www.lagunapottery .com. ✆ **206/682-6162.**

ART GALLERIES

Davidson Galleries ★   This gallery focuses on both contemporary and antique prints by American and European artists and also features contemporary paintings and sculptures with an emphasis on Northwest artists. 313 Occidental Ave. S. www.davidson galleries.com. ✆ **206/624-7684.**

Foster/White Gallery ★★   This gallery represents Dale Chihuly and always has works by this master glass artist. 220 Third Ave. S. www.fosterwhite .com. ✆ **206/622-2833.**

Glasshouse Studio ★   Here, in the oldest glass-blowing studio in the Northwest, you can watch glass art being made and check out the works of numerous local glass artists. 311 Occidental Ave. S. www.glasshouse-studio.com. ✆ **206/682-9939.**

Patricia Rovzar Gallery ★   Bold, colorful, often whimsical art can be seen at this gallery adjacent to the Seattle Art Museum. 1225 Second Ave. www.rovzargallery.com. ✆ **206/223-0273.**

Native American Art

Ancient Grounds ★   This eclectic downtown antiques shop and natural-history gallery sells quality Northwest Coast Indian masks and also Japanese masks, rare mineral specimens, and a wide variety of other rare and unusual pieces from all over the world. An espresso bar is on the premises. 1220 First Ave. ✆ **206/749-0747.**

Flury & Company Ltd. ★   This Pioneer Square gallery specializes in prints by famed Seattle photographer Edward S. Curtis, known for his late-19th- and early-20th-century portraits of Native Americans. The gallery also has an excellent selection of antique Native American art and artifacts. 322 First Ave. S. www.fluryco.com. ✆ **206/587-0260.**

The Legacy Ltd. ★★   In business since 1933, this is Seattle's oldest and finest gallery of contemporary and historic Northwest Coast Indian and Alaskan art and artifacts. 1003 First Ave. www.thelegacyltd.com. ℂ **800/729-1562** or 206/624-6350.

BOOKS

Elliott Bay Book Company ★★★ BOOKSTORE   Seattle's best-known independent bookstore carries an excellent selection of titles, including books on Seattle and the Northwest. 1521 Tenth Ave. www.elliottbaybook.com. ℂ **800/962-5311** or 206/624-6600.

Peter Miller Books ★★★ BOOKSTORE/DESIGN/LIFESTYLE   Anyone interested in architecture and design books and supplies will want to visit this long-established and always-enticing bookstore in downtown Seattle. 2326 Second Ave. www.petermiller.com. ℂ **206/441-4114.**

CRAFTS & HANDMADE GIFTS

The Northwest is a magnet for skilled craftspeople, and shops all around town sell a wide range of high-quality and imaginative pieces. At **Pike Place Market** (p. 82), you can see what area craftspeople are creating and meet the artisans themselves.

Curtis Steiner ★★★ ART/JEWELRY/LOCAL CRAFTS   Curtis Steiner's decorative arts gallery on Ballard Avenue is worth seeking out for handmade pieces in different media that are of exceptional in quality and unique to Washington. 1549 Ballard Ave. NW. www.curtissteiner.com. ℂ **206/297-7116.**

Fireworks Fine Crafts Gallery ★ LOCAL CRAFTS   Playful, bizarre, beautiful—these are just some of the adjectives that can be used to describe the eclectic collection of Northwest crafts here. 210 First Ave. S. www.fireworksgallery.net. ℂ **206/682-9697.**

DEPARTMENT STORES & FLAGSHIPS

Eddie Bauer ★★ OUTDOOR APPAREL   Eddie Bauer got his start here in Seattle back in 1920, and today the chain that bears his name is one of the country's foremost purveyors of outdoor fashions—although these days, outdoor fashion is looking quite a bit more urban. Pacific Place, 600 Pine St. www.eddiebauer.com. ℂ **206/622-2766.**

Filson ★★ OUTDOOR APPAREL   Filson's clothes are meant to last a lifetime, so if you demand only the best, even when it comes to outdoor gear, be sure to check out this local institution. 1555 Fourth Ave. S. www.filson.com. ℂ **866/860-8906** or 206/622-3147.

Nordstrom ★★★ DEPARTMENT STORE   Known for personal service, Seattle-based Nordstrom ranks among the premier department stores in the United States, and this flagship store features all sorts of boutiques, cafes, live piano music, and other features to make your shopping enjoyable. 500 Pine St. www.nordstrom.com. ℂ **206/628-2111.**

Nordstrom Rack ★★★ DEPARTMENT STORE   Nordstrom's discount shop features discontinued lines and one-off clothes and shoes for women, men, and children, all at terrific savings. www.nordstrom.com. 400 Pine St. ℂ **206/448-8522.** Also at 3920 124th St. SE, Bellevue (ℂ **425/746-7200**), and 19500 Alderwood Mall Pkwy., Lynnwood (ℂ **425/774-6569**).

Northwest Pendleton ★★ SPECIALTY APPAREL/ACCESSORIES   For Northwesterners, Pendleton is and always will be the name in classic wool clothing, blankets, and accessories. 1313 Fourth Ave. www.indianblanket.com. ℂ **800/593-6773** or 206/682-4430.

REI ★★★ OUTDOOR APPAREL/RECREATIONAL GEAR   Recreational Equipment, Inc. (REI) is the nation's largest co-op selling outdoor gear, and the company's impressive flagship is a cross between a high-tech warehouse and a mountain lodge. This massive store sells almost anything you could ever need for pursuing your favorite outdoor sport. It also has a 65-foot climbing pinnacle. With all this under one roof, who needs to go outside? 222 Yale Ave. N. www.rei.com. ✆ **888/873-1938** or 206/223-1944.

FOOD

Fran's Chocolates ★★★   Seattle native Fran Bigelow's salted caramels are so fabulously delicious that even President Obama has commented on them. Four Seasons Hotel, 1325 First Ave. www.franschocolates.com. ✆ **800/4122-3726.**

Pike Place Fish Market ★   The guys at this Pike Place Market fishmonger are like a carny act, pulling in the crowds with their "flying fish" performance, throwing big silvery salmon back and forth. Choose one of the fresh salmon to take home, and the guys will pack it up for you in dry ice. Pike Place Market, 86 Pike Place. www.pikeplacefish.com. ✆ **800/542-7732** or 206/682-7181.

MALLS/SHOPPING CENTERS

Pacific Place ★★ SHOPPING MALL   This downtown mall, adjacent to Nordstrom, contains five levels of upscale shop-o-tainment, including Tiffany & Co., bebe, Barney's New York, Coach, MaxMara, six restaurants, and a multiplex movie theater. 600 Pine St. www.pacificplaceseattle.com. ✆ **877/883-2400** or 206/405-2655.

Westlake Center ★★ SHOPPING MALL   In the heart of Seattle's main shopping district, this upscale, urban shopping mall has more than 80 specialty stores along with an extensive food court. The mall is also the southern terminus for the monorail to Seattle Center. 400 Pine St. www.westlakecenter.com. ✆ **206/467-1600.**

SOUVENIRS

Made in Washington ★★ REGIONAL PRODUCTS   Whether it's salmon, wine, or Northwest crafts, you'll find a varied selection of Washington state products in this shop. www.madeinwashington.com. Pike Place Market, 1530 Post Alley (at Pine St.). ✆ **206/467-0788.** Also at Westlake Center, 400 Pine St. (✆ **206/623-9753**).

Ye Olde Curiosity Shop ★ SOUVENIR SHOP   Every inch of this famous tourist trap on the waterfront is covered with souvenirs and crafts, both tacky and tasteful (but mostly tacky). Pier 54, 1001 Alaskan Way. www.yeoldecuriosityshop.com. ✆ **206/682-5844.**

OUTDOOR PURSUITS

It almost goes without saying that this majestically scenic city and region, surrounded by ocean, lakes, and mountains, offers some outstanding recreational opportunities. Get active, the way the Seattleites do, and you'll enjoy the Seattle experience even more.

Biking

Montlake Bicycle Shop, 2223 24th Ave. E. (www.montlakebike.com; ✆ **206/329-7333**), rents bikes by the day for $35 to $90. This shop is convenient to the **Burke-Gilman/Sammamish River Trail** ★★, a 27-mile paved and traffic-free pathway created from an old railway bed. The most convenient place to start a ride is at **Gas Works Park,** on the north shore of Lake Union. From here you can ride north and east, by way of the University of Washington, to **Kenmore Log Boom Park,** at the north end of Lake Washington.

The West Seattle bike path along **Alki Beach** is another good place to ride; it offers great views of the sound and the Olympic Mountains. If you'd like to pedal this pathway, you can rent single-speed bikes at **Alki Kayak Tours,** 1660 Harbor Ave. SW (www.kayakalki.com; ✆ 206/953-0237), which charges $10 per hour. To get there in scenic style, take the water taxi from the downtown waterfront to West Seattle; the dock is right at the Alki Kayak Tours building.

Hiking

Seattleites' favorite spot for a quick dose of nature is **Discovery Park,** 3801 W. Government Way (✆ 206/386-4236), northwest of downtown, at the western tip of the Magnolia neighborhood. Covering more than 500 acres, this park has many miles of trails and beaches to hike—not to mention gorgeous views, forest paths, and meadows.

Sea Kayaking, Canoeing, Rowing & Sailing

If you'd like to try your hand at sea kayaking, standup paddleboarding, rowing, or sailing, head to **Moss Bay Rowing, Kayaking and Sailing Center,** 1001 Fairview Ave. N. (www.mossbay.net; ✆ 206/682-2031), which rents all types of water vehicles at the south end of Lake Union near Chandler's Cove. Rates range from $14 per hour for a single kayak to $20 per hour for a double. From downtown Seattle, this place can be reached on the Seattle Streetcar.

SPECTATOR SPORTS

With professional football, baseball, ice hockey, soccer, and women's basketball teams, as well as the various University of Washington Huskies teams, Seattle is definitely a city of sports fans. **Ticketmaster** (✆ 800/745-3000 or 206/346-1660; www.ticketmaster.com) sells tickets to almost all sporting events in the Seattle area. You'll find Ticketmaster outlets at area Fred Meyer stores.

Baseball

Seattle's most popular professional sports team is the **Mariners** (www.seattlemariners .com; ✆ 206/346-4000 or 346-4001). They play at **Safeco Field,** a stadium with a retractable roof.

Basketball

The **Seattle Storm** (www.wnba.com/storm; ✆ 877/962-2849 or 206/217-9622), of the Women's National Basketball Association, play in **Key Arena. The University of Washington Huskies** women's basketball team has also been very popular for years. For information on both the women's and the men's Huskies basketball games, call ✆ 206/543-2200 or go to www.gohuskies.com.

Football

Winners of the 2014 Super Bowl, the **Seattle Seahawks** (www.seahawks.com; ✆ 888/635-4295 or 425/203-8000) play at **CenturyLink Field,** 800 Occidental Ave. S. (www.centurylinkfield.com; ✆ 206/381-7500), which is adjacent to Safeco Field.

The **University of Washington Huskies** (www.gohuskies.com; ✆ 206/543-2200) play in Husky Stadium on the university campus.

THE PERFORMING ARTS & NIGHTLIFE

Culturally savvy and party-loving, Seattle has a first-rate symphony, a highly regarded opera company, several top-notch theaters, and lots of bars, lounges and nightclubs. To find out what's going on, pick up a free copy of *Seattle Weekly* (www.seattleweekly .com). On Friday, the *Seattle Times* includes a section called "NW Ticket," a guide to the week's arts-and-entertainment offerings.

Bars & Lounges

Alibi Room ★   Tucked away beneath Pike Place Market, this hip bar serves up potent drinks and very good food, and features Friday and Saturday club nights with dance DJs. 85 Pike St. Ste. 410. www.seattlealibi.com. ℭ **206/623-3180.**

Artusi ★★   When you need a hit of Italy, head for this lively aperitivo bar for a grappa or amaro accompanied by excellent *stuzzichini* ("little nibbles"). 1535 14th Ave. ℭ **206/678-2516.**

Bathtub Gin and Co. ★★   All that's missing in this dimly lit, speakeasy atmosphere is the cigarette smoke. Come here for a great cocktail or, on a chilly evening, a signature hot toddy. 2205 2nd Ave. www.bathtubginseattle.com. ℭ **206/728-6069.**

BOKA Restaurant + Bar ★★   This contemporary bar is a beautiful spot to relax and enjoy gourmet bar food and a seasonal cocktail. 1010 1st Ave. www.bokaseattle.com. ℭ **206/357-9000.**

The Central Saloon ★   The oldest saloon in Seattle is a favorite neighborhood hangout with good food and live rock music. 207 1st Ave. S. www.centralsaloon.com. ℭ **206/622-0209.**

Cha Cha Lounge ★   Red lighting, kitschy velvet paintings, piñatas hanging from the ceiling, and some incongruous punk and heavy metal set the scene at this popular bar. 1013 E. Pike St. www.chachalounge.com. ℭ **206/322-0703.**

Fireside Room ★★★   This elegant lounge at the Sorrento Hotel is a romantic spot to stop for a drink, especially on Friday and Saturday nights, when you can hear live music. 900 Madison St. ℭ **206/622-6400.**

Karma Martini Lounge & Bistro ★   The special martinis they shake up at Karma feature a surprising mixture of natural ingredients, including cucumber and Washington apple. 2318 2nd Ave. www.karmaseattle.com. ℭ **206/838-6018.**

Oliver's Lounge ★★   This relaxing bar at the elegant Mayflower Park Hotel serves award-winning martinis and upscale bar food. 405 Olive Way. ℭ **206/623-8700.**

Raygun Lounge ★   It looks kind of unfinished, but that's part of the brainy charm of this spot, which offers dozens of board games you can play while you're eating or drinking (lots of non-alcoholic options). 501 E. Pine St. ℭ **206/852-2521.**

Brewpubs & Wine Bars

Big Time Brewery & Alehouse ★   Seattle's oldest brewpub is done up to look like an old tavern and serves as many as 12 of its own brews at any given time. 4133 University Way NE. www.bigtimebrewery.com. ℭ **206/545-4509.**

Elysian Brewing Company ★★★   Hands-down, Elysian is the best brewpub in Seattle, with especially good stouts and strong ales and a team of creative brewers. 542 First Ave. S. www.elysianbrewing.com. ℭ **206/382-4498.**

The Pike Pub & Brewery ★   In an open, central space inside Pike Place Market, this brewpub makes excellent stout and pale ale, but is best known for its Kilt Lifter Scottish ale. 1415 First Ave. www.pikebrewing.com. ✆ **206/622-6044.**

The Tasting Room ★★   Located in Pike Place Market, this cozy wine bar has the feel of a wine cellar and is cooperatively operated by several small Washington state wineries. You can buy wine by the glass or bottle. 1924 Post Alley. www.winesofwashington .com. ✆ **206/770-9463.**

Dance

Pacific Northwest Ballet ★★★   Seattle's premier dance company presents a wide range of classics, new works, and a yearly *Nutcracker,* with sets and costumes by the late Maurice Sendak, the children's book author. McCaw Hall, 301 Mercer St. www.pnb.org. ✆ 206/441-2424.

Dance Clubs

Baltic Room ★★★   This swanky Capitol Hill hangout for the beautiful people stages a wide range of contemporary dance music (mostly DJs) encompassing everything from electronica to hip-hop and *bhangra* (contemporary Indian disco). 1207 Pine St. www.thebalticroom.com. ✆ **206/625-4444.**

Century Ballroom ★★   With a beautiful wooden dance floor, this is *the* place in Seattle for a night out if you're into swing, salsa, or tango, complete with lessons early in the evening. 915 E. Pine St. www.centuryballroom.com. ✆ **206/324-7263.**

Neighbours ★★   This has been the favorite dance club of Capitol Hill's gay community for years, with different nights of the week featuring different styles of music. 1509 Broadway. http://neighboursnightclub.com. ✆ **206/324-5358.**

See Sound Lounge ★★   With walls of colored lights and a front wall that swings open to let in the summer air, this retro-mod club is one of Belltown's hottest nightclubs, with nightly drink specials. 115 Blanchard St. www.seesoundlounge.com. ✆ **206/374-3733.**

Live Music, Cabaret & Jazz Venues

Dimitriou's Jazz Alley ★★★   The lineup of world-class performers at this large, yet somehow intimate, dinner/jazz club never fails to amaze. 2033 Sixth Ave. www.jazzalley .com. ✆ **206/441-9729.**

The Pink Door Cabaret ★★   There's almost always something out of the ordinary going on here, be it a trapeze artist or accordion player, but Saturday nights are reserved for the fun and naughty burlesque show. Come earlier and you can enjoy a delicious Italian meal in the dining room before the show. 1919 Post Alley. www.thepink door.net. ✆ **206/443-3241.**

The Triple Door ★★★   A sophisticated and enjoyable nightclub and music venue for grown-ups, The Triple Door features an ever-changing and eclectic schedule that features top name performers and the best popular and jazz musicians in Seattle. If you don't come for the music, come to enjoy a cocktail at the Musicquarium Lounge with its enormous aquarium and lively scene. 216 Union St. www.tripledoor.net. ✆ **206/838-4333.**

Opera & Classical Music

Seattle Opera ★★★   Founded in 1963, the Seattle Opera is one of the top opera companies in the U.S., mounting four operas a year at McCaw Hall in Seattle

Downtown & Capitol Hill Performing Arts & Nightlife

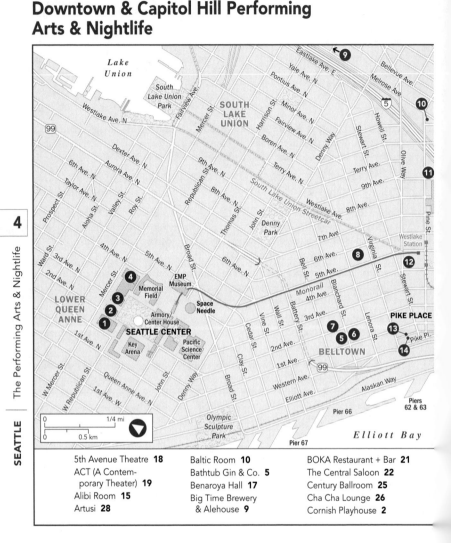

5th Avenue Theatre **18**	Baltic Room **10**	BOKA Restaurant + Bar **21**
ACT (A Contemporary Theater) **19**	Bathtub Gin & Co. **5**	The Central Saloon **22**
	Benaroya Hall **17**	Century Ballroom **25**
Alibi Room **15**	Big Time Brewery & Alehouse **9**	Cha Cha Lounge **26**
Artusi **28**		Cornish Playhouse **2**

Center. Every 4 years, the company mounts Richard Wagner's four-opera cycle, *Ring of the Nibelungen,* a highly anticipated event that draws opera-lovers worldwide. Seattle Center, McCaw Hall, 321 Mercer St. www.seattleopera.org. ℂ **800/426-1619** or 206/389-7676.

Seattle Symphony ★★★   Under Music Director Gerard Schwarz, the Seattle Symphony moved into the top ranks of U.S. orchestras and a new home in the acoustically superb Benaroya Hall in downtown Seattle. Conductor Ludovic Morlot now leads the acclaimed ensemble in a season of classical and pops concerts. Benaroya Hall, 200 University St. www.seattlesymphony.org. ℂ **866/833-4747** or 206/215-4747.

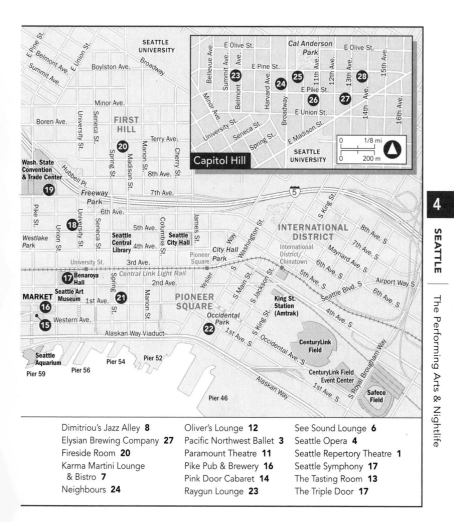

Wash. State Convention & Trade Center

International District/Chinatown

Central Link Light Rail

King St. Station (Amtrak)

CenturyLink Field Event Center

Pier 59, Pier 56, Pier 54, Pier 52, Pier 46

Dimitriou's Jazz Alley **8**
Elysian Brewing Company **27**
Fireside Room **20**
Karma Martini Lounge
& Bistro **7**
Neighbours **24**

Oliver's Lounge **12**
Pacific Northwest Ballet **3**
Paramount Theatre **11**
Pike Pub & Brewery **16**
Pink Door Cabaret **14**
Raygun Lounge **23**

See Sound Lounge **6**
Seattle Opera **4**
Seattle Repertory Theatre **1**
Seattle Symphony **17**
The Tasting Room **13**
The Triple Door **17**

SEATTLE | The Performing Arts & Nightlife

Theater

5th Avenue Theatre ★★★ This elegant playhouse produces some of the liveliest theater in Seattle, including original and Broadway-bound shows and Broadway musicals. 1308 Fifth Ave. www.5thavenue.org. ☏ **206/625-1900.**

ACT (A Contemporary Theatre) ★★ The focus at this energetic venue is on newer plays and playwrights. 700 Union St. www.acttheatre.org. ☏ **206/292-7676.**

Cornish Playhouse (formerly known as Intiman Theatre) ★★★ Serious drama-lovers will love the Tony award–winning Intiman, which has been producing

international classics and contemporary plays for over 3 decades. 155 Mercer St. www.
intiman.org. © **206/443-2222.**

Paramount Theatre ★★★ From Broadway to rock shows, the Paramount offers superb entertainment in a glamorous, historic setting. 911 Pine St. www.stgpresents .org. © **206/467-5510.**

Seattle Repertory Theatre ★★★ Seattle's top professional theater stages everything from the classics to world premières on its two stages. 155 mercer St. www.seattlerep.org. © **877/900-9285** or 206/443-2222.

DAY TRIPS FROM SEATTLE
La Conner & the Skagit Valley ★★★

70 miles N of Seattle

In a competition for quaintest town in Washington, La Conner would leave the other contenders wallowing in the winter mud. This town, a former fishing village, has a waterfront street lined with restored wooden commercial buildings, back streets of Victorian homes, and acres of tulip and daffodil fields stretching out from the town limits. Add to this three museums, numerous plant nurseries and gardening-related stores, art galleries, luxurious inns, and good restaurants, and you have a town that's perfect for a day trip from Seattle.

La Conner dates from a time when Puget Sound towns were connected by water and not by road, and consequently the town clings to the shore of Swinomish Channel. La Conner reached a commercial peak around 1900 (when steamers made the run to Seattle) and continued as an important grain- and log-shipping port until the Great Depression. It never recovered from the hard times of the 1930s, and when the highways bypassed the town, it became a neglected backwater. The wooden false-fronted buildings built during the town's heyday were spared the wrecking balls of the 1960s, and today these old buildings give the town its inimitable charm.

Beginning in the 1940s, La Conner's picturesque setting attracted several artists and writers, and by the 1970s it had become known as an artists' community. Tourism began to revive the economy, and the town's artistic legacy led to the building here of the Museum of Northwest Art, dedicated to the region's many contemporary artists.

What's in a Name?

Although the name sounds like a combination of Spanish and Irish, La Conner is actually named for Louisa A. (LA) Conner, who helped found the town in the 1870s.

Adding still more color to this vibrant little town are the commercial flower farms of the surrounding Skagit Valley. In the spring, tulips carpet the surrounding farmlands with great swaths of red, yellow, and white. The sight is on a par with anything you would ever see in Holland.

ESSENTIALS

GETTING THERE From Seattle, drive north on I-5 and take U.S. 20 west toward Anacortes. La Conner is south of U.S. 20 on La Conner–Whitney Road.

VISITOR INFORMATION Contact the **La Conner Chamber of Commerce,** 606 Morris St. (P.O. Box 1610), La Conner, WA 98257 (www.laconnerchamber.com; © **888/642-9284** or 360/466-4778).

FESTIVALS   From late March to mid-April, the countryside around La Conner is awash with color as thousands of acres of Skagit Valley tulip and daffodil fields burst into bloom in a floral display that rivals that of the Netherlands. The **Skagit Valley Tulip Festival** (www.tulipfestival.org; ✆ **360/428-5959**), held each year during bloom time, is La Conner's biggest annual festival and includes dozens of events.

WHERE TO DINE

Nell Thorn Restaurant & Pub ★ *INTERNATIONAL*   How could you possibly have a restaurant in La Conner without featuring fresh, local, and mostly organic products? Why would you want to, with such delicious bounty so close at hand? You'll get a good meal here no matter what you order, but seafood is always a standout. The upstairs restaurant is a bit more formal, with a more limited menu. Downstairs, in the pub, you can enjoy soups, salads, and sandwiches.

La Conner Country Inn, 205 Washington Ave. www.nellthorn.com. ✆ **360/466-4261.** Main courses $11–$28. Tues–Sun 11:30am–2:30pm and 4–9pm.

Seeds ★ *AMERICAN*   Skagit County is one of the Northwest's most important farming and gardening regions, and this charming bistro on the edge of downtown is housed in a relic of the area's past—a former seed company. You can get breakfast, lunch, or dinner here, and every meal will feature the freshest of local produce and farm products, from naturally nested eggs and seasonal berries and vegetables to grass-fed beef and fresh seafood. There's a bit of everything on the menu, including Washington State wines and beers.

623 Morris St. www.seedsbistro.com. ✆ **360/466-3280.** Main courses $8–$25. Mon–Fri 11:30am–9pm; Sat–Sun 11am–9pm.

EXPLORING LA CONNER & ITS ENVIRONS

The one must-see museum in La Conner is the **Museum of Northwest Art ★★★,** 121 S. First St. (www.museumofnwart.org; ✆ **360/466-4446**), housed in a large contemporary building downtown. The museum showcases works by Northwest artists, particularly Morris Graves, Mark Tobey, and Guy Anderson, all of whom once worked in La Conner. It's open Tuesday through Saturday from 10am to 5pm and Sunday and Monday from noon to 5pm; admission is free.

High atop a hill in the center of town is the **Skagit County Historical Museum ★,** 501 S. Fourth St. (www.skagitcounty.net/museum; ✆ **360/466-3365**), open Tuesday through Sunday from 11am to 5pm; admission is $5 for adults, $4 for seniors and children ages 6 to 12. As the chief repository of Skagit Valley's history, this museum is overflowing with artifacts from daily life over the last century.

Housed in the historic Gerches mansion a few blocks away is the **La Conner Quilt & Textile Museum ★,** 703 S. Second St. (www.laconnerquilts.com; ✆ **360/466-4288**). Here you'll find quilt displays and rooms furnished with antiques. The museum is open Wednesday through Sunday from 11am to 5pm (open daily during Apr); admission is $7.

There is excellent **bird-watching** around the Skagit Valley, especially during the winter months when migratory waterfowl, including trumpeter swans, snow geese, and various raptors, including peregrine falcons and bald eagles, flock to the area's marshes, bays, and farm fields. Eight miles north of La Conner at the **Padilla Bay National Estuarine Research Reserve,** 10441 Bayview-Edison Rd. (www.padillabay.gov; ✆ **360/428-1558**), you can bird-watch along 3 miles of trails through fields and along a dike. The reserve is open daily; the interpretive center is open Wednesday through Sunday from 10am to 5pm. Admission is free.

During the Tulip Festival, stop by **Roozengaarde Flowers & Bulbs**, 15867 Beaver Marsh Rd. (www.tulips.com; ℂ **866/488-5477** or 360/424-8531), the largest grower of tulips, daffodils, and spring bulbs in the U.S., and visit their display garden, tulip fields, and gift shop. **At Christianson's Nursery & Greenhouse,** 15806 Best Rd., Mount Vernon (www.christiansonsnursery.com; ℂ **800/585-8200** or 360/466-3821), you'll find hundreds of varieties of roses and lots of other plants as well. Nearby you can tour the beautiful English country gardens of **La Conner Flats,** 15980 Best Rd. (www.laconnerflats.com; ℂ **360/466-3190**), where high tea is served by reservation.

Shopping is the most popular pastime in La Conner, and up and down **First Street** you'll find lots of great galleries, boutiques, and gift shops.

4 Mount Rainier National Park & Environs ★★★

Paradise: 110 miles SE of Seattle, 70 miles SE of Tacoma, 150 miles NE of Portland

At 14,410 feet, Mount Rainier is the tallest mountain in Washington, and to the sun-starved residents of Seattle and south Puget Sound, the dormant volcano is a giant weather gauge. When the skies clear over Puget Sound, "The mountain is out" is often heard around the region. And when the mountain is out, all eyes turn to admire its broad, snow-covered slopes. Thanks to the region's moisture-laden air, those glaciated slopes remain white throughout the year.

Snow and glaciers notwithstanding, Rainier has a heart of fire. Steam vents at the mountain's summit are evidence that, though this volcanic peak is presently dormant, it could erupt again at any time. If scientists are correct in their calculations that Rainier's volcanic activity occurs in 3,000-year cycles, it may be hundreds of years before another big eruption occurs.

Known to Native Americans as Tahoma, Mount Rainier received its current name in 1792 when British explorer Captain George Vancouver named the mountain for a friend (who never even visited the region). The first ascent to the mountain's summit was made in 1870 by General Hazard Stevens (Stevens Pass is named after him) and Philemon Van Trump, and it was 14 years later that James Longmire built the first hotel on the mountain's flanks. In 1899, Mount Rainier became the country's fifth national park.

ESSENTIALS

GETTING THERE If you're coming from Seattle and your destination is Paradise (the park's most popular area), head for the southwest (Nisqually) park entrance. Take I-5 south to exit 127 and then head east on Wash. 512. Take the Wash. 7 exit and head south toward Elbe. At Elbe, continue east on Wash. 7 At the park entrance, you'll be handed a comprehensive map that includes all trails and facilities. The park entrance fee is $15 per vehicle.

If you don't have a car but still want to visit Mount Rainier National Park, book a tour through **Tours Northwest** (www.toursnorthwest.com; ℂ **888/293-1404** or 206/768-1234), which charges $119 for adults and $87 for children ages 3 to 12 for a 10-hour tour starting in Seattle. These tours operate between late April and early November, and spend most of the day in transit, but you get to see the mountain up close and can do a couple of hours of hiking at Paradise.

Mount Rainier National Park

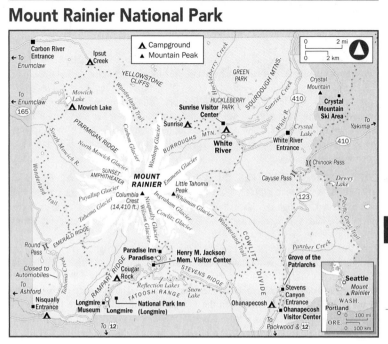

VISITOR INFORMATION For park information, contact **Mount Rainier National Park,** 55210 238th Ave. E., Ashford, WA 98304 (www.nps.gov/mora; ℂ **360/569-2211**). For general information on the area, contact **Visit Rainier** (www.visitrainier.com; ℂ **877/270-7155**).

EXPLORING MOUNT RAINIER NATIONAL PARK

Just past the **main southwest entrance (Nisqually),** is **Longmire,** site of the National Park Inn, the Longmire Museum (with exhibits on the park's natural and human history), a hiker information center, and a ski-touring center that rents cross-country skis and snowshoes in winter.

From here, the road climbs to **Paradise** (elevation 5,400 ft.), a mountainside aerie that affords a breathtaking view. Paradise is the park's most popular destination, so expect crowds. During July and August, the meadows are ablaze with wildflowers, which is why this is such a great place for day hikes. The **Henry M. Jackson Memorial Visitor Center at Paradise** provides panoramic views, and a short walk away is a spot from which you can view Nisqually Glacier. Many miles of other trails lead out from Paradise, looping through meadows and up onto snowfields above the timberline. It's not unusual to find plenty of snow at Paradise as late as July.

In summer, you can continue beyond Paradise to the **Ohanapecosh Visitor Center** (ℂ **360/569-6046**), open daily from late May through early October. Not far from this visitor center, you can walk through the **Grove of the Patriarchs** (see "Hiking & Backpacking," below). Continue around the mountain to reach the turnoff for Sunrise.

Driving counterclockwise around the mountain, you'll come to **Cayuse Pass.** A short detour from this pass brings you to the picturesque **Chinook Pass** area, where there is a good 4.5-mile day-hike loop trail that begins at Tipsoo Lake and circles Naches Peak.

Continuing around the mountain, you'll come to the turnoff for the park's **White River entrance.** This road leads to **Sunrise,** the highest spot in the park (6,400 feet), and site of some of the park's best day hikes. A beautiful old log lodge serves as the **Sunrise Visitor Center** (*𝒞* **360/663-2425**), open daily from late June through early September. From here you can see not only Mount Rainier, but also Mount Baker and Mount Adams. In July and August, the alpine meadows are full of wildflowers. Some of the park's most scenic trails begin at Sunrise. This area is usually less crowded than Paradise.

OUTDOOR ACTIVITIES IN & NEAR THE NATIONAL PARK

HIKING & BACKPACKING   Hikers have more than 240 miles of trails to explore within the park, though the vast majority of park visitors do their hiking at only two places—Paradise and Sunrise. these two alpine areas offer the most scenic day-hiking opportunities, but they can be crowded.

At **Paradise ★★,** the 5-mile **Skyline Trail ★★★** is the highest trail and climbs through beautiful meadows above the tree line. Views of Mount Adams, Mount St. Helens, and the Nisqually Glacier open up along this route. The **Lakes Trail,** of similar length, heads downhill to the Reflection Lakes, with picture-perfect views of the mountain reflected in their waters.

At **Sunrise ★★★** there are also numerous trails of varying lengths. Among these, the 5-mile **Burroughs Mountain Trail** and the 5.5-mile **Mount Fremont Trail** are both very rewarding—the latter even provides a chance to see mountain goats.

The park's single most memorable low-elevation hike is the **Grove of the Patriarchs Trail ★★★.** This 1.5-mile round-trip trail is fairly flat (good for kids) and leads through a forest of huge old trees to a grove of 1,000-year-old red cedars on an island in the Ohanapecosh River. If you've never seen old-growth trees, this is a must. The trail head is near the Stevens Canyon park entrance (southeast entrance).

Another interesting (and easy) low-elevation walk is the **Trail of the Shadows,** a .75-mile loop trail in Longmire. This trail, which circles a wet meadow, leads past bubbling mineral springs.

There are also naturalist-led programs and walks throughout the spring, summer, and fall, and on winter weekends, there are guided snowshoe walks. Check the park newspaper for schedules.

WHITEWATER RAFTING   The Tieton River, which flows down the eastern slopes of the Cascades, is one of the state's most popular rafting rivers. However, the rafting season lasts for only 10 days during the annual August/September drawdown of water from Rimrock Reservoir. Rafting companies offering trips on this river include **Alpine Adventures** (www.alpineadventures.com; *𝒞* **800/723-8386**) and **River Riders** (www.riverrider.com; *𝒞* **800/448-7238** or 206/448-7238). Expect to pay $75 to $90.

WINTER SPORTS   There's good cross-country skiing and snow-shoeing at **Paradise**, where 2-hour **guided snowshoe walks,** with snowshoes provided ($4 suggested donation), are offered daily between mid-December and early January and on winter weekends through March. You'll find a ski touring and cross-country ski and

A Scenic Train Ride on Mount Rainier

From Memorial Day through October, the **Mount Rainier Scenic Railroad ★** (www.mrsr.com; ✆ **888/783-2611** or 360/492-5588) operates vintage steam and diesel locomotives and both enclosed and open passenger cars between the town of Elbe and the southwest entrance to the park. The trips last 1½ to 2 hours and cost $29 for adults, $22 for seniors, $15 for children ages 4 to 12.

snow-shoe rental shop at the **National Park Inn at Longmire** (✆ **360/569-2411**). Snowboarding is popular throughout the year, though there is no lift to get you up the slope, and it's about a 1½-hour climb to the best snowboarding area.

Just outside the park's northeast corner, off Wash. 410, is **Crystal Mountain ★★★** (www.skicrystal.com; ✆ **360/663-3050** for general information, or 888/754-6199 for snow conditions), the state's best all-around ski area due to the variety of terrain. You'll pay $61 for an adult all-day adult lift ticket, $41 for seniors.

WHERE TO STAY & DINE

Within the national park, your first choice for meals should be the dining room at the Paradise Inn. There's also a dining room in Longmire at the National Park Inn. For quick meals, there are snack bars at the Jackson Visitor Center, at Paradise Inn, and at Sunrise Lodge. In Ashford, the **Copper Creek Restaurant,** 35707 Wash. 706 E., Ashford (www.coppercreekinn.com; ✆ **360/569-2326**), makes good berry pies, and breakfast and espresso are served at **Whittaker's Bunkhouse Café,** 30205 Wash. 706 E. (www.whittakersbunkhouse.com; ✆ **360/569-2439**). In summer, you can get pizza, burgers, and beer at **Rainier Basecamp Bar & Grill,** 30027 Wash. 706 E. (www.basecampgrill.com; ✆ **360/569-2727**), next door to Whittaker's. In Elbe, you can get big, juicy burgers from a little white log cabin called **Scale Burgers,** 54109 Mountain Hwy. E. (✆ **360/569-2247**). If you're heading up to the mountain from Seattle, be sure to stop in Eatonville at **Truly Scrumptious Bakery & Café,** 212 Washington Ave. (www.trulyscrumptiousbakery.com; ✆ **360/832-2233**), where you can get a slice of pie, some bread for a picnic, or a sandwich to go.

National Park Inn ★ Open year-round, this historic alpine lodge on the forested slopes near Longmire dates from 1920 and features a full service dining room and general store, both open to the public (there are also guestrooms). Don't expect anything fussy or fancy here; this is a family-friendly, casual dining room with a menu that tries to please everyone, featuring everything from sauteed brook trout and old-fashioned pot roast to mac and cheese. End your meal with warm blackberry cobbler topped with a scoop of vanilla ice cream. You can also order something to drink and enjoy great views of Mount Rainier from the veranda.

Mount Rainier National Park, Longmire, WA 98397. www.mtrainierguestservices.com. ✆ **360/569-2275.** Main courses $8–$20. Daily 7am–7pm.

Paradise Inn ★★ With its cedar-shake siding, huge exposed beams, cathedral ceilings, gigantic stone fireplace, and spectacular mountain views, Paradise Inn is the quintessential Northwest alpine lodge on Mount Rainier. If you want to stay overnight in Mount Rainier National Park, try to get a room at this historic lodge dating from 1917. And if you want a special place to dine, check out the inn's dining room, which is open to the public. The cooking here is above average for a park lodge and utilizes local and regional produce and products, including fresh oysters and fish (and good Dungeness crab cakes). You can also order mushroom strudel, a quesadilla, pork roulade, and pastas with fresh toppings.

Mount Rainier National Park, Paradise, WA 98398. www.mtrainierguestservices.com. ℂ **360/569-2275.** 121 units (33 with shared bathroom). $106 double with shared bathroom; $158–$240 double with private bathroom. Dining room: main courses $14–$28. Dining room daily 7am-8pm. Inn and dining room closed early Oct to late May.

PORTLAND

Given its popularity today, you'd never know that up until about 20 years ago, Portland remained the undiscovered city of the West Coast. Frankly, many Portlanders liked it that way. If you lived in Portland, you knew how special it was and you didn't want to see it spoiled. The slogan "Don't Californicate Oregon" applied to Portland as much as to the rest of the state. Portland wasn't a wealthy city, like San Francisco to the south, and it didn't have the boom-or-bust bravura of Seattle to the north. Although it was the largest inland port on the West Coast, Portland didn't feel connected to the larger world, the way the ocean seaports of San Francisco and Seattle did. It was a quiet, lovely, liberal, and somewhat insular mid-sized metropolis that people loved for its family-friendly neighborhoods and proximity to the ocean, mountains, and high desert. It was a place where residents were aware of their environment and proud of their gardens. The city was progressive enough to install a light rail system back in the 1970s and turn a six-lane highway into downtown's Tom McCall Waterfront Park. There was a large countercultural scene to keep things quirky, and a homegrown arts scene that produced some fine work.

5

As you might have guessed, it was all of these elements that eventually attracted a new wave of residents to Portland. The city has gone from hippie to hipster, and from provincial to pop-culture icon, in a very short time. Watching its evolution has been nothing short of astonishing. Newcomers don't move to Portland because of jobs, they move here because they *want to live here*. A new term has been coined to describe these recent arrivals, "the creative class," describing in part how they create jobs for themselves once they arrive (that's the theory, anyway). Their presence has literally transformed the face of the city. I suppose "independent spirit" is another way to describe the Portland mind-set.

This change has led to a kind of inner-city density the likes of which house-with-big-yard Portland has never known. And what happened to the parking spaces? I suppose micro-apartments and crowded streets are inevitable when you surround yourself with a green belt to help fight sprawl, as Portland did decades ago. It's worked beautifully, and saved the endlessly gorgeous countryside around the city from turning into an endlessly depressing suburban parking lot. But in the process it has squeezed more people and cars into Portland.

You don't come to Portland for its cultural benefits so much as to just hang out. It is the cultural capital of the state, of course, and has long had a lively arts and literature scene. **Powell's City of Books** is one of the finest bookstores in the world and is justifiably a tourist attraction by itself. The

Oregon Symphony can hold its own with any orchestra in the country. Portland was one of the originators (after Seattle) of the phenomenally popular **First Thursday** gallery-hopping idea. The garage-band and grunge music scene is not as feverish as it was a decade ago, but it's still out and about.

FOOD

Speaking of food, everyone and his brother now know that Portland has become a foodie mecca. This is one of the greatest benefits of the "new" Portland, at least for those of us who remember all too vividly when the city had approximately four decent restaurants. The ingredients for great meals were always here—the Pacific Ocean is only 90 minutes away; salmon and steelhead swim up the rivers; just about anything will grow in the fertile Willamette Valley; the vast forests are forageable; and fruits, berries, and nuts have long been staple crops—but it took new chefs with new ideas to turn this local and regional harvest into the kind of exceptional meals that can be had in Portland today. With exceptional Oregon wines to go with them, I might add. Less than an hour away in the wine country, some of the best pinot noirs in the world are being produced. The simple idea of food carts—not just one cart selling hot dogs but dozens of carts selling every kind of cuisine imaginable—also got its start here. But don't assume that all the food in Portland is organic, fat-free, gluten-free, low-salt, vegetarian, free-range, or vegan. Sugar still rules—look at the lines in front of Voodoo Doughnut if you don't believe me—and there's plenty of fat in food cart hits like grilled cheese sandwiches and hot, gooey mac-and-cheese.

GARDENS & PARKS

One of the great things about Portland is that it fosters a green thumb. A visitor can't help but marvel at the beauty of home gardens, and the variety of trees, shrubs, and plants that grow in them. This is the City of Roses, after all, with a yearly Rose Festival complete with floral parades and a fun fair. Travelers should make a point of hanging out in some Portland gardens while they're here. The city has three world-class beauties: the International Rose Test Garden, the Portland Japanese Garden, and Lan Su Chinese Garden. Washington Park and Hoyt Arboretum are endlessly explorable, and Forest Park, which just happens to be the largest urban forest in the country, is crisscrossed with trails that begin at the end of city streets in Northwest and Southwest Portland. All the greenery, and the rain that supports it, is why the air in Portland sometimes smells so sweet and clean.

NEIGHBORHOODS

To get a feel for the Portland of today, the New Portland, hop on a streetcar or the light rail system and go hang out in some Portland neighborhoods. Once upon a time not so long ago, they were just neighborhoods, some better than others, with a strong community spirit. Today, every Portland neighborhood is busy branding itself and, again, rediscovering and reinventing what was always there: A main street or intersection that served local needs. In the New Portland, people flit from one neighborhood to the next because the restaurant/coffeehouse/bakery/microbrewery/boutique phenomenon has spread all over. There are neighborhoods and streets that have been completely transformed, particularly in North Portland, where North Russell Street, North Mississippi, and North Alberta have blossomed in ways unimaginable a few years ago. The Pearl District, created in an old warehouse and light industry area, is one of the most successful urban developments in the country. And downtown Portland remains as attractive and vital as ever. The urban center is not an anonymous warren of designer skyscrapers; it's fairly low-rise (height restrictions prevent tall buildings from usurping the views from the hills) and has a wonderful mixture of architecture and parks to keep it interesting. As you visit residential neighborhoods, don't be surprised if you hear clucking—raising chickens is a new urban pastime in Portland.

So where do people hang out? Portland has more microbreweries than any city in the world, and coffee shops are big small businesses. People order, sip, start to gab with their friends, and never leave except to go to the bathroom. You also hang out at bars during happy hour, which is huge in Portland. I always thought it was because drinks were cheap, but actually it's because the food is half-price.

The nice thing about hanging out in different parts of Portland is that you don't have to travel for miles to do it. The city is really pretty compact and easy to navigate. As you explore, you'll discover what really makes this city so special—its scale, its variety, and its low-key livability. So goodbye Old Portland. I will miss you. But I have to say, the New Portland is a lot more fun and interesting.

ESSENTIALS

Arriving

BY PLANE

Portland International Airport (**PDX;** www.flypdx.com; ✆ **877/739-4636** or 503/460-4234) is located 10 miles northeast of downtown Portland, adjacent to the Columbia River. This is one of the easiest airports in the U.S. to navigate, and it's linked to the city by the easy-to-use MAX light rail system. There's a Travel Oregon **Visitor Information Center** in the baggage claim area where you can pick up maps and brochures and find out about transportation into the city.

GETTING INTO THE CITY

BY CAR   From the airport, follow signs for downtown. From I-205 you'll exit onto westbound I-84, which crosses the Willamette River via the Morrison Bridge exit and brings you into downtown Portland. The trip takes about 20 minutes.

BY LIGHT RAIL   The easiest and least expensive way to get into town is to take the Airport MAX (Red Line) light rail line, operated by **TriMet** (www.trimet.org; ✆ **503/238-7433**). MAX operates daily about every 15 to 30 minutes between 5am and midnight. Buy your ticket from the vending machine on the airport station platform. The fare on MAX is $2.50 for adults and $1 for seniors (or "Honored Citizens," as they're called in Portland). The trip from the airport to Pioneer Courthouse Square in downtown Portland takes about 40 minutes. (Many downtown hotels lie within four or five blocks of Pioneer Square; plan on walking from there since taxis in Portland don't generally cruise for fares.)

BY TAXI   A **taxi** to downtown generally costs between $40 and $45. Taxis are usually available at the lower level Ground Transportation area.

BY TRAIN

Amtrak trains stop at historic **Union Station,** 800 NW Sixth Ave. (www.amtrak.com; ✆ **800/872-7245**), about 10 blocks from the heart of downtown Portland. Taxis are usually waiting to meet trains and can take you to your hotel. If you are renting a car from a downtown car rental office, the agency will usually pick you up at the station. The MAX Yellow and Green lines both run past Union Station and can take you into downtown Portland or across the Willamette River to Portland's east side.

BY BUS

The **Greyhound** bus station is at 550 NW Sixth Ave. (www.greyhound.com; ✆ **800/231-2222** or 503/243-2361), on the north side of downtown near Union Station. You can take MAX from the Greyhound station into downtown. Although you can also easily walk from the station into the heart of downtown, you have to pass through a somewhat rough neighborhood for a few blocks; it's fine during the day, but I wouldn't recommend it after dark or on weekend evenings.

Bolt Bus (www.boltbus.com) is a new, low-cost bus service to Portland from Vancouver, BC and Seattle to the north, and from Eugene to the south. The Bolt Bus conveniently drops off passengers right downtown on SW Salmon Street between 5th and 6th avenues.

Visitor Information

Travel Portland, 701 SW Sixth Ave. (www.travelportland.com; ✆ **877/678-5263** or 503/275-8355), is in Pioneer Courthouse Square in downtown Portland. **Travel Oregon** (www.traveloregon.com; ✆ **503/284-4620**), the state tourism office, has an information desk in the baggage claim area of the Portland Airport.

City Layout

Portland is in northwestern Oregon at the confluence of the Columbia and Willamette rivers. (Contrary to what many people think, Portland is *not* on the Pacific Ocean but about 90 miles east of it.) The **Willamette** (pronounced will-*am*-met) **River,** spanned by eight bridges in the downtown area, cuts through the heart of Portland, dividing it into east and west. **Burnside Street** is the north-south boundary line, dividing the west side into **northwest** and **southwest,** and the east side into **northeast** and **southeast.** The west side rises steadily from the Willamette to about 1,000 ft. in the West Hills, while the residential east side of Portland is relatively flat. Just east of the city, the landscape changes to rolling hills that extend about 50 miles to the Cascade Mountains and Mount Hood, the most prominent peak in the Oregon Cascades (11,235 ft.). The Columbia River, to the north, forms the boundary between Oregon and Washington.

The Greater Metro area also includes Vancouver, Washington, just across the Columbia River to the north of Portland, although that is an entirely separate city. About 2.2 million people live in the combined metropolitan areas.

MAIN ARTERIES & STREETS

I-84 (**Banfield Fwy.** or **Expwy.**) enters Portland from the east. **I-205,** east of the city, bypasses downtown Portland and runs past the airport. **I-5** runs through the city on a north-south axis. **I-405** circles around the west and south sides of downtown. **U.S. 26** (**Sunset Hwy.**) leaves downtown heading west toward Beaverton and the coast. **Ore. 217** runs south from U.S. 26 in Beaverton and connects to I-5.

Neighborhoods in Brief

Everyone who comes to Portland—and even some of us who live here—comments on its many lovely neighborhoods. As the city has grown and diversified, older neighborhoods have been "rediscovered" and their original shopping and retail streets re-invented. The commercial/retail/restaurant areas of several areas, mostly on the east side, are virtually unrecognizable from what they were as recently as the 1990s. Portland has always been community-minded, and the old neighborhoods with their new infill remain the heart and soul of the city.

SOUTHWEST PORTLAND

Downtown Thanks to far-sighted planning efforts, Portland's attractive downtown area has become a model for cities around the country. Compact and pedestrian-friendly, with short 200-square-foot blocks and three historic districts, it's a destination for residents and workers from all over the city. Parks, fountains, public artworks, hotels, restaurants, and a rich texture of building and street materials add to the human-scale appeal. Brick-paved **Transit Malls,** completed in 1978 along SW 5th and 6th Avenues, bisect the main retail and business core.

Starting at the Willamette River, the central downtown area is bounded to the south and north by the curve of I-405. Clustered along the south end are the buildings of **Portland State University** (bounded by I-405, SW Market Street, SW 12th Ave., and SW 5th Ave.). Rising at the north end is the sleek, rhomboid-shaped **U.S. Bancorp Tower** (111 SW 5th Ave.), known locally as "Big Pink." Oregon's tallest building (43 stories), it has a reflective orange-pink facade that plays off the changing light. Downtown extends west to the I-405 Freeway, a monstrosity that cuts right through southwest and northwest Portland at 13th Avenue.

Pioneer Courthouse Square, a brick plaza flanked by the lovely old Pioneer Courthouse, office buildings from the 1920s covered with white glazed terra-cotta tiles (it's officially the Glazed Terracotta Historic District, but nobody knows that except me, and now you), and a large **Nordstrom** store from the 1980s, is a gathering spot called "Portland's living room." Within downtown's Cultural District (along Broadway and the South Park blocks) are the **Arlene Schnitzer Concert Hall,** home of the Oregon Symphony, the **Portland Center for the Performing Arts,** and **Keller Auditorium**—the city's largest performing-arts venues—as well as the **Portland Art Museum** and the **Oregon Historical Society Museum.** The **South Park Blocks,** a tree-lined park-promenade created on land donated by Portland's early settlers, runs from SW Salmon Street through the campus of Portland State to the I-405. **Tom McCall Waterfront Park,** a wide pedestrian esplanade and park, runs along the Willamette River and is the site of numerous festivals (an amusement park is set up here during the Rose Festival). You'd never guess that this popular riverfront greenway was once a six-lane highway.

The **Yamhill National Historic District,** bounded by SW Naito Parkway, Morrison Street, Taylor Street, and 3rd Avenue, is also considered part of downtown Portland. This compact, six-block area, known for its fine examples of late-19th-century cast-iron architecture, marked the southern end of the city's first, waterfront-based commercial core. In the 1950s, when many buildings in the area were demolished for parking lots and to facilitate construction of the present Morrison Street Bridge, the area became isolated from its contemporaneous extension to the north, the area now known as the Skidmore/Old Town Historic District. Restoration and renovation of the remaining buildings began in the 1970s.

Skidmore/Old Town District Portland's original commercial core is bounded by SW Naito Parkway, SW Oak Street, Third Avenue, and NW Davis Street. Running parallel to the Willamette River, and straddling sections of northwest and southwest Portland, this area, along with the Yamhill Historic District to the south (considered a part of downtown), was part of the 1843 land claim that led to the establishment of Portland. From the mid- to late-19th century it served as the city's main riverfront business and entertainment district. **Skidmore Fountain,** a graceful fountain built in 1888—with caryatids holding aloft a bronze basin in the center of an octagonal granite pool with the inscription, "Good citizens are the riches of a city["]—acts as the centerpiece of the district. Cast-iron artifacts from demolished 19th-century Portland buildings are set into an adjacent brick wall and covered arcade that leads to the popular **Portland Saturday Market** (see p. 155). The area began to decline in the 1890s when the logging boom ended and railroads decreased the city's reliance on river trade. **Union Station** (800 NW 6th Ave. near the Broadway Bridge), with its 150-ft. tower proclaiming "Go By Train," was built in 1896 and is a prominent landmark from the railroad era. As the city center shifted west toward higher ground, Old Town gradually became a neglected skid row, and many of the district's brick and cast-iron "commercial palaces" were demolished, leaving gaping holes. Since its designation in 1975 as a National Historic Landmark District, most of the remaining late-19th-century buildings have been restored. Despite the presence of the Portland Saturday Market, the neighborhood has never become a popular shopping district, mostly because some welfare hotels and street people give parts of it a rough edge. With its many clubs and bars, however, it is the city's main nightlife district. The neighborhood is safe during the day, but visitors should exercise caution at night.

Portland Heights Portland Heights, nestled in the hills south of Burnside Street and west of SW Vista, is Portland's oldest and most affluent neighborhood. In gorgeous **Washington Park,** you'll find two of Portland's great gardens (**The International Rose Test Garden** and the **Portland Japanese Garden**) as well as the renowned **Hoyt Arboretum** and the **Oregon Zoo.** This is otherwise primarily a residential neighborhood.

South Waterfront Portland's newest neighborhood is a collection of high-rise offices and condominiums about a mile south of downtown's Tom McCall Waterfront Park. The South Waterfront is home to the lower terminal for the Portland Aerial Tram that glides up to Oregon Health Sciences University (OHSU), the huge medical facility that dominates "Pill Hill" above the South Waterfront. There's otherwise not much here to draw visitors.

NORTHWEST PORTLAND

Chinatown Two carved lions stand in front of the colorful **Chinatown Gate** (NW Fourth Ave. and W. Burnside), erected in 1986 to commemorate 135 years of Chinese contributions to the city of Portland and the state of Oregon. The five-tiered gate marks the official entrance to Portland's low-key Chinatown District, bounded by NW Second and Fifth Avenues, West Burnside, and NW Glisan Street. This small area, with its handful of Chinese groceries and restaurants, is wedged between the Pearl District and Old Town. The neighborhood's main attraction is the impressive **Lan Su Chinese Garden.** Because of its proximity to bars on West Burnside Street and the homeless missions and welfare hotels in Old Town, Chinatown is not a good neighborhood to explore late at night.

Pearl District This relatively new (and recycled) neighborhood of galleries, boutiques, restaurants, cafes, brewpubs, parks, and residential and business lofts and condos is bounded by the **North Park Blocks,** Overton Street, I-405, and Burnside Street. It is rather phenomenal how this former warehouse district has grown up and matured into a really pleasant city neighborhood over the last 20 years. It has all the urban amenities a Portlander requires, including **Powell's City of Books, Jamison Park** with its fountain where kids play in the summer, and public transportation provided by the Portland streetcar. Crowds of people come to the Pearl for **First Thursday** (the first Thursday of every month), when galleries premiere new shows and are open late. The Pearl is Portland's well-planned version of new urbanism and one of the city's main upscale neighborhoods for young families, singles, and boomer retirees.

The Benson Bubblers

Scattered throughout downtown Portland are dozens of cast-bronze four-bubbler drinking fountains installed around 1912 to 1913. They were a gift from Simon Benson, a teetotaling lumber baron who believed a supply of fresh, cool water would help detract from the lure of the saloons. Portland's drinking water comes from Bull Run, a watershed on the northwest slope of Mount Hood, and it is delicious.

Northwest 23rd & Nob Hill   Small in scale and long on charm, **NW 23rd** is the focal point of one of the most attractive neighborhoods in Portland. It's now a hot destination street, known for its shopping, sidewalk cafes, restaurants, and good people-watching. The avenue and its less fashionable twin, **NW 21st,** extend from West Burnside to NW Thurman Street; the blocks between West Burnside and NW Lovejoy streets are the busiest. The upscale commercial aspect of NW 23rd is a fairly recent phenomenon. Two decades ago it was a quiet residential street, a bit shabby around the edges, with little more than a drugstore, a bank, and a couple of stores to serve the needs of the neighborhood. Gradually, the old houses were turned into small shops; existing structures were renovated; and new coffeehouses, boutiques, and restaurants moved in. In the latest phase of development, big "lifestyle" stores like Pottery Barn and Restoration Hardware have grabbed a piece of the commercial action.

The **Nob Hill** neighborhood around NW 23rd Avenue became fashionable in the prosperous 1880s, and there are still many fine Victorian homes to be seen on the streets between NW 17th and NW 25th avenues and NW Everett to NW Thurman streets. These homes are still private residences or have been converted into offices. Farther west, and extending from northwest to southwest, is giant **Forest Park,** one of the largest urban parks in the nation. **Pittock Mansion** is literally the high point of Northwest Portland—it sits about 1,000 feet high in Forest Park and overlooks downtown and east Portland.

NORTHEAST PORTLAND

Irvington   One of Northeast Portland's oldest and most diverse neighborhoods, Irvington is bounded by NE Broadway and NE Fremont between NE 7th and NE 24th. NE Broadway and NE Weidler serve as Irvington's primary commercial streets, with giant **Lloyd Center** mall between them. Like other city neighborhoods, Irvington has undergone an amazing renaissance in the past 2 decades. With its lovely old Victorian and early-20th-century homes on quiet streets shaded by giant trees, it's no wonder that it was "rediscovered" and, after years of being rather run-down, became one of the most expensive residential neighborhoods in Portland.

Alberta Arts District   This newly redefined neighborhood, a few miles north of downtown Portland and a mile to the east of I-5, is Portland's most multicultural and creative neighborhood. Now. It used to be pretty run-down and just called Alberta. Because the old houses here are fairly small and used to be relatively inexpensive, it became a popular neighborhood with young, liberal families. Neighborhood shops are full of alternative-lifestyle fashions, on-the-edge (for Portland) art, and lots of the unexpected and the uncategorizable. Cafes, pubs, and restaurants provide plenty of places for making the scene. On the **Last Thursday** of every month, the neighborhood throws a blocks-long, art-oriented street party. Before all this "urban renaissance" happened, Alberta was an area where African-Americans who came to Portland during World War II to work in the Portland shipyards lived.

North Mississippi District   All these "districts" are new inventions by real estate agents and developers. This area didn't really have a name before it became white, young, and arty. Anchored by the **ReBuilding Center,** a sort of warehouse-sized thrift store full of recycled building materials, the North Mississippi District is 2 miles north of downtown. With plenty of good restaurants, a brewpub, popular music venues, and a couple of great coffeehouses, North Mississippi is a fun neighborhood to explore if you want to get a feel for what it's like to live in the "new" Portland.

SOUTHEAST PORTLAND

Hawthorne   This southeast Portland neighborhood, once a countercultural enclave and still "alternative" around its gentrified edges, is full of eclectic boutiques, moderately priced restaurants, a couple of famous old theaters (the **Aladdin** for live music and performance, and the **Clinton Street,** which has been showing *The Rocky Horror Picture Show* every Saturday night since 1978). Just south of Hawthorne Boulevard, beginning at SE 12th Avenue, you'll find the unique **Ladd's Addition** neighborhood, the oldest planned community in Portland, which has five rose gardens and an unusual (and confusing) street layout. **SE Belmont Street,** just north of Hawthorne Boulevard, and **SE Division Street,** to the south, are two of the city's newly rediscovered and revamped neighborhoods, and both areas are well worth exploring.

Laurelhurst The Laurelhurst neighborhood takes its name from lovely Laurelhurst Park, its centerpiece and showplace. Stretching from about SE 30th to SE 39th and from NE Sandy to NE Belmont, Laurelhurst is a sedate, rather low-key, and family-oriented neighborhood. Development started in the first decades of the 20th century, and the area contains a rich mix of residential architecture styles and sizes.

Sellwood Sellwood is the city's antiques district and has many restored Victorian houses. It's a small-scale area with a real neighborhood feel.

Westmoreland & Eastmoreland Just north of Sellwood, surrounding the intersection of SE Milwaukie Avenue and SE Bybee Boulevard, is the heart of the Westmoreland neighborhood. Westmoreland and adjacent Eastmoreland are primarily residential neighborhoods, mostly laid out and built from the 1920s to 1940s, with a charming mix of bungalows and mansions on curving, tree-lined streets. This area is the home of **Reed College,** a famous liberal bastion. Across from Reed is the beautiful **Crystal Springs Rhododendron Garden.**

5 | GETTING AROUND

By Public Transportation

Portland encourages the use of public transportation, and you can travel around the city via bus, MAX light rail, or the Portland streetcar, all operated by **TriMet** (www.trimet .org; ✆ **503/238-7433**). Buy your 2-hour tickets and day passes on the bus (exact change required), at vending machines at bus and light rail stops, at vending machines on board the streetcar, or at the **TriMet Ticket Office** (701 SW Sixth Ave.), located in Pioneer Courthouse Square behind the waterfall fountain. The office is open Monday through Friday from 8:30am to 5:30pm and Saturdays from 10am to 4pm. Bus and MAX passes and schedules are also available at most Fred Meyer, Safeway, and Albertsons grocery stores throughout the metro area.

BY BUS TriMet buses operate daily over an extensive network. Adult fares are $2.50, $1 for seniors ("Honored Citizens") 65 and older, and $1.65 for children up to age 17. You can make free transfers between the bus and both the MAX light rail system and the Portland streetcar. Tickets are good for 2 hours.

BY LIGHT RAIL The **Metropolitan Area Express (MAX)** is Portland's aboveground light rail system, connecting downtown Portland with the airport (Red Line), the eastern suburb of Gresham (Blue Line), the western suburbs of Beaverton (Red and Blue lines) and Hillsboro (Blue Line), North Portland (Yellow Line), and Clackamas (Green Line). Fares on MAX are the same as on TriMet buses; be sure to

Save Money with TriMet Transportation Passes

A **1-day transportation pass,** which includes all forms of public transportation, costs only $5 for adults, $2 for seniors, and $3.30 for ages 7–17. You can buy a **7-day pass** for $26 adults, $7 seniors, and $8 ages 7–17.

validate your ticket on the platform before you board MAX. There are ticket inspectors who randomly check to make sure passengers have stamped tickets and issue fines to those who don't.

BY STREETCAR **Portland streetcar** (www.portlandstreetcar.org; ✆ **503/238-7433**) runs on two lines, the NS Line and the CL Line. The NS Line is a 4-mile (one way) route from NW Lovejoy and Northrup, through the Pearl District, downtown, and Portland State University to the South Waterfront District. The CL Line is a 4.65-mile (one way) route from SW Market to the Pearl District, across the Broadway Bridge to the Rose Quarter, Convention Center, and OMSI (Oregon Museum of Science and Industry) in northeast and southeast Portland. Both streetcar lines are a great way for visitors to get from downtown to the neighborhoods. Streetcar fares are $1, but that's for the streetcar only; you cannot use a streetcar-only ticket to transfer to buses or MAX.

By Car

CAR RENTALS Portland is a compact city, and public transit will get you to most attractions within its limits. However, if you're planning to explore outside the city— and the Portland area's greatest attractions, such as Mount Hood and the Columbia River Gorge, lie in the countryside within an hour's drive—you'll definitely need a car or a tour company to take you there.

The major car rental companies all have desks at Portland International Airport on the lower level: **Avis** (www.avis.com; ✆ **800/331-1212** or 503/249-4950), **Dollar** (www.dollar.com; ✆ **800/800-3665** or 503/249-4792), **Enterprise** (www.enterprise.com; ✆ **800/261-7331** or 503/252-1500), **Hertz** (www.hertz.com; ✆ **800/654-3131** or 503/528-7900) and **National** (www.nationalcar.com; ✆ **877/222-9058** or 503/249-4900). Outside the airport, but with desks adjacent to the other car rental desks, are **Advantage** (www.advantage.com; ✆ **800/777-5500** or 503/284-6064), **Alamo** (www.goalamo.com; ✆ **877/222-9075** or 503/249-4900), **Budget** (www.budget.com; ✆ **800/527-0700** or 503/249-6331), and **Thrifty** (www.thrifty.com; ✆ **800/847-4389** or 877/283-0898). **Zipcar** (www.zipcar.com) and **Car2go** (www.car2go.com) let you rent a small two-seater car from spots all over Portland, drive it as long as you need to, and return it to a convenient drop-off spot—not necessarily where you picked it up— for a standard rate of 41¢ per minute. You don't have to pay for gas when you use the car. You do need to become a member before you begin using the service, but after the initial charge there is no annual fee.

PARKING Electronic parking meters take coins, credit cards, and debit cards and issue receipts that must be placed on the curbside window of your car. The receipt remains valid elsewhere if you move your car, as long as there is time remaining on it. In most parts of town, you don't have to feed the meters after 7pm, but you do pay for parking on Sundays from 1 to 7pm in some parts of the city. The hourly rate is $1.60.

The city operates **Smart Park** garages at First Avenue and Jefferson Street, Fourth Avenue and Yamhill Street, 10th Avenue and Yamhill Street, Third Avenue and Alder Street, O'Bryant Square, and Naito Parkway and Davis Street. Many downtown merchants and restaurants validate Smart Park tickets for 2 hours if you spend at least $25.

SPECIAL DRIVING RULES You may turn right on a red light after a full stop and left into the adjacent left lane of a one-way street. If a pedestrian is crossing at a white-striped pedestrian crossing, motorists must come to a complete stop until the pedestrian has reached the sidewalk.

By Taxi

You won't find cabs cruising the streets—you or your hotel concierge will have to phone for one. **Broadway Cab** (www.broadwaycab.com; ✆ 503/227-1234) and **Radio Cab** (www.radiocab.net; ✆ 503/227-1212) charge $2.50 for the first passenger, $1 for each additional passenger, and $2.60 per mile.

On Foot

City blocks in Portland are about half the size of most city blocks elsewhere, and the entire downtown area covers only about 13 blocks by 26 blocks. This makes downtown Portland a very easy place to explore on foot. From downtown you can easily walk to the **Pearl District, NW 23rd,** and **Washington Park.** (There are also public transportation options to all those destinations.)

[Fast FACTS] PORTLAND

Area Codes The Portland metro area has two area codes—503 and 971—and it is necessary to dial all 10 digits when making local calls.

Dentist Contact the **Multnomah Dental Society** (www.multnomahdental.org; ✆ 503/513-5010) for a referral.

Doctor If you need a physician referral while in Portland, contact **Legacy Referral Services** (www.legacyhealth.org; ✆ 503/335-3500).

Emergencies For police, fire, or medical emergencies, phone ✆ 911.

Hospitals Two conveniently located area hospitals are **Legacy Good Samaritan Medical Center,** 1015 NW 22nd Ave. (www.legacyhealth.org;

✆ 503/413-7711), and **Providence Portland Medical Center,** 4805 NE Glisan St. (www.providence.org; ✆ 503/215-1111).

Newspapers & Magazines Portland's morning daily newspaper is *The Oregonian.* For arts and entertainment information and listings, consult the "A&E" section of the Friday *Oregonian,* or pick up a free copy of *Willamette Week* at sidewalk newspaper boxes.

Pharmacies Convenient to most downtown hotels, **Central Drug,** 538 SW Fourth Ave. (www.centraldrugportland.com; ✆ 503/226-2222), is open Monday through Friday from 9am to 6pm. **Fred Meyer** and **Safeway** grocery stores have pharmacy departments that are open 7 days a week.

Safety Portland is still a relatively safe city. Take extra precautions, however, if you venture into the Chinatown and Old Town areas at night. Car break-ins and bike thefts are the most common crimes, so don't leave anything valuable in your car, and keep a close eye on your bike.

Smoking Smoking indoors in public places is banned in Oregon.

Taxes Portland is a shopper's paradise—there's no sales tax. However, there's a 12.5% tax on hotel rooms within the city and a 17% tax on car rentals (plus additional fees if you pick up your rental car at the airport, adding anywhere from 10–16%.)

Time Zone Portland is on Pacific time, 3 hours earlier the East Coast.

WHERE TO STAY

The hotel scene, like every other scene in Portland, has changed dramatically in the last quarter-century. For one thing, Portland now has one. The city used to be plain Jane when it came to lodging, but now there is a raft of stylish, comfortable hotels of all levels of sophistication. The large, classic hotels are all downtown, but so are a wide range of mid-size and smaller boutique hotels. Staying downtown is convenient and gives a good taste of Portland's interesting but non-rushed urban scene. Most of the downtown hotels have well-known and popular restaurants and lounges attached to them, and from downtown it's easy to get everywhere by public transportation. I've included a couple of excellent B&Bs (one in Northwest and two in Northeast) that give a good perspective on different Portland neighborhoods. Note that the prices listed below are rack rates—the hotel's official published rates. You can usually lower that rack rate significantly by booking through the hotel's website or a hotel booking site. The prices listed are for a double room in low season (winter) and high season (July–Aug). The **12.5% hotel tax** is not included.

If you arrive without a hotel, check out the last-minute, same-day-only bargains at **Hotel Tonight** (www.hoteltonight.com).

Travel Portland, 701 SW Sixth Ave., Portland, OR 97205 (www.travelportland .com; ✆ **877/678-5263** or 503/275-9293) provides a hotel reservation service for the Portland metro area. For information on **B&Bs** in the Portland area, contact the **Oregon Bed & Breakfast Guild** (www.obbg.org; ✆ **800/944-6196**).

VERY EXPENSIVE

The Benson ★★★ The Benson was built in 1912, the same year the hotel that became the Ace (reviewed p. 120) checked in its first guests. But the two could hardly be more different in scale, scope, and style. The Benson is Portland's premier "old" hotel; it's called "The Residence of the Presidents" because every president from William Taft on has stayed here (George W. being the lone exception). The Benson has some features typical of an older hotel, primarily slightly smaller rooms and bathrooms, but it has also kept up with the times without sacrificing tradition. The lobby is Portland's loveliest, paneled with (now extinct) Circassian walnut from Siberia, with a cozy fireplace area and a Palm Court that hosts a very popular happy hour. The rooms are quiet, both in terms of noise and decor, which can be a relief after all the busy patterns and furniture types in some of Portland's boutique hotels. Here the emphasis is on classic and calm. The beds have TempurPedic mattresses, the service is great, and so is the heart-of-downtown location. **El Gaucho,** the restaurant attached to the Benson, is one of Portland's top steakhouses. (Simon Benson, the timber baron who built the hotel, was the same man who gave Portland the "Benson Bubblers"—those wonderful brass drinking fountains you see all over downtown.)

309 SW Broadway. www.bensonhotel.com. ✆ **800/663-1144** or 503/228-2000. 287 units. $149–$329 double. Valet parking $33. Pets accepted ($25 fee). **Amenities:** 3 restaurants; 2 lounges; bikes; exercise room and access to nearby health club; Wi-Fi (free).

The Nines ★★★ Since its opening in 2008, the Nines has lost none of its cachet. It caused quite a stir initially because it was created on the top nine floors of the old Meier & Frank department store, a Portland retail icon since the 1920s. The Nines, as in "dressed to . . ." honors the defunct fashion emporium (now a Macy's) with fashion-centric artwork, mannequins in the reception area, and bracelet-like drawer handles in the rooms. The hotel lobby is a spacious, light-filled atrium with limousine-long white leather sofas offset by red armchairs. The rooms are fairly large and dressed for fun and sophistication, with fake-jewel shades on swag lamps, cool-blue sofas, and big beds with gleaming white bedspreads. The bathrooms are large and luxurious. Service is a keynote here, with twice-daily maid service and 24-hour room service. Once you're inside, the Nines is a world unto itself. **Urban Farmer,** set off to one side of

Portland Hotels

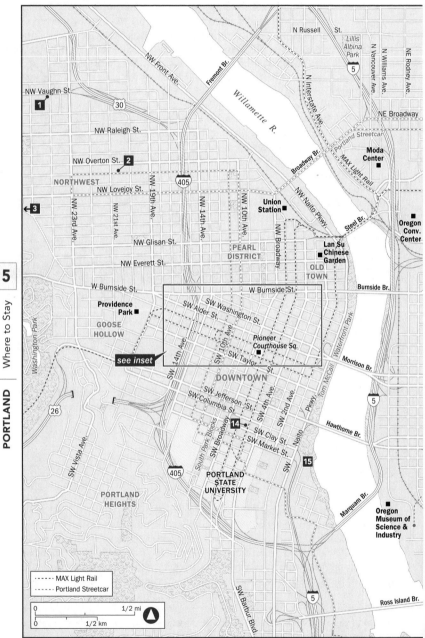

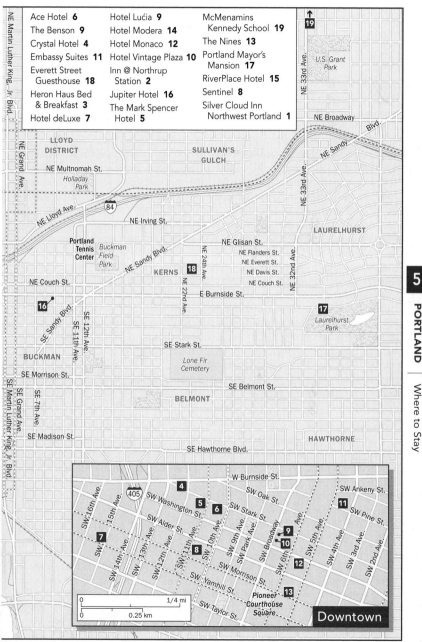

Ace Hotel **6**	Hotel Lucía **9**
The Benson **9**	Hotel Modera **14**
Crystal Hotel **4**	Hotel Monaco **12**
Embassy Suites **11**	Hotel Vintage Plaza **10**
Everett Street Guesthouse **18**	Inn @ Northrup Station **2**
Heron Haus Bed & Breakfast **3**	Jupiter Hotel **16**
Hotel deLuxe **7**	The Mark Spencer Hotel **5**

McMenamins Kennedy School **19**
The Nines **13**
Portland Mayor's Mansion **17**
RiverPlace Hotel **15**
Sentinel **8**
Silver Cloud Inn Northwest Portland **1**

19

U.S. Grant Park

NE Martin Luther King, Jr. Blvd.

NE Broadway

NE Sandy Blvd.

LLOYD DISTRICT

NE Grand Ave.

NE Multnomah St.

Holladay Park

SULLIVAN'S GULCH

NE 33rd Ave.

NE Lloyd Ave.

84

NE Irving St.

LAURELHURST

Portland Tennis Center

Buckman Field Park

NE Glisan St.

NE Flanders St.
NE Everett St.
NE Davis St.
NE Couch St.

NE Sandy Blvd.

KERNS

18

NE 24th Ave.
NE 22nd Ave.
NE 32nd Ave.

NE Couch St.

E Burnside St.

16

SE Sandy Blvd.

SE 12th Ave.
SE 11th Ave.

17

Laurelhurst Park

BUCKMAN

SE Stark St.

Lone Fir Cemetery

SE Morrison St.

SE Belmont St.

SE 7th Ave.
SE Grand Ave.
SE Martin Luther King, Jr. Blvd.

BELMONT

SE Madison St.

HAWTHORNE

SE Hawthorne Blvd.

W Burnside St.

405

SW Oak St.

SW Ankeny St.

4

SW Washington St.

5

SW Stark St.

11

SW Pine St.

6

SW 16th Ave.
SW 15th Ave.

SW Alder St.

SW 9th Ave.
SW Park Ave.
SW Broadway
SW 5th Ave.
SW 4th Ave.
SW 3rd Ave.
SW 2nd Ave.

9

7

SW 14th Ave.
SW 13th Ave.
SW 12th Ave.
SW 11th Ave.
SW 10th Ave.

8

10

SW Morrison St.

12

SW 6th Ave.

SW Yamhill St.

13

Pioneer Courthouse Square

SW Taylor St.

0   1/4 mi
0   0.25 km

Downtown

the lobby, is a farm-to-fork steakhouse, while **Departures,** on the top floor, is a cocktail lounge and Asian-inspired restaurant—the most vegetarian-friendly in the city—with an airport lounge look inside and a rooftop terrace for outdoor drinks and dining.

525 SW Morrison St. www.thenines.com. ℭ **877/229-9995.** 331 units. $259–$699 double. Valet parking $39. Pets accepted ($30 fee). **Amenities:** 2 restaurants; 2 lounges; exercise room; Wi-Fi (free).

EXPENSIVE

Hotel deLuxe ★★   The rooms in this reinvented hotel have the lightest and freshest color schemes in Portland, emphasizing pastel yellows and greens that give a sense of southern California airiness and sun. Years ago this was the Mallory Hotel, which started life pretty grand back in 1912, but by the 1990s was in need of a facelift. (A notable exception being the hotel's famous **Driftwood Room,** a classic and much-cherished time capsule of the 1950s.) The revamped hotel takes on a Golden Age of Hollywood theme (color by Deluxe, remember?) and uses black and white stills from classic movies to decorate the hallways and rooms—each floor is devoted to a separate director. The least expensive rooms are pretty modest in size, but the double-queen rooms and suites are generously large, some with walk-in closets. Bathrooms are white, gray, and gleaming chrome, with marble floors, tiled walls, and pedestal sinks. You can open the windows—a crack, anyway—and won't be bothered by traffic noise. There's a small fitness room with state-of-the-art Technogym equipment. **Gracie's,** the hotel restaurant, serves unfussy American cuisine. The deLuxe is in a slightly off-center part of downtown, just west of the I-5 freeway. Everything downtown, including destination restaurants like **Grüner** (see p. 129) and **Tasty n Alder** (see p. 133), is within a short walking distance, and MAX light rail is about a block away, so you can get all over Portland with ease. The area is filled with some grand old buildings dating from the same era as the hotel. Who knows, you might run into Lauren Bacall or the ghost of Humphrey Bogart right outside your door.

729 SW 15th Ave. www.hoteldeluxe.com. ℭ **866/895-2094** or 503/219-2094. 130 units. $149–$299 double. Parking $28. Pets accepted ($45 fee). **Amenities:** Restaurant; lounge; exercise room; Wi-Fi (free).

Hotel Lućia ★★★   It's not every hotel that uses 40 years' worth of photographs by White House photographer David Hume Kennerly to decorate its lounge and corridors. But the Lućia, downtown Portland's most stylish boutique hotel, has the world's largest collection of Kennerly prints, and they are amazing. Get off the elevator at one floor and there's John and Martha Mitchell, he stern, with a pipe, she madcap, grinning behind dark glasses. Fidel Castro, Ansel Adams, Gerald Ford playing pass-the-straw-under-the-nose with a Japanese geisha—you never know who or what you'll encounter. The hotel's million-dollar art collection also includes many portrait paintings by Gregory Grenon, one of Portland's best-known artists. It's all displayed gallery-style. The rooms are comfortable and wonderfully simple in the best sort of way. There's a glass-topped desk, a comfy leather chair with a brightly colored ottoman, and a big comfortable bed; suites have sofas and more legroom. You can open the windows, a feature I always appreciate. The bathrooms are the same size no matter what type of room you get—they're small, but have cool round aluminum sinks, frosted-glass counters, and make efficient use of the space in a calm, unadorned way. The Gallery Suite features all original art. Restaurant **Imperial ★★** (see p. 130) serves breakfast, lunch, and dinner; there's also a nice cafe for morning pastry and lunchtime sandwiches, and a special room-service ice cream menu so you can order your favorite homemade treats from Salt & Straw ★★ (p. 136).

400 SW Broadway. www.hotellucia.com. ✆ **866/986-8086** or 503/225-1717. 127 units. $129–$309 double; $249–$759 suite. Children 18 and under stay free in parent's room. Parking $30. Pets accepted ($45 fee). **Amenities:** 2 restaurants; lounge; concierge; exercise room; room service, Wi-Fi ($10 per night).

Hotel Modera ★★★   The Modera is a sleek and sophisticated "scene hotel" thoughtfully fashioned from the 1950s-era Portland Motor Lodge. Its mid-century modern footprint and overall minimalist aesthetic has been respected, but reinvented and restyled to reflect today's urban and environmentally aware sensibilities. Portland's first "living wall" (a wall with vertical plantings) graces one side of the revamped entrance courtyard, and the ever-popular outdoor patio of **Nel Centro,** the hotel's restaurant, the other. The Modera's classy lobby is all glass and stone and white walls, with bold pieces of art. Standard rooms are fairly small but comfy and stylish. Decor takes its design cues from mid-century modern's simple shapes, enlivening them with patterned pillows and luxurious bed throws. You can open the windows for a breath of fresh air. The small bathrooms have walk-in showers, white marble countertops, and electric mirrors that don't fog up. Given the limited interiors, this is probably not a hotel where you would hole up for hours in your room—and, with all of downtown right at your doorstep, why would you want to? Nel Centro ("in the center") serves good but overpriced homemade pastas and Italian-inspired meat and seafood dishes. The restaurant's patio firepits draw a busy happy hour crowd.

515 SW Clay St. www.hotelmodera.com. ✆ **877/484-1084** or 503/484-1084. 174 units. $189–$229 double. Valet parking $30. **Amenities:** Restaurant; lounge; access to nearby 24 Hour Fitness; Wi-Fi (free).

Hotel Monaco ★★   Whenever I'm in this big, cheerful hotel, I can never quite forget that it was once the Frederick & Nelson department store. It's been the Hotel Monaco since 1996, when it became the first new hotel in downtown Portland to be fashioned from an existing historic building. Stylistically it's hard to pin down, except that it's as far from minimalist as you can get. The big lobby lounge, with its red walls, tufted fainting couches, and high white arches, has a kind of pleasantly flamboyant Regency-Victorian style, and is a fun and lively spot to enjoy the hotel's complimentary wine and cocktail hour with piano accompaniment. Most of the guestrooms are generously sized suites, with sliding doors to separate bedrooms and living areas. The room decor is more "country" than the public spaces, but what country and era, it's impossible to say. Patterns, textures, colors, and furniture styles are layered together in a busy kaleidoscope that keeps your eyes forever hopping. The bathrooms are more soothing, with marble countertops, wallpaper printed with images of Portland's architecture, and tubs big enough for soaking. The service is exemplary. My only complaints? If you're a business traveler, there is no desk—you have to use a table. But, of course, you're here to play, not to work, right? **Red Star ★** (see p. 133) is a good spot for breakfast, lunch, or dinner. If you just want morning coffee, that's provided in the lobby. The Monaco is only a block from Pioneer Courthouse Square, in the heart of the downtown shopping area, and within easy walking distance of Powell's Books and the Pearl District.

506 SW Washington St. www.monaco-portland.com. ✆ **888/207-2201** or 503/222-0001. 221 units. $99–$300 double; $109–$400 suite. Rates include complimentary evening wine and morning coffee. Valet parking $38. Pets accepted. **Amenities:** Restaurant; lounge; bikes; exercise room; access to nearby health club; Wi-Fi (free).

RiverPlace Hotel ★★ Located on the waterfront esplanade at the south end of Tom McCall Waterfront Park, RiverPlace is the only downtown Portland hotel right on the Willamette River. A low-rise building from the 1980s, it blends in well with the low-rise riverfront condos and businesses around it, and enjoys a unique view of the downtown marina (the Portland dragon boat teams launch from just below the hotel). When the weather opens up, so does the hotel—the lobby area flows through to the Willamette-facing side, and you get a real hit of the unique riverfront location. This is a fashionable and friendly Kimpton property, with Kimpton's eclectic style. The decor has nautical hints here and there, but it is really a creature of the postmodern era, meaning it's a pastiche of contemporary styles and patterns geared for comfort. The bed is always what counts most, and these are wonderful. By far the most inviting accommodations here are the suites, with wood-burning fireplaces and views right out over the river. The courtyard-facing rooms are quieter (the Marquam Bridge spans the river just north of the hotel) and some of them open out onto a garden; there are also self-contained condo units for longer stays. The bathrooms are nice and large, with enough counter space. Every evening there's a complimentary wine hour featuring Northwest vintages. **Three Degrees,** the hotel's restaurant, serves Pacific Northwest cuisine using locally sourced products, and the hotel's outdoor bar area can be a fun mob scene during happy hour on a warm afternoon or evening. It's lovely to stroll along the esplanade out front, or you can borrow one of the hotel's bikes and do a bit of exploring along the riverside bike paths.

1510 SW Harbor Way. www.riverplacehotel.com. (℃ **800/227-1333** or 503/228-3233. 84 units. $169–$409 double. Valet parking $33. Pets accepted ($50 fee). **Amenities:** Restaurant; lounge; bikes; access to nearby health club; Jacuzzi; Wi-Fi (free).

Sentinel ★★★ I liked it in its old incarnation as the Governor Hotel, and I like it even more in its new life as the Sentinel. The hotel occupies two great historic buildings in downtown Portland: The giant, Renaissance palazzo–style former Elks Club (West Wing)—this must have been the grandest Elks Club in the country—and the lovely former Governor Hotel (East Wing). The new decor is the same throughout, but the two buildings offer different room types. Particularly nice are the sixth-floor rooms with private rooftop patios in the East Wing. But I personally like the big windows and original bathroom tile floors in the West Wing. The hotel reopened in 2014 after a 2-year makeover. The rooms are fairly spacious, with dark green walls, built-in white cabinets, leather and wool armchairs, and Pendleton blankets accessorizing the beds. The look is traditional and clubby, but enlivened with some interesting artwork that features images of "movers, shakers and visionaries." The grand lobby, with its coffered plaster ceilings, wouldn't look out of place in Rome. Adjoining it is a **Starbucks** and the house watering hole, **Jackknife Bar. Jake's Famous Crawfish ★★** (see p. 130)—not the original, which is a few blocks away—is also accessible from the hotel. The fitness center is the best of any hotel in Portland. One special touch: As a nod to the age of the building, there's a working Remington typewriter in the lobby area, where you can practice your typing skills as in the days of yore.

614 SW 11th Ave. www.sentinelhotel.com. (℃ **888/246-5631** or 503/224-3400. 100 units. $219–$379 double. Valet parking $36. **Amenities:** Restaurant; lounge; fitness room; Wi-Fi (free).

MODERATE

Ace Hotel ★★ No other hotel captures Portland's independent spirit better than the Ace. It's an environment unto itself, with a Stumptown coffee bar on one side of the lobby and Clyde Commons restaurant on the other. In between, the lobby is anything but fancy-schmancy, so younger travelers won't be intimidated. The hotel was always a working-class hotel, started in 1912. It's on the historic register, so much of it couldn't be altered, except for the room decor, which is what really sets the Ace apart. The hotel skips overstuffed luxury and sticks to the basics without sacrificing comfort, although you have to be willing to look on your stay as a bit of an adventure. The lowest-priced rooms have a sink but share a bathroom (another Ace feature); in the rooms with private bathrooms, you can soak in an original claw foot tub. I love that the beds have woolen Pendleton blankets, a true Oregon touch, and that some of the funky furnishings and artworks are refashioned from found objects. All of it works, and adds a touch of creative ingenuity that the overly decorated boutique hotels miss entirely. There are wall murals in some rooms, turntables with vinyl records in others. For an additional $10, you can enjoy a real breakfast with all kinds of choices. Older visitors probably wouldn't be as comfortable at the Ace, but they would certainly be welcomed.

1022 SW Stark St. www.acehotel.com. © **503/228-2277.** 78 units, 11 with shared bath. $145–$205 double with shared bath, $155–$225 double with private bath. Self-park $25. Pets accepted. **Amenities:** Restaurant; lounge; bikes; access to nearby health club; Wi-Fi (free).

Embassy Suites ★★   The rooms don't have all the fashionista frou-frou of downtown's smaller boutique hotels, or the restrained elegance of the Benson (reviewed on p. 115), but when you enter the lobby of this enormous hotel, you know you have entered someplace special. Built in 1912 as the Multnomah Hotel, it was one of Portland's grandest of grand hotels. Since 1995 it's been the Embassy Suites, one of only two Embassy Suites properties in the U.S. to occupy a historic building. With its moderate prices, generously sized rooms, indoor pool, and complimentary hot breakfast, this is a great hotel choice for families. And the grown-ups can enjoy an evening cocktail hour with a full bar—something I haven't encountered in any other local hotel. All of the rooms were completely refurbished in 2014 and feature big windows that guests can open, always a plus for me, with some nice city views that aren't found in other downtown hotels. Don't be intimidated by that immense lobby—instead, marvel at its intricate columns, gilding, and plasterwork. The downtown location, free Wi-Fi, big exercise room, and historic pizazz of the place are added bonuses.

319 SW Pine St. www.embassyportland.com. © **800/362-2779** or 503/279-9000. 276 units. $109–$259 double w/ full breakfast and complimentary cocktail hour. Valet parking $33; self-parking $18. **Amenities:** Restaurant; lounge; exercise room; Jacuzzi; indoor pool; day spa; Wi-Fi (free).

Heron Haus Bed & Breakfast ★★   Hidden on a hillside in Northwest Portland, Heron Haus has been welcoming visitors since 1986. The 10,000-square-foot Tudor-style house was built in 1904 for salmon baron Frank M. Warren, Sr., whose canneries netted him a fortune (Warrendale in the Columbia Gorge and Warrenton near Astoria were both named for him). With its ivy-covered stucco exterior and spacious rooms with innumerable windows that let in light on even the grayest of Portland days, the house represents an architectural style reminiscent of country manors built in England's Lake District in the late-19th and early-20th centuries. There are original fixtures, woodwork, and built-ins everywhere you look, but bleached oak herringbone-pattern floors, white walls, and light-colored furniture give the interior a more airily "modern" look than other homes of the period. All of the guestrooms on the second and third floors have private bathrooms and gas fireplaces; there are three giant suites, one with a commanding view of Cascade peaks. The rooms all have a comfortable, casual, light-filled ambience that adds to their charm. Northwest

Portland, with its parks and gardens, is a lovely neighborhood to explore. The shops and restaurants of NW 23rd are only a five-minute walk away.

2545 NW Westover Rd. www.heronhaus.com. ✆ **503/274-1846.** 6 units. $155–$225 double w/full breakfast. **Amenities:** Wi-Fi (free).

Hotel Vintage Plaza ★★   I'm not sure what to say about the Hotel Vintage Plaza, because it's undergoing a complete interior makeover. What I can tell you is that this is one of Portland's most highly regarded downtown boutique hotels, with excellent service, and that even in its new incarnation it will carry over the Oregon wine theme that it has used since its opening in 1991. Every room and suite is named for an Oregon vineyard, and delicious Northwest wines are served every evening during a complimentary wine hour. Although the Vintage Plaza was created within a historic building that dates to 1894, it is completely contemporary within, with an atrium next to the lobby. The decor will change, but room configurations will not. The Starlight Rooms are the smallest in terms of square footage, but they're the most romantic and striking rooms in the hotel—each with a sloping, atelier-like glass window-wall that lets you look out on the city and up to the sky. The hotel's smallish bathrooms currently don't have much counter space, but that will change. Expect a bright, up-to-the-minute design scheme that is calmer and more romantic than the busybody decor at Hotel Monaco ★★ (see p. 119), another downtown Kimpton property. An additional draw here is the hotel's restaurant, **Pazzo ★★** (see p. 132).

422 SW Broadway. www.vintageplaza.com. ✆ **800/263-2305** or 503/228-1212. 117 units. $139–$379 double. Rates include complimentary evening wine hour. Valet parking $35. Pets accepted. **Amenities:** Restaurant; lounge; exercise room; Wi-Fi (free).

Inn @ Northrup Station ★★   This boutique hotel right in the heart of the Northwest/Nob Hill/NW 23rd neighborhood is anything but dull. Vivid mix-and-match colors and retro-style furniture enliven the rooms and public areas, almost forcing you to be cheerful. Then again, there's quite a lot to be cheerful about in this hotel, created from a 1970s building and opened in 2002. It's great for families, as some of the rooms can sleep up to five people, and all of the rooms have either a small kitchenette with microwave or a full kitchen. The doors open out to little balconies in the less-expensive back units, and larger patios or balconies in the street-facing units. Parking is free, and the Portland streetcar stops right outside—in fact, guests receive a complimentary daily streetcar pass. The rooms here are not overly large, but they're cozily furnished with sofas, chairs, and tables, and have decent-sized bathrooms with tub-shower combinations. There's a nice rooftop terrace, too, with patio furniture. Reasonable prices, punchy style, and a great location make this one of Northwest Portland's best hotel choices.

2025 NW Northrup St. www.northrupstation.com. ✆ **800/224-1180** or 503/224-0543. 70 units. $129–$229 double w/continental breakfast. Free parking. **Amenities:** Access to nearby health club; complimentary streetcar pass; Wi-Fi (free).

The Mark Spencer Hotel ★   Singers and production crews from the Portland Opera and the casts of touring Broadway shows always stay at the Mark Spencer. Translation: This is a good hotel for extended stays—and for families, as the suites have nice little working kitchens. It's not the most glamorous of downtown hotels, but it's not meant to be. The hotel has been undergoing a gradual refurbishment to freshen up all the rooms and expose some features from the original 1907 structure, like brick walls and beamed ceilings. The one-bedroom suites, with their comfy living rooms and completely separate bedrooms, are the best accommodations here. Is it because of all those performers passing through that the bathroom mirrors are so large and fog-free?

Other helpful features for longer-stay guests include a coin-operated laundry, a small but serviceable fitness room, and an expanded continental breakfast and complimentary evening wine hour. The staff here is pleasant and professional, and the location is central to downtown and the Pearl District.

409 SW 11th Ave. www.markspencer.com. © **800/548-3934** or 503/224-3293. 102 units. $149–$279 double with continental breakfast and afternoon wine reception included. Parking $18. Pets accepted ($15 per day). **Amenities:** Exercise room; coin-operated laundry; Wi-Fi (free).

McMenamins Kennedy School ★★★   Only the McMenamin brothers could have pulled this off—turning an elementary school from 1915 into an all-purpose environment with hotel rooms, restaurants, bars, and a movie theater. This is Portland's version of a casual, family-friendly resort, and I'm giving it three stars not because it's luxurious, but because it is absolutely unique and will give you insight into some of the special qualities that make people fall in love with Portland—namely quirky, down-to-earth, fun-loving originality. Guests here are staying in a school (quite a lovely one), with long hallways and rooms ingeniously fashioned from former classrooms, complete with "cloak rooms," blackboards, and huge windows. This is a historic building with architectural features that can't be altered, so be aware that some guests complain that these big windows let in too much sun in the summer and don't adequately muffle traffic noise from NE 33rd right outside. Newer and quieter rooms have been created in the English (as in literature) Wing behind the school; this wing, with rooms named after books the McMenamin brothers are particularly fond of, opened in 2012. The entire school is available to explore. The big, friendly **Courtyard Restaurant,** open for breakfast, lunch, and dinner, serves an unpretentious menu of burgers, sandwiches, salads, and daily specials, with handcrafted McMenamins ales and regional wines; in nice weather, you can dine outside in the courtyard-garden. The smaller **Cypress Room** has the same menu but features a full bar. Speaking of bars, you can nurse a cocktail in "Detention" or the basement "Boiler Room," decorated with antique plumbing fixtures. The movie theater, in the old auditorium, shows second-run movies every day and evening, and there's a heated soaking pool outside. The Kennedy School has been wonderfully incorporated into the Concordia neighborhood, and locals use the restaurants and bars as much as out-of-town guests.

5736 NE 33rd Ave. www.mcmenamins.com. © **888/249-3983** or 503/249-3983. 57 units. $125–$165 double. Pets accepted ($15 per day). **Amenities:** 2 restaurants; 4 lounges; soaking pool; Wi-Fi (free).

Portland Mayor's Mansion ★★★   When you stay at this imposing Colonial Revival red-brick mansion on Laurelhurst Park in southeast Portland, you are staying in a piece of Portland history. Mayor H. Russell Albee had it built in 1912 for use as his summer home. Albee's architect was A. E. Doyle, the man who designed every significant building in Portland in that era, including the Portland Public Library. This is a grand mansion with most of its original features, and it has been beautifully restored and maintained by owner-innkeeper Dick Kroll. The outstanding quality of the original materials and craftsmanship is augmented by interior decor that features a fine-tuned mix of period antiques, contemporary and Asian artwork, and fine (but not overstuffed or stuffy) furniture. With its white oak and mahogany paneling and staircase, library, solarium, and giant-sized living room, it's definitely an impressive showplace, but it's also comfortable, and guests are encouraged to enjoy its many public rooms. It's also right on Laurelhurst Park, so guests look out onto giant trees, and can literally walk out the door and into the park. The guest rooms, all on the second floor, share the sense of sturdy, well-built luxury that characterizes the rest of the house. For a special treat, book the three-room master suite—it's a small apartment unto itself. The other three rooms are smaller and two of them share a bathroom. The rooms all have big windows that open and are comfortably furnished.

3360 SE Ankeny St. www.pdxmayorsmansion.com. © **503/232-3588.** 4 units, 2 w/private bath. $125–$225 double w/full breakfast included. **Amenities:** Wi-Fi (free).

Silver Cloud Inn Northwest Portland ★ This hotel is on the edge of Portland's trendy Nob Hill neighborhood, and though it's also near an industrial area, it's still an attractive and comfortable place. Although the rooms fronting Vaughn Street are well insulated against traffic noise, I still prefer the rooms on the other side of the building. Reasonable rates are the main draw here, but the rooms are also well designed. The mini-suites have separate seating areas, which makes them good bets for families. The best thing about the hotel is its location within a 5-minute drive (or 15-minute walk) of Forest Park and several of the city's best restaurants. To find the hotel, take I-405 to Ore. 30 W. and get off at the Vaughn Street exit.

2426 NW Vaughn St. www.silvercloud.com. © **800/205-6939** or 503/242-2400. 82 units. $129–$179 double w/full breakfast. Free parking. **Amenities:** Exercise room; access to nearby health club; Wi-Fi (free).

INEXPENSIVE

Crystal Hotel ★ Like the Ace (reviewed on p. 120), the Crystal epitomizes a certain Portland aesthetic that is basic, down-to-earth, and inexpensive. In fact, the rooms with shared bathrooms at the Crystal are the best deals in town. The hotel was created by the McMenamins, the Portland entrepreneur brothers who invented a whole new kind of hotel concept, saving and reinventing historic buildings and turning them into funky, all-in-one environments where you can sleep, eat, drink, and listen to live music. The Crystal Hotel occupies a wedge-shaped building built in 1911. It pays homage to the famous century-old **Crystal Ballroom** ★★★ (see p. 160) across the street, another McMenamins rescue, where just about every famous performer and band coming through Portland has played. Each of the rooms in the hotel draws some decorative inspiration from a song or performance at the Crystal—it might be lyrics printed on the walls, or posters, or hand-painted murals. The rooms themselves are uniformly dark gray with dark accessories—it's not as gloomy as it sounds, and even the shared-bath rooms have wonderful little touches, like a table for two beside the window. On the ground floor, **Zeus Café** serves down-to-earth Northwest food and beer. In the basement there's a speakeasy, **Al's Den,** where you can hear local bands every night of the week. There's also a heated saltwater soaking pool down there. Here's what you have to know about the Crystal: It is right on busy Burnside Street, and you will get more of a trafficky, urban buzz here than at any other hotel in Portland. The hotel wisely provides earplugs in every room, but if a quiet spot is what you're after, you won't find it here. One big plus is that guests can buy tickets for performances at the Crystal Ballroom, even if a show is officially sold out. The hotel's location may be noisy, but it is central to Portland's downtown urban scene.

303 SW 12th Ave. www.mcmenamins.com. © **855/205-3930** or 503/972-2670. 51 units. $85–$105 double with shared bath; $145–$165 double with private bath. Parking $25. **Amenities:** 3 restaurants; 4 lounges; soaking pool; Wi-Fi (free).

Everett Street Guesthouse ★★ This is a good, comfortable, neighborhood B&B that charms with its intimate scale, calm good taste, and rooms decorated with interesting artwork instead of formal spaces loaded with fussy frou-frou. The 1907

Craftsman-style house is typical of the handsome and well-built family homes constructed in Portland during the early 20th century, when wood was plentiful and craftsmanship levels were high. Innkeeper Terry Rusinow, a former gallery owner, has furnished the living room with rich-toned and sturdily comfortable armchairs and a sofa; with its fireplace and glowing fir floors, it's wonderfully welcoming, as is the dining room, where you get a full breakfast (or not, in which case you save $10). On the second floor there's a small common room with a computer, and two modest-sized guestrooms that share a bath. Again, no frilly furnishings or potpourri. The cottage in back is perfect for one or two people who want extra privacy. It has its own entrance, kitchenette, washer-dryer, and private patio, and the same calm good taste prevails. This is a good neighborhood to explore: Laurelhurst Park, restaurants, and movie theaters are within walking distance, and you can get downtown in minutes on nearby public transportation.

2306 NE Everett St. www.everettstreetguesthouse.com. © **503/230-0211** or 503/830-0650. 3 units. $90 double w/continental breakfast; $115 cottage. 2-night minimum (3 nights in cottage). No children. **Amenities:** Bikes; Wi-Fi (free).

Jupiter Hotel ★★ If you're looking for a quiet, room-service-and-fluffy-bathrobes kind of hotel, the Jupiter isn't for you. But if you're an urban adventurer, eager to stash your bags, rent a bike, and explore Portland, the Jupiter will be right up your alley. It will likely fit in with your budget, too. Created in 2004 from a California-style, mid-century modern motor lodge, the Jupiter is what the hotel business calls an "active property"—meaning it caters primarily to a younger crowd (21–45), has an adjoining bar-lounge-restaurant-concert venue (Doug Fir) with a busy outdoor patio that stays open until 2:30am, and lets guests have parties as long as they don't get out of hand. It doesn't try to hide any of this, and offers rooms on the Bar-Patio side (noisier), and on the Chill side (quieter), in addition to providing earplugs in the rooms. The rooms themselves are motel-size, but they've been creatively updated in a way that makes them both comfortable and appealing. Every room has a wall-size mural, some photorealist, some collage, some hand-painted. Furnishing is in a minimalist style that eschews the frou-frou of so many boutique hotels. There's a little table with a chair by the window, platform beds, good lighting, and nicely tiled bathrooms. Colored chalks are provided and you're encouraged to get creative on your room door. Potential downside: windows don't open (guests keep their doors open for air instead), so you're dependent upon an in-room heater or air-conditioner. On a busy summer's night when the hotel's blue wall lights are on, and the guests' doors are open, and the patio bar is in full swing, this is a world unto itself—not for everyone, but possibly for you.

800 E. Burnside St. www.jupiterhotel.com. © **877/800-0004** or 503/230-9200. 81 units. $129–$179 double. Parking $9. Pets accepted ($35 per night). **Amenities:** Restaurant; 2 lounges; rental bikes; access to nearby health club; Wi-Fi (free).

WHERE TO EAT

The Portland restaurant scene is hot, and it's not just because of all the wood-burning ovens that have been cranking out perfect pizzas for the past few years. The city has a national reputation for great restaurants. Driving this renaissance are lots of creative young chefs and their affinity for local produce and wines from the Willamette Valley. Bounteous ingredients can be sourced locally, including organic fruits and vegetables, hazelnuts and walnuts, wild mushrooms, and even Oregon truffles. And that's not to mention those local pinot noir, pinot gris, and pinot blanc vintages.

Portland Restaurants

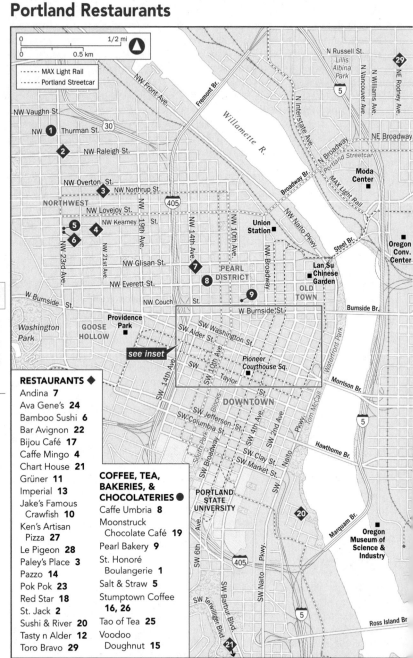

RESTAURANTS ◆

Andina **7**
Ava Gene's **24**
Bamboo Sushi **6**
Bar Avignon **22**
Bijou Café **17**
Caffe Mingo **4**
Chart House **21**
Grüner **11**
Imperial **13**
Jake's Famous
Crawfish **10**
Ken's Artisan
Pizza **27**
Le Pigeon **28**
Paley's Place **3**
Pazzo **14**
Pok Pok **23**
Red Star **18**
St. Jack **2**
Sushi & River **20**
Tasty n Alder **12**
Toro Bravo **29**

**COFFEE, TEA,
BAKERIES, &
CHOCOLATERIES ●**

Caffe Umbria **8**
Moonstruck
Chocolate Café **19**
Pearl Bakery **9**
St. Honoré
Boulangerie **1**
Salt & Straw **5**
Stumptown Coffee
16, 26
Tao of Tea **25**
Voodoo
Doughnut **15**

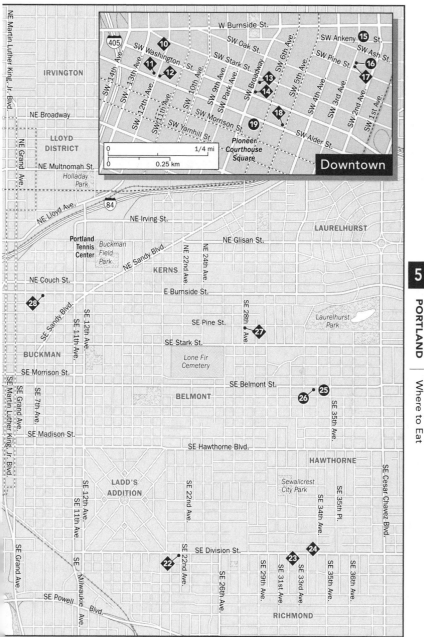

Happy hour is huge in Portland. And it's not just because the drinks are cheap, although that's certainly part of it. It's actually more about the food. Every good restaurant—I mean every one—has a happy hour, with delicious small plates available for about half of their usual price. This is a great way to eat an early dinner for a reasonable price. I won't go into the details of the arcane rules devised by the Oregon Liquor Commission, but restaurants with bars have to offer food with the booze during happy hour. That's one Oregon law I can live with.

The only catch to the Portland dining scene is that it's spread out, and some of the most talked-about restaurants are basically neighborhood spots in residential districts away from the city center. Bear in mind that some of these neighborhood gems don't take reservations (always call first), so, unless you arrive before 7pm or after 9pm, you may end up having to wait a long time for a table.

VERY EXPENSIVE

Andina ★★★ PERUVIAN I confess to being somewhat skeptical when faced with a mile-long menu with dozens of choices. It doesn't seem possible that they could all be worth trying. Andina has such a menu, though, and surprisingly, you could sample just about everything on it and not find a dud. This is one of Portland's top destination restaurants, open since 2003, and it attracts almost fanatical devotion (even after an outbreak of food poisoning in 2013, it remained full to capacity). The reasons for its success? It's big, bold, loud, and serves marvelously fascinating food with tastes that you won't find anywhere else in Portland. It's upscale, too, making it accessible to those food adventurers who find food carts and holes in the wall to be out of their comfort zone. What all this means: Make a reservation as far in advance as you can, or you won't get in. Andina may be famous for its spicy cocktails, but if you want a delicious, non-alcoholic, and very healthy drink, try a glass of Peruvian *chicha morada,* made from purple corn and loaded with antioxidants. Then—well, ask your server to recommend a few small plates and share them. Peru's Latin-based New World cuisine is amazingly diverse and draws from the country's many different food sources: the Pacific, the plains, the mountains, and the jungle. That's why the menu is so long, and why you will want to linger over your special meal at Andina. (By the way, it's easier to get in for lunch, and it's far less of a scene.)

1314 NW Glisan St. www.andinarestaurant.com. ℂ **503/228-9535.** Main courses, lunch $12–$18; dinner $18–$35. Sun–Thurs 11:30am–2:30pm and 5–9:30pm; Fri–Sat 11:30am–2:30pm and 5–10:30pm.

Paley's Place ★★★ NORTHWEST/FRENCH The popularity of Paley's shows no sign of waning, and this destination restaurant in a charming Victorian house is a good spot to try if you're looking for a romantic dinner. It's a bit less formal than it used to be, and now has a bistro side, but you can still cozy up at an intimate table for two and enjoy a quiet fine-dining experience accompanied by great wine. Although diners' opinions can be divided on the cooking and service, Paley's draws far more raves than rants. With his cooking skills and insistence on using only fresh, local ingredients, Vitaly Paley helped start Portland's foodie reputation with this restaurant. A

Juilliard-trained classical pianist and a James Beard award–winning chef, Paley revels in rich, complex flavors. A signature starter is the beef tartare; other appetizers to try are the beef tongue pastrami and the pork, foie gras, and cherry terrine; all the charcuterie is house-made. Because some of the entrees are so rich, half portions are offered, making it easy to share tastes. One specialty dish that won't be found on any other Portland menu is the crispy sweetbreads with cider-braised cabbage and Dijon jus. Other possibilities, depending on the season, might be beef bourguignon served over wide house-made noodles; squid ink risotto with Dungeness crab, braised squid, and spot prawns; or stuffed quail with spice-roasted cauliflower purée. The waitstaff at Paley's is helpful and professional. Reservations are highly recommended.

1204 NW 21st Ave. www.paleysplace.net. (C) **503/243-2403.** Main courses $18–$40; fixed-price menus $50–$70. Mon–Thurs 5:30–10pm; Fri–Sat 5:30–11pm; Sun 5–10pm.

EXPENSIVE

Chart House ★ SEAFOOD   I don't usually recommend chain restaurants, but I'm making an exception for the Chart House for those who want to dine at a Portland restaurant while feasting their eyes on a marvelous view—something that's almost impossible to find elsewhere in Portland's urban restaurant scene. Chart House nabbed this primo hillside location decades ago, and the restaurant has been part of Portland's consciousness since "pre-discovery" days, when the city had only a handful of destination tablecloth restaurants. To accompany that special Chart House view of Portland, the Willamette Valley, and Mount Hood, you can enjoy fish prepared in many different ways. Not all the fish served here is local or even regional, so you can order pistachio-crusted mahi or grilled sea bass with a Meyer lemon glaze. Personally, I would stick to the Pacific salmon or albacore tuna when it's in season. They also do surf-and-turf combinations. The signature dessert is warm lava cake, chocolate outside, chocolate inside, chocolate on top—the sugar rush lasts for hours. If the sun is out, you might want to come here for lunch, or happy hour (daily 4–7pm)—all the better to enjoy that remarkable view.

5700 SW Terwilliger Blvd. www.chart-house.com. (C) **503/246-6963.** Main courses: lunch $12–$27, dinner $23–$37. Mon–Thurs 11:30am–2pm and 5–9:30pm; Fri 11:30am–2pm and 5–10pm; Sat 5–10pm; Sun 10am–3pm and 5–9pm.

Grüner ★★ GERMAN/ALSATIAN   Chris Israel, the chef-owner of this one-of-a-kind downtown restaurant, is something of a legend in the Portland restaurant scene. He opened Grüner in 2008, just when the economy was tanking, but the fact that it weathered the economic storm and is still going strong is a testament to both the food and ambience. In a city full of super-casual restaurants, Grüner stands out for the cool, elegant simplicity of its Bauhausian dining room. Its German- and Alsatian-inspired cuisine (you could call it "alpine") is equally simple and quite delicious. I think this was the first Portland restaurant to serve deviled eggs, those stalwarts of family get-togethers—although these eggs are pickled in beet juice and seasoned with herbs that make them zing. I've always been fond of German cuisine and surprised that so few American restaurants serve it (or good versions of it, anyway). This is the only place I've ever found *Maultaschen*, a Swabian ravioli-like pasta stuffed with pork, beef, and spinach and served in a broth. Instead of a plate of focaccia to nibble on, diners are served a Bavarian-style soft pretzel and dark bread. There's an excellent charcuterie plate that features house-made spicy coppa, salami, rabbit mortadella, country pâté, and liverwurst canapés with grain mustard and cornichons. I also recommend the homemade bratwurst and saucisson sausages with sauerkraut and potatoes. And don't forget to order the spätzle, also delicious. There are some excellent German wines on the menu—nothing tastes better with food like this than a good crisp Riesling or Sylvaner. **Kask,** the restaurant's adjacent bar, is a hopping, happening spot.

527 SW 12th Ave. www.grunerpdx.com. ✆ **503/241-7163.** Main courses $9–$28. Mon–Thurs 11:30am–2pm and 5–9:30pm; Fri 11:30am–2pm and 5–10:30pm; Sat 5–10:30pm.

Imperial ★★ EASTERN EUROPEAN/PACIFIC NORTHWEST Imperial is a fairly new kid on the block when it comes to Portland hotel restaurants, but it's getting a royal buzz because its chef-owner is Vitaly Paley, the force behind the long-running **Paley's Place** ★★★ (p. 128) in Northwest Portland. The name Imperial is a nod to next door **Hotel Lućia**'s ★★★ (see p. 118) previous life as the Imperial Hotel and dining room. But imperial may also have something to do with Imperial Russia, since Paley was born in Kiev and likes to make some of the same dishes his grandmother did. They can be very rich, like the duck meatballs with prunes, aromatic spices, and orange gremolata (duck is featured in other dishes, too). But not all is rich and heavy; offerings like the bay scallop crudo with vinaigrette, grapefruit, and cured steelhead caviar are light, fresh, and still satisfying; a selection of oysters on the half shell is also available. Because Imperial has a big wood-fired grill, grilled and rotisserie meats are a special feature. Try the bone-in pork chop with sage and black-pepper honey, the roasted half chicken, or a dry-aged rib-eye with horseradish butter. After all that, a house-made gelato or sorbet is a perfect way to end your meal.

410 SW Broadway (adjacent to Hotel Lućia). www.imperialpdx.com. ✆ **503/228-7222.** Main courses $14–$32. Mon–Fri 6:30am–10pm; Sat–Sun 8am–2pm and 5–10pm.

Jake's Famous Crawfish ★★ SEAFOOD Some people say "craw" and some people say "cray," but however you pronounce it, crawfish are what Jake's is famous for. And not just any crawfish, but crawfish that come exclusively from Lake Billy Chinook in Oregon's high desert country east of the Cascades. The crawfish season starts there about the end of May and lasts until October. At Jake's, the crawfish are made into a spicy New Orleans/Cajun gumbo-style stew (a good idea, since crawfish aren't the most flavorful of crustaceans). There's a daily list of fresh fish choices, most of them cooked in a fairly unadorned manner. The "Classics" menu is overpriced, but other entrees are reasonably priced. Even if the food won't win any culinary awards, Jake's definitely offers a pretty extraordinary ambience for Portland—an authentic turn-of-the-20th-century restaurant with a gleaming mahogany bar shipped around Cape Horn in the 1880s. There are lovely nude ladies posed above, scenic wall murals, and a wonderfully old-fashioned dining room with tablecloths and professional waiters (you won't see a tattoo or a nose ring on any of them). I would recommend enjoying Jake's unique atmosphere at lunch, when the prices drop by half because the menu is simpler. Another option is happy hour, always popular at Jake's thanks to the gorgeous bar, when you can order plates for $3 to $5. **Jake's Bar and Grill** at 611 SW 10th Ave. (✆ **503/220-1850**) is under the same management and offers many of the same dishes but lacks the original Jake's inimitable ambience.

401 SW 12th Ave. www.jakesfamouscrawfish.com. ✆ **503/226-1419.** Main courses $11–$14 lunch, $15–$47 dinner. Mon–Thurs 11:30am–10pm; Fri–Sat 11:30am–midnight; Sun 3–10pm.

Le Pigeon ★★★ FRENCH Le Pigeon is small and cozy, and dining is at communal tables, which is not to everyone's liking. Since I'm gregarious and never averse to jumping into a conversation, even with complete strangers, the communal table concept works for me. And the food works, too, which is why Le Pigeon has become one of Portland's top destination restaurants. This is rich and skillful cooking, beautifully presented, and enhanced by wine (let the sommelier guide you with wine pairings). The menu changes with the seasons and is based on what is fresh and locally available. Smoked foie gras is one of the staples on the starter list, or you might want to try something like sturgeon pastrami. Only a handful of entrees are offered, including beef cheek bourguignon, duck confit with goat-cheese hummus, and a daily fresh fish special. Foie gras profiteroles for dessert are not for me after a rich meal, but a dish of homemade seasonal berry sorbet is just right. Foodies might want to try the five-course tasting menu with wine pairings. If you want to watch the kitchen in action, sit at the bar.

738 E. Burnside. www.lepigeon.com. © **503/876-8496.** Main courses $22–$38. Daily 5–10pm.

MODERATE

Ava Gene's ★★★ ITALIAN/PACIFIC NORTHWEST   In the past very few years, SE Division between 30th and 35th in the Clinton neighborhood has become a veritable restaurant row, full of casual, family-friendly, neighborhood eateries. Ava Gene's is one of the street's destination restaurants, and with good reason. The sophisticated, Italian-inspired cooking at this contemporary trattoria is delicious, satisfying, and inventive, without being overly complicated. For a fun treat, sit at the chef's counter and watch the non-stop culinary choreography in the kitchen. Ava Gene's menu changes daily, which means everything is fresh that morning. I'd recommend sharing two or three smaller plates and then splitting one of the homemade pasta or protein dishes. You might start with a delicious dish of grilled cauliflower (the kitchen features an open wood-fired grill) with chiles and *tonnato* sauce, followed by beets and avocado with sesame seeds and pickled peppers, and a lettuce salad with sunflower seeds and light lemon-cream dressing. After that, maybe rabbit agnolotti with a light sauce of spring onion and Castelvetrano olives, or halibut with lentils, turnips, and green garlic salsa verde. The service is friendly and attentive. You need to book a table as far in advance as you can; otherwise, you can sit at the chef's counter, which is kept open for walk-ins. Breads and pastries come from Roman Candle Bakery, right next door; you can get a good slab of focaccia there to take home.

3377 SE Division. www.avagenes.com. © **971/229-0571.** Main courses $18–$36. Daily 5–11pm.

Bar Avignon ★★ PACIFIC NORTHWEST/FRENCH   The craft cocktails at this neighborhood restaurant are criminally delicious, and the wine list draws kudos, so you could just come here to drink. But better yet, come here to eat *and* drink. I have friends who come just for the foraged lettuces salad, house-made charcuterie, and artisan cheeses. I find the crispy chicken livers with ramps habit forming. So is the seared pork chop with carrot, arugula, duck egg, and bacon dressing. The menu is short, the food is impeccably fresh, and the touch is light when required and hearty when it needs to be. Share some small plates if you don't want an entree.

2138 SE Division. www.baravignon.com. © **503/517-0808.** Main courses $22–$27. Mon–Thurs 5–10pm; Fri–Sat 5pm–midnight; Sun 5–9pm.

Caffe Mingo ★★ ITALIAN   Portland has countless new restaurants serving all kinds of "new" cuisine, but if you're looking for a little and long-established neighborhood restaurant that serves fine and fairly simple Italian food, head for Caffe Mingo. You must arrive early or late, or be prepared to wait for a table (reservations are accepted only for parties of six or more). The menu changes weekly, and all the fish, meat, and produce come exclusively from local producers and purveyors. Mingo's menu is delightfully limited to just a few choice selections for each course. You might want to start with the potato and onion soup with house-made mascarpone, or one of the fresh salads. I would always recommend the pasta fresca, or daily house-made noodle dish. I also love the pizzas; there are only two to choose from (make mine the fennel sausage with cream, spring onions, and Asiago cheese). There are two *piatti unici* ("unique dishes"), which are meals unto themselves. One might be halibut in broth and vegetables, the other lamb chops with cauliflower and potato purée, mustard greens, and fig molasses. Dessert? I'll have the chocolate *budino* (a cross between cake and pudding) with berry cream and chocolate cookies. The wine list is as selective as the menu.

807 NW 21st Ave. www.caffemingonw.com. *C* **503/226-4646.** Main courses $12–$28. Mon–Thurs 5–10pm; Fri–Sat 5–10:30pm; Sun 4:30–9:30pm.

Pazzo ★★ ITALIAN/PACIFIC NORTHWEST   When a large restaurant can stay in business for almost a quarter of a century, it's doing something right. The food at Pazzo is contemporary Italian, and it's not trend-setting cuisine, but it is always good, making use of local and seasonal ingredients to boost the flavor palette. One of the true tests of a good restaurant, for me, is the Caesar salad, and Pazzo's passes that test with flying colors; this is maybe the best Caesar in Portland. Pazzo excels with its homemade pastas, too, which are great for sharing. The tagliatelle with stinging nettle, spring onion, fava beans, and pecorino cheese that I had on my last visit was *meraviglioso,* as was the pappardelle with veal, pork, and beef ragu. The cioppino with Pacific shrimp and manila clams was less successful, but the desserts were knock-outs. The gelato made with fresh mint was inspired, and the semifreddo (half-frozen pistachio gelato in chocolate cake) was, quite simply, wonderful. This is a big restaurant and draws a lot of customers from the nearby downtown hotels. The service is unobtrusive and professional, the wine list exemplary.

627 SW Washington St. (in Hotel Vintage Plaza). www.pazzo.com. *C* **503/228-1515.** Main courses $19–$36. Mon–Thurs 7:30am–9:30pm; Fri–Sat 7:30am–11pm; Sun 8am–9:30pm.

Pok Pok ★★★ THAI   Like **Ava Gene's,** Pok Pok is a destination restaurant on SE Division's Restaurant Row, and definitely a place to try if you want a hit of Portland's trendsetting food scene. Pok Pok helped start the foodie trend and it's been hot (literally, given the spices used in the cooking) from the very beginning. This is not a dress-up, white-tablecloth place; it's fairly small, opens right onto the street, and you sit at crowded picnic tables with a lot of noise around you. And guess what—that's part of why everyone loves it. The other part, of course, is the food. Many of the dishes are inspired by Thai street food, and the combination of tastes and spices is a good incentive for ordering a variety of plates and sharing. The waitstaff is patient and knowledgeable, and can provide guidance on spice levels (ranging from "not there" to "tongue on fire"). House specialties include *kai yang,* a delicious charcoal-roasted game hen stuffed with lemongrass, garlic, pepper, and cilantro; papaya served with salted black crab; and the must-try chicken wings, marinated in fish sauce and sugar and then deep fried. Pok Pok doesn't take reservations, so be prepared to wait for a table (you can call ahead and get your name on the wait list). While you're waiting for that coveted table to open up, enjoy a cocktail at **Whiskey Soda Lounge,** Pok Pok's bar across the street from the restaurant.

3226 SE Division St. www.pokpokpdx.com. © **503/232-1387.** Main courses $9–$14. Daily 11:30am–10pm.

Red Star ★ AMERICAN/INTERNATIONAL   This is a big downtown restaurant where you can enjoy comfort food in comfortable surroundings. Red Star is attached to the **Hotel Monaco** ★★ (see p. 119), and it has transformed itself from a chop house to a restaurant that offers a medley of internationally inspired small and large plates, all of them good, fresh, and filling. None of them are over-the-top in terms of preparation or presentation (translation: You can bring the family here and they will all find something they like on the menu). First you'll have to tear yourself away from the weeknight happy hour, which lasts from 4 to 8pm and draws a big after-work crowd. Then slide into a booth looking out on 5th and share a few smaller plates, maybe the butternut squash dip paired with hamachi crudo and citrus soy, or the carpaccio with black olive aioli. Then I would recommend fish or meat from the grill—Red Star has a big, wood-burning oven and is known for its wonderfully tender chicken and dry-aged rib-eye steaks. After that, you might not have room for dessert. If you do, try one of the homemade sorbets or ice creams.

503 SW Alder. www.redstartavern.com. © **503/222-0005.** Main courses $18–$36. Mon–Thurs 6:30am–10pm; Fri 6:30am–11pm; Sat 8:30am–midnight; Sun 8:30am–10pm.

St. Jack ★★ FRENCH   It's always been puzzling to me that an upscale destination street like NW 23rd has so few fine-dining restaurants. With the 2014 opening of St. Jack, the situation definitely improved. When this *tres bonne* French bistro and bar moved from its southeast location to northwest, it dropped its lunch menu and became dinner only. Fortunately, the wonderful French cooking survived the journey across the river. Many of the dishes here are classics, with tastes that are delightfully worth rediscovering. I'm talking about cream of tomato soup baked in puff pastry; seared foie gras on brioche; salad Lyonnaise frisée with bacon lardons, poached egg, and bacon-fat croutons; and a cheese plate with an assortment of fabulous French *fromage*. The *plats principaux* are classics, too, and include mussels meunière, roasted trout, oxtail bourguignon, Lyonnaise onion tart, and that delicious old favorite, duck a l'orange. Enjoy a glass of French wine with your French meal and perhaps finish with Proustian, baked-to-order madeleines.

1610 NW 23rd Ave. www.stjackpdx.com. © **503/360-1281.** Main courses $22–$37. Daily 5–11pm.

Tasty n Alder ★★ PACIFIC NORTHWEST   This restaurant is now on everyone's short list of places to try. It's a bustling, unpretentious, shared-plates sort of place with good food and service. The interior is completely unadorned—so Portland—with exposed roof joists and mechanical ducts, and the food is fairly unadorned as well, which is a strong point. For starters, the light and crispy fried oysters are standouts, and the radicchio salad with bacon lardons and a poached egg mixed in is delicious. Although the restaurant is known for its grilled meats, I think the alder plank-smoked salmon is better (certainly far more tender) than the grilled flat iron steak. The entrees are served without sides; you might want to pair your meat or fish with crispy Brussels sprouts or a seasonal root vegetable. Have a glass of wine or a handcrafted beer, end with brûléed banana panna cotta for dessert, and you'll be all set. Tasty's also serves brunch every day.

580 SW 12th Ave. www.tastyntasty.com. ✆ **503/621-9251.** Main courses $15–$44. Sun–Thurs 9am–10pm; Fri–Sat 9am–11pm.

Toro Bravo ★★★ SPANISH   Whether it's **Voodoo Doughnuts ★★** (see p. 136) or a hot restaurant, Portlanders are willing to wait in long lines to get their food fixes, and the lines become social gatherings where enthusiasms are aired and recommendations are shared. That's usually the case at Toro Bravo, which doesn't take reservations. The line starts to form about half an hour before the doors open. There's a reason why this Spanish tapas place is on everyone's top five list: The food is remarkably good and reasonably priced, and the service is attitude-free and topnotch. Try just about anything and you won't be disappointed. While you're deciding, nibble on some toasted almonds with sea salt or some marinated olives and vegetables. Then it's tapas time— share several plates to enjoy the full array of tastes and textures. Highly recommended: salt cod fritters with aioli, fried Spanish anchovies with fennel and lemon, oxtail croquettes with chili mayonnaise, and grilled asparagus with fried ham. The paella with chorizo, shrimp, clams, and mussels is also special. For $30 a head, your table can enjoy the chef's tasting menu, the best way to sample the flavors of this favorite Portland restaurant.

120 NE Russell St. www.torobravopdx.com. ✆ **503/281-4464.** Small plates $2–$14; large plates $8–$20. Sun–Thurs 5–10pm; Fri–Sat 5–11pm.

INEXPENSIVE

Bamboo Sushi ★★ JAPANESE/SUSHI/SASHIMI   I worry about the world's declining fish populations, so a sushi place that only serves sustainably harvested fish from healthy populations is a no-brainer for me. And when the sushi is as fresh and delicious as it is at Bamboo Sushi, I can heartily recommend it to others as well. The eight-piece rolls here are wonderful for sharing—try "The Local" with albacore tuna, jalapeños, and cucumber topped with East Coast red crab and sesame aioli. The assorted sushi and sashimi plates let you sample the freshest fish of the day. There are also many vegetarian options here, including vegetarian sushi.

836 NW 23rd Ave. www.bamboosushipdx.com. ✆ **971/221-1925.** Main courses $11–$25. Daily 5–10pm.

Bijou Café ★ PACIFIC NORTHWEST   Back before there was a "restaurant scene" in Portland, there was the Bijou Café. It doesn't serve dinner, but it's a good spot for breakfast and lunch. This downtown fixture has remained in business because of its fresh, local, organic food, and it offers some specialties that you won't find elsewhere else in Portland, like oyster hash. The French-style omelets are fluffy and delicious. There are also vegetarian choices. I always have the pan-fried oyster or fresh-fish sandwich when I eat lunch here. It's a nice Portland place to know about.

132 SW Third Ave. www.bijoucafepdx.com. ✆ **503/222-3187.** Breakfast and lunch $7–$15. Mon–Fri 7am–2pm; Sat–Sun 8am–2pm.

Ken's Artisan Pizza ★ PIZZA   Here's an idea for a healthy Portland meal: Rent a bike (some hotels offer them to their guests) and pedal over to Ken's Artisan Pizza. It's on one of the city's busiest bike corridors, about a 15-minute ride from downtown, and offers parking for 24 bikes. Then sit back and enjoy the best pizza in town, cooked to blistered-crust perfection in 2 minutes in a wood-fired, igloo-shaped oven. Ten pizza types are available, all of them topped with the freshest ingredients. You can also order a starter or side salad (I'd recommend the roasted vegetable platter). The beer and wine list offers great accompaniments to the pizzas. This is a relaxed, family-friendly place with sidewalk seating in the summer and an interior that features huge beams of old-growth Douglas fir salvaged from the famous Jantzen Beach Big Dipper roller coaster, built in 1923.

304 SE 28th Ave. (at Pine St.). www.kensartisan.com. (© **503/517-9951.** Main courses $12–$16. Mon–Sat 5–10pm; Sun 4–9pm.

Sushi & River ★ JAPANESE/SUSHI This restaurant is comfortable, low-key, and right on the river, serving reliably fresh sushi and rolls in addition to wonderfully authentic tempura and noodle dishes. Plus, it's kind of a secret, even after some 10 years in business, because it doesn't really advertise itself. But locals keep coming back, and there's every reason they should. The light, crispy tempura here is some of the best I've ever had, and the salmon and yellowtail sushi never fail to please. This is not formal Japanese dining, so don't expect tablecloths and dim lighting. There's a large open room with some booths and tables and often just one server to take care of everyone. But you will leave satisfied and feeling like you've made a real discovery.

1181 SW River Dr., #400. (© **503/294-3888.** Main courses $8.50–$17; sushi $5–$7.50. Mon–Fri 11:30am–2pm and 5pm–midnight; Sat 12:30pm–midnight.

Coffee, Tea, Bakeries, Pastry Shops & Chocolatiers

COFFEEHOUSES & CAFES

Coffee is a passion here—we used to say strong coffee helped to speed us up because we were so far behind the East Coast (now that New York comes to Portland for inspiration, the old saying doesn't hold water). In short, you're never far from a good cappuccino or latte in the Rose City. I recommend the following places:

Caffe Umbria ★★★ Started in Seattle by a family from Perugia, this cafe in the Pearl serves, in my opinion, the best lattes in the most sophisticated Italian cafe atmosphere in Portland. There are excellent panini, gelato, and pastries as well, and wine in the evening. 303 NW 12th Ave. www.caffeumbria.com. (© **503/241-5300.** Sun–Wed 7am–7pm, Thurs–Sat 7am–8pm.

Moonstruck Chocolate Café ★★★ At this chocolateria, chocoholics can choose from a variety of hot chocolate drinks and handmade chocolates. There's another Moonstruck downtown at 608 SW Alder St. ((© **503/241-0955**). 526 NW 23rd Ave. www.moonstruckchocolate.com. ((© **503/542-3400**). Mon–Thurs 8am–10pm, Fri–Sat 8am–11pm, Sun 9am–9pm.

Stumptown ★★ Many a Portlander swears by the strong, flavorful coffee at this big, bare downtown cafe with an art-school aesthetic. Whether you go for the French press, a latte, or a double shot of espresso, you're sure to get a kick out of this brew. Other Stumptown locations: Ace Hotel, 1026 SW Stark St. ((© **503/224-9060**); 4525 SE Division St. ((© **503/230-7702**); 3356 SE Belmont St. ((© **503/232-8889**). 128 SW Third Ave. www.stumptowncoffee.com. (© **503/295-6144.** Mon–Fri 6am–6pm, Sat–Sun 6am–7pm.

DINING A LA cart

It's such a simple idea, the food cart, and of course it originated in Portland, where hungry residents don't usually have big budgets for dining out but still like good food. Why not join them, and have lunch the Portland way, "a la cart"? The city has become legendary for its hundreds of food carts (trailers, actually) parked in lots all over town. Look for concentrations of them downtown at **SW Stark Street** and **SW Fifth Avenue, SW Alder Street,** and **SW Ninth** and **SW Tenth** Avenues; **SW Third and Ash** across the river; on the east side, you'll find carts at **NE 10th and Alberta Street, SE 28th Avenue,** and **SE Hawthorne and 38th Avenue.** There are many food-cart standouts, and the carts often serve as a springboard (running board?) for new sit-down restaurants. For spicy Georgian (as in Russia) specialties, try **Kargi Gogo** (www.kargigogo.com), on SW Washington between 9th and 10th avenues. **Tiffin Asha** (www.tiffinasha.com), 1313 NE Alberta St., serves great southern Indian food. **Dalo's** (dalos-kitchen.com), corner of SE Martin Luther King Blvd. and Washington St., serves a mixed vegan platter for $5. But these are just a few possibilities for dining inexpensively at spots around town. For other locations and cartloads of information on Portland food carts, go to www.foodcartsportland.com.

Tao of Tea ★★   Not a coffee drinker? Try this funky teahouse, which specializes in traditional Chinese tea service and feels like it could be in some Kathmandu back alley. 3430 SE Belmont St. www.taooftea.com. ✆ **503/736-0198.** Mon–Sat 11am–10pm, Sun 11am–9pm.

BAKERIES, GELATERIAS & PASTRY SHOPS

Pearl Bakery ★★   One of Portland's first artisan bakeries, Pearl Bakery is famous for its breads and European-style pastries. The *gibassier,* a chewy sweet roll fragrant with anise and orange, is a must-try. The gleaming bakery/cafe is also good for sandwiches, such as a roasted eggplant and tomato pesto on crusty bread. 102 NW Ninth Ave. www.pearlbakery.com. ✆ **503/827-0910.**

St. Honoré Boulangerie ★★★   Not only does this place turn out mouthwateringly authentic French pastries and breads, it makes great coffee and offers a good simple lunch menu, too. They have a new branch at 3333 SE Division (✆ **971/279-4433**). 2335 NW Thurman St. www.sainthonorebakery.com. ✆ **503/445-4342.** Daily 7am–8pm.

Salt & Straw ★★   We are now in the post–Ben & Jerry's and post-post–Baskin-Robbins world of ice cream, a time when people are willing to stand in line for half an hour and think nothing of plunking down $4 for a scoop of homemade ice cream in a flavor unheard of a few short years ago. Salt & Straw is now Portland's ice cream mecca, serving up flavors like salted caramel cupcake, bacon ale, freckled woodblock chocolate, and honey balsamic vinegar with cracked pepper. The Northwest location is also a bakery; the other two locations are "scoop shops": 3345 SE Division (✆ **503/208-2054**); 2035 NE Alberta St. (✆ **503/208-3867**). 838 NW 23rd Ave. www.saltandstraw.com. ✆ **971/271-8168.** Daily 10am–11pm.

Voodoo Doughnut ★★   I'm not a fan of gooey doughnuts, but apparently everyone else in Portland is, because there is always a line here. Voodoo has become a tourist destination where new Portlanders bring their visiting parents and grandparents. Be forewarned that this corner hole-in-the-wall is not in the most savory location, and your wait to get in may be 15 minutes or more; but as I've said elsewhere, standing in line for food is now a Portland thing. Open 24 hours, Voodoo sells voodoo-doll doughnuts (pretzel through the heart, jelly filling), bacon-topped maple bars, vegan doughnuts, and even X-rated doughnuts, packaged in an immediately identifiable pink box. There's a second Voodoo Doughnut across the river at 1501 NE Davis St. (© **503/235-2666**). 22 SW Third Ave. www.voodoodoughnut.com. © **503/241-4704.** Open 24 hrs.

EXPLORING PORTLAND

Ask a Portlander about the city's must-see attractions, and you'll probably be directed to the **Portland Japanese Garden,** the **International Rose Test Garden,** and the **Lan Su Chinese Garden.** Gardening is a Portland obsession, and thanks to the moist and mild weather here, you'll find some of the finest public gardens in the country. Visiting all the city's noteworthy parks and gardens can easily take up two or three days. Seattle, and not Portland, is the place where you're more likely to encounter big museums and splashy traveling art exhibitions. This isn't to say that the Portland Art Museum, which often hosts interesting traveling exhibitions, isn't worth visiting, or that the Oregon Historical Society Museum is not worth your time. They are, but they have a local rather than an international focus. The city's really not so much about spending hours in museums as it is about exploring neighborhoods, parks and gardens, and nearby nature.

Attractions in & Around Downtown Portland

Chapman & Lownsdale Squares ★★ PARK Set aside as public parks in 1852, a year after Portland became an incorporated city, these two adjacent blocks planted with elms, pines, cedars, and ginkgo trees form the green heart of Portland's government quarter. They were the scene of anti-Chinese riots in the 1880s and in the 1920s were sexually segregated to protect women from unwanted advances. **Chapman Square** (btw. SW Madison and SW Main), the former women's park, was named for Judge William Chapman, a founder of *The Oregonian* newspaper. Men were confined to **Lownsdale Square** (btw. SW Main and SW Salmon), named for Daniel Lownsdale, a 19th-century Oregon legislator who was also responsible for building the city's first plank road in 1851. Between the two squares, in the center of SW Main Street, is the graceful and iconic **Thompson Elk Fountain** (1900). Roland Perry's life-size bronze statue of an elk—an animal that reputedly grazed here in the early 1850s—stands atop a pedestal with four granite horse troughs at its base.

Bounded by SW Madison St. and SW Salmon St. and SW 3rd Ave. and SW 4th Ave.

Ira Keller Fountain ★ PLAZA/FOUNTAIN When it was dedicated in 1971, *The New York Times* architectural critic Ada Louise Huxtable called this fountain "the greatest open space since the Renaissance." It's a rather exaggerated claim, but it goes to show you how hot Portland was in terms of urban planning and public art back in the early 1970s. Inspired by the rivers and waterfalls of the Pacific Northwest (although those don't smell like chlorine—yet), this giant, rugged-looking fountain occupies a full city block directly opposite **Keller Auditorium.** Water flowing down through a grassy park planted with pine trees cascades over a series of multilevel concrete cliffs. Square, irregularly placed platforms over the pool act as stepping stones,

Downtown Portland Attractions

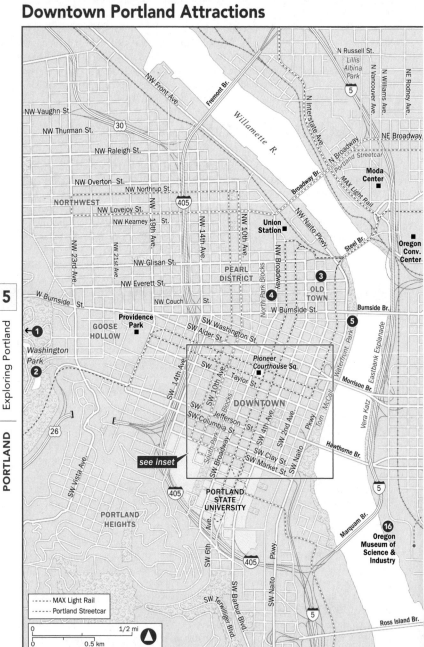

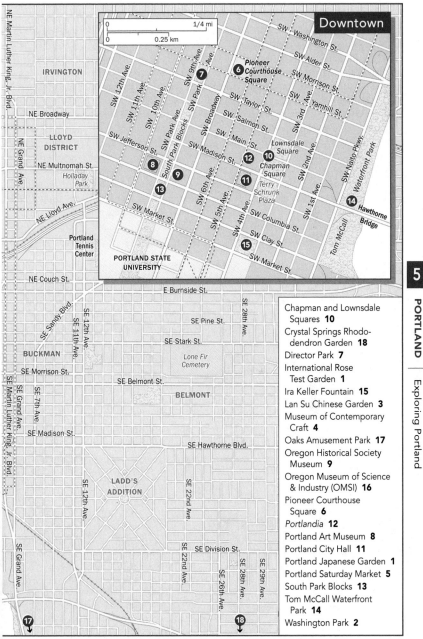

Downtown

Chapman and Lownsdale
 Squares **10**
Crystal Springs Rhodo-
 dendron Garden **18**
Director Park **7**
International Rose
 Test Garden **1**
Ira Keller Fountain **15**
Lan Su Chinese Garden **3**
Museum of Contemporary
 Craft **4**
Oaks Amusement Park **17**
Oregon Historical Society
 Museum **9**
Oregon Museum of Science
 & Industry (OMSI) **16**
Pioneer Courthouse
 Square **6**
Portlandia **12**
Portland Art Museum **8**
Portland City Hall **11**
Portland Japanese Garden **1**
Portland Saturday Market **5**
South Park Blocks **13**
Tom McCall Waterfront
 Park **14**
Washington Park **2**

allowing visitors to get close to the waterfall and even duck behind it. Angela Danadjieva designed the fountain for Lawrence Halprin & Associates.

SW Third Ave. and SW Clay St.

Lan Su Chinese Garden ★★★ GARDEN   Lan Su, in Portland's Chinatown, is not only the best, but the most authentic Chinese garden outside of China. It is a classical Chinese garden, which means that it replicates an urban garden style that came to prominence during the Ming dynasty (1368–1644), when an educated class of scholars, poets, and government officials built walled house-and-garden compounds that were both retreats and private pleasure grounds. In 1999, 65 craftspeople from Suzhou, China (Portland's sister city), came to construct the garden. The intricately detailed architectural components were made in China and shipped to Portland, along with 500 tons of specially chosen rock. The garden opened in 2000. This is not a Western-style garden where plants reign supreme. Instead, two-thirds of the enclosed garden space is comprised of ornate pavilions and halls grouped around a lake and connected by winding paths and zigzagging galleries. As you wend your way through the garden, visiting the ornate pavilions and admiring the constantly changing views, you'll encounter a wonderfully diverse assortment of plants, including specimen trees, rare and unusual shrubs, and perennials.

NW Everett St. and NW Third Ave. www.lansugarden.org. ✆ **503/228-8131.** Admission $9.50 adults, $8.50 seniors, $7 students and children 6–18. Apr–Oct daily 10am–6pm; Nov–Mar daily 10am–5pm.

Museum of Contemporary Craft ★ MUSEUM   Portland has attracted craftspeople for a very long time and is something of a crafts capital of the West Coast. If you visit **Timberline Lodge ★★★** on Mount Hood (p. 170), you'll see an entire alpine lodge furnished by Oregon craftspeople from the 1930s. This museum, founded in 1937 (in a different location), is one of the oldest contemporary craft museums in the U.S. It's a small space that typically hosts select exhibits on two floors of gallery space. These shows can nudge the boundaries of what is considered "craft," sometimes featuring private collections. It's not what I would consider a general-interest museum, but if you appreciate and enjoy contemporary crafts of superlative quality, it is definitely worth your time. The gift shop is one of Portland's best, featuring an array of fine ceramics, glassware, weavings, and jewelry. The museum's location on the **North Park Blocks** makes it easy to fit in with a visit to other galleries in the Pearl District.

724 NW Davis St. on North Park Blocks www.museumofcontemporarycraft.org. ✆ **503/223-2654.** Admission $4 adults, $3 students and seniors. Tues–Sat 11am–6pm (first Thurs of the month until 8pm).

Tea in the Chinese Garden

Tea has been a part of Chinese life and culture for over a thousand years. Introduced first as medicine, tea later became associated with Taoist philosophy. Monks used tea to stay awake during long meditation sessions. By the time teahouses became popular, during the Ming dynasty, tea was firmly established as a social beverage, and serving tea had taken on its own elaborate etiquette. The teahouse located in the two-story **Tower of Cosmic Reflections** in the **Lan Su Chinese Garden** is a perfect spot to sample authentic Chinese tea and teacakes while enjoying a view of the garden.

Oregon Historical Society Museum ★★ MUSEUM   Oregon has a dramatic and fascinating history that began with human habitation at least 12,000 years ago. Most people, however, associate Oregon with the momentous Lewis and Clark Expedition, which traveled down the Columbia and reached the Pacific Ocean in 1805 (see p. 190 for **Fort Clatsop** in the Oregon Coast chapter), and with the Oregon Trail. The same route was used by tens of thousands of immigrants who trekked to a new life in Oregon starting in the 1840s. This downtown museum on the South Park Blocks is the state's main repository of Oregon's history, and it's worth an hour of your time to browse through the exhibits. The temporary shows are sometimes too specialized to be of general interest, but the permanent exhibits display some intriguing artifacts. Go first to the "Oregon, My Oregon" floor, where more than 50 different displays of artifacts and re-created environments tell the story of the state from many different perspectives. Everything from a 9,000-year-old sandal made out of sagebrush to a lunch counter salvaged from Newberry's downtown department store is on display. Also devote some time to the **Northwest Art Gallery,** which presents an overview of Oregon artists.

1200 SW Park Ave. www.ohs.org. © **503/306-5198.** Admission $11 adults, $9 students and seniors, $5 children 6–18. Tues–Sat 10am–5pm; Sun noon–5pm.

Pioneer Courthouse Square ★★★ PLAZA   Any visit to downtown Portland should start on Pioneer Courthouse Square at the corner of SW Broadway and Yamhill Street. The brick-paved square is an outdoor stage for everything from summer outdoor movies to food festivals to flower displays to concerts. It's also a scene of protest rallies, although few of those these days. A few decades ago it was a parking lot, created in 1951 when the Portland Hotel—a Queen Anne–style chateau and an architectural gem—was demolished. Long before that, Pioneer Square was the site of Portland's first schoolhouse. The octagonal cupola of the Classic Revival **Pioneer Courthouse** (701 SW 6th Ave.) at the east end of the square has been a Portland landmark since it was completed in 1873. The first federal building to be constructed in the Pacific Northwest, the courthouse was designed by Alfred Mullet, who also designed the San Francisco Mint. The two large wings on its west facade were added in 1903.

Today, the square, with its **waterfall fountain** and freestanding columns, is Portland's favorite downtown gathering spot, especially at noon, when the **Weather Machine,** a goofy mechanical sculpture, forecasts the weather for the next 24 hours. Amid a fanfare of music and flashing lights, the Weather Machine sends up clouds of mist followed by a sun (clear weather), a dragon (stormy weather), or a blue heron (clouds and drizzle). The **Portland Visitor Information Center** and **Tri-Met ticket office** are located behind and beneath the fountains, and a big **Starbucks** with outdoor tables overlooking the square anchors the corner above. Check the Pioneer Courthouse Square website for upcoming events.

701 SW 6th Ave. www.thesquarepdx.org.

Portlandia ★★ LOCAL LANDMARK/OUTDOOR SCULPTURE   They have the same name, but no, I'm not talking about the TV series that satirizes (sort of) life in Portland. This *Portlandia* is a giantess made out of hammered copper, crouching incongruously atop the entrance to the **Portland Building,** clutching a trident in one hand and reaching toward the street with the other—supposedly welcoming people to the hideous building, or maybe trying to flick them away with her finger. The only hammered-copper giantess larger than *Portlandia* is the Statue of Liberty. Because of the weird way she is positioned, most people don't even notice *Portlandia*. Maybe they are averting their eyes from Michael Graves's Portland Building, the first postmodern structure in the United States, and hated by just about everyone because of its dark interiors and graceless exterior. Classically garbed and emotionless, *Portlandia* went up when the building did, in 1985. She was created by Raymond Kaskey, and yes, she does have a cameo in the opening credits of *Portlandia,* the TV show.

Portland Building at 1120 SW Fifth Ave.

Portland Art Museum ★ ART MUSEUM   Located right across from the **Oregon Historical Society Museum,** the Portland Art Museum was founded in 1892 and is the oldest art museum in the Northwest. It used to be one of the most boring art museums in the Northwest, too, but that changed in the 1990s when dynamic new leadership stepped in and gave the museum some contemporary relevance and muscle. An expansion scheme in 2000 took over the adjacent Masonic Temple and added thousands of square feet of new exhibition space for the museum's permanent collections and traveling shows. The petite collection of small French Impressionists is worth a look, but I would concentrate instead on the **Northwest Native Art** collection, because you otherwise won't see much Native American art in Portland. The contemporary collection in the revamped Masonic Temple is worth a look, too, though I personally find that they have too much work on display, some good, but some mediocre; there are so many pieces hanging in close proximity that it can become a blur. The museum has had some intriguing traveling shows of late, including one of vintage cars and bicycles. The small outdoor sculpture court has some very nice pieces. Plan to spend at least an hour here.

1219 SW Park Ave. www.portlandartmuseum.org. ✆ **503/226-2811.** Admission $15 adults, $12 seniors and college students, free for children 17 and under. Tues–Wed and Sat 10am–5pm; Thurs–Fri 10am–8pm; Sun noon–5pm.

Tom McCall Waterfront Park ★★★ PARK   This grassy, 23-acre park that stretches for about 1½ miles along the Willamette River was once Portland's raucous river port. In 1929, the old downtown wharves were demolished and the first seawall erected; from the 1940s until the 1970s, a major east-west highway plowed through the area. As part of its downtown urban renewal scheme, the city reclaimed the land and named the new park after Tom McCall (1913–1983), an early proponent of land-use planning who served as governor from 1967–1975. The park is frequently used for summertime concerts and festivals, the most famous being the Rose Festival in June, when a Coast Guard ship docks alongside the seawall (an entire fleet used to dock here) and carnival rides are set up. A waterfront esplanade used by strollers, joggers, bicyclists, and Rollerbladers stretches from **RiverPlace** (an upscale retail, hotel, and condominium development with a marina at the south end of the park) to the **Japanese-American Historical Plaza** on the north end, planted with cherry trees and commemorating Portland's Japanese-Americans who were sent to internment camps during World War II. **Salmon Street Springs,** a 100-jet fountain with changing water configurations, is located at Salmon Street and is a favorite cool-off spot for kids on hot summer days.

Along the Willamette River.

Washington Park Attractions

Washington Park ★★★ PARK/GARDENS   Portland is justly proud of its green spaces, and foremost among them is Washington Park. The city bought the land in the Southwest hills in 1871. Unlike **Forest Park** ★★★ (see p. 146), most of Washington

Washington Park Attractions

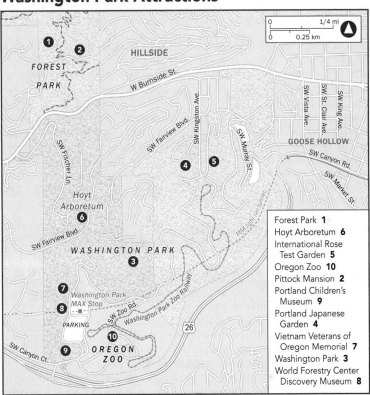

Forest Park **1**
Hoyt Arboretum **6**
International Rose Test Garden **5**
Oregon Zoo **10**
Pittock Mansion **2**
Portland Children's Museum **9**
Portland Japanese Garden **4**
Vietnam Veterans of Oregon Memorial **7**
Washington Park **3**
World Forestry Center Discovery Museum **8**

The Bridges of Multnomah County

Six Portland bridges can be seen by strolling the length of Tom McCall Waterfront Park. The three most notable are the buff-colored **Hawthorne Bridge** (1910), the oldest lift-bridge in the country; the **Morrison Bridge,** which opened in 1887 as a wooden toll bridge—the first span across the Willamette—and was replaced in 1905 and 1958; and the **Steel Bridge,** the world's only telescoping double-deck vertical lift bridge.

Park has been landscaped to serve as a setting for its acclaimed gardens, zoo, and nature-related attractions. Surrounded at its north end by the exclusive Portland Heights neighborhood, the park winds south along the ridge that stretches along the entire west side of the city. This is a great place for hiking, playing tennis, and picnics; in the summer, concerts of all kinds are held in the grassy amphitheater adjacent to the rose garden. SW Kingston Avenue connects the **International Rose Test Garden** and **Portland Japanese Garden** to Hoyt Arboretum, the **World Forestry Center**

Washington Park Choo-Choo

Beloved by generations of kids, the little **Washington Park and Zoo Railway** travels between the zoo and the International Rose Test Garden. Tickets for the miniature railway are $5, free for children 2 and under. There's also a shorter route that just loops around the zoo. It's a kid-sized train, just big enough for adults, with open windows, and it winds its way through the forest.

Discovery Museum, and the **Oregon Zoo.** You could also walk to these attractions, although you'd need most of a day to see them all. MAX, the city's light rail system, includes a stop at Washington Park, providing easy access from downtown to the zoo, the arboretum, and the forestry museum; in the summer a narrow-gauge excursion train runs between the International Rose Test Garden and the zoo.

Entrance at SW Park Pl., 2 blocks west of SW Vista. www.portlandoregon.gov/parks. ✆ **503/823-2525.** Admission free. Daily 5am–10pm.

Hoyt Arboretum ★★ ARBORETUM   Over 900 species of trees, some indigenous to the Pacific Northwest and others imported from around the world, are found in the hills and meadows of this 175-acre arboretum at the south end of Washington Park. Trails wind through well-established stands of magnolias, maples, oaks, hawthorns, cherries, and the most extensive conifer collection in the U.S. There are views of Mount Rainier, Mount St. Helens, and Pittock Mansion along the way. The short **Overlook Trail,** just south of the Washington Park light rail station, leads to the **Visitor Center** (you can also drive there), where visitors will find maps and booklets for self-guided tree tours. **Bristlecone Pine Trail** off Fischer Lane is a 1-mile paved trail with disabled access parking.

The **Vietnam Veterans of Oregon Memorial ★★,** dedicated in 1987, lies at the southwest corner of the arboretum. From a central, bowl-shaped area, an ascending walkway spirals up to six black granite markers inscribed with the names of those reported as dead or missing from 1959 to 1976. Short texts inscribed above the names provide a "living history" of Oregonians during the war years.

Hoyt Arboretum Visitor Center: 4000 SW Fairview Blvd. www.hoytarboretum.org. ✆ **503/865-8733.** Admission free. Visitor Center Mon–Fri 9am–4pm; Sat 9am–3:30pm.

International Rose Test Garden ★★★ GARDEN   Established in 1917, the oldest public rose test garden in the U.S. offers a dazzling display of Portland's favorite flower. Some 8,000 roses representing 525 species grow in fragrant, formal terraces overlooking downtown Portland and Mount Hood. The city's fondness for the genus *Rosa* dates back to 1887 and the founding of the Portland Rose Society, the oldest such group in the U.S. In 1907, rose-loving citizens began a campaign to nickname Portland the "City of Roses," which it's been called ever since.

From the parking lot, steps descend to an information kiosk surrounded by elevated beds of miniature roses. Extending east, and covering two broad terraces, is the **American Garden Rose Selections** garden. The roses being tested here are given a code number rather than a name; four plants of each variety are evaluated for 2 years by an official judge using 13 different criteria. The city of Portland annually awards the best-performing roses with a gold or silver medal. Winners are then given fanciful (and sometimes cutesy) names and moved to the **Gold Award Garden,** located on the

Portland Rose Festival

The **Portland Rose Festival** (www.rose-festival.org), held every year in June, coincides with the roses in the International Rose Test Garden's peak blooming period. It is one of the largest floral-themed extravaganzas in the country, with two parades, the crowning of a Rose Queen (a high school competition), and a fun fair set up in **Tom McCall Waterfront Park ★★★** (see p. 142). This Portland tradition dates back to 1907.

terraces below the **Beach Memorial Fountain.** The fountain is a walk-through, stainless-steel sculpture designed by Portland artist Lee Kelley and named for Frank E. Beach, who spearheaded efforts to nickname Portland the "City of Roses." **Queens' Walk,** on the lowest promenade, is inset with bronze markers for every Rose Festival queen since 1907. Annual and perennial flowers named in Shakespeare's plays are planted in the **Shakespeare Garden,** in the lower southeast corner. The small **Rose Garden Store,** 850 SW Rose Garden Way (🕿 **503/227-7033**), is open in the summer and packed with rose-inspired products.

400 SW Kingston Ave. (in Washington Park). www.rosegardenstore.org. 🕿 **503/823-3636.** Free admission. Daily 7:30am–9pm.

Oregon Zoo ★★★ ZOO   I dislike zoos, even when they're as enlightened as this one, which happens to be Oregon's top tourist attraction. The Oregon Zoo is best known for its elephants, with the most successful breeding herd in captivity. The Africa exhibit is one of the best habitats and includes a manmade rainforest and a savanna populated by zebras, rhinos, giraffes, and hippos. The Alaskan Tundra has grizzly bears, wolves, and musk oxen, while the Cascade Crest exhibit includes a mountain goat habitat. In Steller Cove, Steller sea lions and sea otters are on display. Other exhibits include an intriguing bat house and the Amazon Flooded Forest. And don't miss the naked mole rats, scurrying around in their glass-walled tunnels. In the summer, there are outdoor concerts in the zoo's amphitheater.

4001 SW Canyon Rd. (in Washington Park). www.oregonzoo.org. 🕿 **503/226-1561.** Admission $12 adults, $10 seniors, $8.50 children 3–11. Late-May to early-Sept daily 9am–6pm; early-Sept to Dec and Mar to late-May daily 9am–4pm; Jan–Feb 10am–4pm.

Portland Children's Museum ★ MUSEUM   This museum is full of all kinds of active, hands-on play and discovery lessons that kids love. There are no static exhibits here; it's about diving in and doing. So newborns to 3-year-olds can enjoy a benign magic garden, and older kids can ramp up their activity and imagination levels by creating something from clay, painting in the big garage studio, or donning a hardhat and helping to build a house. They can also push a cart and play at shopping, learn how to care for pets at a pet clinic, climb into a tree house, or learn about nature—which I strongly encourage in this age of passive screen-staring.

4015 SW Canyon Rd. www.portlandcm.org. 🕿 **503/223-6500.** Admission $10 adults and children, $9 seniors, free for children under age 1 (free for all on first Fri of each month 4–8pm). Daily 9am–5pm.

Portland Japanese Garden ★★★ GARDEN   The most authentic Japanese garden outside of Japan occupies a 5½-acre site directly above the **International Rose Test Garden.** Designed by Professor Takuma Tono, a Japanese landscape master from

Tokyo, the garden took 4 years to complete and was opened to the public in 1967 on the site of the old Portland Zoo. The immaculately tended grounds contain superb examples of ancient Japanese gardening styles influenced by Shinto, Buddhist, and Taoist philosophies. Plants, stones, and water are used to create areas of serene and contemplative beauty.

From May through September, you can take an open-sided bus from the parking lot up to the entrance, but I recommend that you walk up the graveled foot path from the lovely **Antique Gate** to the garden entrance.

The **Strolling Pond Garden** is the largest garden on the site, with a picturesque Moon Bridge crossing the Upper Pond. Gracing the **Tea Garden** is a ceremonial tea house constructed in Japan (using pegs instead of nails), reassembled here in 1968. Farther south, the aptly named Zig-Zag Bridge leads through a waterside area planted with May-blossoming Japanese irises to the **Lower Pond,** where giant koi slowly navigate below a waterfall.

The **Natural Garden** covers the south hillside, where stone steps wind down past shallow, meandering waterscapes. The abstract, Zen-inspired **Sand and Stone Garden** is at the end, with weathered stones rising from a bed of gravel that's been raked to suggest the sea. Plantings in the Flat Garden, to the north, are meant to resemble a sake cup and gourd bottle, symbols of pleasure and happiness. The large wooden pavilion behind the Flat Garden is used for special events and provides a majestic view of Portland and Mount Hood from its eastern terrace.

611 SW Kingston Ave. (in Washington Park). www.japanesegarden.com. ℂ **503/223-1321.** Admission $9.50 adults, $7.75 seniors and college students, $6.75 children 6–17. Apr–Sept Mon noon–7pm; Tues–Sun 10am–7pm; Oct–Mar Mon noon–4pm; Tues–Sun 10am–4pm.

World Forestry Center Discovery Museum ★   Trees, beautiful trees. Forests, beautiful forests. We are dependent upon them for our very survival, and we can no longer take them for granted. They are disappearing at an alarming rate and they need all the help and protection they can get. Oregon's economy was founded on logging, and the timber industry, although it no longer has the clout it once did, continues to play an important role in the state. It's also the force behind this museum, which attempts to explain how forests work and how complex they are. Exhibits on the first floor concentrate on the vast forests of the Pacific Northwest, and those on the second floor focus on Russia, China, South Africa, and the Amazon. If you love forests, or want to know more about trees, you will learn something here—but keep in mind that no matter how "sustainable" the practices, the timber industry is about managing forests, not letting them be. There are interesting temporary exhibits staged here throughout the year as well, from photographic exhibits to displays of woodworkers' art.

4033 SW Canyon Rd. www.worldforestry.org. ℂ **503/228-1367.** Admission $9 adults, $8 seniors, $6 children 3–18. Daily 10am–5pm.

Northwest Portland Attractions

You might want to explore urban Northwest Portland by strolling through the **Pearl District,** or down **NW 23rd Avenue** from East Burnside to NW Thurman (see "Neighborhoods in Brief," p. 108). But if you want to enjoy the natural side of Portland, put on some good walking shoes or hiking boots and head up to giant Forest Park.

Forest Park ★★★ PARK   On a 1903 visit to Portland, landscape designer John Olmsted (son of Frederick Law Olmsted, who designed New York's Central Park) drew up a city park plan calling for "a succession of ravines and spurs covered with remarkably beautiful woods." His recommendation led to the establishment of 5,000-acre Forest Park in 1948. One of the largest urban parks in North America, this forest is part of a 9,000-acre park system that forms a wildlife corridor to the Coast Range, dividing the Willamette Valley from the Pacific Ocean. The park is home to more than 50 species of mammals—including rarely seen deer and bobcats—and about 150 species of birds. Some 50 miles of interconnected hiking trails wind up and down the slopes of Forest Park, where a canopy of towering Douglas firs rises above an understory of alders, aspens, hemlock, holly, and maidenhair and sword ferns. White trilliums glow along the paths in the spring. The 33-mile-long **Wildwood Trail** connects Forest Park to **Washington Park** ★★★ (see p. 142) and the **Hoyt Arboretum** ★★ (see p. 144) in Southwest Portland. A few old-growth trees can be found behind the **Portland Audubon Society** (5151 NW Cornell Rd.; www.audubonportland.org; ℭ **503/292-6855**).

Forest Park, Portland, OR 97231. www.forestparkconservancy.org. ℭ **503/823-4492.** There are many ways to access the park and its miles of trails; see the website for information and the entry for Pittock Mansion, below.

Pittock Mansion ★★ HISTORIC HOUSE/PARK/VIEW   The largest and most opulent home in Portland is perched on a 1,000-foot-high crest adjoining **Forest Park,** looking east over the city, the river, and the major peaks of the Cascade Mountains. This is one of the great views in Portland and worth a stop even if you don't visit the mansion. Built for Henry Pittock (1835–1919), who came west on the Oregon Trail in 1853 and eventually amassed a fortune as the publisher of *The Oregonian* newspaper, the mansion was designed by San Francisco architect Edward T. Foulkes and completed in 1914. Stylistically, the structure is a French Renaissance Revival chateau with exterior walls of Italian Tenino sandstone. Visitors can wander through on their own or join a guided tour to learn more about the mansion's history and details of its design, which include Portland's earliest vacuum-cleaning system and walk-in refrigerator. The fine period furnishings and rugs are not original to the house but amply convey the luxurious lifestyle of the prominent Portland family that lived here. Nearly one-third of the mansion is taken up by a magnificent marble staircase and hallway constructed of Italian and domestic marbles. The Jacobean-style library, paneled with Honduran mahogany, has a quatrefoil design plaster ceiling and a fireplace of French Caen stone. The elliptical drawing room, with its elaborate plaster moldings and cornices, commands a 180-degree vista of the city and Mount Hood. Superlative plasterwork and marquetry floors are found in the small, circular Turkish smoking room. On the second floor, a four-room master suite used by Pittock and his wife, Georgiana, is flanked by two smaller suites once occupied by the couple's daughters and their husbands. Trail heads into Forest Park are found at the west end of the parking lot and beyond **Gate Lodge,** the former groundskeeper's house.

3229 NW Pittock Dr. www.pittockmansion.org. ℭ **503/823-3623.** Admission $9.50 adults, $8.50 seniors, $6.50 children 6–18. July–Aug daily 10am–5pm; Sept–Dec and Feb–June daily 11am–4pm. Closed Jan.

Southeast Portland Attractions

Urban adventurers will enjoy southeast Portland's hopping neighborhoods, including **SE Hawthorne, SE Division, Sellwood,** and **Eastmoreland/Westmoreland** (see "Neighborhoods in Brief," p. 108). There is also a heritage amusement park, a superlative garden, and a popular science and technology museum on the east side by the river.

WALKING ALONG THE willamette

It's pronounced Will-*am*-ette, not Will-a-met, and it flows right through the heart of Portland. This river played an important role in the lives of the Native American Multnomah tribe (Portland is in Multnomah County) and was an essential route for the pioneers who trekked across country on the Oregon Trail and poured into the Willamette Valley in the mid-19th century. Pioneers took boats and rafts down this tributary of the Columbia to Oregon City, which marked the end of the Oregon Trail. It was in Oregon City that land claims could be made. The river was deep enough to allow Portland to become a major inland port—hence all the historic drawbridges that you can see downtown. On the west side, you can stroll along the river downtown at **Tom McCall Waterfront Park** ★★★ (see p. 142). On the east side, a paved pathway connects **OMSI** to the **Vera Katz Eastbank Esplanade** to the north. The path from OMSI also heads south 3 miles to **Oaks Amusement Park.** Along the pathway beside the museum, several interesting informational plaques tell the history of Portland and its relationship to the Willamette.

Crystal Springs Rhododendron Garden ★★ GARDEN   After roses, rhododendrons are Portland's favorite flowering shrub. They grow easily in the damp, temperate climate. But forest-loving rhodies are native in Oregon only on a portion of Mount Hood and in the Siskiyou Mountains in southwestern Oregon. Portlanders never saw a rhododendron until some examples arrived from a nursery in England and were exhibited at the Lewis and Clark Exhibition in 1905. Now rhodies are ubiquitous and available in every color and leaf shape imaginable. But all the collecting and hybridizing didn't really begin until 1950, when the first-ever chapter of the American Rhododendron Society was formed in Portland and bought this 7-acre site across from Reed College in Eastmoreland as a garden devoted to rhodies. Lovely year-round, Crystal Springs turns spectacular from April through June, when 600 varieties of rhododendrons and azaleas burst into bloom. From the gatehouse, visitors cross a bridge overlooking a small waterfall and rushing stream and follow paths through the enormous collection of rhodies to **Crystal Springs Lake,** created in 1917 by damming 13 area springs. Congregated near the shoreline and bobbing on the water are coots, widgeons, scaups, wood ducks, mallards, and Canada geese. Paddison Fountain shoots a geyser of water into the lake's South Lagoon. A famous rhododendron show and plant sale is held here on Mother's Day weekend.

SE 28th Ave. (1 block north of SE Woodstock Blvd.). www.rhodies.org. ℂ **503/771-8386.** Admission $3 Mar to Labor Day Thurs–Mon 10am–6pm; free at other times. Apr–Sept daily 6am–10pm; Oct–Mar daily 6am–6pm.

Oregon Museum of Science and Industry (OMSI) ★★ MUSEUM   When I was in school, science was never presented in as interactive, entertaining a manner as it is here. OMSI is all about engaging with science, and it does that with dozens of hands-on exhibits, games, brain teasers, and all the technology you could wish for. I don't think adults would get the same kick out of OMSI as kids do. For little ones, it's a giant science playground with five roomy halls. Earth Hall, a multi-dimensional look at the world we live in, includes exhibits on environmental hazards, natural disasters, and climate change. Life Hall deals with the mysteries of human growth and development. Science Labs gives you a hands-on laboratory experience in chemistry, physics, and technology. The Turbine Hall, devoted to the physical sciences and technology, lets visitors build an aqueduct and program a robot. The Science Playground on the second floor is for kids 6 and younger. There are three additional components to the museum, all of which require separate tickets: **The Empirical Theater** (formerly called the OMNIMAX), the **Kendall Planetarium,** which features astronomy and laser-light shows, and my favorite, the **USS** *Blueback* **submarine** docked in the river right behind the museum.

1945 SE Water Ave. www.omsi.edu. ℂ **800/955-6674** or 503/797-4000. Museum $13 adults, $9.50 seniors and children 3–13; Empirical Theater shows $6–$8.50 adults, $5–$6.50 seniors and children 3–13; submarine tours, planetarium shows, and matinee laser-light shows $5.75; evening laser shows $7.50; discounted combination tickets available. Mid-June to early-Sept daily 9:30am–7pm; early-Sept to mid-June Tues–Sun 9:30am–5:30pm.

ORGANIZED TOURS

Bike Tours

Want to be part of the Portland bike scene, but don't want to do it on your own? Book a ride with **Pedal Bike Tours,** 133 SW Second Ave. (www.pedalbiketours.com; ℂ **503/243-2453**), which offers a wide range of outings, including those that focus on Portland history, brewpubs, and food and coffee. Farther afield, they operate tours of the wine country, the Oregon coast, and the Columbia Gorge. Prices for in-town tours range from $49 to $69 per person. **Portland Bicycle Tours,** 345 NW Everett St. (www.portlandbicycletours.com; ℂ **503/902-5035**), has a basic city tour, as well as tours that focus on Portland green-built buildings, the city's "bikeability," and, of course, brewpubs. Tours cost $40 per person.

Cruises & Sea Kayaking

Portland Spirit (www.portlandspirit.com; ℂ **800/224-3901** or 503/224-3900), a 150-foot yacht, leaves daily year-round from **Tom McCall Waterfront Park** at the foot of SW Salmon Street and cruises west along the Willamette River, offering views of the city skyline and residential areas along the way. It's not terribly exciting terrain, and I have to regretfully report that the meals served on board the lunch and dinner cruises are overpriced and not particularly noteworthy. If you want to see the city by boat, I would recommend taking a basic sightseeing cruise, or the Friday afternoon summer cocktail cruise. Prices range from $28 to $68 for adults and $18 to $63 for children.

For a more active water-level tour of the Willamette, arrange for a sea kayak tour through the **Portland Kayak Company ★★,** 6600 SW Macadam Ave. (www.portlandrivercompany.com; ℂ **503/459-4050**); they operate tours out of the **River-Place Marina** at the south end of Tom McCall Waterfront Park. A 2½-hour tour that circles nearby Ross Island costs $45 to $49 per person. This company also rents sea kayaks, canoes, and standup paddleboards for $10 to $15 per hour.

Bus Tours

If you just want to get an overview of Portland highlights, hop a ride on **Big Pink Sightseeing's** trolley bus, which is operated by **Gray Line of Portland** (www.graylineofportland.com; ℂ **503/241-7373**). From its starting point at **Pioneer Courthouse Square,** the trolley bus makes 12 stops around Portland. If you buy an all-day ticket ($32 for adults, $16 children 6–12), you can hop on and off the bus all day. Each stop has service every 45 to 60 minutes. The trolley operates from late May to mid-October.

Eco Tours of Oregon (www.ecotours-of-oregon.com; ☎ 888/868-7733 or 503/457-0226) runs bus tours to the Oregon coast, wine country, Mount St. Helens, and up the Columbia River Gorge to Mount Hood. Tour prices range from $65 to $90.

With more microbreweries than any other city in the world, Portland has come to be known as Beervana. If you're a lover of craft beers and want to learn more about the local microbrewing scene, book a tour with **Brewvana Portland Brewery Tours** (www.experiencebrewvana.com; ☎ **503/729-6804**), which charges $60 to $74 per person for Friday, Saturday, and Sunday tours that include transportation, tastings, and food. Brewpub tours are also offered on Saturday afternoons by the **Portland Brew-Bus** (www.brewbus.com; ☎ **503/647-0021**), for $45 per person. Slightly more economical brewery tours that utilize TriMet's light rail line and the Portland streetcar are offered by **Pubs of Portland Tours** (www.pubsofportlandtours.com; ☎ **512/917-2464**). Tours cost $30 and stop at four or more breweries or pubs; you'll also have to purchase a TriMet all-day pass ($5).

Walking Tours

Peter's Walking Tours of Portland (www.walkportland.com; ☎ **503/704-7900**), led by Peter Chausse, are a great way to learn more about the city. The downtown visits last 3 hours and take in fountains, parks, historic places, art, and architecture. Tours are by reservation and cost $15 for adults and $10 for teens.

OUTDOOR PURSUITS

Biking

Portland is one of America's most bicycle-friendly cities, with miles of paved paths used by bike commuters and recreational bicyclists. Riding a bike around town, you'll definitely feel like a local, exploring out-of-the-way neighborhoods, pedaling along the banks of the Willamette River, and visiting bike-friendly businesses.

Waterfront Bicycles, 10 SW Ash St., Ste. 100 (www.waterfrontbikes.com; ☎ **503/227-1719**) rents bikes for $9 for 1 hour or $40 per day.

In Tom McCall Waterfront Park, at the foot of SW Salmon Street, you can rent a variety of unusual, family-friendly cycles from **Kerr Bikes** (www.kerrbikes.org; ☎ **503/808-9955**), including three-wheeled and four-wheeled cycles and surreys that carry as many as four adults. Rates range from $10 to $15 per hour. Kerr Bikes is open from March through October; hours vary with the month.

At **Bike Gallery,** 1001 SW Tenth Ave. (www.bikegallery.com; ☎ **503/222-3821**), you can rent a classic commuter bike (with fenders in case of rain) for $28 for 4 hours or $45 for 24 hours.

For mountain-bike rentals, head to **Fat Tire Farm,** 2714 NW Thurman St. (www.fattirefarm.com; ☎ **503/222-3276**), where bikes go for $40 to $125 for a 24-hour rental. Straight up Thurman Street from this bike shop, you'll find the trail head for

Leif Erickson Drive, an old gravel road that is Forest Park's favorite route for cyclists and runners (the road is closed to motor vehicles); the trail is 12 miles long.

Hiking

Hiking opportunities abound in the Portland area. For shorter hikes, you don't even have to leave the city; just head to **Forest Park ★★★** (p. 146), the largest forested city park in the country. Within this urban wilderness, you'll find more than 70 miles of trails. The 30-mile **Wildwood Trail** is the longest trail in the park and will take you all the way up to **Pittock Mansion** in northwest Portland and **Hoyt Arboretum** in southwest Portland. To reach the **Washington Park Arboretum**'s visitor center, 4000 SW Fairview Blvd. (Mon–Fri 9am–4pm; Sat 9am–3pm), drive west on West Burnside Street from downtown Portland and follow signs to the arboretum. You can get a trail map at the visitor center.

SHOPPING

Portland has no sales tax, making it a popular shopping destination for Washingtonians, who cross the Columbia River to avoid paying their state's substantial sales tax.

The Shopping Scene

The blocks around **Pioneer Courthouse Square** are the heartland of upscale shopping in downtown Portland. It's here that you'll find Nordstrom, Macy's, NIKETOWN, Apple, Microsoft, Tiffany, Pioneer Place Mall, and numerous boutiques.

The **Pearl District** and **Nob Hill/Northwest,** both in Northwest Portland, are other destination shopping areas. Most of the Pearl District's best shopping is along NW 10th and 11th avenues going north from West Burnside Street. Here you'll find all kinds of trendy boutiques, art galleries, and home-furnishing stores. The best Nob Hill shopping is along NW 23rd Avenue going north from West Burnside Street. Both neighborhoods have block after block of interesting, often one-of-a-kind boutiques. Along NW 23rd Avenue you'll also find a few national chains like Urban Outfitters, Pottery Barn, and Restoration Hardware.

For shops with a more down-to-earth, funky flair, head southeast to the **Hawthorne District.**

Most small stores in Portland are open Monday through Saturday from 9 or 10am to 5 or 6pm. Shopping malls are usually open Monday through Friday from 9 or 10am to 9pm, Saturday from 9 or 10am to between 6 and 9pm, and Sunday from 11am until 6pm. Many downtown department stores stay open until 8 or 9pm. Most art galleries and antiques stores are closed on Monday.

Shopping A to Z
ANTIQUES

Antiques stores are scattered throughout Portland, but the **Sellwood** neighborhood just east of the Sellwood Bridge is the best place for concentrated shopping. One of the first "streetcar suburbs," it has a number of modest Victorian homes—trolley car drivers lived in many of them—and the quiet, unassuming ambience of a small town. **Antique Row,** on 13th Avenue between SE Malden and Clatsop streets, has the largest concentration of antiques and collectible stores in the state. Victorian, Mission, and Arts and Crafts wood and wicker furniture, linens, glassware, and paintings are among the items you'll find here. There are two large antiques malls (under the same ownership) on Milwaukie Avenue: **Stars,** 7027 SE Milwaukie Ave. (www.stars antique.com; ✆ **503/239-0346**); and **Stars & Splendid,** 7030 SE Milwaukie Ave. (✆ **503/235-5990**).

ART GALLERIES

On the **first Thursday** of the month, galleries in downtown Portland and the Pearl District schedule coordinated openings in the evening from about 6 to 9pm. Stroll from one gallery to the next, meeting artists and perhaps buying an original work of art. On the **last Thursday** of the month, shops and galleries in the **NE Alberta Street** neighborhood stage a similar event.

Augen Gallery ★★★ ART GALLERY   When it opened over two decades ago, the Augen Gallery focused on internationally recognized artists such as Jim Dine, Andy Warhol, and David Hockney. Today the gallery has expanded its repertoire to regional contemporary painters and printmakers as well. 716 NW Davis St. www.augen gallery.com. ✆ **503/546-5056.** Also at 817 SW Second Ave. ✆ 503/224-8182.

Bullseye Gallery ★★★ ART GALLERY   Located in the Pearl District, the Bullseye Gallery is Portland's premier art-glass gallery and shows the work of internationally acclaimed glass artists from around the world. This work goes way beyond pretty vases. 300 NW 13th Ave. www.bullseyegallery.com. ✆ **503/227-0222.**

The Laura Russo Gallery ★★★ ART GALLERY   The focus here is on Northwest contemporary artists, showcasing emerging talents as well as the estates of well-known regional artists. This gallery has been in business for more than 25 years and is highly respected. 805 NW 21st Ave. www.laurarusso.com. ✆ **800/925-7152** or 503/226-2754.

Portland Art Museum Rental Sales Gallery ★★ ART GALLERY   This downtown gallery has a wide selection of works by more than 250 Northwest artists. Sales here help support the Portland Art Museum. 1237 SW 10th Ave. www.portlandart museum.org. ✆ **503/224-0674.**

Quintana Galleries ★★★ ART GALLERY   Quintana is a virtual museum of Native American art, selling everything from Northwest Coast Indian masks to Navajo rugs to contemporary paintings and sculptures by Native American artists. The galleries also carry a smattering of Native American artifacts from both the Northwest and the Southwest. The jewelry selection is outstanding. 124 NW Ninth Ave. www.quintana galleries.com. ✆ **800/321-1729** or 503/223-1729.

BOOKS

Powell's City of Books ★★★ BOOKSTORE   Portland's own Powell's City of Books covers an entire city block three floors deep. It's a longstanding Portland tourist attraction and an all-round fabulous bookstore, with roughly a million books on the shelves. Both new and used are shelved side by side. Pick up a store map to help guide you to the various color-coded rooms. Serious book collectors won't want to miss a visit to the Rare Book Room. City of Books has several satellite stores, including **Powell's Books for Home and Garden,** 3747 SE Hawthorne Blvd.; **Powell's Books on Hawthorne,** 3723 SE Hawthorne Blvd.; and **Powell's Books at PDX,** Portland International Airport, 7000 NE Airport Way, Ste. 2250. 1005 W. Burnside St. www. powells.com. ✆ **800/878-7323** or 503/228-4651. Daily 9am–11pm.

CRAFTS

The Gallery Store at the Museum of Contemporary Craft ★★ ART GALLERY/CRAFTS   On the North Park Blocks at the edge of the Pearl District, this is the nation's oldest not-for-profit art gallery, in business since 1937. It shows only works of clay, glass, fiber, metal, and wood. The bulk of the large gallery is filled with glass and ceramic pieces and fine jewelry. 724 NW Davis St. www.museumofcontemporary craft.org. ℂ **503/546-2654.**

Hoffman Gallery ★ ART GALLERY/CRAFTS   The Hoffman Gallery is on the campus of the Oregon College of Art and Craft, one of the nation's foremost crafts education centers since its founding in 1907. The gallery hosts installations and group shows by local, national, and international artists. The adjacent gift shop has a good selection of handcrafted items and photography. 8245 SW Barnes Rd. www.ocac.edu. ℂ **503/297-5544.**

The Real Mother Goose ★ ART GALLERY/CRAFTS   In business for decades, Mother Goose showcases fine contemporary American crafts, including ceramics, art glass, jewelry, wooden furniture, and sculptural works. Hundreds of craftspeople and artists from all over the U.S. are represented here. 901 SW Yamhill St. www.therealmother goose.com. ℂ **503/223-9510.** Also at Portland International Airport, Main Terminal (ℂ 503/284-9929).

Twist ★★ ART GALLERY/CRAFTS   This large store has quite a massive selection of wildly colorful and imaginative furniture, crockery, glassware, and lamps, and also a limited but impressive selection of handmade jewelry by artists from around the United States. 30 NW 23rd Pl. www.twistonline.com. ℂ **503/224-0334.**

DEPARTMENT STORES & FLAGSHIPS

Columbia Sportswear Company ★★ SPORTSWEAR   The flagship store for Portland's homegrown and highly regarded Columbia Sportswear features outdoor-oriented fashions and accessories for men, women, and children. 911 SW Broadway. www.columbia.com. ℂ **503/226-6800.**

Columbia Sportswear Company Factory Outlet Store ★★ SPORTS-WEAR   This outlet store in the Sellwood neighborhood south of downtown and across the river sells remainders and past-season styles from the local sportswear company, which is one of the Northwest's premier outdoor-clothing manufacturers. You'll pay 30 to 50% less here than you will at the downtown flagship store. 1323 SE Tacoma St. www.columbia.com. ℂ **503/238-0118.**

John Helmer Haberdasher ★★ CLOTHING STORE/HATS   Whether you're looking for a straw boater, a beret, a wide-brimmed Stetson, a felt fedora, a Panama, or a top hat, you'll find it at this classic haberdashery, which opened in 1921. There are also plenty of men's suits, slacks, and sports jackets. The outlay is very traditional, pretty conservative, and definitely Old Portland. 969 SW Broadway. www.johnhelmer.com. ℂ **866/855-4976** or 503/223-4976.

Macy's ★ DEPARTMENT STORE   Macy's took over a historic building overlooking Pioneer Courthouse Square, which it completely renovated and remodeled in 2007. This is the best all-round department store in downtown Portland, with fashion, cosmetics, housewares, jewelry, luggage, and pretty much everything else you look for in a department store. 621 SW Fifth Ave. www.macys.com. ℂ **503/223-0512.**

Nike Factory Company Store ★★ SPORTSWEAR   The Nike outlet is one season behind the current season at NIKETOWN (see below), selling swoosh-brand running, aerobic, tennis, golf, basketball, kids, and you-name-it shoes, clothing, and accessories, all at discounted prices. 2650 NE Martin Luther King Jr. Blvd. www.nike.com. ℂ **503/281-5901.**

NIKETOWN Portland ★★★ SPORTSWEAR The Starbucks of sportswear, Nike is an international super-brand that started right here in the outdoor-loving, sports-oriented Northwest. The Portland flagship store moved to this location in 2013. Like Powell's City of Books, this is a store that doubles as a tourist destination. You'll be greeted upon arrival, and you'll marvel at how little is displayed and how much it all costs. 638 SW Fifth Ave. (at SW Morrison St.). www.nike.com. ℂ **503/221-6453**.

Nordstrom ★★★ DEPARTMENT STORE Directly across the street from Pioneer Courthouse Square, Nordstrom is a top-of-the-line department store that originated in Seattle and takes great pride in its personal service and friendliness. It is devoted almost exclusively to women's and men's fashion; shoppers can find topnotch shoes, jewelry, accessories, and cosmetics here. 701 SW Broadway. www.nordstrom.com. ℂ **503/224-6666**. Also at 1001 Lloyd Center. (ℂ 503/287-2444) and 9700 SW Washington Square Rd., Tigard (ℂ 503/620-0555).

Nordstrom Rack ★★★ DISCOUNT DEPARTMENT STORE They've ratcheted things up and don't have the kind of unbelievable deals that used to lure me here, but you can still find great bargains on high-quality, still-in-fashion looks for men and women. 245 SW Morrison. www.nordstrom.com. ℂ **503/299-1815**.

Portland Outdoor Store ★★ CLOTHING/ACCESSORIES In business since 1919, this Western-wear store is a Portland institution that feels little changed from decades ago. The big neon sign out front and the old general store atmosphere inside are enough to draw even people who aren't into playing cowboy or cowgirl. Look for Pendleton shirts, leather boots and belts, and Western garb that is meant to be worn in real-life situations. 304 SW Third Ave. ℂ **503/222-1051**.

The Portland Pendleton Shop ★ CLOTHING Pendleton wool is as much a part of life in the Northwest as forests and salmon. This company's fine wool fashions for men and women define a casual, comfortable, and warm Northwestern look, and beautiful Pendleton blankets have warmed generations of Northwesterners through long, chilly winters. 900 SW Fifth Ave. www.pendleton-usa.com. ℂ **503/242-0037**.

GIFTS, SOUVENIRS & SPECIALTY STORES

Canoe ★★★ HOUSEWARES/GLASSWARE/HOME DECOR This is the only store in downtown Portland where I actually see people window-shopping. Canoe is simple and sleek and sells only high-quality, well-made items. The emphasis here is on clean, simple, timeless designs. There's a little bit of everything here, although look especially for Finnish and Swedish glassware, furniture, and lighting. 1136 SW Alder St. www.canoeonline.net. ℂ **503/889-8545**.

Made in Oregon ★★ LOCAL SPECIALTIES This is your one-stop shop for all manner of made-in-Oregon gifts, food, and clothing. Every product sold is either grown, caught, or made in Oregon. You'll find smoked salmon, filberts, jams and jellies, Pendleton woolens, and Oregon wines. All branches are open daily. 340 SW Morrison St., Ste. 1300 (in Pioneer Place). www.madeinoregon.com. ℂ **866/257-0938** or 503/273-8719. Also at Portland International Airport (ℂ 503/282-7827) and Lloyd Center mall (ℂ 503/282-7636).

MALLS & SHOPPING CENTERS

Lloyd Center ★★ SHOPPING MALL One of the first covered shopping malls in the country—it opened in 1960—Lloyd Center has kept up with the retail times and remains a popular shopping destination with a Nordstrom, a Macy's, and scores of other small to mid-sized stores, chains, and boutiques. It is also famous for its year-round indoor ice-skating rink. There's a food court and movie theaters, too. My favorite store is **Joe Brown's Caramel Corn** (✆ **503/2872143**), a little slot store beside the skating rink that for over 30 years has been selling absolutely the best caramel corn I have ever found. Between NE Halsey St. and NE Multnomah St., and NE 9th Ave. and NE 15th Ave. ✆ **503/282-2511.**

Pioneer Place ★★ SHOPPING MALL   Just a block from Pioneer Courthouse Square in downtown, this is Portland's most upscale shopping center. Pioneer Place is filled with stores selling designer fashions, jewelry, housewares, bath and cosmetic products, children's games, and much more. There's a food court and movie theaters as well. 700 SW Fifth Ave. (between Third and Fifth aves.). www.pioneerplace.com. ✆ **503/228-5800.**

MARKETS

Portland Farmers Market ★★★ OUTDOOR MARKET   Everyone lights up when they come to this outdoor market, and I don't mean cigarettes. The finest vegetables, fruits, and produce from local farmers brighten shoppers' days, as do foraged mushrooms, handcrafted cheeses, plants, flowers, fish, eggs, spices, jams, jellies, baked goods, and all manner of artisan goodies. Musicians play; people stroll, talk, and sample; and it's Portland all the way. The market is held on Saturdays from 8:30am to 2:30pm on the campus of Portland State University in downtown Portland; it starts up in mid-March and runs until a week before Christmas. South Park Blocks, SW Park and SW Montgomery St. www.portlandfarmersmarket.org.

Portland Saturday Market ★ LOCAL CRAFTS/MARKET   The Portland Saturday Market (held on both Sat and Sun) is a Portland tradition. Every weekend, more than 300 craftspeople sell their wares at this open-air market beside and beneath the Burnside Bridge in Waterfront Park. Some of it is good, some of it is dreck. In addition to the dozens of crafts stalls, you'll find ethnic and unusual foods, and lots of free entertainment. The market is open from the first weekend in March to Christmas Eve, Saturdays 10am to 5pm and Sundays 11am to 4:30pm. Waterfront Park and Ankeny Plaza, SW Naito Pkwy. www.portlandsaturdaymarket.com. ✆ **503/222-6072.**

THE PERFORMING ARTS & NIGHTLIFE

Portland is Oregon's cultural capital, and the city's symphony orchestra, ballet, and opera are all well regarded. A lively theater scene includes plenty of mainstream and fringe theater companies that offer classic and contemporary plays. In summer, festivals move the city's cultural activities outdoors to **Tom McCall Waterfront Park, Washington Park,** and the **Oregon Zoo.**

To find out what's going on during your visit, pick up a copy of *Willamette Week,* Portland's free weekly arts and entertainment newspaper. *The Oregonian,* the city's daily newspaper, also publishes entertainment-related information in its Friday A&E section and in the Sunday edition of the paper.

The Bar & Pub Scene

BARS

Departure ★★   This rooftop bar and restaurant atop **The Nines** hotel in downtown Portland serves good food but also has a remarkable outdoor terrace, very unusual in Portland. People definitely get dressed up to make the scene here, and most of them are under 40. 525 SW Morrison St. www.departureportland.com. ✆ **503/802-5370.**

Portland Performing Arts & Nightlife

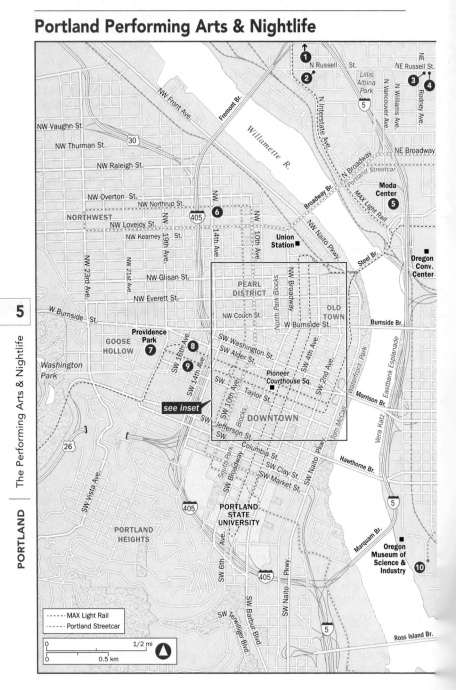

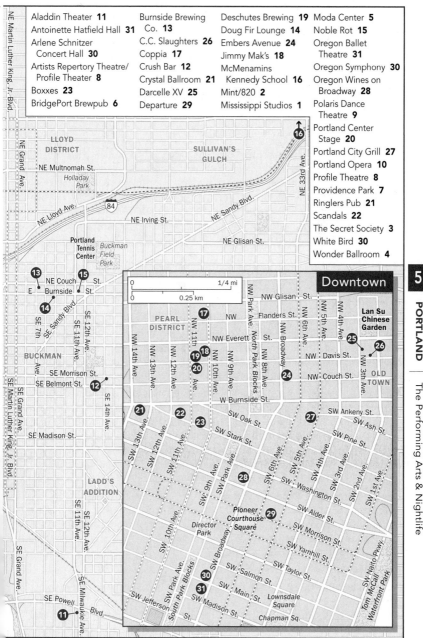

Aladdin Theater **11**
Antoinette Hatfield Hall **31**
Arlene Schnitzer
  Concert Hall **30**
Artists Repertory Theatre/
  Profile Theater **8**
Boxxes **23**
BridgePort Brewpub **6**

Burnside Brewing
  Co. **13**
C.C. Slaughters **26**
Coppia **17**
Crush Bar **12**
Crystal Ballroom **21**
Darcelle XV **25**
Departure **29**

Deschutes Brewing **19**
Doug Fir Lounge **14**
Embers Avenue **24**
Jimmy Mak's **18**
McMenamins
  Kennedy School **16**
Mint/820 **2**
Mississippi Studios **1**

Moda Center **5**
Noble Rot **15**
Oregon Ballet
  Theatre **31**
Oregon Symphony **30**
Oregon Wines on
  Broadway **28**
Polaris Dance
  Theatre **9**
Portland Center
  Stage **20**
Portland City Grill **27**
Portland Opera **10**
Profile Theatre **8**
Providence Park **7**
Ringlers Pub **21**
Scandals **22**
The Secret Society **3**
White Bird **30**
Wonder Ballroom **4**

Downtown

LLOYD DISTRICT
SULLIVAN'S GULCH
PEARL DISTRICT
Lan Su Chinese Garden
OLD TOWN
BUCKMAN
LADD'S ADDITION
Pioneer Courthouse Square
Director Park
Lownsdale Square
Chapman Sq.

5

PORTLAND | The Performing Arts & Nightlife

Mint/820 ★★★   Mixologist Lucy Brennan, owner of this swanky place, single-handedly turned Portland into a town full of cocktail connoisseurs. Using fresh fruit juices, purées, and unusual ingredients, Brennan reinvented the cocktail and set in motion the city's craft cocktail obsession. Beet-infused martini or creamy avocado cocktail, anyone? 816 N. Russell St. www.mintand820.com. ℰ **503/284-5518.**

Portland City Grill ★★   Located way up on the 30th floor of "Big Pink," Portland's tallest building, this restaurant/bar has the best view in all of downtown. Come for the great happy hour so you can catch the sunset and a little live piano music with your singles scene. Unico/U.S. Bancorp Tower, 111 SW Fifth Ave. www.portlandcitygrill.com. ℰ **503/450-0030.**

WINE BARS

Coppia ★★   Located in the heart of the Pearl District, this is Portland's swankiest wine bar. There are lots of good wines, as well as a very creative full menu. Try pasta dishes like risotto with cauliflower, or oxtail agnolotti. Coppia owner Timothy Nishimoto is also a member of Portland's popular band Pink Martini. 417 NW 10th Ave. www.coppiaportland.com. ℰ **503/295-9536.**

Noble Rot ★★★   Located on the fourth floor of a modern Lower Burnside building, this stylish wine bar has a killer view of the downtown Portland skyline. You can get various wine flights, and there are plenty of Oregon vintages available. The wine bar also serves excellent food. Signature menu faves include an endive, beer, blue cheese, and hazelnut salad; onion tart; and a super mac and cheese. (For the record, noble rot is a type of grape fungus utilized in the production of sweet dessert wines.) 1111 E. Burnside St. www.noblerotpdx.com. ℰ **503/233-1999.**

Oregon Wines on Broadway ★★★   With just a handful of stools at the bar and a couple of cozy tables, this tiny place is the best spot in Portland to learn about Oregon wines. On any given night there will be 30 Oregon pinot noirs available by the glass, and five white wines as well. 515 SW Broadway. www.oregonwinesonbroadway.com. ℰ **800/943-8858** or 503/228-4655.

BREWPUBS

Portland, or "Beervana," sits at the epicenter of the Northwest craft brewing explosion.

Brewpubs of all shapes and sizes have become central to Portland's identity, and they are great spots to mix with the locals, order some good food, and taste the extraordinary range of handcrafted beers that are now available.

BREWING UP AN empire

With dozens of brewpubs in the metropolitan area, the McMenamins chain is Portland's biggest brewpub empire. The McMenamin brothers didn't exactly start the Portland brewpub phenomenon, but they have expanded its boundaries and put their stamp on the beer culture of Portland by saving, restoring, and converting several historic buildings—including a former poor farm and an elementary school (see p. 123). They also originated a brewpub concept where patrons can sip beer, eat pizza, and watch a movie. Some of the properties (**Crystal Hotel** ★ and **Kennedy School** ★★★, for example, see p. 124 and p. 123, respectively) now serve as funky hotels with restaurants. The McMenamins' commitment to architectural preservation and their strong belief in family-friendly neighborhood pubs have made their properties popular among all age groups. If I had to recommend one McMenamins' property to visit, it would be Kennedy School. McMenamins' beers can hold their own with any brew in Portland, and the food is filling and tasty, but it's not haute cuisine. For a complete list of the brothers' brewpubs, breweries, and historic hotels, visit **www.mcmenamins.com**.

Downtown

Ringlers Pub ★ BREWPUB With mosaic pillars framing the bar, Indonesian antiques, and big old signs all around, this cavernous place is about as eclectic a brewpub as you'll ever find. A block away are the two associated pubs of **Ringlers Annex,** 1223 SW Stark St. (✆ **503/384-2700**), which occupies a flatiron-shaped building. One of these pubs is below street level with a beer cellar feel, and the other has walls of multi-paned glass. 1332 W. Burnside St. www.mcmenamins.com. ✆ **503/225-0627.**

Northwest Portland

BridgePort Brewpub ★★ BREWPUB Large and perennially busy, this brewpub and restaurant in a former warehouse in the Pearl District is one of Portland's oldest. There are eight or more BridgePort beers on tap and a filling menu of pub food. 1313 NW Marshall St. www.bridgeportbrew.com. ✆ **503/241-3612.**

Deschutes Brewing ★ BREWPUB Located in a converted industrial space, this brewpub has a mountain lodge style similar to that of the famous Timberline Lodge on Mount Hood. There is always a wide range of beers on tap. 210 NW 11th Ave. www.deschutesbrewery.com. ✆ **503/296-4906.**

Southeast

Burnside Brewing Co. ★★★ BREWPUB This gastro-brewpub is a standout because of its creative cooking and industrial-chic decor. Oh yes, the beers are great, too. 701 E. Burnside St. www.burnsidebrewco.com. ✆ **503/946-8151.**

Northeast & North Portland

McMenamins Kennedy School ★★ BREWPUB The local McMenamins brewpub empire took an old Northeast school and turned it into a brewpub, beer garden, movie-theater pub, and even a hotel (see p. 123). Order up a pint and wander the halls to check out all the cool artwork. 5736 NE 33rd Ave. www.kennedyschool.com. ✆ **503/249-3983.**

The Club & Music Scene
ROCK, BLUES & FOLK

Aladdin Theater ★★   This former movie theater now serves as one of Portland's main venues for touring performers. The very diverse musical spectrum represented includes blues, rock, ethnic, country, folk, and jazz. 3017 SE Milwaukie Ave. www.aladdin-theater.com. ✆ **503/234-9694.**

Crystal Ballroom ★★★   The Crystal Ballroom first opened in 1914 and has since hosted performers ranging from early jazz musicians to James Brown, Marvin Gaye, and the Grateful Dead. The McMenamin Brothers (of local brewing fame) renovated the ballroom in 1997 and refurbished its famous "floating" dance floor, which sits on ball bearings. The venue now hosts a variety of performances and special events nearly every night of the week. **Lola's Room,** a smaller version of the Ballroom, is on the second floor and also has a floating dance floor. **Ringlers Pub** occupies the ground floor. 1332 W. Burnside St. www.danceonair.com. ✆ **503/225-0047.** Cover $5–$30.

Doug Fir Lounge ★★   Log cabin styling meets Scandinavian modern at this eclectic underground alt-rock club in the lower Burnside neighborhood of southeast Portland. The club is associated with the **Jupiter Hotel** ★★ (see p. 125). 830 E. Burnside St. www.dougfirlounge.com. ✆ **503/231-9663.** Cover $10–$20.

Mississippi Studios ★   This little performance space in north Portland has become one of the city's premier alternative music venues; the calendar here is both eclectic and affordable. 3939 N. Mississippi Ave. www.mississippistudios.com. ✆ **503/288-3895.** Cover $5–$10.

Wonder Ballroom ★   Originally opened in 1914 as the hall for the Ancient Order of Hibernians (I didn't know Hibernians could dance) and now on the National Register of Historic Places, the Wonder Ballroom is another of Portland's popular restored ballrooms rededicated to everything from hip-hop to swing to bluegrass. Best of all, **Toro Bravo** ★★★ (p. 134), one of my favorite Portland restaurants, is on the same block. 128 NE Russell St. www.wonderballroom.com. ✆ **503/284-8686.** Cover $10–$25.

JAZZ

Jimmy Mak's ★★   This Pearl District club is the best place in Portland to catch live jazz—it's considered one of the best jazz clubs in the country. There are great resident groups on weeknights and guest performers on weekends. 221 NW 10th Ave. www.jimmymaks.com. ✆ **503/295-6542.** Cover $10–$30.

The Secret Society ★★   Gypsy jazz, vintage jazz, Texas swing, big band, jug band, klezmer—you just won't find a more eclectic blend of music than at this second-floor nightclub in north Portland. Not only does this place showcase some of Portland's most distinctive acts, it also does free 6pm shows several nights a week. 116 NE Russell St. www.secretsociety.net. ✆ **503/493-3600.**

CABARET

Darcelle XV ★   In business since 1967 and run by Portland's best-loved drag queen, this cabaret is a campy Portland institution with a female-impersonator show that's been a huge hit for years. There are shows Wednesday through Saturday, catering more to a suburban straight audience than a gay one. 208 NW Third Ave. www.darcellexv.com. ✆ **503/222-5338.** Cover $20.

5

The Performing Arts & Nightlife

PORTLAND

The Gay & Lesbian Nightlife Scene

DANCE CLUBS

Boxxes ★   The crowd here is generally under 30. 1025 SW Stark St. www.boxxes.com. ℂ **503/226-4171.** Cover free–$5.

C.C. Slaughters ★   Popular with a young crowd, this big Old Town nightclub and martini lounge spins different dance sounds every night. 219 NW Davis St. www.ccslaughters pdx.com. ℂ **503/248-9135.** No cover.

Crush Bar ★★   This hetero-friendly Southeast bar attracts a diverse crowd and has DJs spinning dance tunes Friday and Saturday nights. 1400 SE Morrison St. www.crushbar.com. ℂ **503/235-8150.** Cover $5–$10 weekends.

The Embers Avenue   Though primarily a gay disco, Embers is also popular with straights. There are always lots of flashing lights and sweaty bodies going until the early morning. 110 NW Broadway. ℂ **503/222-3082.** Cover $5–$7 weekends.

Scandals ★   A gay Portland institution for more than 30 years, this casual and friendly bar and restaurant has karaoke nights and daily specials and hosts a more mature crowd. 1125 SW Stark St. www.scandalspdx.com. ℂ **503/227-5887.** No cover.

Dance

Oregon Ballet Theatre ★★   OBT is best loved for its performances of *The Nutcracker* every December. The rest of the season includes other classics along with contemporary ballets. Keller Auditorium, 222 SW Clay St. www.obt.org. ℂ **888/922-5538** or 503/222-5538.

Polaris Dance Theatre ★★   It's hard to characterize this company or to fit it into any kind of dance pigeonhole. The choreography is created by resident artists and the dancers have real bodies. The result is engaging, inventive, and sometimes startling works. 1501 SW Taylor St. www.polarisdance.org. ℂ **503/360-1127.**

White Bird ★★★   Fans of modern dance should check out what's being produced by White Bird—and where, as venues can vary. This organization brings in celebrated companies like Twyla Tharp Dance, the Merce Cunningham Dance Company, the Paul Taylor Dance Company, and the Alvin Ailey American Dance Theater, as well as emerging international dance troupes of all kinds. Arlene Schnitzer Concert Hall, 1037 SW Broadway. www.whitebird.org. ℂ **503/245-1600.**

Opera, Dance & Classical Music

Oregon Symphony ★★★   Founded in 1896, the Oregon Symphony is the oldest symphony orchestra on the West Coast. Each year between September and May, the symphony stages several series, including classical, pops, and children's concerts. Under the leadership of conductor Carlos Kalmar, it's become one of the top ensembles in the U.S. Arlene Schnitzer Concert Hall, 1037 SW Broadway. www.orsymphony.org. ℂ **800/228-7343** or 503/228-1353.

Portland Opera ★★   This highly regarded company offers five different productions a year that include grand opera, contemporary opera, chamber opera, and occasionally world premieres. The season runs September through May. Keller Auditorium, 222 SW Clay St. www.portlandopera.org. ℂ **503/241-1407** or 503/241-1802 for box office.

Chamber Music Northwest ★★★ Summer is the time for Portland's annual, outstanding chamber music binge, a month-long series that starts in late June and attracts the world's finest chamber musicians. Performances are held at Reed College and St. Mary's Cathedral. www.cmnw.org. ✆ **503/294-6400.**

The Performing Arts

For the most part, the Portland performing arts scene revolves around the **Portland Center for the Performing Arts (PCPA),** 1111 SW Broadway (www.portland5.com; ✆ **503/248-4335**), which comprises five performance spaces in three buildings. The **Arlene Schnitzer Concert Hall** ★★, 1037 SW Broadway, known locally as the Schnitz, is a restored 1920s movie palace that still displays the original Portland theater sign and marquee out front and is home to the Oregon Symphony. This hall also hosts popular music performances, lectures, and many other special events. Directly across Main Street from the Schnitz, at 1111 SW Broadway, is the **Antoinette Hatfield Hall.** This building, constructed in the 1980s, houses the **Newmark** and **Dolores Winningstad theaters** and **Brunish Hall.** The two theaters host productions by local and visiting companies and performers.

A few blocks away from this concentration of venues is the 3,000-seat **Keller Auditorium,** 222 SW Clay St., home of **Portland Opera,** the **Oregon Ballet Theatre,** and a venue for traveling Broadway shows.

One other downtown performing arts venue worth checking out is the **Old Church** ★★, 1422 SW 11th Ave. (www.oldchurch.org; ✆ **503/222-2031**). Built in 1883, this wooden Carpenter Gothic church is a Portland landmark and serves as a concert venue; every Wednesday at noon it hosts free lunchtime concerts.

Theater

Artists Repertory Theatre ★★ This long-established theater company stages Broadway hits and often includes a world premiere in its season. 1515 SW Morrison St. www.artistsrep.org. ✆ **503/241-1278.**

Portland Center Stage ★★ Portland's largest professional theater company performs in the Gerding Theater at the Armory, a converted armory in the Pearl District. The company stages a combination of classic and contemporary plays and musicals during its September-to-June season. 128 NW 11th Ave. www.pcs.org. ✆ **503/445-3700.**

Profile Theatre ★★ Profile stages the works of only one playwright per year (the hits *and* the flops), allowing theatergoers to see the full spectrum of an artist's creative development. They share space with Artists Repertory Theater. 1515 SW Morrison St. www.profiletheatre.org. ✆ **503/242-0080.**

SPECTATOR SPORTS

Moda Center is home to the Portland Trail Blazers and is the main focal point of Portland's **Rose Quarter.** In addition to the Moda Center, this sports and entertainment neighborhood includes Veterans Memorial Coliseum (once the Trail Blazers' home, now host to a junior ice hockey team) and several restaurants and bars. Tickets to events are sold through the **Rose Quarter** box office (www.rosequarter.com; ✆ **503/797-9619**). To reach the stadiums, take the Rose Quarter exit off I-5. Parking is expensive, so you might want to consider the MAX light rail line from downtown Portland. **Providence Park** (www.providenceparkpdx; ✆ **503/554-5400**), near downtown, is a much-smaller outdoor sports venue used for soccer and Division I football. It's easily reached by MAX light rail.

Basketball

The NBA's **Portland Trail Blazers** (www.nba.com/blazers; ℭ **503/797-9600**) do well enough every year to have earned a very loyal following. Unfortunately, they have a habit of not quite making it all the way to the top. The Blazers pound the boards at the Moda Center (see above). Call for current schedule and ticket information.

Soccer

Major League Soccer's **Portland Timbers** (www.portlandtimbers.com; ℭ **503/553-5550**), play at **Providence Park,** 1844 SW Morrison St., near downtown Portland (see above).

DAY TRIPS FROM PORTLAND

Why do you think everyone loves Portland so much? Of course it's the city itself, but it's also because of what's just outside the city. Some of the most beautifully diverse landscapes in the country (okay, let's say the world) can be visited and enjoyed on day trips from Portland. Below, I've provided a handful of options that range from the dramatic splendor of Mount Hood and the Columbia River Gorge to the rural, rolling hills of the wine country. You could also make a day trip to the Oregon coast. Astoria, Seaside, Cannon Beach, Lincoln City, and the Three Capes Scenic Loop—all described in chapter 6—are excellent day trip possibilities.

THE WINE COUNTRY

Newberg: 25 miles SW of Portland; Dundee: 27 miles SW of Portland; McMinnville: 38 miles SW of Portland

Oregon is famous for its pinot noirs, but these exceptional wines are produced in such small quantities that they usually can't be found outside the region. They are part and parcel of Portland's palate and available at every good restaurant and wine store—even supermarkets. If you want to sample a few of Oregon's exemplary wines and enjoy some scenic countryside at the same time, spend an afternoon or weekend visiting the wineries in what Portlanders simply call the "wine country."

Wine is grown in more than one area of Oregon, but the part of the wine country closest to Portland is in the **North Willamette Valley,** which begins in the town of **Newberg** and extends south to **McMinnville** along Ore. 99W. Throughout this region you'll find good restaurants and inns, so you'll never be too far between wining and dining or sipping and sleeping.

Essentials

GETTING THERE You'll find the heart of wine country between Newberg and McMinnville, along Ore. 99W, which heads southwest from Portland.

VISITOR INFORMATION The **Willamette Valley Visitors Association** (www.oregonwinecountry.org; ℭ **866/548-5018**) is a good source of information on this area. For more about the Oregon wine scene, including a calendar of winery events, pick up a copy of *Oregon Wine Press* (www.oregonwinepress.com), a monthly magazine available at area wine shops and wineries. The **Willamette Valley Wineries**

STICK TO THE pinots

For the most part, you can forget about cabernet sauvignon, merlot, and zinfandel while you're here. **The Willamette Valley** just isn't hot enough to produce these varietals. With the exception of southern Oregon wineries and a few Willamette Valley wineries that buy their grapes from warmer regions, Oregon wineries have, thankfully, given up on trying to produce cabs and zins. The wines of the Willamette Valley are primarily the cooler-climate varietals traditionally produced in Burgundy, Alsace, and Germany. Pinot noir is the uncontested leader of the pack, with pinot gris running a close second. gewürztraminer and Riesling are also produced, and with the introduction of early ripening Dijon-clone chardonnay grapes, the region is finally beginning to produce chardonnays that can almost compete with those of California. A handful of wineries also make sparkling wines, which are often made from pinot noir and chardonnay grapes.

Association (www.willamettewines.com; ℂ 503/646-2985) publishes a free map and guide to the local wineries. You can pick up a copy at almost any area winery.

FESTIVALS   The most prestigious festival of the year, and certainly the most expensive ($900 a ticket) is the **International Pinot Noir Celebration,** in McMinnville (www.ipnc.org; ℂ 800/775-4762 or 503/472-8964), held every year on the last weekend in July or first weekend in August. The 3-day event includes tastings, food, music, and seminars. This high-end event is for wine and food connoisseurs and snobs and has to be reserved far in advance. It's better to simply make your own tour of the vineyards.

Touring the Wineries

Forget pretentiousness, grand villas, celebrity wineries, and snobbish waiters—this is not Napa Valley. Oregon wineries for the most part are still small establishments. Although in recent years more and more well-capitalized wineries have been opening with the sole purpose of producing high-priced pinot noir, many of the region's wineries are still family-owned and -operated and produce moderately priced wines.

Wine country begins only a few miles west and southwest of Portland. Approaching the town of Newberg on Ore. 99W, you leave the urban sprawl behind and enter the rolling farm country of Yamhill County. These hills form the northern edge of the Willamette Valley and provide almost ideal conditions for growing wine grapes. The views from these hills take in the Willamette Valley's fertile farmlands as well as the snow-capped peaks of the Cascades.

For anyone simply interested in tasting a little Oregon wine, the wineries along Ore. 99W are a good introduction. Those with more than a passing interest will want to explore the wineries that are located up in the hills a few miles off the highway.

At most wineries, you'll be asked to pay a tasting fee, usually $5—this fee is often waived if you buy some wine. In the past few years, as pinot noir prices have risen into the $40 to $60 range, tasting room fees have also been creeping up. At some of the more prestigious wineries, you may have to pay a tasting fee between $10 and $20.

The Wine Country

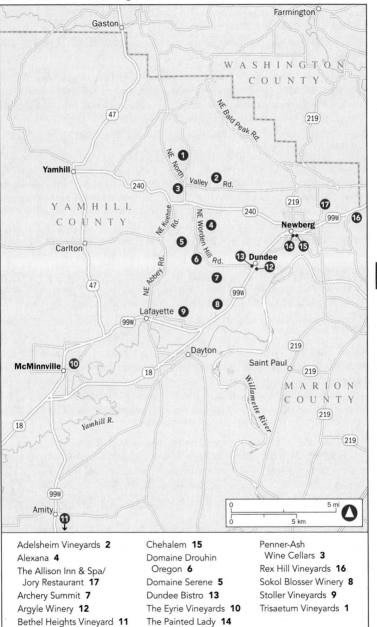

The Best Wineries

Adelsheim Vineyard ★   This winery has been around since the 1970s and consistently produces well-regarded pinots. The single-vineyard wines here are the standouts. You can call ahead to arrange a tour ($40–$150).

16800 NE Calkins Ln, Newberg. www.adelsheim.com. *C* **503/538-3652.** Tasting fee $15. Daily 11am–4pm.

Alexana ★★   The wines at Alexana are made by Lynn Penner-Ash, one of Oregon's top winemakers (her own winery is just a short drive away), and they are every bit as good as the wines from her own label. Pinot noirs include an estate bottling and a vintage from Shea, considered one of the best vineyards in the state.

12001 NE Worden Hill Rd., Newberg. www.alexanawinery.com. *C* **503/537-3100.** Tasting fee $15. Daily 11am–5pm.

Archery Summit ★★★   With big wines, a big winery, and a big reputation, Archery Summit is one of Oregon's premier producers of pinot noir. Only pinot noir is produced, and the grapes all come from Archery Summit's own vineyards. Wines are aged almost exclusively in new-oak barrels and spend time in some of the only barrel-aging caves in the state.

18599 NE Archery Summit Rd., Dayton. www.archerysummit.com. *C* **503/864-4300.** Tasting fee $15–$45. Daily 10am–4pm. West of Dundee on Ore. 99W; turn right on Archery Summit Rd.

Argyle Winery ★★★   Located right on the highway in Dundee, this winery is best known for its sparkling wines and chardonnay, but also produces pinot noir. Due to traffic congestion in Dundee, this winery is best visited when heading east on Ore. 99W.

691 Ore. 99W, Dundee. www.argylewinery.com. *C* **888/427-4953** or 503/538-8520. Tasting fee $10–$22. Daily 11am–5pm.

Bethel Heights Vineyard ★★★   Set high on a hill and surrounded by more than 50 acres of grapes, Bethel Heights primarily produces chardonnays and fabulous pinot noirs.

6060 Bethel Heights Rd. NW, Salem. www.bethelheights.com. *C* **503/581-2262.** Tasting fee $5. Feb–Nov Tues–Sun 11am–5pm; Dec Sat–Sun 11am–5pm; Jan by appointment. From Ore. 221 in Lincoln, take Zena Rd. west and turn right on Bethel Heights Rd.

Chehalem ★   At this tasting room, on the eastern edge of downtown Newberg, you can sample the wines of one of Oregon's most respected wineries. Reliable pinot noirs can be found here, as can good chardonnay, pinot gris, and pinot blanc (a less common white wine). You'll also find Riesling and Grüner Veltliner here. Tours of the nearby winery are offered Wednesday through Saturday at 11am ($25); reservations are required.

106 S. Center St., Newberg. www.chehalemwines.com. *C* **503/538-4700.** Tasting fee $15, tours $25. Daily 11am–5pm.

Domaine Drouhin Oregon ★★★   Years ago, when France first heard that Oregon wineries were making pinot noir, most French winemakers scoffed. Not Maison Joseph Drouhin of Burgundy; the family bought land in the Red Hills of Dundee and planted vines. Today the Burgundian-style wines of Domaine Drouhin Oregon are superb examples of old-world winemaking—silky, seductive, and well balanced. Tours of the winery ($25) are available by reservation.

6750 Breyman Orchards Rd., Dayton. www.domainedrouhin.com. *C* **503/864-2700.** Tasting fee $10, tours $25. July–harvest (Oct) daily 11am–4pm; other months Wed–Sun 11am–4pm.

West of Dundee on Ore. 99W; turn right on McDougall Rd. and right again onto Breyman Orchards Rd.

Domaine Serene ★★★ Located across the road from Domaine Drouhin Oregon, this is another of Oregon's top wineries, with an impressive winemaking facility and the impressive prices ($42–$75) to prove it. Great ratings from *Wine Spectator* have made these wines some of the most sought after in the state. Pinot noir, chardonnay, and Syrah are produced here.

6555 NE Hilltop Lane, Dayton. www.domaineserene.com. ✆ **866/864-6555** or 503/864-4600. Tasting fee $15–$60. Wed–Mon 11am–4pm. West of Dundee on Ore. 99W; turn right on McDougall Rd. and right again onto Breyman Orchards Rd.

The Eyrie Vineyards ★★ This winery is the oldest producer of pinot noir in Oregon and was responsible for putting Oregon on the international wine map in 1979 and 1980, when its 1975 pinot noir won major competitions in France. Eyrie was also the first vineyard in America to produce pinot gris, which has since become one of Oregon's top white wines.

935 NE 10th Ave., McMinnville. www.eyrievineyards.com. ✆ **888/440-4970** or 503/472-6315. Tasting fee $5. Wed–Sun noon–5pm.

Penner-Ash Wine Cellars ★★★ Winemaker Lynn Penner-Ash has been on the Oregon wine scene for years, and her winery between Newberg and Yamhill is one of the more impressive facilities in the area. Set high on a hill with a stupendous view, it would be worth a visit even if Penner-Ash didn't produce such excellent wines. The pinot noirs and Syrahs here are out of this world. Tours are offered on Saturday and Sunday at 10am.

15771 NE Ribbon Ridge Rd., Newberg. www.pennerash.com. ✆ **503/554-5545.** Tasting fee $10–$15. Wed–Sun 11am–5pm. From Ore. 240 between Newberg and Yamhill, drive north on NE Ribbon Ridge Rd.

Rex Hill Vineyards ★★★ Set amid mature vineyards on the outskirts of Newberg, Rex Hill is a good first stop in wine country. One of the oldest wineries in Oregon, Rex Hill focuses on higher end pinot noir, which can be outstanding. Also look for good chardonnay and pinot gris for less than $20.

30835 N. Ore. 99W, Newberg. www.rexhill.com. ✆ **800/739-4455.** Tasting fee $10. Daily 10am–5pm.

Sokol Blosser Winery ★★★ Sokol Blosser sits high on the slopes above the west end of Dundee. Off-dry whites are a strong point here, and the Evolution, a blend of nine different grapes, shouldn't be missed. A walk-through a showcase vineyard provides an opportunity to learn about the growing process, and tours of the winery ($20) are given on Saturday and Sunday by reservation.

5000 Sokol Blosser Ln., Dundee. www.sokolblosser.com. ✆ **800/582-6668** or 503/864-2282. Tasting fee $5–$15. Daily 10am–4pm. Southwest of Dundee off Ore. 99W.

Stoller Vineyards ★★ This large, LEED-certified winery produces not only good chardonnay and pinot noir; with an array of photovoltaic panels on the roof, it also produces electricity. The owners are also co-owners of Chehalem winery (see above), one of the most highly respected wineries in the state. Stoller has a cottage and farmhouse available for rent, with a 2-night minimum.

16161 NE McDougall Rd., Dayton. www.stollervineyards.com. ✆ **503/864-3404.** Tasting fee $10–$15. Daily 11am–5pm. Southwest of Dundee off Ore. 99W.

Trisaetum Vineyards ★★★ Few Willamette Valley wineries produce Riesling, but it's one of the specialties at Trisaetum. In any given vintage, the winery will produce several styles, from dry to sweet. Excellent pinot noir is also produced. Try to get a look at the winery's impressive barrel caves.

18401 Ribbon Ridge Rd., Newberg. www.trisaetum.com. ℭ **503/538-9898.** Tasting fee $10. Wed–Mon 11am–4pm.

Where to Stay
NEWBERG
The Allison Inn & Spa ★★★ Every detail in this luxurious boutique resort inn has been carefully designed to enhance your experience of staying in the Oregon wine country. Natural wood, handcrafted furniture, and fine fabrics lend a calm, earthy glow to the large guestrooms. Balconies and terraces look out on Willamette Valley vistas of vineyards, rolling farmland, trees, and mountains. Original art graces the public spaces, the rooms, and the landscaped gardens. Spa-style bathrooms have sliding panels so you can soak and look out at your fireplace and the scenery outside. Of course, there's also a luxurious on-site spa, with an indoor swimming pool. The inn's restaurant, **Jory ★★★,** is highly acclaimed (see below) The Allison is the only resort in the wine country; its high prices reflect the level of comfort and service you'll find here.

2525 Allison Ln., Newberg. www.theallison.com. ℭ **877/294-2525** or 503/554-2525. 85 units. $350–$400 double. Pets accepted ($50 fee). **Amenities:** Restaurant; lounge; fitness center; Jacuzzi; indoor pool; spa; Wi-Fi (free).

Where to Eat
NEWBERG
Jory Restaurant ★★★ NORTHWEST **The Allison Inn**'s stylish restaurant, under the direction of Chef Sunny Jin (formerly of the French Laundry in Napa), adheres to the same high standards you'll find throughout the resort's property. The windowed walls look south across the Willamette Valley toward the farms and woodlands where much of the food is sourced. Fresh vegetables and herbs are also planted and harvested in the chef's garden on the grounds of the hotel. The menu is seasonal, so you might find starters like roasted delicata squash soup with maple-bacon dumplings, or a freshly picked salad. The preparations are kept fairly simple: If fresh halibut with asparagus is on the menu, the flavors of both will come through clearly; the lamb loin will be perfectly seared. The wine list here is exemplary and features lots of Oregon pinot noirs, some from the Allison's own vineyards. You should reserve in advance here, and request a booth with a view. If you're a real foodie, you might want to sit at the chef's counter and watch the workings of the kitchen.

In The Allison Inn & Spa, 2525 Allison Ln., Newberg. www.theallison.com. ℭ **503/554-2526.** Main courses $14–$45. Mon–Sat 6:30–10:30am, 11:30am–2pm, and 5:30–9pm; Sun 6:30am–2pm and 5:30–9pm.

The Painted Lady ★★★ FRENCH/NORTHWEST ["]Painted Lady" is not a hostess, but the name given to brightly colored Victorian houses like the one that hosts this excellent restaurant in downtown Newberg. The menu makes creative use of local and seasonal Willamette Valley meat, vegetables, and fruits, and Pacific Ocean seafood. Halibut might be crusted with valley hazelnuts (long a local crop), gnocchi might be served with foraged wild mushrooms, locally grown rabbit might be accompanied by a purée of squash and cauliflower from a nearby farm, and a delicious cheesecake dessert might come with blueberry compote. Wines from local vineyards are featured, of course. The bounty of the region is on full display in the three- and four-course fixed price meals that are served here. Advance reservations are a must.

201 S. College St., Newberg. www.thepaintedladyrestaurant.com. © **503/538-3850.** Prix-fixe menus $70–$75. Wed–Mon 5–10pm.

DUNDEE

The Dundee Bistro ★ NORTHWEST   A favorite stop for visitors touring local vineyards near Dundee, this delightful bistro occupies space next to the **Ponzi Wine Bar.** "Bistronomy"—high-quality food served in a casual, inexpensive fashion—is the philosophy here. All the culinary buzzwords are in play: local, seasonal, sustainable, organic. Garbanzo bean and nettle soup might be your starter, followed by homemade pastas, which are worthy second courses or entrees. The carbonara here has oyster mushrooms and leeks. (Those oyster mushrooms, locally foraged, are also used for the mushroom pizza.) You can get a local microbrew or wine to accompany your meal. You'll eat well here, and there's a kid's menu, too.

100-A SW Seventh St., Dundee. www.dundeebistro.com. © **503/554-1650.** Main courses $11–$24. Daily 11:30am–9pm.

MOUNT HOOD ★★★

Government Camp: 56 miles E of Portland; Timberline Lodge: 60 miles E of Portland

Regal, snow-capped Mount Hood is Portland's mascot, or icon, visible from the city on clear days and an integral part of Portlanders' consciousness. At 11,235 feet, this dormant volcano in the Cascade Range is the tallest mountain in Oregon—and also the busiest, since it's a renowned winter ski destination and a year-round outdoor playground within an easy day trip of Portland.

The mountain is just one feature—albeit the most spectacular one—of the 1.1 million-acre **Mount Hood National Forest.** Within the forest are some 95 campgrounds and 50 lakes stocked with rainbow, cutthroat, steelhead, and brown trout. The scenic, free-flowing rivers (the Sandy and the Salmon being the most prominent) are known for their fishing, rafting, swimming, and tubing. Both forest and mountain are crisscrossed by an extensive trail system for hikers, cyclists, and horseback riders.

All of this is almost literally in Portland's front yard, about 60 miles east of downtown. A day trip to **Timberline Lodge** serves as a remarkable introduction to the grandeur that is Oregon.

Essentials

GETTING THERE   From Portland, drive east on I-84 to exit 16 (Wood Village) and continue east on U.S. 26 to Government Camp; from there, a well-marked road leads to Timberline Lodge.

VISITOR INFORMATION   For more information on Mount Hood, contact the **Hood River Ranger Station,** 6780 Ore. 35, Parkdale, OR 97041 (www.fs.fed.us/r6/mthood; © **541/352-6002**), which has maps and provides information on permits and road conditions. Online you can also check out www.mthood.info. The commercial site **Mount Hood Territory** (www.mthoodterritory.com) is also packed with useful information, including tips on traveling around the mountain.

Mount Hood

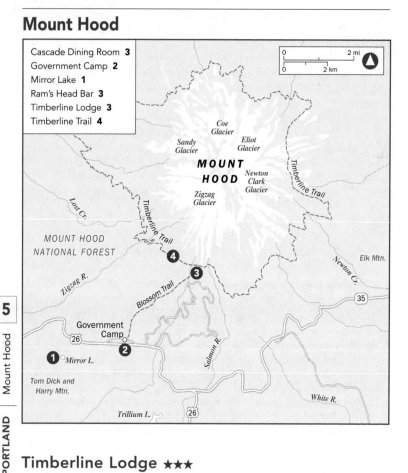

Cascade Dining Room **3**
Government Camp **2**
Mirror Lake **1**
Ram's Head Bar **3**
Timberline Lodge **3**
Timberline Trail **4**

Coe Glacier
Sandy Glacier
Eliot Glacier
MOUNT HOOD
Newton Clark Glacier
Zigzag Glacier
Timberline Trail

Lost Cr.
Timberline Trail
MOUNT HOOD NATIONAL FOREST
Elk Mtn.
Zigzag R.
Newton Cr.
Blossom Trail
35
Government Camp
26
Mirror L.
Tom Dick and Harry Mtn.
Salmon R.
White R.
Trillium L.
26

Timberline Lodge ★★★

Timberline Lodge is one of the greatest and most iconic mountain lodges in the U.S. Constructed during the Great Depression as a WPA project, this classic alpine ski lodge is a paean to the materials and superlative craftsmanship of a bygone era. Both massive and intimate, it has lost nothing of its grandeur or period charm since President Franklin D. Roosevelt came out to inaugurate it. Timberline's enormous stone fireplace, huge exposed beams, and wide-plank floors are as impressive as they ever were—even more so, because this size and quality of wood is no longer available. Woodcarvings, imaginative wrought-iron fixtures, weavings, hand-hooked rugs, and handmade furniture complete the rustic picture.

Staying at Timberline is an atmospheric treat, but it is not a place that was built with the kind of over-the-top luxury some travelers expect today. The simple, cozy rusticity in most of its rooms is not a stylistic gimmick but the real McCoy. The smallest rooms lack private bathrooms, and windows in most rooms were built for durability rather

Exploring Around Timberline Lodge

Besides having a fabulous view of Mount Hood and the surrounding Cascades, and great skiing (see "Hitting the Slopes" box, above), Timberline Lodge is surrounded by wildflower meadows that burst into bloom in July and August. (Hikers should stay on the trails, because this environment above the timberline is a very fragile ecosystem.)

In summer you can ride the lift up to the Palmer Snowfield behind the lodge, even if you aren't skiing. The **Magic Mile Skyride,** which operates daily from 11am to 2pm (until 3pm Friday through Sunday), costs $15 for adults and $9 for seniors and children 7 to 14. By the way, don't forget to bring a jacket or sweater, even if it's August.

than view-power. The lodge has an array of restaurants and lounges that are open to the public, and overnight guests have use of a heated outdoor pool (always nice in the winter, with the snow piled up around it).

Timberline Lodge, OR. www.timberlinelodge.com. ℂ **800/547-1406** or 503/272-3311. 70 units, 10 with shared bathroom. $125 double with shared bathroom; $165–$300 double with private bathroom. **Amenities:** 4 restaurants; 3 lounges; exercise room; Jacuzzi; year-round outdoor pool; sauna; Wi-Fi (free).

Where to Eat

Cascade Dining Room ★★ NORTHWEST/INTERNATIONAL   The Cascade Dining Room in Timberline Lodge is the best restaurant on Mount Hood. It does not have a view, however, and dinner here can be quite expensive (try it at lunch instead). In keeping with the times, the restaurant now tries to be as much "farm to table" as possible, and also uses only locally sourced meats and poultry. The menu is also seasonal. If morel mushrooms are available, definitely try them. Bacon-wrapped pork belly with Dungeness crab is another delicious appetizer. For main courses, the Oregon lamb rib-eye and the bone-in pork chop are both top-notch, and there is always fresh fish on the menu. Some dishes are a bit too complicated, but the overall cooking skill here is quite high.

In Timberline Lodge, Timberline Lodge, OR. www.timberlinelodge.com. ℂ **503/272-3391.** Reservations required for dinner. Main courses $17–$48; lunch buffet $17. Mon–Fri 7:30–10:30am, 11am–2pm, and 5:30–8pm; Sat–Sun 7:30–10:30am, 11am–3pm, and 5:30–8pm.

Ram's Head Bar ★ AMERICAN   The restaurant-bar on Timberline's mezzanine level has the big-window mountain view that the Cascade Dining Room lacks, so naturally everyone wants to come here to sit and stare at the snowpack. The experience doesn't suffer when you add signature cheese fondue and a glass of wine, or a pint of microbrew produced at **Mt. Hood Brewing** just down the road. There are other all-day, anytime choices, too, like delicious clam chowder, charcuterie from Olympic Provisions (a top purveyor in Portland), and artisan cheeses that aren't in a fondue pot. The scene is relaxed and fun and always busy on weekends.

In Timberline Lodge, Timberline Lodge, OR. www.timberlinelodge.com. ℂ **503/272-3391.** Main courses $12–$19. Mon–Thurs 2–11pm; Fri–Sun 11am–11pm.

Columbia Gorge

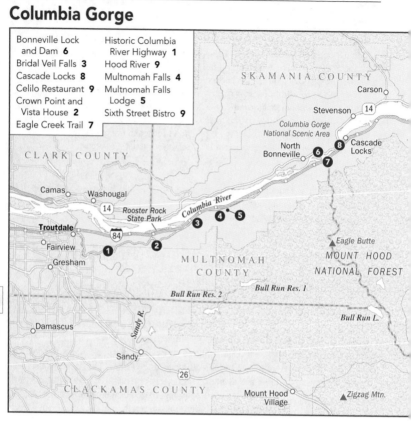

Bonneville Lock and Dam **6**
Bridal Veil Falls **3**
Cascade Locks **8**
Celilo Restaurant **9**
Crown Point and Vista House **2**
Eagle Creek Trail **7**
Historic Columbia River Highway **1**
Hood River **9**
Multnomah Falls **4**
Multnomah Falls Lodge **5**
Sixth Street Bistro **9**

THE COLUMBIA GORGE ★★★

Columbia Gorge National Scenic Area: Begins 18 miles E of Portland

Stretching from the Sandy River in the west to the Deschutes River in the east, the **Columbia Gorge National Scenic Area ★★★** is one of the most breathtakingly dramatic landscapes in the United States. Carved out over countless eons by enormous glaciers and floods of unimaginable power, this miles-wide canyon with its mile-high basalt cliffs is flanked on its north (Washington) side by **Mount Adams** and on its south (Oregon) side by **Mount Hood,** two Cascade peaks that rise more than 11,000 feet. With a string of dramatic waterfalls, including iconic **Multnomah Falls ★★★** (Oregon's highest and most famous waterfall), and forests of Douglas fir rising up from the banks of the Columbia River, the Gorge is a year-round recreational area. Hiking trails lead to hidden waterfalls and cliff-top panoramas while windsurfers race across wind-whipped waters at Hood River, the windsurfing capital of the United States. You can explore and enjoy this unforgettable stretch of the Columbia Gorge on an easy day trip from Portland.

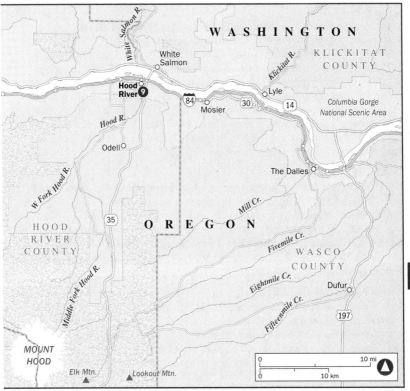

Essentials

GETTING THERE   I-84 and the Historic Columbia River Highway both pass through the Gorge on the Oregon side of the Columbia River. The most scenic route utilizes both highways and is described in the driving tour below.

VISITOR INFORMATION   For information on the Gorge, contact the Columbia River Gorge Visitor's Association, P.O. Box 324, Corbett, OR 97019 (www.crgva.org; ℂ **800/984-6743**), or the **Columbia River Gorge National Scenic Area**, 902 Wasco St., Ste. 200, Hood River, OR 97031 (www.fs.usda.gov/crgnsa; ℂ **541/308-1700**). The **Multnomah Falls Forest Service Visitor Center** (ℂ **503/695-2372**) at Multnomah Falls Lodge has maps of hiking trails and is a great source of information on attractions in the Gorge.

Scenic Driving Tour

Though I-84 is the fastest road through the Columbia Gorge, the Gorge is best appreciated at a more leisurely pace on the **Historic Columbia River Highway ★★★,** which begins 16 miles east of downtown Portland at the second Troutdale exit off I-84.

Opened in 1915, this winding, two-lane highway was a marvel of engineering at the time and opened the Gorge to tourism.

CROWN POINT

Your first unforgettable view of the Gorge comes at the **Portland Women's Forum State Scenic Viewpoint ★★★** at **Crown Point,** which provides a 30-mile vista that is nothing short of spectacular. Topping Crown Point is historic **Vista House,** 40700 E. Historic Columbia River Hwy. (www.vistahouse.com; ✆ **503/695-2240**), an octagonal stone structure perched 733-ft. above the river. It was originally built as a way station for travelers along the scenic highway back in 1918. Step into this lovely building to have a look at its architecture and exhibits that tell the story of the construction of the historic highway and the geology of the Gorge. There's also a coffee shop and a gift shop. Vista House is open 10am to 4pm from March through October, but Crown Point is open year-round, weather permitting.

WATERFALLS

From Crown Point, the historic highway drops down into the Gorge and passes several beautiful waterfalls. The first of these is 249-foot **Latourell Falls ★,** a diaphanous wisp of water that cascades over basalt cliffs stained lime-green by lichen. A 2.3-mile loop trail leads from this waterfall up to the smaller **Upper Latourell Falls.** Continuing east, you'll come to **Shepherd's Dell Falls, Bridal Veil Falls, Mist Falls,** and **Wahkeena Falls,** all of which are either right beside the historic highway or a short walk away.

MULTNOMAH FALLS

At 620 feet from the lip to the lower pool, **Multnomah Falls ★★★** is the tallest waterfall in Oregon and the fourth tallest in the United States. In addition to being the tallest, it's also the most famous waterfall along the historic highway, and the state's most visited natural attraction (in other words, expect crowds). A steep trail leads up to the top of the falls; partway up there's a picturesque arched bridge directly in front of the falls.

The historic **Multnomah Falls Lodge** has a restaurant, snack bar, and gift shop, as well as a **National Forest Visitor Center** with information on the geology, history, and natural history of the Gorge.

BONNEVILLE DAM & EAGLE CREEK

Just after the historic highway merges with I-84 is exit 40, the exit for **Bonneville Lock and Dam ★** (✆ **541/374-8820**). The visitor center here has exhibits on the history of this dam, built in 1938. One of the most important features here is the fish ladder, which allows adult salmon to return upriver to spawn. Underwater windows let visitors watch the fish as they pass through the ladder (note that salmon runs have been greatly diminished—because of this dam, in part). To see how trout, salmon, and steelhead are raised before being released into the river, visit the adjacent **Bonneville Fish Hatchery,** 70543 NE Herman Loop (www.dfw.state.or.us; ✆ **541/374-8393**). A **Sturgeon Viewing Center ★★** allows you to marvel at several immense sturgeons through an underwater window. At this same exit off I-84 (and at Eagle Creek), you'll find access to a section of the **Historic Columbia River Highway State Trail,** a paved multiuse trail that connects the town of Cascade Locks with Bonneville Dam. This trail incorporates abandoned sections of the Historic Columbia River Highway and is open to hikers and bikers. Near the western trail head, you'll also find the trail to **Wahclella**

HITTING THE slopes

There are five downhill ski areas on Mount Hood, though two of these are tiny operations that attract primarily beginners and families. There are also many miles of marked cross-country ski trails. Although opening and closing dates have been readjusted in recent years because of unpredictable weather, the ski season on Mount Hood typically begins around Thanksgiving and runs through March or April. There is also summer snowboarding on the Palmer Snowfield at **Timberline Ski Area.** The single most important thing to know about skiing anywhere in Oregon is that you'll have to have a **Sno-Park permit** ($4/day), which allows you to park in plowed parking areas on the mountain. Permits are available at ski shops and at convenience stores. To visit Mount Hood in the winter, check the website for the **Hood River Ranger Station** (www.fs.usda.gov/mthood) for current weather conditions; you may need snow tires or chains.

Mount Hood Meadows ★★★ (www.skihood.com; ✆ **503/337-2222** or 503/227-7669 for snow report), 12 miles northeast of Government Camp on Ore. 35, is the largest ski resort on Mount Hood, with more than 2,000 skiable acres, 2,777 vertical feet of slopes, five high-speed quad lifts, and a wide variety of terrain. This is the closest Mount Hood comes to having a destination ski resort.

Timberline Ski Area ★★ (www.timberlinelodge.com; ✆ **503/272-3158** or 503/222-2211 for snow report) is the highest ski area on Mount Hood and has one slope that is open throughout the summer, though it can be slushy and attracts snowboarders and not downhill skiers. Mount Hood Meadows is better for general skiing during the winter season, but this is the site of historic **Timberline Lodge.**

If you're interested in cross-country skiing, head to **Mount Hood Meadows Nordic Center ★★** on Ore. 35 ort **Teacup Lake ★★★,** across the highway from the turnoff for Mount Hood Meadows. Teacup Lake is maintained by a local ski club (www.teacupnordic.org) and has the best system of groomed trails on the mountain.

Falls ★, a little-visited yet very picturesque waterfall tucked back in a side canyon. The trail to the falls is less than a mile long and relatively flat.

Beyond Bonneville Dam is **Eagle Creek,** the single best spot in the Gorge for a hike. The **Eagle Creek Trail ★★★** leads past several waterfalls; if you have time for only one hike in the Gorge, it should be this one.

Not far beyond Eagle Creek is **Bridge of the Gods,** a steel suspension bridge that connects Oregon and Washington at the site where, according to a Native American legend, a natural bridge used by the gods once stood. Geologists now believe that the legend is based in fact; there is evidence that a massive rock slide may have once blocked the river at this point.

CASCADE LOCKS

Just beyond Bridge of the Gods, you'll come to **Cascade Locks.** It was at this site that cascades once turned the Columbia River into a raging torrent that required boats to be portaged a short distance downriver. Built in 1896, the Cascade Locks allowed steamships to pass unhindered and made traveling between The Dalles and Portland much easier. With the construction of the Bonneville Lock and Dam, the cascades were flooded, and the locks became superfluous.

The **Cascade Locks Marine Park** at 355 WaNaPa St. serves as the ticket office for the stern-wheeler *Columbia Gorge* ★★ (www.portlandspirit.com; ✆ **800/224-3901** or 503/224-3900), which makes 1- and 2-hour sightseeing cruises and lunch, brunch, and dinner trips on the river (daily except Wed) from May through October. These cruises provide a great perspective on the Gorge. Fares for the 2-hour scenic cruises are $28 for adults and $18 for children. (I don't recommend the more expensive meal cruises because the food is not particularly good.)

HOOD RIVER

Located 62 miles east of Portland, and easily accessible from I-84, the town of **Hood River** is a good place to end your day trip in the Columbia Gorge before heading back to Portland. Long before windsurfing was invented and Hood River began to bill itself as the "Windsurfing Capital of the World," this small Columbia Gorge town was primarily a lumber town and shipping depot for the apples, peaches, pears, cherries, and plums grown in the vast fruit orchards in **Hood Valley.** You can still drive into Hood Valley and buy sweet Bing and Rainier cherries and other fresh-picked fruit at farm stands along Ore. 35, but it's the windsurfing on the Columbia River that draws recreational enthusiasts from around the globe.

The conditions for windsurfing are ideal at this juncture in the mighty river. Every summer, hot air rising over the desert to the east of the Cascade Range sucks cool air up the Columbia River Gorge from the Pacific, and the winds howl through what is basically a natural wind tunnel. They used to curse these winds in Hood River. Not anymore. Windsurfing and kiteboarding have given the town a new lease on life. Pull into the riverside park and watch the action as riders unfurl their sails and kites, zip up their wetsuits, and launch themselves into the melee of hundreds of other like-minded souls shooting back and forth across a mile of windswept water. Aerial acrobatics like flips and 360-degree turns are common sights.

Many of the town's old Victorian and Craftsman houses have now been restored, giving Hood River a historic atmosphere to complement its lively windsurfing scene.

For more information, contact the **Hood River County Chamber of Commerce,** 720 E. Port Marina Dr., Hood River, OR 97031 (www.hoodriver.org; ✆ **800/366-3530** or 541/386-2000), located near the river at exit 63 off I-84.

Hood River sits at the juncture of I-84 and Ore. 35, which leads south to connect with U.S. 26 near the community of Government Camp.

ROOSTER ROCK STATE PARK

If it's a hot summer's day and you're returning to Portland via I-84, you may want to take a dip in the river at **Rooster Rock State Park** ★, with its long sandy beach, and, in a remote section of the park, a clothing-optional stretch. Whether you stop or not, you'll easily spot this riverside monolith, which the explorers Lewis and Clark used as a landmark on their journey down the Columbia to the Pacific Ocean in 1805. Rooster Rock State Park is 13 miles west of Multnomah Falls on I-84.

GORGE TOURS

Because the Columbia River Gorge is so scenic, you might want to leave the driving to someone else so you can take it all in. If so, contact **Martin's Gorge Tours** (www.martinsgorgetours.com; ✆ **877/290-8687** or 503/349-1323). Various tours focus on waterfalls, wildflowers, or wine and cost $49 to $85 per person.

Where to Eat

Celilo Restaurant ★★ NORTHWESTERN   The dinner menu is more interesting, but since you're on a day trip through the Gorge, lunch is probably what you'll have at this upscale and upbeat Hood River restaurant. It's the best place to eat in the Gorge, with a stylish, design-conscious, lots-of-wood interior that evokes a lodge-y Northwest scene. Menus change often, but lunch offerings of locally sourced food typically include a selection of sandwiches: oyster po' boy, pulled pork, barbecued steak, or a Mediterranean vegetarian wrap. There's a good burger, too. Some of the produce is foraged locally, so look for dishes with freshly picked forest mushrooms or greens. There's a good wine and beer list to accompany your meal.

16 Oak St., Hood River. www.celilorestaurant.com. © **541/386-5710.** Main courses $10–$25. Daily 11:30am–3pm and 5–9:30 or 10pm.

Multnomah Falls Lodge ★ AMERICAN   Considering the number of diners served here, this wonderfully scenic old lodge-style restaurant does a pretty good job with its food and service. The building was constructed in 1925 at the base of Multnomah Falls. I'd recommend calling ahead for a reservation and having lunch here on your day trip through the Columbia Gorge. If you're not the designated driver, you might enjoy a huckleberry daiquiri first. The rainbow trout is not wild, but it is from the Northwest, and the grilled salmon is worth trying. There's also mac and cheese, prime rib, a tostada made with Oregon pink shrimp, and a vegetarian choice. For a peek at the thundering falls while you dine, try to get a table in the conservatory room or, in summer, out on the patio.

Historic Columbia River Hwy. (or I-84, exit 31), Corbett. www.multnomahfallslodge.com. © **503/695-2376.** Main courses $13–$25. Daily 8am–9pm.

Sixth Street Bistro ★ AMERICAN/INTERNATIONAL   This two-tiered restaurant is all about enjoying good, sturdy food in a casual environment. On the first floor there's outdoor patio dining, and a lounge with a balcony above. The windsurfing crowd fills this place on summer weekends, sometimes just to enjoy a microbrew. The lunch menu features big club and BLT sandwiches and wraps. Dinner ventures a bit farther afield, with chicken Marsala and baby back ribs joined by Pad Thai noodles and a teriyaki stir-fry. Vegetarian and gluten-free items are also available.

509 Cascade Ave., Hood River. www.sixthstreetbistro.com. © **541/386-5737.** Main courses $7–$18. Sun–Thurs 11:30am–9:30pm; Fri–Sat 11:30am–10pm.

6

THE OREGON COAST

'll never forget the first time I saw, heard, and smelled the Pacific Ocean on the Oregon coast. The pounding roar of the breakers as they rolled into shore; the driftwood-strewn white-sand beach with its giant, forested headland and offshore monoliths; the sharp, salty breath of the sea—it was all so powerful, a sensory massage that put life in a new perspective that was both enlarging and humbling at the same time.

I thought I had died and gone to heaven. Actually, I'd only gone to Oceanside, a tiny hamlet on the Three Capes Scenic Loop between Tillamook and Pacific City. A friend had an old, lopsided, cedar-shingled beach cottage that had been in the family for decades. It had a delicious damp smell to it—the smell of a house that never entirely dried out—and a wood-burning fireplace, a little kitchen and a couple of tiny bedrooms. Oceanside had one sort-of store, a motel, a tavern, and not much else. That's how much of the coast was before the surging real-estate boom that started in the late 1980s and didn't stop until the crash of 2008. When you "went to the beach," as Oregonians said, it was to reconnect with nature, walk on shoreline where you were the only person for miles, explore the wind-socked headlands, get soaked by the rain, make love, read books and play games, fix seafood dinners (or go out to one of the very few restaurants), dream by the fire, and let the lullaby of the sea tug you into a deep sleep.

And that's what a trip to the Oregon coast is still about—except that now you don't have to stay in a motel and do your own cooking, unless you want to, because every kind of accommodation is available, from yurts to luxury hotels; every town has at least one or two restaurants; and all the hotels have giant-screen TVs and free Wi-Fi so you can tune out the very nature you came here to enjoy. What hasn't changed, despite all the new building, is that every inch of the Oregon coast remains open to the public. There are no private beaches anywhere along the 363 miles (584 km) of coastline that stretches from Astoria in the north to Brookings in the south. That's why it's sometimes called "the People's Coast."

As for the weather—well, that may be changing, but you still need to bring a fleece, a hoodie, and a windbreaker, no matter what time of year you visit. Maybe a wet suit, too.

I'm kidding. Sort of.

WEATHER

This is not a coast where you can swim and it's not a coast where you can sunbathe. The very idea is preposterous. This is a coast where people come to *watch storms*, for heaven's sake. The bigger the better. That's not to say that the weather is never benign. August and September are the "calmest" and warmest months, but there can be periods of calm and sunshine throughout the year. And because of the topography of headlands and valleys, the weather blowing in off the Pacific can change from one mile to the next, one *moment* to the next. In July and August, hot weather inland can pull in fogs that don't burn off until the afternoon.

SHORELINE

This is a coastline of remarkable grandeur and endless natural drama, with vast white-sand beaches stretched between massive, forested headlands, along enormous bays and fifty miles of non-stop sand dunes. The surf pounds and surges against offshore haystacks, sea stacks, and monoliths, all of which were gnawed away from the mainland over countless eons by winds and the relentless chomping of the sea. The northern and central stretches of forested shoreline are considered temperate rainforest.

U.S. 101, also called the **Coast Highway,** is the backbone of the Oregon coast. It runs parallel to the ocean, with some inland stretches, and is one of the most scenic highways in the world. The highway is graced at several points by bridges designed in the 1930s by the great bridge engineer Conde McCullough.

In this chapter, I give you the highlights of the Oregon coast. The towns of most interest to first-time visitors—**Astoria, Cannon Beach,** and **Newport**—can be day trips from Portland. Although I didn't have space in this chapter to describe all the

Watching the Whales

Every spring and winter, gray whales migrate along the Oregon coast, often passing within easy viewing distance. Though whalers nearly harpooned them to extinction, these 50-foot-long, 30-ton leviathans recovered following government protection. Now, approximately 18,000 whales ply the 6,000-mile route between the Bering Sea and Mexico, the longest-known migration of any mammal. Southbound whales pass the Oregon coast from early December to early February, peaking at about 30 whales per hour in the last half of December. Northbound whales are less concentrated, passing from March through June and peaking in late March. Several hundred gray whales live along the Oregon coast year-round. If you want to whale-watch, bring binoculars and try to position yourself on high ground so you can see the "blow," the steamy exhalation whales make when they surface. Whale-watching excursions are available in Depoe Bay (p. 209).

6 The Oregon Coast

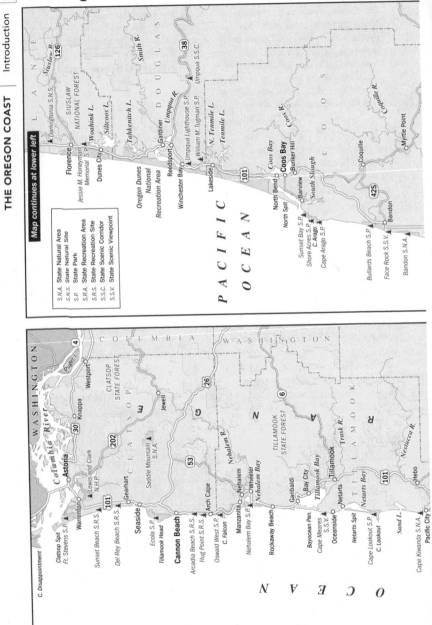

Map continues at lower left

S.N.A. State Natural Area
S.N.S. State Natural Site
S.P. State Park
S.R.A. State Recreation Area
S.R.S. State Recreation Site
S.S.C. State Scenic Corridor
S.S.V. State Scenic Viewpoint

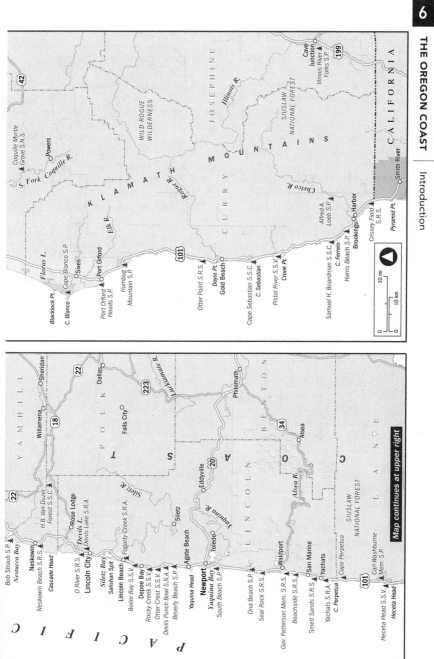

lighting the way: HISTORIC LIGHTHOUSES ON THE OREGON COAST

Of the nine original lighthouses on the Oregon Coast, seven are open to the public and most are still active. If you time it right, you'll get to go inside, take a tour, maybe go up the stairs to the watch room or even higher to the lantern room. (There are also two privately built lighthouses, but neither is open to the public.) The nine original beacons are wave-and-wind-lashed repositories of Oregon's rich coastal history, and among the more interesting buildings you'll see as you travel along the Oregon coast. I've listed most of them in this chapter, but here's a quick run-down of where they are, from north to south.

o **Tillamook Rock Lighthouse** (p. 192): Built on a rocky island 1.2 miles offshore of Tillamook Head, lit in 1880, decommissioned 1957. The lighthouse can be seen from **Ecola State Park** (p. 198) and from Highway 101 south of Cannon Beach; not open to the public.

o **Cape Meares Lighthouse** (p. 201): The shortest lighthouse on the coast is accessible from **Cape Meares State Scenic Viewpoint** (p. 201), the most northerly cape of the **Three Capes Scenic Loop** (p. 200).

o **Yaquina Head Lighthouse** (p. 216): At 93 feet high, it's the tallest lighthouse on the Oregon coast and part of the **Yaquina Head Outstanding Natural Area** (p. 216).

o **Yaquina Bay Lighthouse** (p. 215): The oldest surviving lighthouse on the Oregon coast was built in 1871 and stands on the southern end of **Newport**

(p. 209), just north of the Yaquina Bay Bridge.

o **Heceta Head Lighthouse** (p. 220): The most photographed lighthouse on the Pacific Coast is located off Highway 101 about 12 miles north of **Florence** (p. 220).

o **Umpqua River Lighthouse** (p. 225): Almost identical to Heceta Head (they were built from the same plans), this lighthouse was built on the bluffs overlooking the beach in what is now **Umpqua Lighthouse State Park** (p. 224).

o **Cape Arago Lighthouse:** This lighthouse, built in 1907, is located about 4 miles south of Charleston between **Sunset Bay State Park** (p. 225) and **Shore Acres State Park** (p. 225) on the Cape Arago Highway southwest of Coos Bay.

o **Coquille River Lighthouse** (p. 229): Built on a rocky islet in 1896 and unique, with its cylindrical tower attached to the east side of an elongated, octagonal room, this lighthouse was active until 1939; located in **Bullards Beach State Park** (p. 229) about 2 miles north of **Bandon** (p. 226).

o **Cape Blanco Lighthouse:** Towering above the westernmost point in Oregon, Cape Blanco Lighthouse sits 245 feet above the ocean and is the oldest continuously operating light in Oregon (built in 1870); located in **Cape Blanco State Park** about 4½ miles north of **Port Orford.**

wonders of the wonderful Oregon coast, I hope you will consider driving the entire length, from Astoria to Brookings. Such a trip could be done in 2 days, but I would draw it out over 5 days and savor every scenic mile along the way.

THE NORTH COAST

Starting right at the Columbia River, the border between Oregon and Washington, Oregon's North Coast extends down to Neskowin, close to Lincoln City. This stretch of the coast is backed by the Cascade Range, a line of low (but snowy in winter) mountains that you have to pass over to reach the Pacific. Because it can be easily reached from Portland and I-5, the North Coast is one of the most visited parts of the Oregon coast. There is no end of dramatic sea-scenery and long, white-sand beaches here, but there's also history, for the explorers Lewis and Clark rafted down the Columbia in 1805 and set up their winter camp at **Fort Clatsop,** near present-day Astoria. And **Astoria** itself is the oldest settlement this side of the Mississippi.

Astoria ★★

95 miles NW of Portland

History runs deep in Astoria. In fact, you could say that Oregon's Euro-centric history started right here, where the mighty Columbia River spills into the Pacific Ocean. First, in the winter of 1805/1806, the explorers Lewis and Clark built Fort Clatsop 5 miles south, establishing an American claim to what would become the Oregon Country. Five years later, in 1811, fur traders working for John Jacob Astor arrived at the mouth of the Columbia to set up a fur-trading fort that was named Fort Astoria, in Astor's honor, and became the first permanent American settlement west of the Mississippi. Astoria served as an important shipping port for the huge loads of timber cut in Oregon's virgin old-growth forests and shipped around the world. And because no real roads existed along the Oregon coast, Astoria became a port for the passenger and cargo ships sailing from New York around the Cape of Good Horn, and for the steamers that worked their way up the Oregon coast from San Francisco. Back then, the river teemed with unimaginable numbers of salmon, and when the salmon-canning boom hit in the 1880s, Astoria became a hustling and bustling little city—the second largest in Oregon—and wealthy merchants, sea captains, timbermen, and fish barons began building the ornate, Victorian-style homes that still dot the steep hillsides. Finnish, German, Swedish, and Norwegian immigrants poured into the burgeoning city to work in the canneries and lumber mills and on fishing boats. World War II saw another maritime boom for Astoria, but the city's fortunes waned, and by the 1960s Astoria was a pretty sorry-looking place.

It had incredible potential as a tourist destination, but, as the resources that fueled its growth dwindled or dropped away, it lost its economic oomph and couldn't do much more than struggle along. Now that is changing, and people are talking about an Astoria renaissance. There's a strong community focus here, and as more people have discovered or rediscovered Astoria and the scenic splendor of the Columbia River, old homes and derelict buildings have been restored and taken on a new life. The changeover began with the restoration of the Liberty Theater downtown, a venue that now attracts a wide variety of performers, and the revitalization of the old waterfront area, which is now more accessible because of the 5-mile-long Astoria Riverwalk trail. New hotels have been built, old hotels and historic properties have been restored, and restaurants, coffee houses, and brewpubs have sprung up. Hopefully, as this transformation takes shape, Astoria will not lose its old working-class heritage. There are still buildings here like Suomi Hall, the Finnish community's social center, but other historic places like the old Finnish bathhouse have disappeared.

Because this old city is located just inland from the river's giant, 14-mile-wide mouth, it is more a river port than a beach town. The Coast Guard is a major employer and presence in town, and there's still a big commercial and recreational fishing industry. One new development is that about a dozen cruise ships heading up to Alaska or down to California now dock at Astoria and send their 2,000 or 3,000 passengers into the town for the day or just an afternoon (another reason why new businesses are opening). More controversial is a proposal to turn the city into a port for exporting natural gas. Environmentalists rightly fear that this project will do irreparable harm to the river, and the community is fiercely divided on the issue.

For visitors, Astoria's greatest attraction lies in its hillsides of restored Victorian homes and the scenic views across the Columbia to the hills of southwestern Washington. The combination of historical character, scenic vistas, a lively arts community, and some interesting museums make this one of the most intriguing towns on the Oregon coast.

ESSENTIALS

GETTING THERE From Portland, take U.S. 30 west. From the north or south, take U.S. 101.

GETTING AROUND Astoria has a fairly small downtown core, so you can walk just about everywhere, including to the waterfront. On weekends and in summer (noon–7pm) the restored 1913 **Astoria Riverfront Trolley ★★** (© **503/325-8790;** fare $1) runs between Pier 39 and the Astoria Red Lion Inn, making several stops along the way; the round trip takes about an hour. The 5-mile Astoria **Riverwalk ★★★,** a flat, paved trail between the Port of Astoria and 40th Street, is a perfect way to explore Astoria's revitalized waterfront on foot or by bike.

VISITOR INFORMATION Contact or visit the **Astoria-Warrenton Area Visitor Center,** 111 W. Marine Dr. (www.oldoregon.com; © **800/875-6807** or 503/325-6311), open Monday through Saturday 9am to 5pm (daily summer).

FESTIVALS Astoria is a community-minded city with many local festivals and events that draw visitors from all over. The annual **Fisher Poets Gathering** (www.fisher poets.org; © **503/338-2438**), held in late February (usually at Clemente's restaurant, see p. 186), celebrates the poetry of commercial fishermen and women; you have to be a fisherperson to read your poetry, but everyone is welcome to attend. In late April, the **Astoria Warrenton Crab, Seafood & Wine Festival** (www.oldoregon.com) draws big crowds to the Clatsop County Fairgrounds. In June, the fairgrounds are also the site of the fun-and-food-loving **Scandinavian midsummer Festival** (www.astoriascanfest .com). Also in June, but held at the Liberty Theater, is the celebrated **Astoria Music Festival,** with a surprisingly sophisticated lineup of classical and pop performances. The **Astoria Regatta** (www.astoriaregatta.org; © **800/535-8767** or 503/861-2288), held every year in mid-August, is the city's biggest festival and includes lots of sailboat races. For a complete listing of all the festivals in the area, visit **www.oldoregon.com**.

WHERE TO STAY

Cannery Pier Hotel ★★★ Hands-down, this is Astoria's best hotel. It is beautifully designed and service-oriented, but, because this is Astoria, there is nothing stiff or sniffy about it. The hotel, which opened in 2005, was built atop one of Astoria's old

Astoria

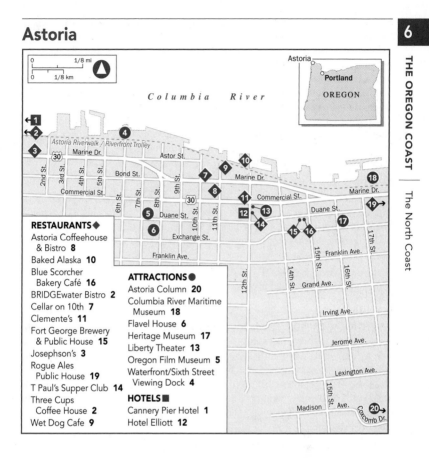

RESTAURANTS◆

Astoria Coffeehouse
& Bistro **8**
Baked Alaska **10**
Blue Scorcher
Bakery Café **16**
BRIDGEwater Bistro **2**
Cellar on 10th **7**
Clemente's **11**
Fort George Brewery
& Public House **15**
Josephson's **3**
Rogue Ales
Public House **19**
T Paul's Supper Club **14**
Three Cups
Coffee House **2**
Wet Dog Cafe **9**

ATTRACTIONS●

Astoria Column **20**
Columbia River Maritime
Museum **18**
Flavel House **6**
Heritage Museum **17**
Liberty Theater **13**
Oregon Film Museum **5**
Waterfront/Sixth Street
Viewing Dock **4**

HOTELS■

Cannery Pier Hotel **1**
Hotel Elliott **12**

cannery piers right on the Columbia River, and it takes advantage of its location by offering wonderful river views from every room. The 1-bedroom corner suites with windows on two sides and a walk-out balcony offer the best outlooks; in one of these you could sit for hours, mesmerized, looking out at the mighty Columbia, the ships and the vast span of the Astoria–Megler Bridge (binoculars are provided in every room). Every room has a gas fireplace to cozy things up and a clawfoot-style soaking tub, and shutters that open out from the tub area to the living area and the view beyond. The decor uses light woods and natural fabrics to create an upscale but unobtrusive Northwest style. In the morning, a barista is on hand to make your special coffee drink with breakfast; there's a spa where you can soak in a warm pool or get a massage or facial; and if it's a nice day, you can hop on one of the complimentary bikes and go for a spin along Astoria's 6-mile River Walk. All in all, this place is just plain great.

10 Basin St. www.cannerypierhotel.com. © **888/325-4996** or 503/325-4996. 46 units. $179–$629 double w/continental breakfast and evening wine and appetizers included. **Amenities:** Bikes; exercise room; sauna; spa; free Wi-Fi.

Hotel Elliott ★   The sign painted at the top of this 6-story building, the tallest in downtown Astoria, says simply, "HOTEL ELLIOTT. WONDERFUL BEDS." The building dates from 1924 and it has always been a hotel, though never quite as nice a hotel as it is now, after its complete overhaul, refurbishment, and reopening in 2005 as a boutique hotel. The re-do bridged the gap between the old hotel and the new one by retaining some of the great vintage features, like Douglas fir doors and detailing, but restyling the room interiors to reflect modern tastes (the beds are new but still wonderful). A muted color palette enhances the sense of calm, and all the windows have been double-paned so the rooms are quiet. Bathrooms have granite counters, tub-shower combinations, and heated floors. Downstairs, to one side of the lobby, there's a pleasant wine bar; in the morning, this is where a continental breakfast is served. On a nice afternoon or evening, head up to the roof garden for a view out over Astoria.

357 12th St. www.hotelelliott.com. ⓒ **877/378-1924** or 503/325-2222. 32 units. $99–$329 double w/continental breakfast included. **Amenities:** Lounge; exercise room; free Wi-Fi.

WHERE TO EAT

The "Astoria renaissance" everyone is talking about definitely extends to the city's ever-expanding restaurant scene. Until just 5 years ago, Astoria was a city with a couple of decent restaurants. Now the area around the restored Liberty Theater at 12th and Commercial has several worthwhile dining spots, and there are also a couple of good places on or near the waterfront.

Baked Alaska ★ NORTHWEST/PIZZA Everyone loves this casual waterfront restaurant and pizzeria, and it's easy to see and taste why. The restaurant takes up an entire pier and offers the most amazing water- and bridge-views—especially from the outdoor tables at the very end, where you'll find the bar (happy hour daily from 3 to 6pm). There's a limited number of soups, salads, and small plates on offer, including oysters on the half shell and a really delicious clam chowder. For mains, lunch or dinner, try one of the signature Baked Alaska sandwiches, created by the chef when he had only one pizza oven and had to be creative. The sandwiches are made with hand-tossed pizza dough, folded and baked in the oven, and filled with smoked salmon, iron steak, grilled chicken breast, pork belly, or vegetables. The handcrafted, brick-oven pizzas here are also worth trying (gluten-free crusts available), and so are the Alaskan cod fish and chips.

1 12th St. www.bakedak.com. ⓒ **503/325-7414.** Main courses $10–$25. Daily 11am–10pm.

BRIDGEwater Bistro ★★ NORTHWEST A step up in the sophistication level from Baked Alaska, this large, attractive bistro in a former cannery near the upscale Cannery Pier Hotel offers an all-purpose, gluten-free-friendly lunch and dinner menu (90% of the menu can be modified to be gluten-free). Even the fish and chips are gluten-free, although you'd never know it. If you're coming for dinner, you might want to the try the Northwest Potlatch, a signature bouillabaisse with Dungeness crab, salmon, crabs, mussels, and scallops in a tomato-pancetta-ginger stock. There are many options here, from small plates to burgers and fresh fish. There's also a good wine and beer list and a good Sunday brunch with seafood specialties.

20 Basin St. www.bridgewaterbistro.com. ⓒ **503/325-6777.** Main courses $10–$32. Mon–Sat 11:30am–8 or 9pm; Sun 11am–8 or 9pm.

Clemente's ★★ SEAFOOD/PACIFIC NORTHWEST This corner restaurant in the "urban renaissance" section of downtown Astoria is casual, like all Astoria restaurants, but it has a crisp formal touch, too, with cloth napkins and heavy cutlery whether you're having lunch or dinner. Clemente's has been around for several years, and it has grown up in that time to become an excellent restaurant for fresh seafood and produce from local suppliers. The menu changes seasonally. For a really satisfying lunch, I would recommend the fresh fish sandwiches; the oyster and halibut are both great and served on chewy rustic bread with non-greasy fries and house-made catsup. You can order fish and chips made from freshly caught halibut, salmon, cod, or oysters. Clemente's, with its airy dining room and cool bar area, is very much a local venture and a good spot to know about.

1198 Commercial St. www.clementesrestaurant.com. $\textcircled{C}$ **503/325-1067.** Main courses $10–$28. Tues–Sun 11am–3pm and 5–9pm.

T Paul's Supper Club ★ AMERICAN/PACIFIC NORTHWEST A touch of whimsy prevails in this cheerful, casual bistro in downtown Astoria. It's not what you might think of as an old-style supper club, but rather a good spot to stop in for lunch or dinner or in between for a snack or a meal. The menu is all over the place, with Caribbean, Mexican, Southern, and Pacific Northwest offerings. One of their most popular offerings is the whopping Boom Boom Salad with chicken or shrimp served on a bed of greens with chopped apple, pear, strawberry, and red onion with bacon and cheese. The burgers and sandwiches are good and, in keeping with the old supper-club shtick, several kinds of steak are available.

360 12th St. www.tpaulssupperclub.com. $\textcircled{C}$ **503/325-2545.** Main courses $9–$28. Mon–Thurs 11am–9pm; Fri–Sat 11am–11pm.

EXPLORING ASTORIA

Astoria is the oldest settlement west of the Rockies, and there's more history here and in the surrounding vicinity than anywhere else along the Oregon coast. Two

---

COFFEE, BEER, WINE & more

Here's a list of some other good spots in Astoria to check out for coffee, beer, smoked salmon, and baked goods.

Smoked Fish & Deli To be in the know in Astoria, you have to know about **Josephson's,** 106 Marine Dr. (www.josephsons.com; $\textcircled{C}$ **800/772-3474** or 503/325-2190), a local seafood-smoking company that opened in 1920 and sells smoked salmon by the pound. It has a take-out deli counter with clam chowder, smoked seafood on rolls, and more.

Coffee For the best latte in town, head down to **Three Cups Coffee House,** 279 West Marine Dr. ($\textcircled{C}$ **503/325-7487**), the coffee house that shares space with Columbia Coffee Roasters. In downtown Astoria you can get good espresso at the **Astoria Coffeehouse & Bistro,** 243 11th St. (www.astoriacoffeehouse.com; $\textcircled{C}$ **503/325-1787**).

Brewpubs Astoria is big on brewpubs. Downtown on the waterfront, there's the **Wet Dog Cafe,** 144 11th St. (www.wetdogcafe.com; $\textcircled{C}$ **503/325-6975**), and at the east end of town, there's the **Rogue Ales Public House,** Pier 39, 100 39th St. (www.rogue.com; $\textcircled{C}$ **503/325-5964**), where you can sometimes watch sea lions just outside the window. Some of the most unusual brews in town are on tap at the **Fort George Brewery & Public House,** 1483 Duane St. (www.fortgeorgebrewery.com; $\textcircled{C}$ **503/325-7468**).

Bakery The **Blue Scorcher Bakery Café,** 1493 Duane St. (www.bluescorcher.com; $\textcircled{C}$ **503/338-7473**), is Astoria's best bakery.

Wine The **Cellar on 10th,** 1004 Marine Dr. (www.thecellaron10th.com; $\textcircled{C}$ **503/325-6600**), is a well-stocked wine shop that has weekly tastings and occasional winemaker dinners.

worthwhile museums (Columbia River Maritime Museum and the Flavel House) will give you a flavor of this port and cannery-city's thriving past, and nearby Fort Clatsop, where the explorers Lewis and Clark wintered in 1805, takes you back even further. But look around the downtown core and you'll see the "new" Astoria reclaiming its old buildings for new uses. And if you have time, drive around some of the old neighborhoods where Victorian-era homes are slowly being reclaimed.

Astoria Column ★★ LANDMARK/VIEW   Constructed in 1926 atop Coxcomb Hill, the landmark Astoria Column stands 125-feet tall and was patterned after Trajan's Column in Rome. On the exterior wall, a mural depicts the history of the area. There are 164 steps up to the top of the column, and on a clear day the view makes the climb well worth the effort. On the way to the Astoria Column, stop by **Fort Astoria,** on the corner of 15th and Exchange streets. A log blockhouse and historical marker commemorate the site of the trading post established by John Jacob Astor's fur traders.

Coxcomb Hill (drive up 16th St. and follow the signs). www.astoriacolumn.org. (✆ **503/325-2963.** Admission by donation. Daily dawn–dusk.

Columbia River Maritime Museum ★★ MUSEUM   Without the Columbia River—the second-largest river in U.S.—there would be no Astoria, and this small, well-done museum in a shingle and glass-fronted building on the riverfront captures the history of the river's exploration, navigation, and commercial uses. Centuries before the Columbia had a name, explorers from different nations had their eye on this mighty waterway, and the museum's collection of rare European maps, dating from the early 1500s to 1792 (when Captain George Vancouver successfully sailed up the river), is something map-lovers will especially enjoy. The problem for most of those explorers, and the problem for vessels today, was that high seas and the Columbia Bar, a shifting sandbar at the river's entrance, made entering the river so treacherous that the area became known as "the graveyard of the Pacific." The museum has a collection of vessels—a Coast Guard rescue ship, a fishing trawler, a sailboat, and the lightship *Columbia*—that illustrate the types of boats found on the Columbia. One vessel on display is a small Japanese fishing boat washed up on a nearby beach after the Japanese tsunami of 2012. Another display features two cannons (or carronades, as they are called) washed ashore after a shipwreck in 1846 and discovered in 2013 after a violent storm uncovered them. There's a section devoted to the enormous salmon canneries in Astoria that began operation in the mid-19th century and lasted until the 1940s. Give yourself about 2 hours if you want to see all the river- and sea-related exhibits in this fascinating museum.

1792 Marine Dr. www.crmm.org. (✆ **503/325-2323.** Admission $10 adults, $8 seniors, $5 children 6–17. Daily 9:30am–5pm. Closed Thanksgiving and Christmas.

Flavel House ★★ MUSEUM/HISTORIC HOUSE   Many fortunes were made in 19th-century Astoria, and the enterprising Captain George Flavel made his by operating the first pilot service to guide ships across the treacherous Columbia River Bar. In 1885, after making his millions, Captain Flavel (1823–1893) had this imposing Queen Anne–style house built for his wife and three children. (As a side note, Captain Flavel was 30 when he married 14-year-old Mary Christina Boelling, the daughter of a German immigrant who ran a boarding house in Astoria.) Your ticket is a calling card that you present when you step into this enormous and ornate home. It's a self-guided tour with docents along the way to answer your questions. How tall are those ceiling anyways? At least 14 feet. The wood used everywhere and for everything, including the commodes, is mostly Douglas fir. Some of the furniture is original, some of it is typical of the period. This was certainly a far more formal age than our own, though the house, with its giant dining room, sitting room, and library, has a lived-in look. (The last daughter, Nelly, lived in the house until 1936.) Enormous it might be, but Mrs. Flavel and her two daughters, even though they moved in rather elevated social circles in Astoria and San Francisco, did all the cooking, most of the cleaning, and washed the dishes themselves. The house and its occupants present a rather fascinating portrait of a certain strata of upper-middle-class society in the rough-and-tumble Pacific Northwest of the late-19th and early-20th century, so you may want to watch the 13-minute video in the ticket office (the former carriage house). The nine trees in the Victorian-style garden around the house—a giant sequoia redwood, a camperdown elm, four cork elms, a bay laurel, a pear tree, and a ginkgo—were obtained by Captain Flavel on his voyages and planted after the house was built.

441 Eighth St. www.cumtux.org. © **503/325-2203.** Admission $6 adults, $5 seniors and students, $2 children 6–17. May–Sept daily 10am–5pm; Oct–Apr daily 11am–4pm.

Heritage Museum ★ MUSEUM   If you have a real interest in the history of Astoria and Clatsop County, this local-history museum housed in the former Astoria City Hall is worth a visit. There's nothing outstanding here, but you'll find collections of Native American and pioneer artifacts as well as archival photographs of the city at various points in its development and the people and personalities who put it on the map.

1618 Exchange St. www.cumtux.org. © **503/325-2203.** Admission $6 adults, $2 children 6–17. May–Sept daily 10am–5pm; Oct–Apr Tues–Sat 11am–4pm.

Waterfront ★★★ HISTORIC NEIGHBORHOOD/PARK   The city of Astoria has worked hard to revitalize its historic Columbia River waterfront and to make it accessible to residents and visitors. There are several places in or near downtown where you can enjoy the views and watch the wildlife (sea lions, bald eagles, herons) and ships from docks that once housed the city's canneries and waterfront businesses. At the **Sixth Street Viewing Dock,** a raised viewing platform provides impressive views of the massive Astoria–Megler Bridge stretching for more than 4 miles across the mouth of the river from Oregon to Washington. At the east end of town, the old cannery on **Pier 39,** 100 39th St. (www.pier39-astoria.com; © **503/325-2502**), was originally built in 1875 and was home to Bumble Bee Seafoods. Today, the restored and spiffed-up cannery is the oldest building on the waterfront, and inside you'll find historic photos of the cannery and **Bridgewater Bistro** (reviewed p. 186); nearby, built on the site of another cannery building, is the upscale **Cannery Pier Hotel** (reviewed p. 184). Sea lions often congregate on the breakwater adjacent to Pier 39. On weekends and daily from June through August (noon–7pm), the restored 1913 **Astoria Riverfront Trolley** (© **503/325-8790;** fare $1) runs between Pier 39 and the Astoria Red Lion Inn, making several stops along the way; the round trip takes about an hour. The 5-mile Astoria **Riverwalk** ★★★, a flat, paved trail between the Port of Astoria and 40th Street, is a perfect way to explore Astoria's revitalized waterfront on foot or by bike.

ASTORIA AFTER DARK

The major performing-arts venue in Astoria is the **Liberty Theater,** 1203 Commercial St. (www.liberty-theater.org; © **503/325-5922**), a beautifully restored 1920s movie palace that now hosts a surprising array of performers and performances throughout the year. If you're here in the summer, you might enjoy a performance of *Shanghaied in Astoria,* a musical melodrama that is staged each year by the **Astor Street Opry**

THE goonies IN ASTORIA

Call me an intellectual snob, but I had never heard of *The Goonies* before I visited the **Oregon Film Museum,** 732 Duane St. (www.oregonfilm museum.org), housed in the old Clatsop County Jail across from the Flavel House and administered by the Clatsop Historical Society. I now know that this 1985 film is something of a cult classic for kids, and that parts of it were filmed in Astoria. This ingenious little museum allows you to make short films of yourself (or selves) using three different Goonie-type sets; the museum will send you a video download of your film. So far, about 30 movies have been filmed in Oregon, and you'll find information and clips of some of them here, plus general information on the movie-making business. What is a gaffer, anyway? Half of the building is not a stage set but the real cells used in the Clatsop County Jail—and in *The Goonies* movie. Kids 8 and older, and particularly those who have seen *The Goonies*, might kick a kick out of this place. Admission is $6 for adults, $2 for ages 6 to 17. Hours are October through April daily 11am to 4pm, May through September daily 10am to 5pm.

Company, 129 W. Bond St. (www.shanghaiedinastoria.com; ✆ **503/325-6104**). Performances are usually held from early July to mid-September.

Fort Clatsop–Lewis & Clark National Historic Park ★★★

5 miles S of Astoria

ESSENTIALS
GETTING THERE From Astoria, head south on U.S. 101 and follow signs.

VISITOR INFORMATION The park's **visitor center** (www.nps.gov/lewi; ✆ **503/861-2471**) is open year-round, mid-June to Labor Day daily 9am to 6pm; Labor Day to mid-June daily 9am to 5pm. Here you'll find interpretive displays, a good bookstore, and park rangers who can provide information on nearby attractions, hiking trails, and other parks.

"Ocian in view! O! The joy!" William Clark wrote in his journal as he stood on a spit of land just south of present-day Astoria in the fall of 1805. He was feeling exultant after the arduous journey he'd undertaken with Meriwether Lewis and the Corps of Discovery, traveling over 2,500 miles west from St. Louis, across the northern plains, over the Rockies, and down the Columbia River to the Pacific. They had achieved their goal and fulfilled Thomas Jefferson's mandate to find a passageway to the west. But Clark had yet to deal with the weather on the northern Oregon coast. After building Fort Clatsop, where the Corps spent the winter, Clark wrote, "O! How horrible is the day waves brakeing with great violence against the shore . . . all wet and confined to our shelters." Throughout that long winter, there were only 5 days when it didn't rain.

An accurate replica of their shelter, a log stockade which they named Fort Clatsop after the local Clatsop Indians who had befriended them, is what you'll see at this national park. Though archaeologists have never been able to pinpoint the exact location of Fort Clatsop, this replica was built within a few yards of where they believe the original fort stood. The design was based on notes and sketches in William Clark's journal.

It's not a large fort. It was built quickly, and it's very basic, with wooden gates at either end and two rows of small, adjoining cabins facing each other across a central courtyard (which would have been mud instead of the bark chips that are there now), and it provides a glimpse of what life was like for these now-legendary explorers during that endlessly wet winter more than 200 years ago. Sacagawea, the 16-year-old Shoshone woman who made the trek with French-Canadian Toussaint Charbonneau and their infant son, occupied the first cabin to your right upon entering. Lewis and Clark shared the cabin next to them. The Corps slept about eight men to a cabin on the other side. These bare, unfinished cabins had an open firepit at one end with a flue for the smoke, hand-hewn wooden beds, and not much else. (You'll appreciate the luxury of a warm dry bed and a hot shower after a visit here.) From mid-June through Labor Day, park rangers clad in period clothing give demonstrations of some of the daily activities that took place at the fort, including flintlock use, buckskin preparation, and candle making.

A path leads down from the fort to a nearby canoe launch area. The explorers traveled south from Fort Clatsop as far as present-day Seaside—where they boiled seawater to make salt and marveled at a beached whale (Sacagawea insisted on accompanying the men to see it)—and north to Cape Disappointment in Washington State. Both of these sites are part of the Lewis and Clark Historical Park, as is the 6.5-mile **Fort to Sea Trail,** which ends in Seaside. Over on the Washington side of the Columbia, there are two installations by artist Maya Lin that were commissioned as part of the Lewis and Clark bicentennial.

On the short trail from the visitor center to the fort, you'll pass a bronze statue of Sacagawea with her baby on her back. This is a long-overdue tribute to the young Shoshone woman who traveled with the expedition as an unpaid guide and interpreter. She was all of 16 and had given birth just 3 months before the Corps of Discovery set off. Our ideas about "history" and history makers have changed drastically over the last couple of decades. The Native Americans who inhabited the coastal regions of the Northwest had a rich and long-evolved culture of their own that preceded the arrival of Lewis and Clark by thousands of years. But however you view their achievements, Lewis and Clark and the men—and woman—who accompanied them, made an incredible journey through an area previously unknown to whites, and their arrival at this spot on the Oregon coast in 1805 marks the beginning of a new era in the settlement of the West.

92343 Fort Clatsop Rd. (off U.S. 101, 5 miles southwest of Astoria). www.nps.gov/lewi. © **503/861-2471.** Admission $3 adults, free for children 15 and under. Mid-June to Labor Day daily 9am–6pm; Labor Day to mid-June daily 9am–5pm.

Cannon Beach ★★★

7 miles S of Seaside, 112 miles N of Newport, 79 miles W of Portland

Weathered cedar-shingle cottages and buildings, picket fences draped with drifts of nasturtiums, quiet gravel lanes, interesting little art galleries and shops, good restaurants and coffee shops, and a long, flat, gorgeous sand beach presided over by massive monoliths, called sea stacks, rising from the surf—what more could you want from an Oregon beach town? If it weren't for all the other people who also think Cannon Beach is the most wonderful place on the Oregon coast, this would be a misty version of heaven. Some say that Cannon Beach suffers from chronic quaintness; others

CANNON BEACH trivia

- **Cannon Beach** was named for a cannon that washed ashore after the U.S. Navy schooner *Shark* wrecked on the coast north of here in 1846.
- Rising 235 feet above the water, Cannon Beach's **Haystack Rock** is the most photographed monolith on the Oregon coast.
- The area's offshore rocks are protected nesting grounds for sea birds. Watch for tufted puffins, something of a Cannon Beach mascot.
- Tillamook Rock is the site of the **Tillamook Rock Lighthouse** (aka "Terrible Tilly"), which was frequently battered by huge storm waves that sent large rocks crashing through the light, 133 feet above sea level. The lighthouse was decommissioned in 1957 and is now used as a columbarium.

complain that it has become too upscale and expensive for its own good. Once, after all, it was the Oregon coast's most renowned artists' community. But now Cannon Beach is as much about upscale shopping in tasteful, tucked-away plazas as it is about being in touch with nature in the form of the Pacific Ocean. But with so many utilitarian and ticky-tacky towns along the coast, I personally think that well-groomed and always-presentable Cannon Beach is one of the top beach towns on the Oregon coast. Despite the crowds, it still has a village atmosphere, and summer throngs and traffic jams can do nothing to assault the dramatic, in-your-face beauty of Haystack Rock, the famous monolith that rises like a giant plum pudding from the pounding waves of the Pacific.

ESSENTIALS

GETTING THERE Cannon Beach is on U.S. 101 just south of the junction with U.S. 26. From Portland, it takes about 1½ to 2 hours to get there by car.

VISITOR INFORMATION The **Cannon Beach Visitor Center,** 207 N. Spruce St. (intersection of Sitka and Spruce; www.cannonbeach.org; © **503/436-2623**) is open daily from 9am to 5pm.

GETTING AROUND The town stretches for about 3 miles between the ocean and Highway 101, and is easily walkable. **Hemlock Street,** the main drag in downtown Cannon Beach, is the town's commercial hub, with a concentration of galleries, boutiques, restaurants, and candy and ice cream stores. The **Cannon Beach Shuttle** provides van service up and down the length of town and operates daily with seasonal hours. Look for signed shuttle stops. The fare is $1.

FESTIVALS The **Savor Cannon Beach** (www.savorcannonbeach.com) food and wine festival in early March is a popular event, with food and wine tastings throughout the town. In early June, the **Sandcastle Day** contest turns the beach into one vast canvas for sand sculptors from all over the region. This is a well-known Oregon coast event and draws thousands of visitors. In early November, the **Stormy Weather Arts Festival** celebrates the arrival of winter storms with gallery shows and performances. For a current listing of events, visit **www.cannonbeach.org**.

Cannon Beach

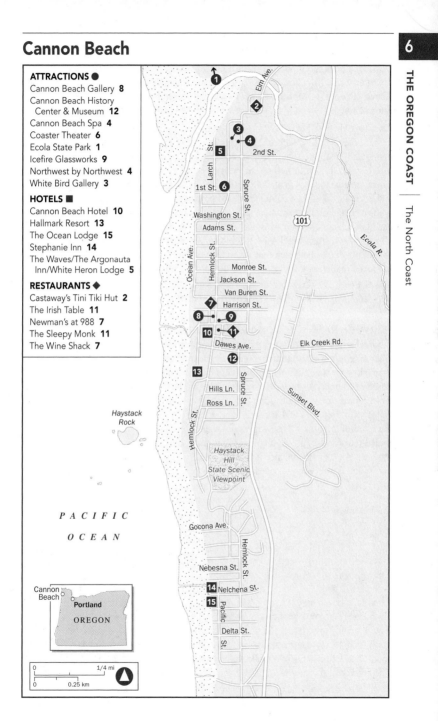

ATTRACTIONS ●
Cannon Beach Gallery **8**
Cannon Beach History
  Center & Museum **12**
Cannon Beach Spa **4**
Coaster Theater **6**
Ecola State Park **1**
Icefire Glassworks **9**
Northwest by Northwest **4**
White Bird Gallery **3**

HOTELS ■
Cannon Beach Hotel **10**
Hallmark Resort **13**
The Ocean Lodge **15**
Stephanie Inn **14**
The Waves/The Argonauta
  Inn/White Heron Lodge **5**

RESTAURANTS ◆
Castaway's Tini Tiki Hut **2**
The Irish Table **11**
Newman's at 988 **7**
The Sleepy Monk **11**
The Wine Shack **7**

Elm Ave.
2nd St.
Larch St.
1st St.
Spruce St.
Washington St.
Adams St.
101
Ecola R.
Hemlock St.
Ocean Ave.
Monroe St.
Jackson St.
Van Buren St.
Harrison St.
Dawes Ave.
Elk Creek Rd.
Spruce St.
Hills Ln.
Ross Ln.
Sunset Blvd.
Hemlock St.

Haystack
Rock

Haystack
Hill
State Scenic
Viewpoint

PACIFIC

OCEAN

Gocona Ave.
Hemlock St.
Nebesna St.
Nelchena St.
Pacific St.
Delta St.
St.

Cannon
Beach
Portland
OREGON

0   1/4 mi
0   0.25 km

WHERE TO STAY

If you're heading here with the whole family or plan to stay a while, consider renting a house, a cottage, or an apartment. Offerings range from studio apartments to large luxurious oceanfront houses, and prices span an equally wide range. Contact **Cannon Beach Property Management** (www.cbpm.com; © **877/386-3402**) for more information.

Cannon Beach Hotel ★★ This shingle-sided hotel in an older Cannon Beach neighborhood has no lack of character. It is, in fact, one of the oldest hotels on the coast, and celebrated its 100th anniversary in 2014. But there's nothing creaky or funky about it now, in its present incarnation as a comfortable, well-designed B&B. There are nice touches in all the public areas: fresh flowers, a wood fire, big armchairs, and a sense of Zen-like calm. The hotel property includes a few century-old cottages with river-rock fireplaces and a newer Courtyard wing with suites and Jacuzzis, so you can choose various room sizes and configurations depending on your needs. I personally like the historic hotel—a rarity in Cannon Beach. You are not on the beach here, or looking out at the beach, but it's minutes away, and the surrounding neighborhood has some real charm. In the summer, the on-site cafe serves lunch and dinner.

1116 S. Hemlock St. www.cannonbeachhotel.com. © **800/238-4107** or 503/436-1392. 37 units. $159–$259 double w/continental breakfast (for rooms in hotel only). **Amenities:** Restaurant; free Wi-Fi.

Hallmark Resort ★ The buildings of this double-decker, tri-sided resort are grouped around a central parking lot that detracts from the views from the less expensive units, but the location is pretty spectacular no matter where you are and adds drama to your stay. Hallmark Resort occupies a high bluff looking down on the famous beach of Cannon Beach with Haystack Rock in the distance. The possibilities here run from family-friendly guestrooms that sleep 6 and have full kitchens to oceanfront suites with fireplaces and Jacuzzis. The oceanfront suites with walk-out balconies are the stand-outs here for those who really want a special experience. I like the whites and muted tones and light wood colors of the decor here, because they don't detract from the view but seem to enhance it. The resort has a big recreation center with two indoor pools, and it offers spa services. The staff here is really friendly and helpful.

1400 S. Hemlock St. www.hallmarkinns.com. © **888/448-4449** or 503/436-1566. 129 units. $129–$389 double, Pets accepted ($20). **Amenities:** Exercise room; 2 Jacuzzis; 2 indoor pools; sauna; spa; free Wi-Fi.

The Ocean Lodge ★★★ What a great place to stay in Cannon Beach! The wide, sandy beach is right below this mid-sized inn—you have direct access to it from the ground-floor rooms—and the views are panoramic vistas down to Haystack Rock. Everything is sturdy, well-built, and nicely designed here, and the rooms are furnished with classic good taste and a minimum of frills and fuss but have everything you need for a cozy beach stay. Even if the winds are raging and the rain is pouring, you can comfortably curl up in your room and enjoy the fire or soak in your Jacuzzi. The rooms have kitchenettes, coffee and cookies are always available downstairs, and there's a good (self-serve) continental breakfast in the morning that you can take it to your room. The lodge is fairly upscale but very relaxed and casual, and the staff is terrific. The commercial center of Cannon Beach is about ¾ mile away.

2864 S. Pacific St. www.theoceanlodge.com. © **888/777-4047** or 503/436-2241. 45 units. $279–$429 double w/continental breakfast included. Pets accepted ($19 per night). **Amenities:** Access to nearby health club; free Wi-Fi.

Stephanie Inn ★★★ An air of elaborate, service-oriented formality prevails at this well-known inn and its fine-dining restaurant. I mention this because it is rather unusual on the mostly very casual Oregon coast. But the Stephanie caters to people who want the best and are willing to pay a very pretty penny for it. Couples looking for an upscale, perfect-in-every-detail experience love the Stephanie, which was built in 1993 and is considered one of the top-of-the-line Oregon coast hotels. The beds have fine linens, TempurPedic mattresses, and of course there's evening turn-down service with chocolates. Every room has a Jacuzzi and gas fireplace. And almost every room has a view—but even if it doesn't, there's a downstairs in the library where you can enjoy the ocean right outside the windows. The room decor here is very traditional, more home-like than beach-like, and when you're in your room, you feel cocooned from the elements—until you open the door and step out onto your balcony or patio for an instant hit of the Pacific. The Stephanie serves a full breakfast and offers evening wine and hors d'oeuvres to its guests. The restaurant (reviewed on p. 197) is a fine-dining haven. And here's something special to consider if you decide to stay at this highest-of-high-end beach hotels: For $59 they will build you your very own bonfire on the beach.

2740 S. Pacific St. www.stephanie-inn.com. © **800/633-3466** or 503/436-2221. 41 units. $379–$619 double w/full breakfast included. No children under 12. **Amenities:** Restaurant; access to nearby health club; free Wi-Fi.

The Waves/The Argonauta Inn/White Heron Lodge ★ it's impossible to describe all the accommodation possibilities at these three very different properties, all of them managed by The Waves. The best thing to know is that they are all really close to the beach—in fact, some are almost *on* the beach—at the north end of town near Ecola State Park, and also so close to the town center that you can easily walk there. The Waves, the largest property, is a cluster of oceanfront buildings with an assortment of rooms that mostly have great views and are decorated in a casual, comfortable beach style, some with fireplaces and Jacuzzis. The Argonauta Inn consists of five cottages, one of them dating from 1906, that have one or two suites within them and little yards; these are the most atmospheric and reminiscent of what Oregon beach cottages used to be like. The two beachfront units that make up White Heron Lodge look out on a grassy lawn with the pounding Pacific just beyond. So take your pick and choose the amenities you want—there's something here for single travelers, couples, and families.

188 W. Second St. www.thewavescannonbeach.com. © **800/822-2468** or 503/436-2205. 55 units. The Waves $89–$209 double; White Heron Lodge $159–$349 suite; Argonauta $119–$479 suite. 3-night minimum July–Aug; 2-night minimum on weekends Sept–June. **Amenities:** Jacuzzi; free Wi-Fi.

WHERE TO EAT

This being the Oregon coast, where every hotel room seems to have a kitchenette, you may opt to stay in and cook your own meals while you watch the waves. But this is also Cannon Beach, where you'll find more good restaurants than anywhere else except Newport and Yachats. For a bottle of wine to take back to your room and enjoy on the balcony overlooking the beach, stop in at **The Wine Shack,** 124 N. Hemlock St. (www.beachwine.com; © **800/787-1765** or 503/436-1100), or **Laurel's Cannon Beach Wine Shop,** 263 N. Hemlock St. (© **503/436-1666**). For good locally brewed beer, visit **Bill's Tavern & Brewhouse,** 188 N. Hemlock St. (© **503/436-2202**).

Savor Cannon Beach

The 4-day **Savor Cannon Beach** festival (www.savorcannonbeach.com) in early March, an annual celebration of Pacific Northwest wine and regional cuisine, includes six wine tasting events and many other related community activities. Approximately 40 Northwest wineries pour tastings at shops, galleries, restaurants and hotels in Cannon Beach during the wine walk on Saturday of the festival.

Castaways Tini Tiki Hut ★ CARIBBEAN/CAJUN/CREOLE/FUSION   In Cannon Beach, land of the year-round fleece and hoodie, this little cottage-restaurant is a local fave, maybe because it likes things spicy and kinda fun. The ingredients may be the ubiquitous crab, shrimp, and seafood of the Oregon coast, but it's cooked up in different ways: the crab turned into fritters, the shrimp curried, and the fish and shellfish in the jambalaya seasoned Cajun style. The flavors of Hawaii and Thailand also make cameo appearances here. If seafood doesn't swim with you, try the Haystack Chicken, named after Cannon Beach's most iconic landmark, or the macaroni and cheese with Andouille sausage. The portions here are large, so you may want to share. And the cocktail menu is fun, too, with some rum-based delights.

316 N. Fir St. ℂ **503/436-8777.** Main courses $16–$23. Wed–Sun 5–9pm.

The Irish Table & The Sleepy Monk ★★ IRISH/COFFEE   This little shingle-sided cottage-like building in "midtown" Cannon Beach is a shared-space operation. By day it's The Sleepy Monk coffee house, where you can get a good organic brew and a pastry to go with it. At night, it becomes The Irish Table, one of Cannon Beach's best-loved (and smallest) restaurants. The Irish Table has a small menu with maybe five starters (a good cheese board, a couple of fresh salads, a couple of seafood appetizers) and as many entrees. The food is perhaps more Irish-inspired than typically Irish, but may include vegetarian shepherd's pie with wild mushrooms, lamb chops with a Dijon reduction sauce, a seared flatiron steak, and a fresh fish selection. A few rich desserts are offered, and hot drinks with Irish whiskey. Arrive early or be prepared to wait in line.

1235 S. Hemlock St. ℂ **503/436-0708.** Main courses $20–$29. Sleepy Monk Fri–Tues 8am–4pm; Irish Table Fri–Tues 5:30–10pm.

Newman's at 988 ★★★ FRENCH/ITALIAN   The Newman of Newman's 988 is John, the first chef to put Stephanie Inn on the coastal culinary map. He opened his own fine-dining restaurant in a small yellow cottage in "midtown" Cannon Beach. Part of the experience of a meal here is the presentation, which is less fussy now than it used to be at Stephanie Inn. The menu is French- and Italian-inspired but relies exclusively on the freshest ingredients of the Pacific Northwest. For appetizers, try the foie gras pasta with Oregon black truffle mushrooms or the crab cakes with parsley, lemon, and shallot aioli. There is a daily ravioli, and lobster ravioli, one of Newman's signature dishes, is always on the menu. Duck breast; marinated lamb rack; and beef medallions with pancetta, onions, and Gorgonzola are typical entree choices. Newman also offers a daily tasting menu and a fine selection of wines to accompany your meal.

988 S. Hemlock St. www.newmansat988.com. ℂ **503/436-1151.** Main courses $20–$30. Daily 5:30–9pm (closed Mon mid-Oct to July 3). Closed mid-Jan to early Feb.

Stephanie Inn ★★★ PACIFIC NORTHWEST   The restaurant at the Stephanie Inn provides the most formal fine-dining experience on the North Coast. It's not for everyone, but if you want a special-occasion restaurant with white linen and attentive service, this is it. (You don't have to be staying at the inn to dine here, nor do you have to dress up, but you should at least be "smart-casual.") The second-floor dining room is all wood and windows, though it does not look out on the Pacific. The menu changes often based on what's seasonal and fresh. If they're available, share the seared scallops as an appetizer; there are two large ones served with roasted grapes, walnuts, pancetta, aged Gouda fondue, and crispy shallots. On my last visit I had a delicate and delicious creamy asparagus soup with crème fraiche followed by a filet of wild Alaskan halibut with organic wild rice and grilled asparagus and a citrus/apple/fennel salad. The recommended wine pairing was perfect. The Meyer lemon curd tart was a mighty temptation, but I was too full to try it. This is the sort of restaurant where your server actually asks if everything is cooked to perfection—and usually, it is. There is a nightly four-course, fixed-price dinner that offers a considerable savings over a la carte choices.

2740 S. Pacific St. www.stephanie-inn.com. ℂ **800/633-3466** or 503/436-2221. Main courses $42–$48, fixed-price menu $69. Daily 5:30–8pm (until 8:30pm Sat).

EXPLORING CANNON BEACH

Cannon Beach ★★★ OUTDOOR RECREATION/BEACH   Wide, flat, sandy Cannon Beach is a wonderful place to take a long, invigorating beach walk. Haystack Rock adds an undeniably dramatic focal point to the beach, and when the tide is out, you can explore the tide pools at its base. But please don't disturb the sea urchins and starfish, and don't climb up on the monolith—every year, careless climbers have to be plucked off the rock because the tide has come in and stranded them. Besides walking, kite flying and beachcombing are the most popular Cannon Beach pastimes, but you can also enjoy the beach in a variety of other ways. Between Memorial Day and Labor Day, guided horseback rides to Cove Beach and Haystack Rock are offered by **Sea Ranch Stables,** 415 Fir St. (www.cannon-beach.net; ℂ **503/436-2815**), at the north entrance to Cannon Beach. Rides cost $65 to $130.

Cannon Beach History Center ★ MUSEUM   On the surface, Cannon Beach may not look as though it has much history, but from Lewis and Clark's visit to the story of the cannon that gave the town its name, there is a bit to learn about this town's past. The story of Cannon Beach is told in well-designed exhibits. A hands-on reproduction of a Native American longhouse is a hit with kids.

1387 S. Spruce St. www.cbhistory.org. ℂ **503/436-9301.** Admission free. Wed–Mon 1–5pm.

More Beaches Near Cannon Beach

Three miles south of town is **Arcadia Beach State Recreation Site** ★★, one of the prettiest little beaches on the north coast. Another mile farther south you'll find **Hug Point State Recreation Site** ★★, which has picnic tables, a sheltered beach, and the remains of an old road that was cut into the rock face of this headland. **Oswald West State Park** ★★★, 10 miles south of Cannon Beach, is one of my favorites of all the parks on the Oregon coast. A short trail leads to a driftwood-strewn cobblestone beach on a small cove. Headlands on either side of the cove can be reached by hiking trails that offer wonderful views. The waves here are popular with surfers, and there's a walk-in campground.

Ecola State Park ★★★ OUTDOOR RECREATION/STATE PARK   Hikers, whale-watchers, surfers, and beachcombers flock to this gorgeous coastal park that wraps around Tillamook Head and features 9 miles of Pacific Ocean shoreline. The hikes include an 8-mile segment of the **Oregon Coast Trail** that is also a part of the **Lewis and Clark National Historic Trail. Indian Beach** marks the start of the new **Clatsop Loop Trail,** a 2.5-mile interpretive trail that gives you the chance to walk on the south side of Tillamook Head, and in the footsteps of Captain Clark and members of the Corps of Discovery. Salal, salmonberry, and some of the region's largest Sitka spruce trees thrive in this area. (One large Sitka spruce is estimated to have germinated in the 1600s and was almost 200 years old when Clark walked the trail.)

In addition to Indian Beach, popular with surfers and tide-pool explorers, there is secluded **Crescent Beach.** The park also has several picnic areas perched on bluffs high above the crashing waves. The 1-mile stretch of trail between the main bluff-top picnic area and Indian Beach is particularly scenic, passing through old-growth forest with good views of the ocean and beaches far below. Ecola is a good spot to observe coastal wildlife. During the winter and spring, you can see migrating gray whales from one of the promontories overlooking the ocean. During the migration seasons, a popular whale-watching program features trained volunteers to help you spot the grays. In July and August it's a good idea to arrive early because parking can be difficult.

84318 Ecola State Park Rd. (north of Cannon Beach). www.oregon.gov/oprd/parks. ✆ **800/551-6949** or 503/436-2844. Daily dawn–dusk. Day-use fee $5 per vehicle.

CANNON BEACH NIGHTLIFE

The **Coaster Theater,** 108 N. Hemlock St. (www.coastertheatre.com; ✆ **503/436-1242**), the best-known professional theater on the Oregon coast, presents a season of dramas, comedies, and musicals.

cannon beach SHOPPING & SPA-ING

For many Cannon Beach visitors, shopping is the town's greatest attraction. In the heart of town, along **Hemlock Street,** you'll find dozens of densely packed small shops and galleries offering original (and not-so) art, fine (and not-so) crafts, souvenirs, gifts, and casual fashions. And because this is a fairly upscale getaway town, relaxing in a spa is also possible.

Galleries   Northwest by Northwest, 232 N. Spruce St. (www.nwbynwgallery .com; ✆ **800/494-0741** or 503/436-0741) features works by established Northwest artists. **White Bird Gallery,** 251 N. Hemlock St. (www.whitebird gallery.com; ✆ **503/436-2681**), sells colorful contemporary art and fine crafts.

Icefire Glassworks, 116 E. Gower St. (http://cbgallerygroup.com/icefire-glass works; ✆ **888/423-3545** or 503/436-2359) is a glassblowing studio south of downtown. **Cannon Beach Gallery,** 1064 S. Hemlock St. (www.cannonbeacharts .org; ✆ **503/436-0744**) is operated by a local arts organization and mounts shows in a wide variety of styles but which tend to be heavy on beach landscapes.

Spa   Want to turn a Cannon Beach getaway into a truly relaxing escape? Book a massage or a skin or hydrotherapy treatment at the **Cannon Beach Spa,** 232 N. Spruce St. (www.cannonbeachspa.com; ✆ **888/577-8772** or 503/436-8772). Prices run between $80 and $105 for an hour-long massage.

Manzanita ★★

14.5 miles S of Cannon Beach

As the crowds have descended on Cannon Beach, people seeking peace and quiet and a slower pace have migrated south to the community of Manzanita. Located south of Neahkanie Mountain, Manzanita enjoys a setting similar to Cannon Beach, but without the many haystack rocks. There isn't much to do except walk on the beach and relax, which is exactly why most people love Manzanita.

The beach at Manzanita stretches for 5 miles, from the base of Neahkanie Mountain to the mouth of the Nehalem River, and is a favorite of both full-body-wetsuit-clad surfers and windsurfers (who also windsurf in the quieter waters of Nehalem Bay just across Nehalem Spit from the ocean).

WHERE TO STAY

If you want to rent a vacation house in Manzanita, contact **Manzanita Rental Company** (www.manzanitarentals.com; ✆ **800/579-9801** or 503/368-6797).

Coast Cabins ★★★   To call them "cabins" is something of a misnomer—at least if you associate "cabin" with a little rustic cottage from an earlier era. These two-story cedar-shake and glass-fronted cabins are gorgeously sited and outfitted to enhance a quiet but luxurious beach stay. You're not on the ocean, but close to it, and the wooded setting gives you a real hit of the Oregon coast. What I love about this place is that the cabins are so simple and well designed, inside and out. Comfortably luxurious, they are set up for couples and individuals looking for a romantic and revivifying retreat. The decor includes original art, wool area rugs woven in Tibet, clean-lined and unobtrusive Scandinavian-style fixtures and furniture, and private outdoor hot tubs. Like all good things, these cabins have been "discovered" and are hard to book in July and August, so plan ahead, or enjoy them off-season.

635 Laneda Ave. www.coastcabins.com. ✆ **800/435-1269** or 503/368-7113. 5 units. $215–$375 double. 2-night minimum on weekends and throughout the summer. Pets accepted ($30 deposit, plus $25 per night). **Amenities:** Access to nearby health club; free Wi-Fi.

The Inn at Manzanita ★★   Nestled among pines and spruce trees within a lovely coastal garden, this contemporary, cedar-sided inn is right in Manzanita but has all the charm and privacy you could want, plus easy access to the beach. There are four different buildings within the complex, and each room is styled differently, but the "room themes" here are low-key and fairly unobtrusive. There's a different outlook from every room, too, but all of them have fireplaces and balconies, and some have kitchenettes. Gardening on the Oregon coast is not easy, so the park-like grounds and garden here is a special feature.

67 Laneda Ave. www.innatmanzanita.com. ✆ **503/368-6754.** 14 units. $179–$229 double, 2-night minimum on weekends and July to Labor Day; 3-night minimum on some holidays. Pets accepted ($15 per night). **Amenities:** Access to nearby health club; free Wi-Fi.

WHERE TO EAT

For lattes and the latest news, head to **Manzanita News & Espresso,** 500 Laneda Ave. (✆ **503/368-7450**). At the end of the day, wind down at **Vino Manzanita,** 387-D Laneda Ave. (✆ **503/368-8466**), a cozy little wine bar.

Bread and Ocean ★★ NORTHWEST   The lunch menu is small—cold sandwiches (fresh tuna, barbecued beef brisket, or a Dagwood on ciabatta); panini with an

TILLAMOOK AND ITS FAMOUS cheese

About 27 miles south of Manzanita, U.S. 101 veers inland about 2 miles from the ocean and comes to the town of **Tillamook.** There's really no reason to stop in Tillamook except to visit the **Tillamook Cheese Factory,** 4175 U.S. 101 N. (www.tillamookcheese.com; ✆ **800/542-7290** or 503/815-1300). It's the most popular tourist attraction in a flat, lush, coastal valley long known as one of Oregon's foremost dairy regions. Tillamook cheese is ubiquitous everywhere in the state—until the recent advent of artisan cheeses, it was the *only* real cheese to be had. At the factory, visitors can observe the cheese-making process (cheddars are the specialty), buy Tillamook ice cream, and browse through

a large gift shop where all manner of cheeses and other edible gifts are available. The factory is open daily from 8am to 8pm in the summer, otherwise 8am to 6pm.

Located on the same side of U.S. 101 is the **Blue Heron French Cheese Company,** 2001 Blue Heron Dr. (www.blueheronoregon.com; ✆ **800/275-0639** or 503/842-8281). Created within an old dairy barn, Blue Heron stocks the same sort of comestibles as the Tillamook Cheese Factory, though the emphasis here is on brie (which, however, is not made locally). Blue Heron is open daily from 8am to 8pm in summer and 9am to 6pm in winter.

array of deli specialties; homemade soup—but everything made here is delicious. Maybe that explains why it has been Manzanita's favorite lunch spot since it opened in 2003. That and the baked goods. This is the place to come for a packed picnic-lunch box that you can take to the beach. Dinner is served Friday through Sunday only, and features barbecue on Friday and Saturday nights. Everyone in town seems to show up for coffee and pastries in the morning.

154 Laneda Ave. www.breadandocean.com. ✆ **503/368-5823.** No credit cards. Main courses $$8.50–$24. Wed–Thurs 7:30am–2pm; Fri–Sat 7:30am–2pm and 5–9pm; Sun 8am–2pm and 5–8pm.

EXPLORING MANZANITA

It's about the beach and nothing but the beach.

Nehalem Bay State Park ★★ OUTDOOR RECREATION/STATE PARK/ BEACH   Just south of town, this state park encompasses all of Nehalem Spit and provides access to both Manzanita beach and Nehalem Bay. The park includes a **campground** and has a 1.75-mile paved bike path, a horse camp, and horse trails. At the south end of the spit, more than 50 harbor seals can often be seen basking on the beach. To reach the seal area requires a 5-mile round-trip hike.

9500 Sandpiper Ln., Nehalem. www.oregon.gov/oprd/parks. ✆ **503/368-5154.** Day-use fee $5 per vehicle. Daily 8am-5pm.

Three Capes Scenic Loop ★★★

The Three Capes Scenic Loop, a 35-mile byway off of U.S. 101, begins just west of downtown Tillamook and leads south along the coast past Cape Meares, Cape Lookout, and Cape Kiwanda to end near Pacific City. Together these capes offer some of the most spectacular scenery on the northern Oregon coast. All three capes are state parks, and all make great whale-watching spots in the spring.

ESSENTIALS

GETTING THERE To start the loop, follow Third Street south out of Tillamook and watch for the right turn for Cape Meares State Scenic Viewpoint. You can also access the loop from the south at Pacific City.

EXPLORING THE THREE CAPES SCENIC LOOP

The road from Tillamook takes you along the shore of **Tillamook Bay** and around the north side of Cape Meares. Just around the tip of the cape, you'll come to **Cape Meares State Scenic Viewpoint ★★★,** the site of the **Cape Meares Lighthouse** (open daily Apr–Oct 11am–4pm). The views from atop this rocky headland are superb.

Continuing south around the cape, you come to the residential community of **Oceanside,** with its white-sand beach and offshore monoliths known as the **Three Arch Rocks.** At the north end of the beach, a pedestrian tunnel leads through a headland to a secluded beach.

Three miles south of Oceanside, you'll come to **Netarts Bay,** famous for its excellent clamming and crabbing.

Continuing south, the scenic byway leads to **Cape Lookout State Park ★★** (www.oregon.gov/oprd/parks; ℂ **503/842-4981**), where you'll find a campground, picnic areas, beaches, and several miles of hiking trails. The most breathtaking trail leads 2½ miles out to the end of Cape Lookout, several hundred feet above the ocean. There is a $5 day-use fee here.

Cape Kiwanda ★★, just north of Pacific City, is preserved as **Cape Kiwanda State Natural Area.** At the foot of the cape's sandstone cliffs, it's possible to scramble up a huge sand dune to the top of the cape for dramatic views of this rugged piece of shoreline. The base of the cape is the staging area for Pacific City's dory fleet. These flat-bottomed commercial fishing boats are launched from the beach and plow through crashing breakers to get out to calmer waters beyond. When the day's fishing is done, the dories roar into shore at full throttle and come to a grinding stop as high up on the beach as they can. This is Oregon's only such fishing fleet, and it's celebrated each year on the third weekend in July with the annual Dory Days Festival. If you'd like to go out in one of these dories and fish for salmon, ling cod, or albacore tuna, contact **Haystack Fishing** (www.haystackfishing.com; ℂ **866/965-7555** or 503/965-7555; $180 per person, two-person minimum). Trips are offered June through September.

WHERE TO STAY

In Pacific City

Inn at Cape Kiwanda ★★ Every room has an ocean view—but in many of them, you have to look across a parking lot to see it. That's the one drawback, for me, at this otherwise comfortable and well-run hotel across the street from the busy beach at Cape Kiwanda Natural Area. The pluses are big view windows (the corner rooms are best), private balconies, and gas fireplaces. The furnishings here remind me of a suburban home, with a style that leans toward the traditional. The Pelican Pub & Brewery, which runs the inn, is right across the street.

33105 Cape Kiwanda Dr. www.innatcapekiwanda.com. ℂ **888/965-7001** or 503/965-7001. 35 units. $139–$329 double; $229–$359 suite. 2-night minimum on holidays, and on weekends July–Aug. Children 18 and under stay free in parent's room. Pets accepted ($20). **Amenities:** 2 restaurants; lounge; bikes; exercise room; free Wi-Fi.

WHERE TO EAT
In Oceanside
Roseanna's Cafe SEAFOOD/INTERNATIONAL   Oceanside was the first coast town I ever stayed in in Oregon, and it didn't have a restaurant—or much of anything except simple cottages and a great beach. When Roseanna's opened in the early 1980s, it became a favorite spot for locals and those driving along the Three Capes Scenic Loop. Unpretentious and with a fabulous view, it was the only spot for miles around that attempted to do more than fish and chips or burgers. Over the years, this little restaurant in a simple building from the early 1900s hasn't changed much, and it remains a favorite spot. The food is comfortable and filling if not haute cuisine; special sauces are created to complement just about everything from seafood to pasta. Roseanna's is famous for its desserts, so you may want to sample the fresh huckleberry pie or other sweets. The restaurant doesn't take reservations, so be prepared to wait for a table.

1490 Pacific Ave. www.roseannascafe.com. © 503/842-7351. Reservations not accepted. Main courses $8–$30. Sun–Thurs daily 9am–8pm; Fri–Sat 9am–9pm.

In Pacific City
The Grateful Bread Bakery & Restaurant ★   This bright, pleasant bakery-bistro, known for its fresh-baked bread and pastries, has long been my favorite lunch spot in Pacific City. This is a place that uses as much unprocessed, organic, and sustainable food as possible and always has vegetarian options. The lunch menu is limited mostly to sandwiches (made with that delicious bread), salads, and grilled fish. Try the vegetarian chili, a stuffed focaccia sandwich, or one of their pizzas. They also make a good latte (for the coast). Service can be slow, but because you're at the coast to unwind, that shouldn't be a problem.

34805 Brooten Rd., Pacific City. © 503/965-7337. Main courses: $10–$12. Thurs–Mon 8am–3pm.

Pelican Pub & Brewery ★ PUB FOOD   When was the last time you sat in a pub with a view of crashing surf, an enormous sand dune, and an offshore monolith? Pelican Brewery offers some delicious and award-winning brews—Irish Handcuffs, Doryman's Ale, and Kiwanda Cream Ale among them—and a fabulous Cape Kiwanda view to go with them. And food, too, the kind that goes well with beer and a day at the beach. The lightly breaded and salted fried calamari is a favorite way to start a meal here. I also like the blackened salmon salad, the Tsunami Stout Chili (made with pork and beef and topped with Tillamook cheese), the seafood quesadilla, and the wild mushroom pie. Pasta and gourmet pizzas are available, too. This is a very laid-back place that welcomes kids.

33180 Cape Kiwanda Dr. www.pelicanbrewery.com. © 503/965-7007. Main courses $12–$24. Sun–Thurs 8am–10pm; Fri–Sat 8am–11pm.

THE CENTRAL COAST
Easy access from Portland and I-5 through the Coast Range gives the Central Coast a leg-up in popularity. **Lincoln City** is one of the coast's most-visited and family-friendly destinations, and **Newport,** home the excellent Oregon Coast Aquarium, two lighthouses, and the historic neighborhood of Nye Beach, is the most interesting town along this part of the coast. Whale-watching expeditions leave from the tiny harbor at **Depoe Bay,** and the old town of **Florence,** along the Siuslaw River, has some real historic character. **Yachats,** with its exceptionally beautiful beach, is one of the more affluent communities along the Central Coast.

heading up CASCADE HEAD

Rising 1,770 feet above sea level, **Cascade Head** is one of the highest headlands on the coast. The headland—with lush coastal rainforest of Sitka spruce and Douglas fir covering its lower flanks and treeless, windswept meadows above—juts out into the sea between the small community of Neskowin (10 miles south of Pacific City on U.S. 101) and the larger town of Lincoln City. On its south side, this rare example of a maritime prairie rises above the Salmon River estuary, and the entire headland is home to native grasses and wildflowers as well as elk, deer, bald eagles, falcons, and great horned owls. The area around Cascade Head is so unique that it has been designated a UNESCO Biosphere Reserve. From a trail head on its south side, the 6-mile **Nature Conservancy**

Cascade Head Trail ★★★ climbs up the side and over the top of this magnificent headland all the way to Neskowin. The trail provides spectacular vistas of the Salmon River, the Coast Range, and the Pacific. To reach the trail head, turn west from U.S. 101 onto Three Rocks Road (just north of the Salmon River) and follow it about 2½ miles to Knight County Park at the end. Park there and walk back to Savage Road, where you'll find a half-mile boardwalk trail that takes you to the trail head. There's an initial 1,000-foot elevation gain, after which the trail becomes relatively easy. This is a fragile ecosystem, so stay on the trail. No dogs or bikes are allowed. The Nature Conservancy's preserve has been set aside primarily to protect the habitat of the rare Oregon silverspot butterfly.

Lincoln City ★

88 miles SW of Portland, 44 miles S of Tillamook, 25 miles N of Newport

Despite its name, Lincoln City is not a city at all but a collection of five small towns that grew together over the years and now stretch for miles along the coast. The result is that there's no specific town center, and little to distinguish Lincoln City from a commercialized stretch of suburban highway. Motel rates here, though often high for what you get, are generally better than those in coast towns with more charm and better beaches

Thanks in part to the arrival of a big casino in Lincoln City, the stretch of U.S. 101 between Otis to Depoe Bay, which includes Lincoln City, has become congested sprawl, and a summer weekend in Lincoln City can mean coping with bumper-to-bumper traffic. If at all possible, come during the week or during the off season to avoid the endless traffic and the crowds.

Once you get off U.S. 101, however, Lincoln City has neighborhoods as charming as any on the coast, and at the south end of town, in the Taft District, the city has been working hard to bring back a historical character and provide an attractive, pedestrian-friendly area.

Just north of town, in an area known as Road's End, you'll find a long, uncrowded beach with spectacular views to the north.

ESSENTIALS

GETTING THERE   Ore. 22 from Salem merges with Ore. 18 before reaching the junction with U.S. 101. From Portland, take U.S. 99W to McMinnville and then head west on Ore. 18.

VISITOR INFORMATION   The **Lincoln City Visitor Center,** 540 NE U.S. 101 (www.oregoncoast.org; ✆ **541/994-3302**), is open Wednesday to Monday 10am to 4pm.

FESTIVALS   Annual **kite festivals** include the Summer Kite Festival in late June and the Fall Kite Festival in early to mid-October. In addition, Lincoln City has an annual **Sandcastle Building Contest** each year in early August. On the nearby Siletz Indian Reservation, the **Nesika Illahee,** the annual Siletz Pow Wow, takes place on the second weekend in August. For a current listing of events in Lincoln City visit **www.oregon coast.org.** Music lovers can enjoy excellent performances by chamber groups, ensembles, and soloists at the **Cascade Head Music Festival** (www.cascadeheadmusic.org) held in July.

WHERE TO STAY

In addition to the town's many hotels and motels, Lincoln City has plenty of vacation rental houses and apartments offering good deals, especially for families. For information, contact **Horizon Rentals** (www.horizonrentals.com; ✆ **800/995-2411** or 541/994-2226) or **Pacific Retreats** (www.pacificretreats.com; ✆ **800/473-4833** or 541/994-4833). Rates generally range from around $75 to $250 nightly for houses for 4 to 12 people.

Ester Lee Motel ★   This is what a modest, ocean-facing Oregon coast motel used to be like in simpler days, when being at the beach was more about being at the beach than it was about fancy upgraded amenities in a hotel room. I still like the Ester Lee for that very reason. Located at the south end of Lincoln City, this vintage motel and cottages makes absolutely no claims to have glamor or glitz. It's basic, both inside and out, but the rooms have spectacular views (no balconies, however). And the Ester Lee is probably the least expensive place to stay in Lincoln City. Most units have kitchens and fireplaces (some of them wood-burning, with free firewood). Pay a little more and you can book a cozy cottage that sleeps from two to seven people. There's a paved access down to the beach, and grocery stores, restaurants, and the casino are about 4½ miles to the north.

3803 S. U.S. 101. www.esterlee.com. ✆ **888/430-2100** or 541/996-6111. 44 units. Motel $65–$169 double. **Amenities:** Free Wi-Fi.

Looking Glass Inn ★   The Looking Glass is a good choice for families and those who want to be near the beach but don't have to be right on it. Only a couple of the rooms here have rather tame partial views of the wild Pacific, seen over parking lots and nearby buildings, but the entrance to the beach on Siletz Bay is only one block away. What this all means is that you can get a nice, clean room in this well-maintained and pet-friendly property for less money. The complex of brown, shingle-sided with white-trim buildings is what much Oregon coast lodging used to look like. The rooms have been comfortably freshened up; all have kitchenettes, and all are suites, some with fireplaces, a few with whirlpool soaking tubs. Even Fido or Fifi is well-treated here, with his or her very own beach-bed and dining bowls. Speaking of dining, the famous Mo's chowder house is right across the street from the Looking Glass, and the inn will give you a coupon for a free bowl of Mo's famous clam chowder.

861 SW 51st St. www.lookingglass-inn.com. ✆ **800/843-4940** or 541/996-3996. 36 units. $79–$249 double w/continental breakfast included. Pets accepted ($15 per night). **Amenities:** Free Wi-Fi.

Starfish Manor Hotel ★★   From your balcony or whirlpool tub, you'll have a view of miles of beach, and the ceaseless sound of the Pacific will lull you to sleep. If there's a storm, or the weather's chilly, you can turn on your fireplace and feel cozily protected and warm. That's what Starfish Manor is all about. This boutique hotel specializes in romantic getaways, the kind where you can happily hole up in your oceanfront room and reinvigorate your relationship with a loved one, or with yourself and nature. There aren't any kids around, and no barking dogs. The studios and suites are sweet and welcoming, with upscale features like kitchenettes with cherrywood cabinets and granite countertops, and those two-person whirlpool tubs with ocean views. The hotel is at the north end of Lincoln City, away from the day-trippers and casino traffic.

2735 NW Inlet Ave. www.onthebeachfront.com. ℂ **800/972-6155** or 541/996-9300. 17 units. $159–$425 suite. No children, no pets. **Amenities:** Free Wi-Fi.

WHERE TO EAT

Bay House ★★★ NORTHWEST   The Bay House is one of a rare handful of fine-dining restaurants on the Oregon coast—by which I mean white linens on the table, impeccable service, outstanding cuisine beautifully presented, and a worldly selection of fine wines to pair with your food choices. It's been around since 1937, with various owners and chefs, and now it's expanded to include a nice cocktail lounge and wine bar in addition to its glass-fronted dining room with an eye-popping view of Siletz Bay and the Salishan Spit. So if you are going to be staying on the Central Oregon coast, anywhere from Lincoln City to Depoe Bay, and you want a special dining experience, this is the place. You might want to start with some smoked-salmon ravioli, or Medjool dates (currently on the menu of every upscale restaurant in the Northwest) with bleu cheese and citrus-arugula salad. There are typically four entrees on the menu: fish or seafood, beef, duck or game bird, and vegetarian. The wine list includes some 2,000 selections. You may want to try the tasting menu, although if you do, the entire table has to order it.

5911 SW U.S. 101. www.thebayhouse.org. ℂ **541/996-3222.** Reservations recommended. Main courses $27–$44, tasting menu $62. Wed–Sun 5:30–9pm.

Blackfish Cafe ★ SEAFOOD/AMERICAN   My verdict is out on Blackfish. I'm still hoping it will return to its once high standards, because Lincoln City needs a nice, unpretentious little restaurant like this. But my recent visit left me wondering what had happened. The food felt like it had been rushed, the service was spotty, and my plate had a chip in it. Normally I wouldn't be too finicky, but the devil, as they say, is in the details. So I don't want to write this busy restaurant off, but I want you to be aware that it may be experiencing problems (on the coast it is notoriously difficult to find good chefs and service staff). I would suggest trying Blackfish for lunch instead of dinner, and I would stick to the basics, such as the good chowder, fish and chips, and crispy fried oysters. You won't go wrong with those.

2733 NW U.S. 101. www.blackfishcafe.com. ℂ **541/996-1007.** Reservations recommended. Main courses $10–$30. Wed–Mon 11:30am–9pm.

Kyllo's Seafood & Grill ★★ SEAFOOD   It's big, it's loud, it's right on the beach, it's family-friendly, and they don't take reservations so there's always a line for dinner on weekends and during the busy summer months. If you don't want to wait, ask if you can be seated at the bar—the full menu is available, and you can still look out through the giant windows toward the tiny D River (Oregon's shortest) and the beach beyond. I have been eating at Kyllo's for years, and I've never had a bad meal. But I always stick pretty much to the basics, like pan-fried Willapa Bay oysters, a halibut sandwich, crab cakes, or fish and chips. The fish and shellfish is always fresh, and your meal comes with various sides that will more than adequately fill you up. This bright, contemporarily styled restaurant isn't about fine dining, but it's the best place to eat in Lincoln City.

1110 NW First Court. www.kyllosrestaurant.com. ✆ **541/994-3179.** No reservations accepted. Main courses $9–$30. Daily 11:30am–9pm.

Otis Cafe ★ AMERICAN   For years, the area around Cascade Head and Lincoln City has been where I usually hang out on the coast, and for years, the little Otis Cafe has been the spot where locals and in-the-knowers go for a big, old-fashioned breakfast or a filling lunch with a piece of marionberry pie for dessert. It's nothing more than a cheerful roadside diner, 5 miles north of Lincoln City, but over the years it's been "discovered" by Portland beach weekenders, so it's now busier than ever and savvy enough to sell *The New York Times* in addition to the local Lincoln City *News Guard*. But, thankfully, the food remains resolutely old-fashioned: liver and onions (yes, really), chicken-fried steak and grilled oysters for dinner, burgers, BLTs, and tuna melts for lunch. And let us not forget the gooey cinnamon bun for breakfast.

1259 Salmon River Hwy. (Ore. 18), Otis, OR 97368. www.otiscafe.com. ✆ **541/994-2813.** Main courses $6–$14. Daily 7am–8pm.

EXPLORING LINCOLN CITY

Beach ★ OUTDOOR RECREATION/OCEAN BEACH   Lincoln City's 7½-mile-long beach is the town's main attraction. This is not a beach for swimming, but for walking, beachcombing, and, because of the steady winds, the best kite flying on the Oregon coast. Among the better beach-access points are the **D River State Wayside,** on the south side of the D River (the shortest river in Oregon), and the **Road's End State Wayside,** at the north end of Lincoln City. Road's End is also a good place to explore tide pools. You'll find more tide pools on the beach at NW 15th Street.

Chinook Winds Casino Resort ★ CASINO   This massive casino run by the Confederated Tribes of Siletz Indians and located right on the beach at the north end of town offers blackjack, poker, slot machines, keno, and bingo, and a video-game room for the kids. Big-name entertainers perform nightly year-round. There's a hotel and restaurants on site.

1777 NW 44th St. www.chinookwindscasino.com. ✆ **888/244-6665** or 541/996-582. Admission free. Daily 24 hrs.

Donald's Secret Spot for an Old-Fashioned Shrimp Cocktail

Whenever I'm at the beach, I get a craving for an old-fashioned shrimp cocktail. You know what I'm talking about, right? A shrimp cocktail is not a drink, it's a scoop of sweet, tiny, tender little Oregon bay shrimp slathered with cocktail sauce. You can order these in restaurants, of course, but I always go to **Barnacle Bill's Seafood Market,** 2174 NE Hwy. 101 (✆ **541/994-3022**), an open-fronted seafood store right on the highway. It's been around forever, and the fresh fish, Dungeness crabs, and seasonal razor clams have gotten steadily more expensive, but this is where you can still get a shrimp cocktail served in a paper cup with a plastic spoon and a bag of crackers for $5. Barnacle Bill's is open daily 9:30am to 4:30pm.

Connie Hansen Garden ★★ GARDEN Gardening on the Oregon coast can be a difficult and often impossible proposition, given the salty air, rocky/sandy soil, and sometimes gale-force winds, so this charming and distinctive coastal cottage garden in a residential section of Lincoln City is both a surprise and a delight for garden lovers. It was created over a 20-year period by its namesake, Connie Hansen, a San Francisco transplant who moved to Lincoln City in 1973. Though small, the garden is planned in such a way that it seems much larger, and surprises are found at every turn of the meandering paths that run through it. Visit in the spring for the primroses, irises, and rhododendrons; in the summer to enjoy a panoply of colorful and unusual perennials; and in the fall to marvel at the burnished colors in the heather berms. Rare trees and shrubs add interest throughout the year. The garden is so unobtrusive from the road that you could pass by and never notice it. To find it, turn off U.S. 101 onto NW 33rd and look for the sign and small parking lot.

1931 NW 33rd St. www.conniehansengarden.com. ℂ **541/994-6338.** Admission by donation. Garden daily dawn–dusk, visitor center Tues, Sat 10am–2pm.

Depoe Bay ★★

13 miles S of Lincoln City, 13 miles N of Newport

Unlike other coastal towns in Oregon, Depoe Bay isn't centered around a strollable beach, but around a giant bay and a tiny harbor. In fact, Depoe Bay claims to be the smallest harbor in the world—all of 6 acres. Yet this miniscule and very protected port is home to more than 100 fishing boats and Coast Guard cutters. All of these boats must leave or enter the harbor through a narrow channel that's little more than a crack in the rocky coastline. During stormy seas, it's almost impossible to get in or out of the harbor safely.

Shell mounds and kitchen middens around the bay indicate that Native Americans long ago called this area of the Central Oregon coast home. In 1894, the U.S. government deeded the land surrounding the bay to a Siletz Indian known as Old Charlie Depot. Charlie had taken his name from the army depot where he worked. Old Charlie later changed his name to Depoe, and when a town was founded here in 1927, it took the name Depoe Bay.

Though most of the town is a bit off the highway, you'll find a row of touristy souvenir shops, restaurants, and charter-fishing and whale-watching companies on the inland side of U.S. 101, above the harbor. A sidewalk on the other side of the highway serves as a promenade along this rocky section of the Oregon coast.

ESSENTIALS

GETTING THERE From the north, the most direct route is Ore. 99W/18 to Lincoln City, and then south on U.S. 101. From the south, take U.S. 20 from Corvallis to Newport, and then go north on U.S. 101.

VISITOR INFORMATION Contact the **Depoe Bay Chamber of Commerce,** 223 SW U.S. 101 (www.depoebaychamber.org; ℂ **877/485-8348** or 541/765-2889).

FESTIVALS Memorial Day is the time for the **Fleet of Flowers,** during which local boats carry flower wreaths out to sea in memory of loved ones. In mid-September the town holds its annual **Salmon Bake,** a great opportunity to enjoy some traditionally prepared salmon. For more information, visit **www.depoebaychamber.org**.

WHERE TO STAY

Channel House ★★★ Lock me in the Cuckoo's Nest and throw away the key. I won't mind. This extraordinary suite, at the top of the Channel House, is perched right above the ocean—and I mean *right above*. I don't think there's a room anywhere on the Oregon coast that is closer to the water, except the equally fabulous suites on the first and second floors. Lie in bed and the ocean is right there in front of you with no intervening beach, just a bit of rocky shoreline. From these suites, you can step outside and watch the boats making their tricky entrances and departures to and from Depoe Bay . . . while sitting in your outdoor whirlpool. It's hard not to love Channel House, because it has everything you could possibly want for a memorable coast experience. The decor is tasteful, upscale, and comfy; there are fireplaces to ward off any chill or induce romance or reverie; the kitchens are modern; and the views—well, once you see them, you'll know why I want to be locked in the Cuckoo's Nest.

35 Ellingson St. www.channelhouse.com. © **800/447-2140** or 541/765-2140. 12 units. $100–$350 double w/continental breakfast included. **Amenities:** Free Wi-Fi.

Inn at Arch Rock ★★ Channel House is all contemporary luxury, and the Inn at Arch Rock is more like a wonderfully comfortable beach cottage with an emerald-green lawn above the cliffs and crashing surf. And some of the rooms here have views that, although not as close to the water, rival them for sheer eye-popping splendor. The original buildings in this small complex were cottages built in the 1930s; later, a motel-like building was added and, as of 2014, another new wing is being added. The best rooms are on the second floor—especially #12 with corner windows and a cushioned bench below them that lets you sit or lounge with a book, with the ocean just below. There are some nice older features, like wood-burning fireplaces from the 1950s and a little staircase that takes you down to a small, surf-churned beach.

70 NW Sunset St. www.innatarchrock.com. © **800/767-1835** or 541/765-2560. 13 units. $79–$139 double w/continental breakfast. Pets accepted ($10 per night). **Amenities:** Free Wi-Fi.

WHERE TO EAT

If you're in need of a pick-me-up while passing through Depoe Bay, stop by the **Pirate Coffee Company,** 10 Vista St. (www.piratecoffeecompany.com; © **541/765-4373**).

Restaurant Beck ★★★ NORTHWEST Restaurant Beck is one of the three upper-echelon fine-dining restaurants along the Oregon coast, the other two being the **Bay House** ★★★ (p. 205) near Lincoln City and the dining room at the **Stephanie Inn** ★★★ (p. 197). The presence of an award-winning chef, Justin Wills, and a location in the luxurious Whale Cove Inn (a sister property to the Channel House in Depoe Bay, above), has put Beck on the map. And the imaginative cooking, too, of course. Wills is up-to-date with all the current foodie farm-to-table or sea-to-table trends. Foraged wild greens might show up in your salad, your halibut may be a hay-smoked crudo with wild mushroom and ramp kimchi, and your troll-caught Oregon king salmon may come with fried reindeer moss and smoked steelhead roe. And how about dried matsutake mushroom ice cream? You just won't find this kind of culinary creativity and experimentation anywhere else on the coast. It's a social-media-savvy "Follow us on Facebook and Twitter" kind of place that treats the chef like a celebrity and dining as an experience to share—via Instagram. This is highly unusual on the laid-back, low-key Oregon coast.

At Whale Cove Inn, 2345 S. US. 101. www.restaurantbeck.com. © **541/765-3220.** Main courses $26–$31. Wed–Mon 5–9pm.

Tidal Raves ★★ SEAFOOD Tidal Raves, at the south end of Depoe Bay, has been around for years and, because it sticks mostly to classic preparations of fresh seafood with a few creative spin-offs, has had a loyal following since it opened. Part of the appeal here is the incredibly dramatic view that goes along with the professional service and casual yet sophisticated atmosphere. Three worthwhile signature dishes are Dungeness crab cakes, fish tacos, and a spinach and oyster bisque. More innovative is the red curry barbecue shrimp.

279 NW U.S. 101. www.tidalraves.com. © **541/765-2995.** Main courses $13–$26. Daily 11am–9pm.

EXPLORING DEPOE BAY

The town of Depoe Bay doesn't attract visitors because it has a long, beautiful beach. The coastline hereabouts is rocky and unwalkable. Aside from whale-watching and standing on the highway bridge to observe the boat traffic passing in and out of the world's smallest harbor, the most popular activity here, especially when the seas are high, is watching the **spouting horns.** Similar to blowholes, spouting horns can be seen all along the coast, but nowhere are they more spectacular than along the coastline at Depoe Bay, right across from the main tourist strip on U.S. 101. These geyserlike plumes occur in places where water is forced through narrow channels in basalt rock. As the channels become more restricted, the water shoots skyward under great pressure and can spray 60 feet into the air. If the surf is really up, the water can spray a long distance, and more than a few unwary visitors have been doused by a spouting horn.

Whale-Watching ★★★ OUTDOOR RECREATION/WILDLIFE TOUR   Gray whales *(Eschrichtius robustus)* are migratory mammals that make an annual journey from the Bering Sea to their birthing grounds in Baja California and back again. But there's a resident pod of grey whales that makes its home in the waters of Depoe Bay for 10 months of the year. Small wonder that whale-watching is the top attraction in Depoe Bay. Visitors come from around the world to catch a glimpse of these behemoths of the sea. You can whale-watch from many shore observation spots or take one of the whale-watching charters out for a closer look. It's a thrilling and unforgettable sight when you see breeching whales in their natural habitat. Whale-watching trips aboard comfortable cruisers or speedy Zodiacs depart throughout the day from Depoe Bay. Bring your sea legs and your binoculars. **Tradewind Charters,** with a kiosk right on Highway 101 in "downtown" Depoe Bay (www.tradewindscharters.com; © **800/445-8730** or 541/765-2345), offers 1- or 2-hour whale-watching excursions; prices are $18 to $35 adults, $16 to $30 seniors, $9 to $15 ages 5 to 12.

To learn more about gray whales, stop in at Depoe Bay's **Whale Watching Center,** 119 U.S. 101 (www.oregon.gov/oprd/parks; © **541/765-3304**), perched on the cliff above the entrance to the harbor. Rangers and volunteers are on hand to point out gray whales if they are visible, and there are interesting displays about *Eschrichtius robustus.* Memorial Day to Labor Day, the center is open daily from 9am to 5pm; other months open Wednesday through Saturday from 10am to 4pm and Sunday from noon to 4pm.

Newport ★★★

12 miles S of Depoe Bay, 24 miles N of Yachats, 58 miles W of Corvallis.

As Oregon coast towns go, Newport has something of a split personality. This lively community of 10,000 on Yaquina Bay is both a working port, with the largest commercial fishing fleet in Oregon, and a tourist destination, home to the Oregon Coast Aquarium, the top attraction on the coast. Along the downtown bayfront, dockworkers unloading fresh fish mingle with vacationers licking ice-cream cones as fishing boats. pleasure craft, and Coast Guard cutters ply the waters of the bay. The air smells of fish and shrimp, and freeloading sea lions doze on the docks, waiting for their next meal. Directly across the street, art galleries, souvenir shops, and restaurants crowd together.

The busy bayfront is the center of Newport. The aquarium and Hatfield Marine Science Center are on the south side of Yaquina Bay, reached by the beautiful arched span of the Yaquina Bay Bridge, opened in 1936 and one of seven bridges on the Oregon coast designed by Conde McCullough. At the north end of town is the historic neighborhood of Nye Beach, where many of the charming old cottages and heritage buildings date from the early 1900s, when Newport was developing as one of the coast's first ocean resorts. Nye Beach is home to the Newport Performing Arts Center, a popular year-round venue for performances and art events of all kinds. Newport is also home to two historic lighthouses, which are just 3 miles apart.

In the late 1800s, before all the fishing and the aquarium and the saltwater taffy shops, Newport got its start as an oystering community, and oysters are still important to the local economy. They're raised in oyster beds along Yaquina Bay Road, east of town.

Though in recent years Newport has come close to matching the overdevelopment of Lincoln City, this community on the shore of Yaquina Bay still manages to offer a balance of industry, history, culture, beaches, good restaurants, and family attractions. It's one of the most interesting towns you'll find on the Oregon coast.

ESSENTIALS

GETTING THERE Newport is on U.S. 101 at the junction with U.S. 20. From Portland, take I-5 south to Corvallis and head west on U.S. 20; the drive to Newport takes about 2½ hours.

VISITOR INFORMATION Contact the **Greater Newport Chamber of Commerce,** 555 SW Coast Hwy. (www.newportchamber.org; © **800/262-7844** or 541/265-8801).

FESTIVALS In February, the **Seafood and Wine Festival** is one of the coast's premier events. Artists and craftsmen showcase a variety of art, sculpture, photography, pottery, and jewelry; Pacific Northwest wineries pour the wines; and culinary professionals serve the seafood. For more information, contact the Newport Chamber of Commerce (www.newportchamber.org).

WHERE TO STAY

Elizabeth Street Inn ★★ Even your car has a view at this well-done, in-town hotel built in 2000. That's because there's a covered parking lot (a boon in car-crowded Newport in the summer) on the lobby level. There are no bad views here; every room looks out on the long, scenic stretch of Nye Beach directly below. The decor is tasteful and unobtrusive. Every room has at least a sofa; all have fireplaces and kitchenettes. The white bed linens are crisp and fresh. It all adds up to a room you can really relax in. Two other pluses: the full breakfast and the large, indoor, saline pool. Plus, you can leave your car to enjoy the view and walk everywhere in Nye Beach.

2332 SW Elizabeth St. www.elizabethstreetinn.com. © **877/265-9400** or 541/265-9400. 68 units. $109–$329 double w/full breakfast. Pets accepted ($25 fee). **Amenities:** Exercise room; Jacuzzi; indoor saline pool; free Wi-Fi.

Newport Belle Bed & Breakfast ★ For a nautical night on Newport Bay, walk up the gangplank of the Newport Belle, the only sternwheel B&B in North America. This is a unique and charming floating B&B, with 5 rooms, or cabins, all

Newport

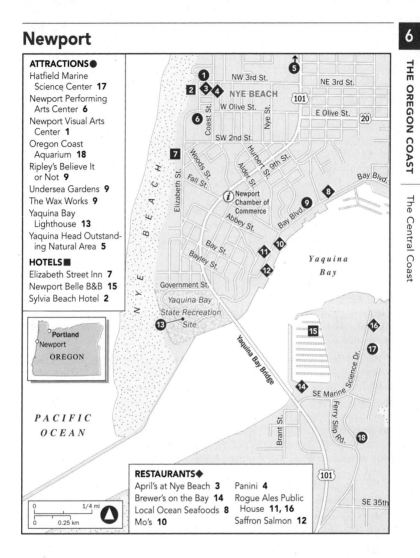

ATTRACTIONS●

Hatfield Marine Science Center **17**

Newport Performing Arts Center **6**

Newport Visual Arts Center **1**

Oregon Coast Aquarium **18**

Ripley's Believe It or Not **9**

Undersea Gardens **9**

The Wax Works **9**

Yaquina Bay Lighthouse **13**

Yaquina Head Outstanding Natural Area **5**

HOTELS■

Elizabeth Street Inn **7**

Newport Belle B&B **15**

Sylvia Beach Hotel **2**

Portland
Newport
OREGON

NW 3rd St.
NE 3rd St.
NYE BEACH
101
W Olive St.
E Olive St.
20
SW 2nd St.
Coast St.
Nye St.
Woods St.
Hubert St.
Alder St.
9th St.
Fall St.
Elizabeth St.
Newport Chamber of Commerce
Bay Blvd.
Abbey St.
Bay Blvd.
Bay St.
Bayley St.
Government St.
Yaquina Bay State Recreation Site
Yaquina Bay
N Y E   B E A C H
Yaquina Bay Bridge
Yaquina Bay
SE Marine Science Dr.
Ferry Slip Rd.
Brant St.
PACIFIC OCEAN
0   1/4 mi
0   0.25 km
101
SE 35th

RESTAURANTS◆

April's at Nye Beach **3**   Panini **4**

Brewer's on the Bay **14**   Rogue Ales Public

Local Ocean Seafoods **8**   House **11, 16**

Mo's **10**   Saffron Salmon **12**

with private bathrooms. The rooms, on two decks, are small but have nice touches like beadboard wainscoting, a little table and two chairs, and windows that let in lots of light and give you a sense of being right on the bay (which you are). The decor is quasi-Victorian but kept fairly simple. The public areas on the top deck include a parlor and a sunroom where you can enjoy a complimentary glass of wine in the evening. People with major mobility issues would probably find it difficult to navigate the boat's staircases.

2126 SE OSU Dr., Newport, OR 97365. ℂ **800/348-1922** or 541/867-6290. www.newportbelle .com. 5 units. $150–$165 double w/breakfast included. Pets accepted ($25 per night). No children. Closed Nov to mid-Feb. **Amenities:** Access to nearby health club; free Wi-Fi.

Sylvia Beach Hotel ★★★   Sylvia's isn't for everyone, but if it's for you, you'll absolutely love it and never want to leave. It's not for everyone because it has no TVs, no telephones, and no Wi-Fi. But if you're prepared and in the right mood, the funky charm of this century-old hotel right on Nye Beach is absolutely unique. Usually I'm not that crazy about "theme" rooms, but because the theme at Sylvia Beach is literary, I love it. (Sylvia Beach, in case you don't know, was an American woman with the famous bookstore in Paris, known for championing the likes of James Joyce.) Every room here is dedicated to a different writer: the Colette room is all French elegance, the Mark Twain room is all masculine swagger, and the Dr. Seuss room is bright, bold, and funny. It's impossible to describe all the different room configurations and bathrooms—each one is different, and the original nooks and crannies are all intact, including a fabulous second-floor library where you can relax by the fire with your favorite book as the waves pummel the beach below. A full breakfast is included, and the hotel's **Table of Content** restaurant serves a good fixed-price dinner for $25. Oh, and by the way, Shelley, the resident tortoiseshell cat, is definitely people-friendly.

267 NW Cliff St. www.sylviabeachhotel.com. ℂ **888/795-8422** or 541/265-5428. 20 units. $115–$220 double w/full breakfast. 2-night minimum on weekends. **Amenities:** Restaurant; no TV, phone, or Wi-Fi.

WHERE TO EAT

In addition to its beach and marine-centric attractions, Newport has some good restaurants. In fact, on a coast not known for its great restaurants, Newport shines like a lighthouse beacon. I hope you like seafood because, as you might expect, there's a lot of it on the menus here.

April's at Nye Beach ★★ NORTHWEST/MEDITERRANEAN   In a charming old building right across from the Sylvia Beach Hotel, April's is a place that locals love and always recommend to visitors. You won't find fresher food or produce anywhere. The chef, April Wolcott, picks fresh seasonal herbs and produce from her Buzzard Bay farm, chooses fish as soon as it's brought to the dock on the Bayfront, and uses only top-grade Niman Ranch beef. The emphasis on farm-to-fork means that the daily specials are just that. In addition to seafood and steaks, April's is known for handmade pasta with sauces made from scratch in house. The wine list favors Pacific Northwest and Italian vintages. The atmosphere here, with April's husband Kent doing the meeting and greeting, is warm and relaxed. There's also an excellent selection of regional wines at reasonable prices.

749 NW Third St. www.aprilsatnyebeach.com. ℂ **541/265-6855.** Main courses $16–$28. Wed–Sun 5–9pm. Closed late Nov–Jan.

Local Ocean ★★★ SEAFOOD   Both simple and sophisticated, this glass-fronted restaurant on the Bayfront serves fish and seafood so fresh that you can ask what boat it just came in on. The front opens out onto the sidewalk for summer dining, otherwise it's small tables in the colorful, streetside dining room with a showcase of fresh seafood to greet you as you enter. All of the seafood is locally sourced and sustainably harvested; no farmed fish is served. My suggestion here is to order three small plates and share them: maybe the fresh mixed-greens salad, an order of panko-crusted pan-fried oysters, and a couple of fish tacos. The fish and seafood is cooked with a minimum of fuss but has some nice spicy additions in the fish tacos. This is my favorite restaurant in Newport, but it doesn't take reservations, and at peak times you will probably have to stand in line. If you have the time, do it.

213 SW Bay Blvd. www.localocean.net. ☏ **541/574-7959.** Main courses $9–$24. Daily 11am–8pm (until 9pm in summer)..

Mo's ★ SEAFOOD   Years ago, when I first visited Mo's, I was amazed to find that the clam chowder was so thick that I could stand my spoon upright and it wouldn't fall over. Mo's is still serving chowder like that. That is what Mo's has always been known for and what keeps the crowds returning. Mo's is an Oregon coast institution, and if you have kids in tow it's good to know about, because it's relatively inexpensive com-pared to other coast fish restaurants. There are now Mo's up and down the coast (in Cannon Beach, Lincoln City, and Florence), but this was the first, and it has expanded exponentially over the years and now has an overflow Annex with the same menu and better views. I would stick with the basics here: seafood sandwiches, fish and chips, or seafood dinners. Be prepared to wait on weekends year-round and every day in sum-mer. The seating is casual, the portions hearty, the quality good, and the cooking unsurprising.

622 SW Bay Blvd. www.moschowder.com. ☏ **541/265-2979.** Main courses $8–$18. Daily 11am–10pm.

Panini ★ COFFEE/PIZZA/BAKERY   This funky little spot in Nye Beach makes the best lattes I've found on the entire Oregon coast—and believe me, I've looked and tasted a lot of them. They also make really good pizzas and have a bakery that turns out some delectable rolls (try the one filled with raisins) and pastries to accompany your coffee. I like this spot because it is so completely unpretentious, down-to-earth, and friendly—a real throwback, nowadays, to an earlier time. There are a couple of small tables and some room at a counter, but that's it. Panini's serves the Nye Beach locals in the Nye Beach way—up-to-date but untrendy.

232 NW Coast St. ☏ **541/265-5033.** Pizza/snacks $14–$20. Daily 7am–7pm.

Saffron Salmon ★★ NORTHWEST   Located on the public pier next to the Coast Guard station, Saffron Salmon is about dining on fresh seafood while enjoying a great sea view. Yes, burgers are available for fish-haters, but wouldn't you rather enjoy mus-sels and frites, or cod fish and chips, or a fresh filet of salmon sandwich? Pasta lovers can order garlic prawns on linguine, or smoked salmon on egg noodles. For a bit of everything from the sea, try the spicy seafood stew. While you're dining, you won't be able to keep your eyes off the sea lions and fishing boats just beyond the giant window.

859 SW Bay Blvd. www.saffronsalmon.com. ☏ **541/265-8921.** Main courses $15–$26 Thurs–Tues 11:30am–2:15pm and 5–8:30pm. Closed early to late Nov.

EXPLORING NEWPORT

Bayfront ★★ NEIGHBORHOOD   The Bayfront is tourist central for Newport. Here you'll find restaurants, ice-cream parlors, saltwater-taffy shops, chowder houses, and souvenir stores. The Bayfront is also home to commercial fishermen, seafood processing plants, art galleries, and numerous sea lions, who love to lounge on the floating docks adjacent to Undersea Gardens (from the adjacent pier, you can observe them at fairly close range).

The Bayfront is also where you'll find Newport's three tourist traps: **Ripley's Believe It or Not!, The Wax Works,** and **Undersea Gardens,** where a scuba diver feeds fish in a large tank beneath a boat moored on the Bayfront. Geared toward kids, all three of these places share the same address and phone number: **Mariner Square,**

250 SW Bay Blvd. (www.marinersquare.com; © **541/265-2206**). Admission for each is $12 for adults and $7 for children 5 to 12, or $25 for adults and $15 for children to visit all three. Enter at your own risk, and don't come grousing to me if you're disappointed with what you find inside.

Hatfield Marine Science Center Visitor Center ★ AQUARIUM   Located near the Oregon Coast Aquarium, this marine research facility of Oregon State University has a few interesting exhibits on life in Oregon's coastal waters. It's academic and science-oriented, geared to current topics in environmental and marine research, but the giant Pacific octopi are definitely worth visiting, and there are other marine-related exhibits as well. If your time in Newport is limited, visit the Oregon Coast Aquarium and don't worry about missing this.

2030 SE Marine Science Dr. www.hmsc.oregonstate.edu. © **541/867-0226.** Admission by suggested $5 donation. Memorial Day to Labor Day daily 10am–5pm; Labor Day to Memorial Day Thurs–Mon 10am–4pm.

Nye Beach ★★★ NEIGHBORHOOD   Newport was one of the earliest beach resort destinations in Oregon, and it was in Nye Beach that the first hotels and vacation cottages were built. Today, this neighborhood, north of the Bayfront along the beach, has been given a new pedestrian-only street and is home to hotels, good restaurants, some interesting shops, and, of course, miles of sandy beach. There's public parking at the turnaround on Beach Drive. The works of local and regional artists are showcased at the **Newport Visual Arts Center,** 777 NW Beach Dr. (www.coastarts.org; © **541/265-6540**). The center is open Tuesday through Sunday from 11am to 6pm. Just a few blocks away, the **Newport Performing Arts Center,** 777 W. Olive St. (www.coastarts.org; © **541/265-2787**), hosts local and nationally recognized ensembles, performers and art exhibits.

Oregon Coast Aquarium ★★★ AQUARIUM   He's not here now, but there was an international hoo-haw back in 1996 when Keiko, the orca whale star of *Free Willy,* arrived via UPS at his new home, a huge aquarium built expressly for him at the Oregon Coast Aquarium. I was one of the lucky journalists who got to cover Keiko's arrival, and I was nearly sidelined by the crush of photographers racing to get their shots of Keiko as he was raised in a hydraulic harness from his tank on the back of a flatbed truck, swung over the new aquarium, and lowered into the water. It was a whale of a good story, and for years, Keiko was the superstar of the aquarium, with a cadre of handlers who tried to rehabilitate him for life in the wild. This meant trying to restore the natural hunting instincts that had been sucked out of him during his years as a performer in a too-small, too-warm tank in Mexico. Eventually Keiko was released into an underwater pen in an Icelandic fjord, but he never learned how to hunt for his own food and died in 2003 of various complications. His story has always haunted me—for instance, the incredible amount of time and money spent by humans trying to restore the instincts that humans had robbed him of in the first place—and, to me, Keiko still haunts the Oregon Coast Aquarium, where for years he was able to swim in a much larger tank, one filled with seawater instead of chlorine, than he'd ever lived in before. He didn't have to perform, but he was still surrounded by the humans who lined up in droves to watch him through underwater viewing windows.

All of which has nothing to do with the Oregon Coast Aquarium today, which remains one of the top aquariums in the country, and is definitely worth at least a couple hours of your time. Keiko's tank has been reconfigured with a walk-through acrylic tunnel that allows you to watch the far less loveable sharks that now hungrily patrol the waters where Keiko once swam. The aquarium does a great job of telling about aquatic life in Oregon's cold coastal waters and along its dramatic and varied shoreline. One outdoor exhibit is a walk-through aviary with tufted puffins, a beautiful and endangered shore bird. Another exhibit follows the course of a raindrop from mountain stream to sea, illustrating the journey with examples of the fish and animals found along the way. Though it rarely spreads its tentacles the full 20 feet, the giant Pacific octopus is another featured attraction. Sandy beaches, rocky shores, salt marshes, kelp forests, and the ocean waters of the Pacific—Oregon's interlinked coastal ecosystems are amazing and beautiful, and full of the creatures you will see or learn about in this fascinating aquarium.

2820 SE Ferry Slip Rd. www.aquarium.org. © **541/867-3474.** Admission $20 adults, $18 seniors and ages 13–17, $13 children 3–12. Memorial Day to Labor Day daily 9am–6pm; Labor Day to Memorial Day daily 10am–5pm.

Yaquina Bay State Recreation Site ★★★ LIGHTHOUSE/LANDMARK/ HISTORIC SITE   The older of Newport's two lighthouses, **Yaquina Bay Lighthouse,** is just north and west of the Yaquina Bay Bridge. This 1871 lighthouse, the oldest building in Newport, is unusual in that the light is in a tower atop a two-story wood-frame house. The building served as both home and lighthouse, and supposedly is haunted—but they say that about just about every lighthouse on the Oregon coast.

846 SW Government St. www.oregon.gov/oprd/parks. © **800/551-6949.** Admission free. June–Sept daily 11am–5pm; winter daily noon–4pm.

NEWPORT PERFORMING ARTS & NIGHTLIFE

The **Newport Performing Arts Center,** 777 W. Olive St. (www.coastarts.org; © **541/265-2787**), hosts a year-round roster of performances and events.

If you're in the mood for a good pint of microbrew ale, visit **Rogue Ales Public House,** 748 SW Bay Blvd. (www.rogue.com; © **541/265-3188**). There's a second Rogue pub, **Brewer's on the Bay** over near the Oregon Coast Aquarium at 2320 OSU Dr. (© **541/867-3664**).

Yachats ★★★

24 miles S of Newport, 26 miles N of Florence, 138 miles SE of Portland

Located on the north side of 800-foot-high Cape Perpetua, the village of Yachats (pronounced *yah*-hots) is something of an artists' community that also attracts a goodly number of affluent retirees and what passes these days for "counterculturists." When you get your first glimpse of Yachats's setting, you will likely agree that there's more than enough oceanfront splendor here to inspire anyone. Although there really aren't any non-natural attractions in this village of about 700 people, the natural ones more than suffice.

Yachats is a Chinook word meaning "dark waters at the foot of the mountains," and that sums up perfectly the setting of this small community, one of the few on the Oregon coast that could really be considered a village (it has no major commercial development of any kind). The tiny Yachats River flows into the surf on the south edge of town, where Cape Perpetua, the highest point on the Oregon coast, rears its forested head, and to the east stand the steep, forested mountains of the Coast Range. The shoreline on which the town stands is rocky, with little coves here and there where you can find agates among the pebbles paving the beach. Tide pools offer hours of exploring, and in winter, storm

DON'T MISS YAQUINA HEAD outstanding NATURAL AREA

One place you really don't want to miss is the **Yaquina Head Outstanding Natural Area ★★★,** a laborious name but an apt one for this fascinating piece of coastline, 3 miles north of Newport at 750 NW Lighthouse Dr. (www.blm.gov/or/resources/recreation/yaquina/index.php; ✆ **541/574-3100**). At 93 feet, the still-functioning **Yaquina Head Lighthouse,** the area's gleaming white focal point, is the tallest lighthouse on the Oregon coast and one of the most easily accessible to visitors. The light began operation in 1874, replacing the earlier Yaquina Bay Lighthouse overlooking Yaquina Bay in Newport (see p. 209). Displays in the adjacent **Yaquina Head Interpretive Center** (open daily 10am–4:30pm) cover everything from the life of lighthouse keepers and their families to the sea life of tide pools. But this is also a wonderful spot to view seabirds and other sealife. Cormorants and pigeon guillemots roost on the steep slopes, and harbor seals lounge on the offshore rocks, and in early winter and spring you may be able to spot a migrating gray whale. A stairway leads down to a cobblestone beach below the lighthouse, where you can explore tide pools at low tide (there's even a wheelchair-accessible tide-pool trail). Centuries ago, Native Americans lived along this rocky cove, harvesting shellfish and other foods from the sea. Admission is $7 per car. The grounds are open daily from 8am to 8pm; tours of the lighthouse are given at noon, 1, 2, and 3pm.

waves create a spectacular show. Uncrowded beaches, comfortable motels, and a couple of good restaurants add up to a great spot for a quiet getaway.

ESSENTIALS

GETTING THERE   From the north, take Ore. 34 west from Corvallis to Waldport, and then head south on U.S. 101. From the south, take Ore. 126 west from Eugene to Florence, and then head north on U.S. 101.

VISITOR INFORMATION   Contact the **Yachats Area Chamber of Commerce,** 241 U.S. 101 (www.yachats.org; ✆ **800/929-0477** or 541/547-3530).

WHERE TO STAY

In addition to the hotels listed below, plenty of rental homes are available in Yachats. Contact **Ocean Odyssey** (www.ocean-odyssey.com; ✆ **800/800-1915** or 541/547-3637), or **Yachats Village Rentals** (www.97498.com; ✆ **888/288-5077** or 541/547-3501). Rates for most vacation homes range from around $140 to $225 per night.

The Fireside Motel ★   Located adjacent to Overleaf Lodge, its more upscale sister property, the Fireside is a good choice for families and travelers who aren't interested in on-site spa amenities and want good value for their dollar. The basic difference between the two properties is that not all of the rooms at the Fireside have views and fireplaces. Also, they do not have the floor-to-ceiling sliding glass doors and private balconies that the Overleaf has, so if you get a balcony room and step outside, you're right next door to your neighbor. That said, the rooms here have many of the same comfortable appointments, many have equally stunning ocean views, and some of them have special features like tongue-in-groove beamed ceilings and kitchenettes.

MY ENCOUNTER WITH THE ghost AT HECETA HEAD LIGHTSTATION

I had heard it was haunted, of course, but just about every lighthouse or lighthouse-affiliated building on the coast makes that claim. But one clear, moonlit night I was awakened from my slumbers at this historic B&B by the strange sound of something dropping or rolling down the stairs. Chills ran down my spine—until the room became so warm that I had to remove the blankets. Thump, thump, thump. I didn't get a whole lot of sleep, and the next morning when I walked bleary-eyed into the breakfast room and asked who else had been awakened by all that thumping, everyone looked at me as if I were crazy. Whatever it was that had gone bump in the night apparently didn't bump loud enough to rouse the other guests. But when I did some research

on the topic, I discovered that the "manifestations" of the ghost were often the sound of a ball slowly rolling down the stairs and rooms that suddenly became suffocatingly warm. I suppose it *could* have been the furnace snapping on (the manager assured me it wasn't), but I prefer to believe that it was the resident ghost, an older woman dressed all in black and sometimes seen, broom in hand, in the upstairs rooms. I was so taken with the stories I heard (the level-headed local contractor, who climbed a ladder to do some work on the upper floors, saw the lady in black gliding toward him and fled in terror, never to return) that I turned the lady in black into Rue, the ghost that forever sweeps and haunts the Heceta Head B&B in my play *Oregon Ghosts*.

The continental breakfast is not as big and varied as the Overleaf's, and there is a smaller and much less fancy lobby and overall ambience.

1881 U.S. 101 N. www.firesidemotel.com. ✆ **800/336-3573** or 541/547-3636. 43 units. $80–$165 double. w/continental breakfast. Pets accepted ($10 per night). **Amenities:** Access to adjacent spa; free Wi-Fi.

Heceta Head Lightstation ★★   You want picturesque? You want photogenic? You want historic? You want haunted? Stay here, in one of the last remaining lighthouse keeper's houses on the Oregon coast. It's a white Victorian clapboard house with an open front porch, and it sits in an improbably tidy green lawn with a picket fence on a forested cliff not far from the Heceta Head Lighthouse, with views for miles. When houses like this were built, they didn't have "picture windows" or private balconies. If you got through the winter without the roof blowing off, you were lucky. The house has been a B&B for several years now, and it's an enjoyable place to stay with lots of handcrafted (but non-fancy) period details, like the wooden staircase to the rooms on the second floor. The rooms all have different outlooks but share a comfortable, period-inspired look. There's a lounge and public kitchen downstairs, and you're served a big breakfast in the morning. So it's no wonder that the Heceta Head Lightstation fills up quickly and you have to make a reservation well in advance of your trip. Once here, you're fairly isolated, so plan accordingly. And be sure to visit the Heceta Head Lighthouse as part of your stay.

92072 U.S. 101 S.0 www.hecetalighthouse.com. ✆ **866/547-3696** or 541/547-3696. 6 units, 4 with private bathroom. $133–$315 double w/full breakfast included. 2-night minimum on weekends. No children under 10. **Amenities:** Free Wi-Fi.

Ocean Haven ★★ The address of this enviro-friendly ocean retreat is Yachats, but it's really about 8 miles south, perched on a bluff in a Marine Protected and Shore-bird Conservation Area. Ocean Haven is about the ocean, and the fragile ocean and shore ecosystem, so you won't find giant-screen TVs (though you can still surf with the free Wi-Fi). What you will find is a charming rustic retreat committed to sound environmental practices. Oh, and some pretty spectacular views, too, especially in the North or South View rooms with their walls of glass. For super-natural romantic charm, book the little cabin with its wood-burning fireplace and ocean-facing deck. Wood-paneled walls give a lovely warmth to all the rooms and cabin; the furniture includes recliners and window-bunks. You can walk to the beach and lots of nearby tide pools.

94770 U.S. 101, Yachats, OR 97498. www.oceanhaven.com. ℂ **541/547-3583.** 5 units. $110–$165 double. **Amenities:** Free Wi-Fi.

Overleaf Lodge ★★ Even finicky travelers who eschew the modern motel-resorts that line the Oregon coast will probably like Overleaf Lodge. The location, directly beside a rocky stretch of coastline about a mile north the center of Yachats, is superb. The sound of the surf is always in your ears (at night when the tide is in and the waves are crashing on the rocks below, you'll really feel the power of the Pacific), and most of the rooms have private balconies or patios so you can sit outside and enjoy the spectacle of the sea. The rooms were all refurbished in 2014 and have a fresh, upgraded look and feel that provides comfort and style. The bathrooms and vanity areas have granite countertops (but plastic tubs) and the furniture is a sturdy, generic rendition of Arts and Crafts style. The larger rooms have two big comfortable armchairs, a fireplace, and a full kitchen; there's a comfy recliner in the smaller rooms. The spa area is also well done, with two heated soaking pools and separate sauna areas for men and women. One of the nicest features in this hotel is the coastal path right behind it, which is easy to walk and takes you along a highly scenic section of the ocean to a long sand beach. And the complimentary breakfast is very generous and filling.

280 Overleaf Lodge Lane. www.overleaflodge.com. ℂ **800/338-0507** or 541/547-4880. 54 units. $135–$295 double w/continental breakfast included. **Amenities:** Spa, exercise room; heated indoor soaking pools; sauna; free Wi-Fi.

WHERE TO EAT

On my never-ending quest for truth, justice, and a decent cup of coffee, I discovered **Green Salmon Coffee and Tea House,** 220 U.S. 101 N. (www.thegreensalmon.com; ℂ **541/547-3077**), where you can get organic, fair-trade coffee, baked goods, and light meals.

Heidi's Italian Dinners ★★ ITALIAN Heidi Travaglia moved to Yachats from New Jersey over 2 decades ago and started her career as a caterer with a deli and take-out pizza. She now serves dinners only—and they are the best Italian dinners in Yach-ats (it's wise to make a reservation here). The restaurant is in a charming little cottage beside the beach in "downtown" Yachats. One of her specialties is *cioppino,* an Italian seafood stew with cod, prawns, scallops, calamari, and shrimp in a spicy tomato base. Another is Dungeness crab ravioli. But this is also where you'll find real spaghetti and meatballs in a marinara sauce. There are only about 9 dishes on the menu, and they change every couple of weeks. You can enjoy a good Italian wine with your Italian dinner.

84 Beach. ℂ **541/547-4409.** Main courses $14–$23. Summer Wed–Sun 4:30am–8:30pm; winter Fri–Sun 5–8:30pm.

Luna Sea Fish House ★★ SEAFOOD   Lots of people think this is the best fish house on the entire coast because it serves only wild-caught fish. The owner, Robert Anthony, is a seasonal salmon fisherman and a Dungeness crabber who supplies his small, simple restaurant beside Highway 101 with the freshest of the fresh. This is cozy but not a fancy place in any way, shape, or form. The tablecloths are blue-and-white-checked oilcloth. There's a heated tent outside to handle larger summer crowds. The fresh catch is served grilled or fried, and the presentation is not exactly artful. Fresh grilled albacore tuna or other seasonal fresh fish is typically served over a big helping of salad. The salmon fish and chips are wonderful. Lua Sea in some ways reminds me of the way the Oregon coast used to be: simple, unpretentious, real. They serve breakfast as well.

153 U.S. 101 N. www.lunaseafishhouse.com. ℂ **541/547-4794.** Main courses $11–$16. Daily 9am–9pm (8pm in winter; 10pm Fri–Sat summer).

Ona ★ SEAFOOD/AMERICAN   Ona is about casual fine dining. It's the most sophisticated of Yachats's restaurants in that you can order a well-made cocktail before dinner, and choose from a good wine list at dinner. The window-lined dining room is a pleasant spot with an outdoor deck for summer dining. People come to Ona for dishes like fresh Dover sole wrapped over Dungeness crab and bay shrimp with a pinot gris cream reduction. The grilled oysters and fried rockfish used for the fish and chips are panko crusted and delicious. The Dungeness crab cakes are stuffed with lots of crab and served with a capered remoulade. Ona also make a great three-meat meatloaf using grass-fed beef, lamb, and pork. This is a good spot for a romantic dinner or a better-than-average lunch—the kind that makes you want to linger a bit.

131 U.S. 101. www.onarestaurant.com. ℂ **541/547-6627.** Main courses $10–$30. Mon–Fri 11am–9pm; Sat–Sun brunch 11am–3pm and 4–9pm.

EXPLORING YACHATS

Gray whales come close to shore near Yachats on their annual spring migration, and several take up residence throughout the summer at the mouth of the Yachats River. You can see them in the spring from Cape Perpetua, South of Cape Perpetua, **Neptune State Scenic Viewpoint,** at the mouth of Cummins Creek, and **Strawberry Hill Wayside**.

Built in 1927 in the shape of a cross, the **Little Log Church & Museum,** 328 W. Third St. (ℂ **541/547-3976**), is a repository of local history and still serves as a community gathering point. The museum is generally open from noon to 3pm (closed Thursdays).

Cape Perpetua Scenic Area ★★★ NATURE/OUTDOOR RECREATION/LIGHTHOUSE   Looming over tiny Yachats is the impressive bulk of 800-foot-high Cape Perpetua, the highest spot on the Oregon coast. Because of the cape's rugged beauty and diversity of natural habitats, it has been designated a scenic area. The visitor center houses displays on the natural history of the cape and the Native Americans who for thousands of years harvested its seafood. Within the scenic area are 26 miles of hiking trails, tide pools, ancient forests, scenic overlooks, and a campground. Guided hikes are offered (weather permitting) when the visitor center is open. If you're here on a clear day, be sure to drive to the top of the cape for the highest and eye-poppingest vista on the coast. There's good access to the tide pools via a short Oceans-ide trail from the pull-off at the north end of the scenic area. At the **Devil's Churn,** a spouting horn caused by waves crashing into a narrow fissure in the basalt shoreline sends geyserlike plumes of water skyward, and waves boil through a narrow opening in the rocks.

Cape Perpetua Visitor Center, 2400 U.S. 101. www.fs.fed.us/r6/siuslaw. (*C*) **541/547-3289.** Admission $5 per vehicle. Summer daily 10am–5:30pm; spring and fall daily 10am–4pm; winter Wed–Sun 10am–4pm.

Florence ★★

12 miles S of Heceta Head, 50 miles S of Newport, 60 miles W of Eugene

The sprawl along Highway 101 just north of Florence may make you wonder if you're on the Oregon coast or driving along a mall-laden suburb in Anywhere, USA. But head down from the highway toward downtown Florence, and you'll encounter one of the few communities on the Oregon coast that retains a semblance of historic character. Set on the banks of the Siuslaw River, Florence's Old Town is lined with restored wooden commercial buildings that house restaurants and shops. The **Oregon Dunes National Recreation Area** (see p. 222) starts just south of Florence—hence town's claim to be "Gateway to the Oregon Dunes."

HECETA HEAD LIGHTHOUSE, SEA LION CAVES & carnivorous plants

On the stretch of U.S. 101 between Yachats and Florence there are three attractions that have long lured travelers along the Oregon coast. Ten miles south of Cape Perpetua, **Heceta Head Lighthouse State Scenic Viewpoint ★★★** is worth a stop to see **Heceta Head Lighthouse,** the most photographed lighthouse on the Oregon coast, and the breathtaking seascape of pounding surf and offshore haystack rocks. Heceta (pronounced "huh-*see*-tuh") Head is a rugged headland named for Spanish explorer Captain Bruno Heceta. The old lighthouse keeper's home is now a bed-and-breakfast (see **Heceta Head Lightstation ★★,** p. 217). Between Memorial Day and Labor Day, free tours are given of the lighthouse keeper's house Thursday through Monday between noon and 5pm. There is a $5 day-use fee to use the park.

One mile south of Heceta Head, **Sea Lion Caves ★★,** 91560 U.S. 101 N. (www.sealioncaves.com; (*C*) **541/547-3111**), is the largest sea cave in the United States and has been a popular tourist attraction since 1932. The 300-foot-long cave and a nearby rock ledge are the only year-round mainland homes for Steller sea lions, the larger of the two species of sea lion (bulls can weigh almost a ton). Although you're likely to see quite a few of the sea lions here at any time of year, it is during the fall and winter that the majority of them move into the cave. A combination of stairs, pathways, and an elevator lead down from the bluff-top gift shop to a viewpoint in the cave wall. The best time to visit is late in the afternoon, when the sun shines directly into the cave and the crowds are smaller. Admission is $14 for adults, $13 for seniors, $8 for children 3 to 12. The caves are open daily from 9am to 5pm.

Another 6 miles south is the **Darlingtonia State Natural Site ★,** a small botanical preserve protecting a bog full of rare *Darlingtonia californica* plants, insectivorous pitcher plants also known as cobra lilies. You'll find this fascinating preserve on Mercer Lake Road; there's a turn-off sign from Highway 101. There's no admission or set opening hours.

Florence got its start in the 1850s, soon after the California Gold Rush, when premium lumber from Oregon forests was cut and floated down the Siuslaw (sigh-*oo*-slaw) River and shipped south to San Francisco. The town apparently didn't have a name, or couldn't decide on one, until a piece of debris from the shipwrecked *Florence* drifted ashore and spurred someone's imagination.

Although the Florence waterfront has a picturesque charm, I would recommend that you visit Florence for a stroll and lunch, rather than making it an overnight stop.

ESSENTIALS

GETTING THERE   Florence is on U.S. 101 at the junction with Ore. 126 from Eugene.

VISITOR INFORMATION   For more information on Florence, contact the **Florence Area Chamber of Commerce,** 290 U.S. 101 (www.florencechamber.com; ✆ **541/997-3128**). Their office is open Monday to Friday 9am to 5pm, Saturday 10am to 2pm, and Sunday 11am to 3pm.

WHERE TO EAT

Mr. Coffee Finder (that's me) recommends **Siuslaw River Coffee Roasters,** 1240 Bay St. (www.coffeeoregon.com; ✆ **541/997-3443**), for a decent cuppa. **Lovejoy's Restaurant & Tea Room,** 195 Nopal St. (www.lovejoysrestaurant.com; ✆ **541/902-0502**) serves a traditional English tea.

Bridgewater Fish House and Zebra Bar ★ AMERICAN   For a reliably good meal and a hit of old Florence, this big, busy restaurant is a good choice. It occupies the most prominent building on Bay Street, a 1901 false-fronted general store built in 1901, and it has retained the atmosphere of that era. When it's available, and if you want to eat like a real Oregonian (or like Oregonians used to eat), order the whole steamed Dungeness crab, still in its shell, and start cracking. These sweet, delicious crabs are pretty much unavailable outside of the Pacific Northwest. Bridgewater's is good with fish, though not all of it is from local waters, and they also make good pastas.

1297 Bay St. www.bridgewaterfishhouse.com. ✆ **541/997-1133.** Main courses $10–$25. Daily 11am–11pm.

La Pomodori ★★ ITALIAN   For the best food in town, head over to 7th and Maple, where La Pomodori cooks up Italian food with a Northwest twist. This is where you can get bruschetta, a caprese salad, sausage gnocchi, and chicken cacciatore. But you can also get Italo-Northwest hybrids like a Reuben on focaccia or Tuscan halibut (served on a bed of spinach with pinenuts and tomatoes). The atmosphere is cozy, and the prices are reasonable for the top quality of the food. It's a good idea to make a reservation at least a day in advance.

1415 Seventh St. www.lapomodori.com. ✆ **541/902-2525.** Main courses $10–$24. Tues–Fri 11:30am–2pm and 5–8pm; Sat 5–8pm.

Maple Street Grille ★ AMERICAN   This small cottage-restaurant in Old Town combines charm with its comfort food. And good comfort food at that. Where else can you get good, old-fashioned pot roast with carrots, onions, mashed potatoes and gravy? Or bacon-wrapped meatloaf? But they've kept up with the culinary times and also offer a few Asian-inspired specialties, pulled-pork sliders, lettuce wraps, and fish or meat skewers. Fresh fish is always on the menu. And the classic burgers are nice and juicy.

If you're strolling in Old Town and want a French-press coffee or cocktail, this is a nice spot for that, too.

165 Maple St. www.maplestreetgrille.com. ✆ **541/997-9811.** Main courses $10–$23. Tues–Sat 11am–9pm.

EXPLORING FLORENCE & ENVIRONS

Old Town ★★ NEIGHBORHOOD/HISTORIC DISTRICT   Florence's Old Town, on the north bank of the Siuslaw River, is one of the most charming historic districts on the Oregon coast and the town's chief attraction. The restored wood and brick buildings housing shops, galleries, and restaurants capture the flavor of a late-19th/early-20th-century fishing and logging village. There's a promenade along the river, and a tiny park with a view down the riverfront at the site of the old ferry crossing.

Siuslaw Pioneer Museum ★ MUSEUM   The pioneer settlers in the Siuslaw River area were primarily loggers and fishermen, and the river was their chief means of transportation (and remained so until the 1930s). Housed in a former church building, this museum tells the story of early life in and around Florence with historic displays that include period rooms and artifacts. There's a small Native American collection, too. For an interesting couple of hours, take the historic walking tour that begins at the museum and winds through Old Town Florence; you can pick up a brochure or download the walking-tour map from the museum's website.

278 Maple St. www.siuslaw pioneermuseum.com. ✆ **541/997-7884.** Admission $3. May–Sept daily noon–4pm, closed Mon rest of year. Closed Dec 25–Jan 1.

THE SOUTH COAST

Oregon's South Coast begins just about where the **Oregon Dunes** do. You could use Florence as the starting point for the South Coast, but more typically Reedsport is considered where this special section of the coast begins, extending all the way down to Brookings on the northern California border. This stretch of coastline isn't exactly remote, but it's away from major inland cities and doesn't have many highways that cut through the coastal mountains and connect it to I-5. Once you get here, trusty U.S. 101 continues down the coast, taking you to Bandon, Gold Beach, Brookings, and into California.

Oregon Dunes National Recreation Area ★★

The Oregon Dunes Recreation Area begins just S of Florence and ends north of Coos Bay

The Oregon Dunes National Recreation Area starts just south of Florence and stretches for almost 50 miles. Recreation is the key word here; the dunes are magnets for all kinds of outdoor activities. Within this vast area of shifting sands—the largest sand dunes on the West Coast—there are numerous lakes, popular sports fishing and water-skiing destinations, but there are also places set aside for racing dune buggies, dirt bikes, and other off-road vehicles (ORVs) through the sand dunes.

The Umpqua River divides the national recreation area roughly at its midway point. Along the banks of the river are the little towns of Gardiner, Reedsport, and Winchester Bay. **Gardiner** was founded in 1841 when a Boston merchant's fur-trading ship wrecked near here. An important mill town in the 19th century, Gardiner has several stately Victorian homes. **Reedsport** is the largest of these three communities, and the town of **Winchester Bay** is known for its large fleet of charter-fishing boats. If you want a dunes experience, I would recommend that you explore the dunes on day trips.

ABOUT THE dunes

The first Oregon dunes were formed between 12 and 26 million years ago by the weathering of inland mountain ranges, but it was not until about 7,000 years ago, after the massive eruption of Mount Mazama (today's Crater Lake), that they reached their current size and shape. That volcanic eruption emptied out the entire molten-rock contents of Mount Mazama, and in the process created the caldera that became Crater Lake, the deepest lake in the U.S.

Due to water currents and winds, the dunes are in constant flux. Currents move the sand particles north each winter and south each summer, while constant winds off the Pacific Ocean blow the sand eastward, piling it up into dunes. Over thousands of years, the advancing dunes have swallowed up whole sections of forests, isolating some groves as remnant tree islands, turning others into parched patches of skeleton forest.

Freshwater trapped behind the dunes formed numerous **freshwater lakes,** many of which are now ringed by campgrounds and vacation homes. These lakes are popular for fishing, swimming, and boating. Lakes within the recreation area include **Cleawox Lake, Carter Lake, Beale Lake,** and **Horsfall Lake.**

European beach grass is changing the natural dynamics of this unusual ecosystem. Introduced to anchor sand dunes and prevent them from inundating roads and river channels, the beach grass has been much more effective than anyone ever imagined. Able to survive even when buried under several feet of sand, the plant has covered many acres of land and formed dunes that effectively block sand from blowing inland off the beach. As Pacific winds blow sand off the dunes into wet, low-lying areas, more vegetation takes hold. The result is that, today, only 20% of the dunes are open sand (the figure was once 80%). It is predicted that within 50 years, the Oregon dunes will be completely covered with vegetation and will no longer be the barren, windswept expanses of sand seen today.

ESSENTIALS

GETTING THERE   The dunes can be accessed at marked turn-offs all along Highway 101 between Florence and Coos Bay.

VISITOR INFORMATION   For more information on the dunes, contact the **Oregon Dunes National Recreation Area Visitor Center,** 855 U.S. 101, Reedsport, OR 97467 (www.fs.fed.us/r6/siuslaw; ✆ **541/271-6000**). From mid-May to mid-September, this visitor center is open daily from 8am to 4:30pm; other months, it is closed on Saturday and Sunday.

There is a $5-per-car day-use fee within the recreation area.

EXPLORING THE DUNES

There are numerous ways to explore and enjoy the dunes and surrounding area.

CAMPING & WATER SPORTS   **Jessie M. Honeyman Memorial State Park** ★★ (www.oregon.gov/oprd/parks; ✆ **541/997-3641**), 3 miles south of Florence, is a unique spot with a beautiful forest-bordered lake and towering sand dunes. The park offers camping, picnicking, hiking trails, and access to Cleawox and Woahink lakes. On Cleawox Lake, there is a swimming area and a boat-rental facility. The dunes adjacent to Cleawox Lake are used by off-road vehicles.

Umpqua Lighthouse State Park (www.oregon.gov/oprd/parks; © **541/271-4118**), near the Umpqua River Lighthouse ★★★ (see below), is the site of 500-foot-tall sand dunes that are the tallest in the United States. The park offers picnicking, hiking, and camping amid forests and sand dunes.

ELK VIEWING   One mile east of Reedsport on Ore. 38, at the **Dean Creek Elk Viewing Area ★,** you can spot 100 or more elk grazing on meadows that have been set aside as a preserve. In summer the elk tend to stay in the forest, where it's cooler.

GOLF   The 18-hole **Sandpines Golf Links,** 1201 35th St. (www.sandpines.com © **800/917-4653**), plays through dunes and pine forest and is one of Oregon's most popular courses. During the summer, you'll pay $79 for 18 holes. Alternatively, try the 18-hole **Ocean Dunes Golf Links,** 3345 Munsel Lake Rd. (www.oceandunesgolf .com; © **800/468-4833** or 541/997-3232), which also plays through the dunes and charges $25 to $42 for 18 holes during the summer.

HIKING   There are several places to wander among these sand dunes. If you have time only for a quick walk, head to **Carter Lake Campground,** where you can continue on from the Taylor Dunes viewing platform. The beach is less than a mile beyond the viewing platform, and roughly half this distance is through dunes. From this same campground, you can hike the **Carter Dunes Trail.** The beach is 1½ miles away through dunes, forest, and meadows known as a *deflation plain.* A 3.5-mile loop trail leads from the **Oregon Dunes Overlook** out to the beach by way of Tahkenitch Creek, a meandering stream that flows through the dunes and out to the ocean. Another mile south of the Oregon Dunes Overlook, you'll find the **Tahkenitch Creek Trail Head,** which accesses an 8-mile network of little-used trails that wander through dunes, forest, marshes, and meadows. However, for truly impressive dunes, the best route is the **John Dellenback Dunes Trail ★★,** which has its trail head a half-mile south of **Eel Creek Campground** (11 miles south of Reedsport). This 5.4-mile round-trip trail leads through an area of dunes 2 miles wide by 4 miles long.

HORSEBACK RIDING   **C&M Stables,** 90241 U.S. 101 N. (www.oregonhorse backriding.com; © **541/997-7540**), located 8 miles north of Florence, offers rides on the beach and through the dunes. A 1-hour dune ride costs $40 to $45, and a 2-hour ride on the beach costs $60 to $65.

OFF-ROAD VEHICLES   About 30% of the sand dunes are open to **off-road vehicles (ORVs),** which are also known as ATVs (all-terrain vehicles), and throngs of people flock to this area to roar up and down the dunes. If you'd like to do a little off-roading, you can rent a miniature dune buggy or ATV from **Sand Dunes Frontier,** 83960 U.S. 101 S. (www.sanddunesfrontier.com; © **541/997-5363**), 4 miles south of Florence. Guided tours of the dunes are offered by Sand Dunes Frontier and **Sandland Adventures,** 85366 U.S. 101 S. (© **541/997-8087;** www.sandland.com), 1 mile south of Florence (this company has a little amusement park as well). The tours cost about $12 to $50. One-person dune buggies and ATVs rent for about $45 per hour. Down at the southern end of the recreation area, you can rent vehicles from **Spinreel Dune Buggy Rentals,** 67045 Spinreel Rd., North Bend (www.ridetheoregondunes.com; © **541/759-3313**), located just off U.S. 101, about 9 miles south of Reedsport.

SANDBOARDING   Sandboarding is basically snowboarding in the sand, and at **Sand Master Park,** 87542 U.S. 101 N., Florence (www.sandmasterpark.com; © **541/997-6006**), you (or your teenage kids) will find 40 acres of sculpted sand dunes designed to mimic a wintertime snowboard park (lots of jumps and rails). June through mid-September, the park is open daily from 9am to 6:30pm; other months, it's open Monday, Tuesday, and Thursday through Saturday from 10am to 5pm, and Sunday noon to 5pm. The park is closed from mid-January through February. Sand boards rent for $10 to $25.

UMPQUA RIVER LIGHTHOUSE   In Winchester Bay, you can visit the historic **Umpqua River Lighthouse** ★★★. The original lighthouse was at the mouth of the Umpqua River and was the first lighthouse on the Oregon coast. It fell into the Umpqua River in 1861 and was replaced in 1894 by the current lighthouse. Adjacent to the lighthouse is the **Visitors Center & Museum,** 1020 Lighthouse Rd. (ⓒ **541/271-4631**), a former Coast Guard station with historical exhibits and an information center. At the museum, you can arrange to join a tour of the lighthouse. Tours are offered May through October daily between 10am and 4pm and cost $3 for adults and $2 for children 6 to 16. Across the street from the lighthouse is a **whale-viewing platform;** the best viewing months are November through June.

VIEWPOINTS   The easiest place to get an overview of the dunes is at the **Oregon Dunes Overlook,** 10 miles south of Florence. Here you'll find viewing platforms high atop a forested sand dune that overlooks a vast expanse of bare sand. Another easy place from which to view the dunes is the viewing platform on the **Taylor Dunes Trail,** which begins at the **Carter Lake Campground,** 7½ miles south of Florence. It is an easy ½-mile walk to the viewing platform.

Cape Arago Highway ★★★

Coos Bay tries hard, but it simply is not the sort of Oregon coast town that I would recommend to visitors. South of Coos Bay, however, you'll find three state parks and a protected marine estuary that preserve some of the most breathtaking shoreline on the entire south coast.

U.S. 101 begins a 50-mile inland stretch at Coos Bay, not reaching the ocean again until Bandon, so start your exploration of this beautiful stretch of coast by heading southwest from Coos Bay on the Cape Arago Highway.

SUNSET BAY STATE PARK ★

In 12 miles you'll come to **Sunset Bay State Park** (www.oregon.gov/oprd/parks; ⓒ **800/551-6949** or 541/888-4902), with one of the few beaches in Oregon where the water actually gets warm enough for swimming (although folks from warm-water regions may not agree). Sunset Bay is almost completely surrounded by sandstone cliffs, and the entrance to the bay is quite narrow, which means the waters here stay fairly calm. Picnicking and camping are available, and there are lots of tide pools to explore.

SHORE ACRES STATE PARK ★★★

Continuing on another 3 miles brings you to **Shore Acres State Park** (www.oregon .gov/oprd/parks; ⓒ **800/551-6949** or 541/888-4902), once the estate of local shipping tycoon Louis J. Simpson, who spent years developing his gardens. His ships would bring him unusual plants from all over the world, and eventually the gardens grew to include a formal English garden and a Japanese garden with a lily pond. His enormous mansion was demolished long ago, but the formal gardens and sunken lily pond built atop the cliffs overlooking the Pacific remain, and are a rare and wondrous sight in coastal Oregon. From the gardens, you can walk down to a tiny cove with rock walls, sculpted by the waves into unusual shapes, rising up from the water. The water off the

south slough NATIONAL ESTUARINE RESEARCH RESERVE

Four miles down Seven Devils Road from Charleston, you'll find the remarkably beautiful **South Slough National Estuarine Research Reserve ★★★** (www.southsloughestuary.org; ℭ **541/888-5558**). In 1972, the South Slough inlet of the Coos River became the first federally protected estuary in the U.S., and once you see it, you'll understand why these 5,000 acres of tidal flats, vast marshes, and meandering channels are so important to the health of the coastal ecosystem. Stop in at the Interpretive Center for a map and directions to the 1.75-mile trail that takes you through the characteristic estuarine habitats. It's an easy hike, and the pristine coastal scenery is absolutely glorious.

park is often a striking shade of blue, and **Simpson Beach,** in the little cove, just might be the prettiest beach in Oregon. There is a $5 day-use fee here.

CAPE ARAGO STATE PARK ★★

Cape Arago State Park (www.oregon.gov/oprd/parks; ℭ **800/551-6949**) is the third of this trio of parks. Just offshore from the rugged cape lie the rocks and small islands of Simpson Reef, which provide sunbathing spots for hundreds of seals (including elephant seals) and sea lions. The barking of the sea lions can be heard from hundreds of yards away, and though you can't get very close, with a pair of binoculars you can see the seals and sea lions quite well. The best viewing point is at **Simpson Reef Viewpoint.** On either side of the cape are coves with quiet beaches (the beaches are closed from March to June to protect young seal pups). Tide pools along these beaches offer hours of fascinating exploration during other months.

Bandon ★★★

24 miles S of Coos Bay, 54 miles north of Gold Beach

Once known primarily as the cranberry capital of Oregon (you can see the cranberry bogs south of town along U.S. 101), Bandon is now better known for its world-class Bandon Dunes Golf Resort. It's also set on one of the most beautiful stretches of coastline in the state, where the Coquille River empties into the Pacific. Just south of town, the beach is littered with boulders, monoliths, and haystack rocks that seem to have been strewn by some giant hand. Sunsets are stunning.

During the steamboat age, Bandon was a popular stopping-off point for passengers traveling between San Francisco and Seattle (there was no I-5 or U.S. 101 back then). The town became known as the "Playground of the Pacific." A devastating fire in 1936 put an end to Bandon's playground days. Today, a waterfront boardwalk connects Bandon with the Coquille River and the historic Coquille Lighthouse, one of only a handful of buildings to survive the fire. But even with its post-fire buildings, Bandon exerts a charm all its own and has the quaint feel of a historic seaside village that attracts artists, craftspeople, backpackers, retirees, and lots and lots of golfers.

ESSENTIALS

GETTING THERE Bandon is on U.S. 101. From the I-5 at Roseburg, head west on Ore. 42 to Coquille, where you take Ore. 42S to Bandon.

VISITOR INFORMATION   For more information, contact the **Bandon Chamber of Commerce,** 300 Second St. (www.bandon.com; ℃ 541/347-9616).

FESTIVALS   Bandon is the cranberry capital of Oregon, and every year in September the harvest is celebrated with the **Bandon Cranberry Festival.**

WHERE TO STAY

Bandon Dunes Golf Resort ★★★   You don't have to be a golfer to stay here, but you may feel like a fish out of water if you don't. That said, Bandon Dunes Golf Resort can be enjoyed as a resort with luxurious accommodations and resort amenities, although those are also geared to golf and golfers. Secluded duplex and multi-unit cottages are nestled around a pond and in quiet forest settings, and rooms and suites are available at the inn. Unlike most hotels and resorts along the coast, the units here do not have kitchens, but you can get terrific meals at the fine-dining restaurant in the lodge and the casual Pacific Grill in the clubhouse. The decor throughout is a kind of upscale Arts and Crafts utilizing natural woods and fabrics, with big Morris-style armchairs and flatscreen TVs. Guests can buy golf packages or receive a discount on individual courses.

57744 Round Lake Dr. www.bandondunesgolf.com. ℃ **888/345-6008.** 186 units. $100–$390 double. **Amenities:** 5 restaurants; 3 lounges; exercise room; four 18-hole golf courses and one 13-hole par-3 course; Jacuzzi; free Wi-Fi.

Bandon Inn ★   The super-friendly and super-economical Bandon Inn sits on the south bank of the Coquille River overlooking Bandon's Old Town. Rooms in the inn's two buildings are fairly large and decorated in a quasi-country, semi-traditional style that doesn't have much to do with the Oregon coast and better evokes the feeling of an inn on the Eastern Seaboard, with mix-and-match patterns and colors. All the rooms have microwaves and refrigerators, some have balconies, and there are thoughtful amenities like in-room coffeemakers and free local and long-distance U.S./Canada telephone calls. From the inn, a stairway leads down to Old Town with its shops and restaurants.

355 U.S. 101. www.bandoninn.com. ℃ **800/526-0209** or 541/347-4417. 57 units. $89–$155 double; Pets accepted ($15 per night). **Amenities:** Free Wi-Fi.

Best Western Inn at Face Rock Resort ★   Get one of the deluxe rooms here with its own little protected patio, and you'll spend hours sitting contentedly looking out at the glimmering Pacific just across Beach Loop Drive. The Best Western complex sits on 8 acres adjacent to the Old Bandon Golf Links, and it was where golfers often stayed before Bandon Dunes Golf Resort opened in 1999. It's a well-kept and attractive property, dating from 1979, with a big indoor pool open 24 hours. The rooms are comfortable, fairly large, and have full-length tubs in the bathrooms. The decor won't win any awards, but everything is spic-and-span and the prices are very reasonable. From the hotel, there's a path that will take you right down to the beach at Face Rock.

3225 Beach Loop Dr. www.innatfacerock.com. ℃ **800/638-3092** or 541/347-9441. 74 units. $79–$269 double w/full breakfast included. Pets accepted ($20 fee). **Amenities:** Restaurant; lounge; bikes; exercise room; Jacuzzi; indoor pool; sauna; free Wi-Fi.

WHERE TO EAT

When it's time for a latte or espresso, stop in at **Bandon Coffee Cafe,** 365 Second St. SE (www.bandoncoffee.com; ℃ **541/347-1144**), in a cottage on the edge of Old Town. For a quick meal of incredibly fresh fish and chips, you can't beat **Bandon Fish**

Market, 249 First St. SE (www.bandonfishmarket.com; © **541/347-4282**), which is right on the waterfront and has a few picnic tables. Also here on the waterfront, you can get cooked Dungeness crab at **Tony's Crab Shack,** 155 First St. (www.tonyscrab shack.com; © **541/347-2875**).

Alloro Wine Bar ★★★ ITALIAN   Co-owners Jeremy Buck and Lian Schmidt lived, studied, and cooked in Italy before moving to Bandon to open their Oregon coast version of an Italian *enoteca,* a place devoted to good food and wine. There's no question about it, this little red wood-frame restaurant in Old Town is the most sophisticated spot to dine in Bandon. It's not fancy, but it draws a pretty upscale crowd that includes a mix of locals and golfers from all over the world who have come to play at Bandon Dunes Golf Resort. As you would expect from food professionals, everything they use here is fresh, local, and seasonal—or imported from Italy. Main courses emphasize local seafood (wild salmon, ling cod, albacore tuna, halibut, Dungeness crab, locally caught spot prawns) but rabbit, duck, pork, and steak dishes are also on the menu. And if you love pasta, as I certainly do, try one of the homemade pasta dishes—your choices might include pappardelle with local oxtail ragu; orecchiette with Italian sausage ragu; and fusillata with clams, shrimp, and peas in a garlic-saffron cream. Preparation here is simple rather than complicated. All these dishes can be enjoyed with a glass or bottle of fine Oregon or Italian wine. It's best to make a reservation if you want to dine here.

375 Second St. SE. www.allorowinebar.com. © **541/347-1850.** Main courses $12–$27. Summer daily 4–9 or 10pm; other months Thurs–Sun 4–9pm. Closed Jan to mid-Feb.

The Gallery ★★★ PACIFIC NORTHWEST/AMERICAN   For a fine-dining experience in a country club setting, this restaurant overlooking the 18th hole at the upscale Bandon Dunes Golf Resort hits a hole in one. You can expect fine service, fine food, and fine wine here, and you don't have to be a golfer or a guest at the resort to enjoy it. The chef creates seasonal menus that take advantage of local seafood, game, and produce. Start with some fresh oysters on the half shell or a salad of organic mixed greens with grape tomatoes and cherry vinaigrette. For your main course, try the scallops with pancetta or the Northwest steelhead with orzo and arugula with pine nuts. You can also order a steak; duck breast confit; or roast chicken with taro, kale, and winter squash. The food here is creative without being overly fussy, and it is artfully presented. A sommelier is on hand to help you with your wine choices. It's best to reserve in advance.

Bandon Dunes Golf Resort, 57744 Round Lake Dr. www.bandondunesgolf.com. © **888/345-6008.** Main courses $24–$39. Daily 7am–10pm.

The Loft Restaurant & Bar ★★ PACIFIC NORTHWEST   The Loft is a small, simple space on the second floor of a building on the Bandon riverfront in Old Town, and the food is remarkably good. The first floor serves as a deli (great spot for picnic provisions), wine shop, and bakery. The dinner menu upstairs typically has about seven entrees. I love the smoked salmon goat-cheese tart with beets and walnuts, but being a burger fan, I also love the grass-fed beef burger with truffle aioli. And being a connoisseur of chicken pot pies, I can honestly say that I've never had one quite as good as the Loft's, made with free-range chicken and wild local mushrooms. Each dish is created with local, organic produce and locally sourced fish (roasted butterfish is another specialty) and meat. It all adds up to a charmingly tasty meal in a charmingly unpretentious restaurant with a lovely view. Just so you know, there's a good wine list and a full bar.

315 First St. SE. www.theloftofbandon.com. ✆ **541/329-0535.** Main courses $16–$26. Restaurant summer Wed–Sun 5–9pm; shorter hours other months; deli summer daily noon–6pm.

6

THE OREGON COAST

The South Coast

Lord Bennett's Restaurant and Lounge ★ AMERICAN   A favorite spot for Sunday brunch, and a special-occasion-dinner, dress-up restaurant that has long been a local favorite, Lord Bennett's is housed in a contemporary structure with big windows looking out over the ocean. This is a fairly sedate place with good fresh seafood (try the pan-fried oysters from Coos Bay), steaks, chops, chicken, and a handful of pasta dishes, including a vegetarian version. If you come for brunch, enjoy the corned-beef hash, cranberry French toast, and lemon blueberry pancakes. To get the most out of that ocean view, stop by for lunch—it's less crowded and less expensive.

1695 Beach Loop Dr. (next to the Sunset Motel). www.bandonbythesea.com/lord_ben.htm. ✆ **541/347-3663.** Main courses $12–$22. Mon–Thurs 5–9pm; Fri–Sat 11am–2pm and 5–9pm; Sun 10am–2pm and 5–9pm.

EXPLORING BANDON

The easily strollable **Old Town** area contains a small concentration of shops, crafts galleries, and restaurants. The Bandon area is known for its scenic viewpoints and state parks, its wildlife watching opportunities, and its golf.

Beach Loop Road ★★★ SCENIC DRIVE/OCEAN BEACH   Head out of Bandon on **Beach Loop Road,** where shoreline monoliths have been sculpted by wind and waves into contorted spires and twisted shapes. All of these rock formations have names, and all of them are art of **Oregon Islands National Wildlife Refuge.**

The first good place to view the rocks and get down to the beach is at **Coquille Point,** at the end of 11th Street. Here you'll find a short, paved interpretive trail atop a bluff overlooking the beach, rock monoliths, and the mouth of the river. A long staircase leads down to the beach. From here you can see **Table Rock** and the **Sisters.**

Face Rock, the area's most famous profile, makes an appearance at **Face Rock State Scenic Viewpoint.** Yes, it does resemble a face gazing skyward, and old Native American legend claimed that the rock is a "she"—a princess turned to stone by an evil sea spirit. Nearby are rocks that resemble a dog, a cat, and kittens (called, no surprise, **Cat and Kittens**). A trail leads down to the beach from the viewpoint, so you can explore some of the rocks at low tide.

South of the rocks, along a flat stretch of beach backed by dunes, there are several beach access areas, all of which are within **Bandon State Natural Area.**

Bullards Beach State Park ★★★ STATE PARK/LIGHTHOUSE/SCENIC AREA   Across the river from downtown Bandon, **Bullards Beach State Park** (www.oregon.gov/oprd/parks; ✆ **541/347-3501**) has beaches, a marsh overlook, hiking and horseback-riding trails, a picnic area, a campground, and a boat ramp. Fishing, crabbing, and clamming are all very popular.

Coquille River Lighthouse ★★★ LIGHTHOSE/HISTORIC BUILDING   The squat, sturdy and rather charming Coquille River Lighthouse, first lit in 1896, is located on the rocky, windy north bank of the Coquille River in Bullards Beach State Park. This is one of the few lighthouses to be hit by a ship: in 1903 an abandoned schooner plowed right into the light. Early May through mid-October, tours of the lighthouse are offered daily between 11am and 5pm.

GOLF ★   The premier courses are found at Bandon Dunes Golf Resort (see below), but there are other, less expensive courses in Bandon. **Bandon Crossings Golf Course,** 87530 Dew Valley Lane (www.bandoncrossings.com; ✆ **888/465-3218** or

world-class golf AT BANDON DUNES
GOLF RESORT

Golf may be a dying sport, but don't tell that to the passionate linksters who descend on Bandon from all over the world to play world-class golf at **Bandon Dunes Golf Resort ★★★**, 57744 Round Lake Dr. (www.bandondunesgolf .com; *℃* **800/742-0172**). This is not your typical parkland golf course but an oceanfront links course modeled after the legendary courses in Scotland and Ireland, where the game originated. The motto at Bandon Dunes is "Golf as it was meant to be," and what that means is that you walk the course (with or without a caddie) and the course follows the natural contours of the coastal landscape with its dunes, shore pines, gorse, and winds off the Pacific. In all, there are five courses at Bandon Dunes, designed by the likes of David McLay Kidd, Tom Doak, Bill Coore and Ben Crenshaw. They are both scenic and rugged, and playing here is an experience like no

other. Since opening in 1999, Bandon Dunes has become one of the top golf destinations in the world, its courses compared to Pebble Beach, Carnoustie, and Pine Valley—and, some would say, better than all of them. Scattered throughout the 9,000-acre resort are lodges and secluded, upscale cottages (see "Where to Stay," p. 227), although you don't have to stay here to play here. There is also a fine-dining restaurant (see "Where to Eat," p. 227). Seasonally adjusted greens fees, per course, range from $75 to $250 for resort guests, and from $100 to $295 for golf-only guests. No golf carts are allowed; caddies are available and charge $80 to $100 per bag. All proceeds from playing the 13-hole, par 3 Bandon Preserve course benefit the Wild Rivers Coast Alliance, and there is also a college-scholarship fund for caddies.

541/347-3232), is an 18-hole course 5 miles south of town on U.S. 101. Green fees are between $45 and $75 in the summer. The **Old Bandon Golf Links,** 3235 Beach Loop Dr.; *℃* **541/329-1927**), offers a scenic 9 holes not far from famous Face Rock. The green fee is $20 for 9 holes. This course rents 1880s and 1920s vintage golf clubs for golfers who want to play the game the way it used to be.

West Coast Game Park Safari   In the interests of full disclosure, I have to say that I have issues with zoos and places like this. West Coast Game Park Safari bills itself as America's largest wild-animal petting park, and that's why I have problems with it. In a world of poachers and disappearing habitats, I understand the need for protection and conservation, but wild animals are wild animals, and when you destroy their natural instincts (to flee humans, for example), you destroy their spirit and ability to survive in the wild. That's what happened with Keiko, the orca whale star *of Free Willy,* who was taken to the Oregon Coast Aquarium (see p. 214) for a well-meant but unsuccessful rehabilitation after being abducted from his pod and forced to spend years as a performer. Here, depending on what young animals they have at the time of your visit, humans are allowed to play with leopard, tiger, or bear cubs. It is a tourist attraction where many families like to stop, and that's all I'll say about it.

46914 U.S. 101 S. (7 miles south of Bandon). www.westcoastgameparksafari.com. *℃* **541/347-3106.** Daily summer 9am–6pm (call for hours in other months). $18 adults, $17 seniors, $10 ages 7–12, $7 for ages 2–6.

Insider's Tip for Local Jams and Jellies

Every time I am in this neck of the ocean I make a point to stop at **Misty Meadows,** 48053 U.S. 101 (www.oregon jam.com; ☏ **541/347-2595**), which is not a retirement community but a wonderful store that sells jams and jellies made from locally harvested fruits. And boy, are they good—on toast, an English muffin, a buttered crumpet, ice cream, or as a condiment to meats and fish. I'm talking cranberry, marionberry, blackberry, huckleberry, salal, cherry, and other fruits. Sugar-free varieties are available, and they also have honey, syrups, and barbecue rubs. Misty Meadows is open daily 9am to 5pm. Look for it south of Bandon on the east side of U.S. 101 (after West Coast Game Park Safari).

Outdoor Exploring

BIRDWATCHING ★★★   More than 300 species of birds have been spotted in the Bandon vicinity, making this one of the best sites in Oregon for bird-watching. The **Oregon Islands National Wildlife Refuge,** which includes 1,853 rocks, reefs, and islands off the state's coast, includes the famous monoliths of Bandon. Among the birds that nest on these rocks are rhinoceros auklets, storm petrels, gulls, and tufted puffins. The puffins, with their large, colorful beaks, are the most beloved of local birds, and their images show up on all manner of local souvenirs.

The **Bandon Marsh National Wildlife Refuge** (www.fws.gov/oregoncoast/bandonmarsh/index.htm; ☏ **541/347-1470**), at the mouth of the Coquille River, is another good spot for bird-watching. In this area, you can expect to see grebes, mergansers, buffleheads, plovers, and several species of raptors.

WHALE-WATCHING ★★★   At Bandon, as elsewhere on the Oregon coast, **gray whales** migrating between the Arctic and Baja California, Mexico, pass close to the shore and can often be spotted from land. The whales pass Bandon between December and February on their way south and between March and May on their way north. Gray days and early mornings before the wind picks up are the best times to spot whales. Coquille Point (at the end of 11th Street) and the bluffs along **Beach Loop Road** are the best vantage points.

"Honey, Is That a T-Rex Beside the Highway?"

Yes, dear, it is. The giant T-Rex, frozen in its voracious rampage, stands beside U.S. 101 about 12 miles south of Port Orford, and it will certainly get your attention—or, more likely, that of your kids. The **Prehistoric Gardens & Rainforest,** 36848 U.S. 101 S. (www. prehis toricgardens.com; ☏ **541/332-4463**), is a lost world of life-size dinosaur replicas. Though they aren't as realistic as those in *Jurassic Park,* they'll make the kids squeal with delight (or terror). The gardens are open in the summer daily from 10am to 6pm; other months, call for hours. Admission is $10 for adults, $9 for seniors, and $8 for children 3 to 12. If you don't want to venture inside, you can get your T-Rex photo op right by the side of the road.

Gold Beach ★★★

32 miles S of Port Orford, 54 miles N of Crescent City, CA

Let's look history in the eye before we move on to the golden delights of Gold Beach today. There are a couple of big backstories that have had a major influence on the development of the town and the surrounding region. In 19th-century California, gold prospectors struggled through rugged mountains in search of pay dirt, but when they arrived in Oregon, they discovered they could scoop it up off the beach. The black sands at the mouth of the Rogue River were high in gold, and it was this gold that gave Gold Beach its name. The white, gold-greedy settlers inevitably came in conflict with the local Tututni tribe, whose forbearers had lived in the region for at least 8,500 years. Violence erupted in 1856, but within the year the Rogue River Indian Wars had come to an end, and the Tututnis were removed to a reservation.

When the gold played out, commercial fishermen moved in to take advantage of the river's incredible salmon and steelhead runs (Zane Grey wrote about this period in his novel *Rogue River Feud*). A Scotsman named David Hume became the "Salmon King" of the Rogue, opening canneries that shipped out 16,000 crates of salmon a year. The efficiency of the commercial fishermen's nets and traps quickly decimated the local salmon population, and a hatchery had to be constructed to replenish the runs. Another backstory.

Today, the chief delight of is the wild and scenic **Rogue River** that empties into the Pacific at Gold Beach. The Rogue is, to my mind, one of the great rivers of the West, perhaps of the world. You'll see it far below, glittering if the day is bright, darkly mysterious if the weather is foggy or rainy, as you cross the Art Deco Patterson Bridge that spans the north and south banks above the river's wide estuary. There is, of course, a beach at Gold Beach, though it's not really the area's main attraction. That is, and always will be, the Rogue, the most famous fishing and rafting river in the state.

GETTING THERE   Gold Beach is on U.S. 101 between Brookings and Port Orford. Coming from the north, the nearest highway connection to I-5 is Ore. 42 from Roseburg to Bandon. Coming from the south, you must either follow U.S. 101 north from California or take U.S. 199 southwest from Grants Pass, Oregon, and then continue north on U.S. 101 to Gold Beach via Brookings.

VISITOR INFORMATION   The **Gold Beach Visitor Center,** 94080 Shirley Lane (www.goldbeach.org; © **800/525-2334** or 541/247-7526), in South Beach Park at the south end of town, is open Monday to Saturday 9am to 5pm.

WHERE TO STAY

Ireland's Rustic Lodges & Gold Beach Inn ★★★   I love these charming little cabins built in 1936, because they remind me of what the entire Oregon coast used to be like before modern motels, hotels, and luxury resorts sprang up. The cabins couldn't be simpler or cuter, with a double bed in an alcove, a couple of easy chairs, a wood-burning fireplace, and a small bathroom with a shower. In the day, stars like Clark Gable would come up here to fish and chill. The rustic cabins are now part of a larger, 19-acre oceanfront property that includes the adjacent Gold Beach Inn, with two newer buildings. The cabins with their knotty pine walls have all the charm; the rooms in the other buildings have the views—and great views at that. Those rooms have walls and ceilings of Douglas fir, gas fireplaces, and nondescript but comfy easy chairs. There are also separate houses that are perfect for family reunions or large groups. The grounds here are full of old trees, grassy lawns, and trails down to the

The Rogue is a fabled fishing and rafting river, and over the last century, fishing lodges have been built along the Rogue's south bank in or near the wild and scenic stretch of the river. The lodges are a bit difficult to reach—sometimes accessible only by hiking or jet boat—and their season is limited, but you might want to consider staying at one of these unique and unforgettable spots. The lodges are typically fairly rustic and cater to people who are taking guided rafting trips down the Rogue, or serve as overnight stopovers along the rafting trips. See the "Rafting the Rogue" box, p. 236). Three good lodges to consider are **Cougar Lane Lodge,** 4219 Agness Rd. (🕿 **541/247-7233**); **Lucas Pioneer Ranch & Fishing Lodge,** 3904 Cougar Lane (www.lucaslodgeoregon.com; 🕿 **541-247-7443**); and **Half Moon Bar Lodge,** 3140 Juanipero Way (www.thehalfmoonbarlodge.com; 🕿 **541/842-2821**).

beach. There is also a wonderful patio area with three hot tubs (no kids after 10pm) and a solarium. For the price and the view—and the inimitable historic cachet of the little cabins—Ireland's can't be beat.

29346 Ellensburg Ave. (U.S. 101). www.irelandsrusticlodges.com. 🕿 **877/447-3526** or 541/247-7718. 40 units. $49–$255 double w/full breakfast included. Pets accepted ($10). **Amenities:** 3 Jacuzzis; free Wi-Fi.

Jot's Resort ★   Families and travelers on a budget who want a water view and some extra amenities will enjoy Jot's. The views here are not of the ocean but the mighty Rogue River, its historic bridge, and the fishing and jet boats that make their way up and down the river. This is a motel-style property with acres of asphalt parking lot around it, but once you're in your room you can slide open the glass doors and step out onto a balcony. Decor is pretty plain, but every room has a comfortable bed, a dining table, and two upholstered chairs. Various room types and configurations are available, from standard rooms to fairly spacious condo units. There's an outdoor and an indoor pool, a reasonably priced restaurant, and the hotel will arrange for jet boat rides and charter fishing boats and guides for you.

94360 Wedderburn Loop. www.jotsresort.com. 🕿 **800/367-5687** or 541/247-6676. 140 units. $60–$135 double. Pets accepted ($10–$25 per night). **Amenities:** Restaurant; lounge; indoor and outdoor pools; free Wi-Fi.

Tu Tu' Tun Lodge ★★★   If we had a four-star rating, I'd give it to Tu Tu' Tun. For a truly memorable southern Oregon experience, this sublime lodge on the sublimely beautiful Rogue River, 7 miles east of Gold Beach, can't be beat. Designed by architects, and open since 1970, Tu Tu' Tun's rooms all have balconies or patios that look out on a wide stretch of one of Oregon's most scenic rivers. The hotel has rooms that are luxuriously comfortable, with handcrafted wood detailing, Arts and Crafts–style furnishings, all-natural fabrics, and a romantic, sophisticated ambience that sets it apart from every other hotel in the area. Spring for a fireplace room if you can—these are wood-burning fireplaces—and for added allure, book one of the rooms with an outdoor soaking tub. All kinds of amenities are part of the Tu Tu' Tun experience, including evening wine and hors d'oeuvres and a delicious breakfast. For an additional fee you can enjoy dinner (summer only) at communal tables that seat eight. The lobby/lounge area with its big fireplace and Arts and Crafts–style furniture leads out to a patio area overlooking an outdoor pool and lawn that in turn leads down to a stretch of the beach. Jet boats arrive at the lodge's dock in the summer, so guests can take a ride up the river from here. If you're looking for the best, this is it.

96550 N. Bank Rogue River Rd. www.tututun.com. (*) **800/864-6357** or 541/247-6664. 21 units. $150–$445 double w/full breakfast, evening wine and hors d'oeuvres included. No children under 10 May–Sept. **Amenities:** Restaurant (dining room closed for dinner Nov–Apr); lounge; access to nearby health club.; outdoor pool; spa services; free Wi-Fi.

WHERE TO EAT

Coffee alert: The best coffee in Gold Beach is at **Rachel's Coffee House** in the Gold Beach Bookstore at 29707 Ellensburg Ave. ((*) **541/247-7733**).

Anna's by the Sea ★★ NEW AMERICAN Anna's is not like other restaurants along Highway 101 that serve the inevitable "fisherman's platter" or fish and chips. For one thing, it's a block off the highway, and for another thing, it's really small, seating only 14 people. It also serves double duty as Gold Beach's only wine bar and wine store, with a surprisingly large selection of mostly European vintages. The chef-owner, with a bit of tongue-in-cheek, calls his cooking "nouvelle Canadian prairie cuisine." Whatever you call it, it's usually on the mark when it comes to taste. The cheeses offered as a starter are all made in-house, and if you order one of fresh, crisp salads, he might go outside and cut some of the fresh greens. Only four main courses are offered (five in the summer). I would recommend the breast of duck served over mashed potatoes or the wild-caught shrimp with truffle oil. On some weekend nights, a guitar player provides soft music. It can all be a bit eccentric (bone china, heavy cutlery, but if you don't have wine, your water is served in a plastic cup), but you'll get a meal unlike any place else in Gold Beach.

29672 Stewart St. www.annasbythesea.com. (*) **541/247-2100.** Main course $17–$29. Oct–June Wed–Sat 5–8pm; July–Sept Tues–Sat 5–8pm.

Nor'wester Seafood ★ SEAFOOD/STEAK Nor'wester has the best view in Gold Beach—it's in the port area with a big, busy dining room that overlooks the mouth of the Rogue and its fleet of fishing boats—and also the most consistently reliable food. There aren't many surprises in this popular steak and seafood place. I would go for the fresh fish of the day, especially if it's locally caught salmon (spring through summer). Black cod is used for the fish and chips; the oysters (lightly breaded and pan-fried) come from Willapa Bay in Washington. This is a fairly expensive restaurant but remains popular with locals and visitors because of its reliability.

10 Harbor Way (in the Port of Gold Beach). www.norwesterseafood.com. (*) **541/247-2333.** Main courses $23–$34. Daily 5–9pm.

Spinner's ★★ SEAFOOD/AMERICAN Spinner's has been around for a long time and is known for the consistency and reliability of their cooking. This is where locals go to celebrate special occasions because it has a nice, smart-casual atmosphere. Fish, steaks, and chops are on offer at Spinner's, but I personally would always go for the fish, and especially the cedar-planked fresh wild salmon roasted on cedar and served with a zinfandel sauce. The pasta with local Dungeness crab is also good.

29430 Ellensburg Ave. www.spinnersrestaurant.com. (*) **541/247-5160.** Main courses $9–$32. Daily 4:30–9pm.

EXPLORING THE GOLD BEACH AREA

As with so many other coastal towns, the attractions of Gold Beach are not in the town itself but in the surrounding area. The Rogue is the focal point here.

Curry Historical Museum ★ MUSEUM   This diminutive local history museum has displays of Native American and pioneer artifacts as well as re-created environments such as a miner's cabin that provide an overview of the history of the area.

29419 Ellensburg Ave. www.curryhistory.com. ✆ **541/247-9396.** $2 adults, 50¢ children. Tues–Sat 10am–4pm. Closed Jan.

Hiking   There's an abundance of outstanding hiking trails in the area, including the following:

o The trail head for the 6-mile **Rogue River Walk** ★★★ begins 7 miles from the south end of the Patterson Bridge, east on Jerry's Flat Road. The trail provides spectacular views of the Rogue as it weaves through areas with spring wildflowers, myrtlewood groves, and over bridges. There are benches along the way to rest, do some bird watching, and take in the view.

o At the **Frances Schrader Old Growth Trail** ★★★, 10 miles up Jerry's Flat Road/ South Bank Rogue River Road near the Lobster Creek Campground, you can take a 1-mile loop trail through a stand of majestic, old-growth trees, including a grove of Port Orford cedars; these trees are native to a limited range in southwest Oregon and northwest California.

o Not far from the Old Growth Trail, you'll find the **Myrtle Tree Trail** ★★★. Along this .25-mile trail, you'll find the world's largest myrtle tree, 88 feet tall and 42 feet in circumference. From U.S. 101 in Gold Beach, drive east on Jerry's Flat Road, (FS Road #33) toward Agness. At approximately 9½ miles, turn left on FS Road #3310, cross the bridge over the river, and turn right on Silver Creek Road (FS Road #3533) and watch for signs. Park at the turn-out on the right side of road; the trail head is on the left side of the road.

For more information on hiking in the Gold Beach area and specific directions to the trail heads, contact the Siskiyou National Forest's **Gold Beach Ranger Station,** 29279 Ellensburg Ave. (www.fs.fed.us/r6/rogue-siskiyou; ✆ **541/247-3600**). The Gold Beach Visitor Center (see p. 232) can also help direct you to the trail heads.

Jerry's Rogue River Museum ★★ MUSEUM   At the Port of Gold Beach and affiliated with the gift shop for Jerry's Rogue Jets (see below), this is the more modern and informative of the two museums in Gold Beach. It focuses on the geology and cultural and natural history of the Rogue River with small collections of Indian and pioneer artifacts, and it has a menagerie of stuffed animals found on the Rogue.

29880 Harbor Way (Port of Gold Beach). ✆ **541/247-4571.** Admission free. July–Aug daily 9am–9pm; rest of year Mon–Sat 9am–5pm, Sun 10am–5pm.

Jet Boat Rogue River Tour ★★★ OUTDOOR RECREATION/BOAT TOUR   For most visitors, a jet-boat trip up the Lower Rogue is the easiest way to see a portion of this fabled river. Powerful, shallow-draft hydrojet boats use water jets instead of propellers, allowing them to cross rapids and riffles that are only a few inches deep. **Jerry's Rogue Jets,** 29880 Harbor Way (www.roguejets.com; ✆ **800/451-3645** or 541/247-4571), leaves from the Port of Gold Beach on the south side of the bridge and offers three different trips. The 64-mile **Historic Mail Boat Trip** follows the route mailboats have taken up the Rogue, delivering mail and cargo, since 1895. The 80-mile **Whitewater Journey** pushes farther up the river to a section of whitewater rapids. On the 104-mile **Wilderness Whitewater** ★★★ trip, you get to enter the wild and scenic section of the Rogue, accessible only to jetboats, rafters, and hikers. Prices range from $50 to $95 for adults, $25 to $45 for children ages 4 to 11. The

RAFTING THE rogue

A guided **white-water rafting trip** down the wild and scenic Rogue is an unforgettable experience, but it takes some planning, and the rafting season is fairly short. Rafting trips generally start near Agness, about 35 miles up the Rogue from Gold Beach, or Merlin, 130 miles west of Gold Beach near Grants Pass. White-water-rafting companies offer half-day, full-day, or multiday trips that stop at rustic river lodges or campsites along the riverbanks (your guides do most of the work, setting up camp and preparing meals). Area rafting companies include **Rogue Wilderness Adventures** (www.wildrogue.com; ℂ **800/336-1647** or 541/479-9554); **Galice Resort,** 11744 Galice Rd., Merlin (www.galice.com; ℂ **541/476-3818**); **Orange Torpedo Trips,** 210 Merlin Rd., Merlin (www.orangetorpedo.com; ℂ **866/479-5061** or 541/479-5061); and **Rogue River Raft Trips,** Morrison's Lodge, 8500 Galice Rd., Merlin (www.rogueriverraft.com; ℂ **800/826-1963** or 541/476-3825). Expect to pay around $70 to $80 for a half day and $85 to $95 for a full day. Three-day lodge or camping trips are in the $650 to $1000 range.

longer trips include a stop for lunch (additional $8–$10 charge) at one of the fishing lodges on the Rogue (you can make arrangements to stay overnight at the lodge and be picked up by jet boat the next day). Knowledgeable and Coast Guard–certified guides accompany every jetboat trip and provide commentary on the wildlife and geology of the river. You may see deer, black bear, river otters, or bald eagles along the way. This is a safe adventure that everyone will enjoy.

Nesika Beach ★ OCEAN BEACH When you want to get out on the beach, head north of town across the Rogue River to Nesika Beach. To reach the best stretch of this beach, take the North Nesika Beach turnoff and then continue north to the end of the road. Alternatively, continue a little farther north to Old Coast Road, where you'll find a steep trail down to the beach.

SHOPPING

The largest bookstore on the Oregon coast, **Gold Beach Books ★★★,** 29707 Ellensburg Rd. (www.oregoncoastbooks.com; ℂ **5431/247-2495**), stocks all the current bestsellers but also has a big selection of new and used books on subjects of local, regional, and state interest, plus a rare-books room. **Rachel's Coffee House** occupies part of this space on Gold Beach's main drag.

If you want to take home some local salmon, albacore or steelhead, **Fishermen Direct Seafood,** 29975 Harbor Way (www.fishermendirect.com; ℂ **888/523-9494** or 541/247-9494), in the Cannery Building at the port, can package it up and freeze it for you.

PLANNING YOUR TRIP

This guidebook is a little unusual in that it covers two major Pacific Northwest cities and the Oregon coast. In other words, it's not a complete guide to the Pacific Northwest but a selective guide to the three places most people want to visit and are most curious about. In this chapter you'll find some useful preliminary information about each place to help you start planning your trip. There is more specific information in the individual chapters devoted to Seattle, Portland, and the Oregon coast. In those chapters you will find information on airports, local transportation options, where to find information, festivals and special events, and so on. Here I'm dealing with the bigger picture and recapping some useful information.

GETTING TO SEATTLE

By Plane

Seattle-Tacoma International Airport (SEA), 17801 International Blvd., Seattle, WA 98158 (www.portseattle.org/sea-tac; ✆ **206/787-5388**), commonly called "Sea-Tac," is Washington's main airport and is served by about 20 national and international airlines. There are direct international flights to many cities, including London, Amsterdam, Paris, Beijing, Tokyo, and Seoul. For information on getting from the airport into Seattle, see "Arriving" in chapter 4, p. 48.

By Car

Seattle is 110 miles (177 km) from Vancouver, British Columbia; 176 miles (285 km) from Portland; 810 miles (1,303 km) from San Francisco; 1190 miles (1915 km) from Los Angeles; and 285 miles (459 km) from Spokane.

   I-5 is the main north-south artery through Washington, running south to Portland and Los Angeles and north to the Canadian border. **I-405** is Seattle's east-side bypass and accesses the cities of Bellevue, Redmond, and Kirkland on the east side of Lake Washington. **I-90** connects Seattle to Spokane in eastern Washington. **Wash. 520** connects I-405 with Seattle just north of downtown and also ends at I-5.

   All the major car-rental agencies have offices in Seattle and at or near Seattle-Tacoma International Airport, including:

     Advantage (www.advantage.com; ✆ **800/777-5500**)
     Alamo (www.alamo.com; ✆ **877/222-9075**)

Avis (www.avis.com; © 800/331-1212)
Budget (www.budget.com; © 800/527-0700)
Dollar (www.dollar.com; © 800/800-3665)
Enterprise (www.enterprise.com; © 800/261-7331)
Fox Rent A Car (www.foxrentacar.com; © 800/225-4369)
Hertz (www.hertz.com; © 800/654-3131)
National (www.nationalcar.com; © 877/222-9058)
Thrifty (www.thrifty.com; © 800/847-4389)

By Train

Amtrak (www.amtrak.com; © 800/872-7245) service runs from Vancouver, British Columbia, to Seattle and from Portland and as far south as Eugene, Oregon on the *Cascades* (a high-speed, European-style Talgo train). The train takes about 4 hours from Vancouver to Seattle and 3½ to 4 hours from Seattle to Portland.

There is also Amtrak service to Seattle from San Diego, Los Angeles, San Francisco, and Portland on the *Coast Starlight,* and from Spokane and points east on the *Empire Builder.* Amtrak also operates a bus between Vancouver and Seattle. Trains arrive and depart from the historic **King Street Station,** 303 South Jackson St., near the Pioneer Square area of downtown Seattle.

By Bus

Greyhound (www.greyhound.com; © 800/345-3109) provides long-distance bus service to Seattle from cities around the U.S. The Seattle Greyhound Station is located in downtown Seattle at 811 Stewart St.

If you're traveling between Portland and Seattle or Vancouver, BC and Seattle, **Bolt Bus** (www.boltbus.com; © 877/265-8287) offers cheap rates and free onboard Wi-Fi. Bolt Bus picks up and deposits passengers on 5th Avenue S. and S. King Street in the International District, close to the King Street Amtrak station.

GETTING AROUND SEATTLE

For a complete summary of all your transportation options in Seattle, see "Getting Around" in chapter 4, p. 52.

Central Seattle—including downtown, Belltown, Seattle Center, South Lake Union, the waterfront, and Pioneer Square—is fairly compact and walkable. There is also a good bus system, a streetcar that connects downtown to South Lake Union, and a light-rail system that connects Seattle to the airport and makes some stops along the way.

If you're staying in downtown Seattle, a car is unnecessary. Parking is difficult and expensive, and Seattle traffic jams are awful. If you are planning a day trip to Mount Rainier National Park (p. 100), however, a car is necessary. And a car makes getting to Seattle neighborhoods like Ballard, Fremont, and Capitol Hill easier (though you still have to find a parking space when you get there).

One of the most important benefits of belonging to the **American Automobile Association** (www.aaa.com; © 800/222-4357) is that it supplies members with free maps and emergency road service. In Seattle, there's an AAA office in the University District at 4554 9th Ave. (www.aaawa.com; © 800/452-1643 or 206/633-4222). Members of AAA also can get detailed road maps of Oregon by calling their local AAA office.

In Washington, as in Oregon, you may turn right on a red light after a full stop, and if you are in the far-left lane of a one-way street, you may turn left into the adjacent left lane of a one-way street at a red light after a full stop. Everyone in a moving vehicle is required to wear a seat belt.

GETTING TO PORTLAND

By Plane

Portland International Airport (PDX) is Oregon's biggest and busiest airport and is served by major national and two international airlines. The airport has direct international service to Amsterdam and Tokyo and direct service to New York, Chicago, Denver, and several other airports throughout the U.S. For information on getting from the airport into Portland, see "Arriving" in chapter 5, p. 107.

By Car

The distance to Portland from Seattle is 176 miles (285 km); from Spokane, 350 miles (563 km); from Vancouver, British Columbia, 285 miles (459 km); from San Francisco, 640 miles (1,030 km); and from Los Angeles, 1,015 miles (1,633 km).

I-5 runs through the length of Oregon and continues north toward the Canadian border and south to Los Angeles, passing through the heart of Portland. **I-84** runs from Idaho and points east into Oregon, ending in Portland.

By Train

Amtrak's (www.amtrak.com; ✆ **800/872-7245**) *Coast Starlight* train connects Portland with Seattle, San Francisco, Los Angeles, and San Diego. In Portland, it stops at historic **Union Station,** 800 NW Sixth Ave., about 10 blocks from the heart of downtown. Between Portland and Seattle there are both regular trains and modern Talgo trains, which make the trip in 3½ to 4 hours versus 4½ hours for the regular train. The Talgo train, called *Cascades,* runs between Eugene, Oregon and Vancouver, British Columbia.

By Bus

Greyhound (www.greyhound.com; ✆ **800/231-2222** in the U.S.; ✆ **001/214/849-8100** outside the U.S.) connects Portland with cities nationwide. The Greyhound bus station is at 550 NW Sixth Ave., close to the train station.

Bolt Bus (www.boltbus.com) is a low-cost bus service to Portland from Vancouver, BC and Seattle to the north, and from Eugene to the south. The Bolt Bus drops off passengers right downtown on SW Salmon between 5th and 6th avenues. Bolt Bus makes the trip between Seattle and Portland in about 3½ hours and offers free Wi-Fi on board.

GETTING AROUND PORTLAND

For a complete summary of all your transportation options in Portland, see chapter 5, p. 107.

You don't need a car while in Portland because the city is well served by public transportation (light-rail, streetcar, buses). However, if you want to take day trips to the Columbia Gorge National Scenic Area (p. 171), the wine country (p. 163), or Mount Hood (p. 169), or explore the Oregon coast, a car is necessary.

Major rental-car companies with offices in or near Portland International Airport or in downtown Portland include Alamo, Avis, Budget, Dollar, Enterprise, Hertz, National, and Thrifty.

One of the most important benefits of belonging to the **American Automobile Association** (www.aaa.com; ✆ **800/222-4357**) is that it supplies members with free maps and emergency road service. In Portland, AAA is located at 600 SW Market St. (www.oregon.aaa.com; ✆ **800/452-1643** or 503/222-6767). Members of AAA also can get detailed road maps of Oregon by calling their local AAA office.

In Oregon, you may turn right on a red light after a full stop, and if you are in the far-left lane of a one-way street, you may turn left into the adjacent left lane of a one-way street at a red light after a full stop. Everyone in a moving vehicle is required to wear a seat belt.

Oregon is one of only two states in the U.S. with no self-service gas stations. So when you pull into a gas station, an attendant will fill your tank.

GETTING TO THE OREGON COAST

By Car

A car is the only way to see and explore the Oregon coast, and driving the Coast Highway (U.S. 101) is part of the Oregon coast experience. There are virtually no public transportation options along U.S. 101. (There is Amtrak and Greyhound bus service only to cities along inland I-5.)

From Portland, there are fairly direct routes to Astoria (p. 183) via **U.S. 30**; to Cannon Beach (p. 191) via U.S. 26; and to Depoe Bay (p. 207) via U.S. 99W and Ore. 18. Trip time from Portland to these destinations on the North Coast is about 1½ to 2 hours.

Other routes that head west from I-5 to U.S. 101 on the coast are **Ore. 126** from Eugene to Florence (p. 220); **Ore. 42** and **Ore. 42S** from Roseburg to Bandon; and Ore. 199 from Grants Pass to Brookings/Gold Beach.

If you are heading to the Central Coast (chapter 6, p. 202), you might consider flying into the **Eugene Airport (EUG)**, served by Allegiant Air, Delta Connection, Alaska/Horizon Air, and United Express, and renting a car there. This will save you about 110 miles (177 km) of driving from Portland.

If you are headed to Oregon's South Coast (chapter 6, p. 222), you might consider flying into the **Rogue Valley International–Medford Airport (MFR),** served by Allegiant Air, Alaska/Horizon Air, and SkyWest Airlines (Delta Connection and United Express), and renting a car there. This will save you about 275 miles (443 km) of driving from Portland.

Yurt-ing Along the Coast

State parks along the coast offer a variety of camping alternatives. Top among these are yurts (circular domed tents with electricity, plywood floors, and beds), which make camping in the rain a lot more comfortable. Yurts, which rent for $35 to $76 a night, can be found at 14 coastal parks.

TIPS ON COASTAL ACCOMMODATIONS

From boutique hotels to B&Bs, golf resorts, Rogue River fishing lodges, and rustic cabins, the Oregon coast has as a wide variety of accommodations. Summer (June–September) is the high season, when rooms are most expensive and campgrounds are full. From October to May, prices drop and everything along the coast is less busy.

FAST FACTS: SEATTLE, PORTLAND & OREGON COAST

Area Codes In Oregon, you need to include the area code when dialing local calls. The area code for Portland is 503. For the Oregon coast, the area code is 541.

ATMs The easiest and best way to get cash in the United States is from an ATM (automated teller machine). The **Cirrus** (www.mastercard.com; 📞 **800/424-7787**) and **PLUS** (www.visa.com) networks span the country; you can find them everywhere in

Seattle, Portland, and along the coast. You'll find ATMs at banks, gas stations, supermarkets, and convenience stores.

Business Hours Banks are generally open Monday through Friday from 9am to 5pm, and some branches are also open Saturday 9am–noon. Stores are open Monday through Saturday from 10am to 6pm (until 9pm at malls), and Sunday from noon to 5pm. Bars are allowed to be open until 2am.

Car Rental See "Getting Around: By Car," p. 237.

Customs Every visitor 21 years of age or older may bring in, free of duty, the following: (1) 1 liter of alcohol; (2) 200 cigarettes, 100 cigars (but not from Cuba); and (3) $100 worth of gifts. These exemptions are offered to travelers who spend at least 72 hours in the United States and who have not claimed them within the preceding 6 months. It is forbidden to bring into the country almost any meat products (including canned, fresh, and dried meat products, such as bouillon and soup mixes). Generally, condiments including vinegars, oils, pickled goods, spices, coffee, tea, and some cheeses and baked goods are permitted. Avoid rice products, as rice can often harbor insects. Bringing fruits and vegetables is prohibited because they may harbor pests or disease. International visitors may carry in or out up to $10,000 in U.S. or foreign currency with no formalities; larger sums must be declared to U.S. Customs on entering or leaving, which includes filing form FinCEN 105. For details regarding U.S. Customs and Border Protection, consult your nearest U.S. embassy or consulate, or **U.S. Customs** (www.customs.gov).

Disabled Travelers

Thanks to provisions in the Americans with Disabilities Act, most public places are required to comply with disability-friendly regulations—almost all public establishments (including hotels, restaurants, and museums, but not certain National Historic Landmarks). in Portland, all modes of public transportation—bus, light rail, streetcar—provide accessible entrances. In Seattle, newer buses are accessible, as are the light-rail and the streetcar from downtown to South Lake Union.

Because it has few steep streets, Portland is a particularly wheelchair-friendly city. Seattle, with its steep downtown streets, is more difficult.

In Seattle, Portland, and along the Oregon coast, many hotels have handicapped accessible rooms. In state parks and national forests, you'll find paved trails designed to accommodate wheelchairs. At **Yaquina Head Outstanding Natural Area** (p. 216) on the Oregon coast outside of Newport, there are even wheelchair-accessible tide pools.

The **America the Beautiful—National Park and Federal Recreational Lands Pass—Access Pass** gives travelers with visual impairments or those with permanent disabilities (regardless of age) free lifetime entrance to federal recreation sites administered by the National Park Service. This includes national parks, monuments, historic sites, recreation areas, and national wildlife refuges. The America the Beautiful Access Pass can only be obtained in person at a National Park Service facility that charges an entrance fee, such as Fort Clatsop–Lewis & Clark National Historical Park. You need to show proof of a medically determined disability. For more information, go to www.nps.gov/fees_passes.htm, or call the United States Geological Survey/USGS (✆ **888/275-8747**), which issues the passes.

Doctors To find a doctor, check with the front desk or concierge at your hotel or look in the yellow pages of the local telephone book under "Physician."

Drinking Laws The legal age for purchase and consumption of alcoholic beverages is 21; proof of age is required and often requested at bars, nightclubs, and restaurants, so it's always a good idea to bring ID when you go out. Do not carry open containers of alcohol in your car or in any public area that isn't zoned for alcohol consumption. The police can fine you on the spot. Don't even think about driving while intoxicated.

Aside from on-premises sales of cocktails in bars and restaurants, hard liquor can be purchased only in liquor stores. Beer and wine are available in convenience stores and grocery stores. Brewpubs tend to sell only beer and wine, but some also have licenses to sell hard liquor.

Drugstores/Pharmacies Fred Meyer, a major grocery chain in Washington and Oregon, has a pharmacy in many of its stores. Also look for Walgreen's (Washington and Oregon) and Bartell (Washington only). Many prescription drugs have different names outside the U.S., so it's important to know what the drug's name is in the U.S.

Electricity Like Canada, the United States uses 110 to 120 volts AC (60 cycles), compared to 220 to 240 volts AC (50 cycles) in most of Europe, Australia, and New Zealand. Downward converters that change 220–240 volts to 110–120 volts are difficult to find in the United States, so bring one with you.

Embassies & Consulates All embassies are in Washington, D.C. If your country isn't listed below, call for directory information in Washington, D.C. (📞 **202/555-1212**), or check **www.embassy.org/embassies**.

The embassy of **Australia** is at 1601 Massachusetts Ave. NW, Washington, D.C. 20036 (www.usa.embassy.gov.au; 📞 **202/797-3000**).

The embassy of **Canada** is at 501 Pennsylvania Ave. NW, Washington, D.C. 20001 (www.canada international.gc.ca/washington; 📞 **202/682-1740**). There is a consulate in Seattle.

The embassy of **Ireland** is at 2234 Massachusetts Ave. NW, Washington, D.C. 20008 (www.embassy ofireland.org; 📞 **202/462-3939**).

The embassy of **New Zealand** is at 37 Observatory Circle NW, Washington, D.C. 20008 (www.nzembassy.com; 📞 **202/328-4800**). There is a consulate in Seattle.

The embassy of the **United Kingdom** is at 3100 Massachusetts Ave. NW, Washington, D.C. 20008 (http://ukinusa.fco.gov.uk; 📞 **202/588-6500**). There is a consulate in Seattle.

Emergencies Call 📞 **911** to report a fire, call the police, or get an ambulance anywhere in the U.S. This is a toll-free call.

Family Travel For recommendations of kid-friendly attractions and family-friendly activities, see "Seattle, Portland & the Oregon Coast for Families" under "Suggested Itineraries" in chapter 2. In general, you will find Seattle, Portland, and the Oregon coast very kid-friendly.

Insurance For information on traveler's insurance, trip cancellation insurance, and medical insurance while traveling, visit www.frommers.com/planning.

Internet & Wi-Fi The Pacific Northwest is very tech-savvy. Nearly all hotels and B&Bs in Seattle, Portland, and along the Oregon coast offer free Wi-Fi to guests. other places to get access to the Internet are cafes and public libraries. Do not expect Wi-Fi or Internet access at campgrounds or in state parks.

LGBT Travelers Gay and lesbian travelers will generally feel very welcome in Seattle, Portland and along the Oregon coast. Same-sex marriage is now legal in Washington state and is expected to be legalized in Oregon in the near future.

Mobile Phones If you have a U.S. mobile phone and network, it's a good bet that your phone will work in in Seattle, Portland, and along the Oregon coast, but T-Mobile, Sprint, and Nextel are weak in rural areas and in some places along the coast. If you're visiting from another country, be sure to find out about international calling rates and roaming charges before using your phone in the United States. You could ring up a huge phone bill with just a few calls and texts

Newspapers & Magazines *The Oregonian* (www.oregonlive.com) is Portland's daily paper. *Portland Monthly* (www.portlandmonthly.com) is a good lifestyle monthly. *Willamette Week* (www.willametteweek.com) is a free weekly news, arts, and entertainment newspaper.

The *Seattle Times* (www.seattletimes.com) and *Seattle Post-Intelligencer* (www.seattlepi.com) are Seattle's daily newspapers. *Seattle Weekly* (www.seattleweekly.com) is the city's free news, arts, and entertainment weekly.

Packing The Pacific Northwest is a very casual place. Seattle has more "dress up" kinds of places than Portland does, and the Oregon coast is about staying dry and comfortable in cool, wet weather. The weather can be warm in the summer, but typically cools down considerably at night. In the winter, there is frequent rain, and temperatures tend to hover in the 40s and 50s. When you're packing, think layers. To keep yourself covered, bring a fleece jacket, a hoodie, and a rain jacket.

Passports Every air traveler entering the U.S. is required to show a passport. For more information on passports, see the following:

Australia Australian Passport Information Service (⟨℡⟩ **131-232,** or visit www.passports.gov.au).

Canada Passport Office, Department of Foreign Affairs and International Trade, Ottawa, ON K1A 0G3 (www.ppt.gc.ca; ⟨℡⟩ **800/567-6868**).

Ireland Passport Office, Setanta Centre, Molesworth Street, Dublin 2 (www.foreignaffairs.gov.ie; ⟨℡⟩ **01/671-1633**).

New Zealand Passports Office, Department of Internal Affairs, 47 Boulcott St., Wellington, 6011 (www.passports.govt.nz; ⟨℡⟩ **0800/225-050** in New Zealand or 04/474-8100).

United Kingdom Visit your nearest passport office, major post office, or travel agency, or contact the **Identity and Passport Service (IPS),** 89 Eccleston Square, London, SW1V 1PN (www.ips.gov.uk; ⟨℡⟩ **0300/222-0000**).

United States To find your regional passport office, check the U.S. State Department website (http://travel.state.gov/passport) or call the **National Passport Information Center** (⟨℡⟩ **877/487-2778**) for automated information.

Police Call ⟨℡⟩ **911** for emergencies. If 911 doesn't work, dial 0 (zero) for the operator and state your reason for calling.

Safety Seattle and Portland are generally very safe cities, but exercise the usual cautions. Car break-ins and bike theft are not uncommon, so do not leave items in your car in plain view, and if you're riding a bike, make certain you have a good lock and don't leave the bike unattended for long periods of time. State parks along the coast are generally very safe, but again, don't leave anything valuable in your car. This is particularly important to remember at the waterfall parking lots in the Columbia River Gorge area.

Senior Travel Don't be shy about asking for discounts, but always carry some kind of identification, such as a driver's license, that shows your date of birth. Almost all attractions, theaters, and tour companies offer senior discounts.

The U.S. National Park Service offers an **America the Beautiful–National Park and Federal Recreational Lands Pass–Senior Pass,** an annual pass that gives seniors 62 years and older entrance to all properties administered by the National Park Service—national parks, monuments, historic sites, recreation areas, and national wildlife refuges—for an annual fee of $80. The pass must be purchased in person at any NPS facility that charges an entrance fee. Besides free entry, the America the Beautiful Senior Pass also

offers a 50% discount on some federal-use fees charged for such facilities as camping, swimming, parking, boat launching, and tours. For more information, contact the **United States Geological Survey** (**USGS;** www.nps.gov/fees_passes.htm; ⟨℡⟩ **888/275-8747**), which issues the passes.

Smoking Smoking is prohibited in restaurants and bars in Washington and Oregon. Most hotels are now smoke-free as well.

Taxes The United States has no value-added tax (VAT) or other indirect tax at the national level. Every state, county, and city may levy its own local tax on all purchases, including hotel and restaurant checks and airline tickets. These taxes will not appear on price tags. Tthere's no sales tax in Oregon, but there is a 14.5% tax on hotel rooms. You may also have to pay taxes on a rental car in Portland. The sales tax in Washington is currently 6.5%, but because of complex tax laws, it may be as high as 9.5% in some municipalities. The hotel tax in Seattle is 15.6%.

Telephones Local calls require 10 digits (so include the area code). **To make calls within the United States and to Canada,** dial 1 followed by the area code and the seven-digit number. **For other international calls,** dial 011 followed by the country code, city code, and the number you are calling.

For **directory assistance** ("Information"), dial 411 for local numbers and national numbers in the U.S. and Canada. For **long-distance information,** dial 1, then the appropriate area code plus 555-1212.

Time Washington and Oregon are on Pacific Standard Time, 3 hours earlier than New York.

Daylight saving time (summer time) is in effect from 1am on the second Sunday in March to 1am on the first Sunday in November, and moves the clock 1 hour ahead of standard time.

Tipping In hotels, tip **bellhops** at least $1 per bag ($2–$3 if you have a lot of luggage) and tip the **room-cleaning staff** $1 to $2 per day (more if you've left a big mess for him or her to clean up). Tip the **doorman** or **concierge** only if he or she has provided you with some specific service (for example, calling a cab for you). Tip the **valet-parking attendant** $1 every time you get your car.

In restaurants, bars, and nightclubs, tip **service staff** and **bartenders** 15% to 20% of the check, tip **checkroom attendants** $1 per garment, and tip **valet-parking attendants** $1 per vehicle.

As for other service personnel, tip **cab drivers** 15% of the fare; tip **skycaps** at airports at least $1 per bag ($2–$3 if you have a lot of luggage); and tip **hairdressers** and **barbers** 15% to 20%.

Toilets You won't find public toilets or restrooms on the streets in Seattle or Portland, so head for cafes, hotel lobbies, bars, restaurants, museums, department stores, railway and bus stations, and gas stations. Large hotels and fast-food restaurants are often the best bet for clean facilities.

Visas Citizens from some countries must have (1) a valid passport that expires at least 6 months later than the scheduled end of their visit to the U.S.; and (2) a tourist visa. For information about U.S. Visas go to **http://travel.state.gov** and click on "Visas." Or go to one of the following websites:

Australian citizens can obtain up-to-date visa information from the **U.S. Embassy Canberra,** Moonah Place, Yarralumla, ACT 2600 (℘ **02/6214-5600**), or by checking the U.S. Diplomatic Mission's website at http://canberra.usembassy.gov/visas.html.

British subjects can obtain up-to-date visa information by calling the **U.S. Embassy Visa Information Line** (℘ **09042-450-100** from within the U.K. at £1.20 per minute; or ℘ **866-382-3589** from within the U.S. at a flat rate of $16, payable by credit card only) or by visiting the "Visas to the U.S." section of the American Embassy London's website at http://london.usembassy.gov/visas.html.

Irish citizens can obtain up-to-date visa information through the **U.S. Embassy Dublin**, 42 Elgin Rd., Ballsbridge, Dublin 4 (http://dublin.usembassy.gov; ℘ **1580-47-VISA** [8472] from within the Republic of Ireland at €2.40 per minute).

Citizens of **New Zealand** can obtain up-to-date visa information by contacting the **U.S. Embassy New Zealand,** 29 Fitzherbert Terrace, Thorndon, Wellington (http://newzealand. usembassy.gov; ℘ **644/462-6000**).

Visitor Information Contact **Travel Oregon** (www.traveloregon.com; ℘ **800/547-7842**) or **Travel Portland,** 701 SW Sixth Ave., Portland, OR 97205 (www.travelportland.com; ℘ **877/678-5263** or 503/275-9293). Larger towns along the Oregon coast have either a tourist office or a chamber of commerce that provides information; see "Visitor Information" sections in the Oregon Coast chapter for addresses. For information on **camping** in Oregon state parks, contact the **Oregon State Parks Information Center,** 725 Summer St. NE, Ste. C, Salem, OR 97301 (www.oregon.gov/oprd/parks; ℘ **800/551-6949** or 503/986-0707).

For more information about Seattle, contact **Seattle's Convention and Visitors Bureau,** 701 Pike St., Suite 800 (www.visit seattle.org; ℘ **206/461-5800**). This organization operates the **Seattle Visitor Center** inside the Washington State Convention and Trade Center, 7th Avenue and Pike Street (℃ **206/ 461-5840**); and the **Market Information Center,** Southwest Corner of 1st Avenue and Pike Street in the Pike Place Market (℃ **206/461-5840**). For additional information on other parts of Washington, contact **Washington State Tourism** (www.experience wa.com; ℃ **800/544-1800**).

Wi-Fi See "Internet & Wi-Fi," earlier in this section.

AIRLINE WEBSITES

MAJOR AIRLINES

Air Canada
www.aircanada.com

Alaska Airlines
www.alaskaair.com

American Airlines
www.aa.com

Budget Airlines
www.budgetair.com

Delta Air Lines
www.delta.com

Frontier Airlines
www.frontierairlines.com

Hawaiian Airlines
www.hawaiianair.com

JetBlue Airways
www.jetblue.com

Southwest Airlines
www.southwest.com

United Airlines
www.united.com

US Airways
www.usairways.com

Index

W

Wahclella Falls, 174–175
Walking tours
  Portland, 150
  Seattle, 88–89
Washington Park, 14, 142–143
Washington Park and Zoo
  Railway, 144
Washington Park Arboretum, 13,
  86–87
Washington State Ferries, 52–53,
  77
Waterfront, 189
The Waterfront, 50
Water taxis, Seattle, 52
Weather, Oregon coast, 178–179
Weather Machine, 141
West Coast Game Park Safari,
  230
Westlake Center, 92
Westmoreland & Eastmoreland,
  112
West Seattle, 52
Whale-watching, 4, 231
  Depoe Bay, 15, 209
  Oregon coast, 179
  Oregon Dunes, 225
Whale Watching Center, 209
Whiskey Soda Lounge, 133
White Bird, 161
White Bird Gallery, 198
White River entrance, 102
White-water rafting
  Gold Beach, 236
  Mount Rainier National Park,
   102
Wildwood Trail, 147, 151
Willamette River, 148
Willamette Valley wineries, 163–
  168
Winchester Bay, 222
Wine country, near Portland, 163–
  169
Wing Luke Asian Museum, 87
Winter sports, Mount Rainier
  National Park, 102–103
Wonder Ballroom, 160
Woodland Park Zoo & Rose
  Garden, 87–88
World Forestry Center Discovery
  Museum, 146

Y

Yachats, 26, 215–220
Yamhill National Historic District,
  109
Yaquina Bay Lighthouse, 4, 13,
  182
Yaquina Bay State Recreation
  Site, 23, 25
Yaquina Bay State Recreation
  Site, 215
Yaquina Head Interpretive Center,
  216
Yaquina Head Lighthouse, 23, 25,
  31, 182, 216

Yaquina Head Outstanding
  Natural Area, 23, 25, 31, 182,
  216
Ye Olde Curiosity Shop, 92

Accommodations

Ace Hotel (Portland), 6, 120–121
Ace Hotel (Seattle), 60–61
Alexis (Seattle), 58
The Allison Inn & Spa (Newberg),
  168
Arctic Club Hotel (Seattle), 5, 56
Bandon Dunes Golf Resort, 227
Bandon Inn, 227
The Benson (Portland), 6, 115
Best Western Inn at Face Rock
  Resort, 227
Cannery Pier Hotel (Astoria), 7,
  184–185
Cannon Beach Hotel, 194
Channel House (Depoe Bay), 7,
  207–208
Coast Cabins (Manzanita), 199
Crystal Hotel (Portland), 124
The Edgewater (Seattle), 5, 56–57
Elizabeth Street Inn (Newport),
  210
Embassy Suites (Portland), 6, 121
Ester Lee Motel (Lincoln City),
  204–205
Everett Street Guesthouse
  (Portland), 124–125
Executive Hotel Pacific (Seattle),
  5, 61
The Fireside Motel (Yachats), 216–
  217
Four Seasons Hotel (Seattle), 5,
  57
Gaslight Inn (Seattle), 62
Grand Hyatt (Seattle), 58–59
Hallmark Resort (Cannon Beach),
  194
Heceta Head Lighthouse (near
  Yachats), 7, 217
Heron Haus Bed & Breakfast
  (Portland), 121–122
Hotel Ändra (Seattle), 5, 59
Hotel deLuxe (Portland), 6, 118
Hotel Elliott (Astoria), 185–186
Hotel Five (Seattle), 62–63
Hotel Lucia (Portland), 6, 118–119
Hotel Max (Seattle), 61–62
Hotel Modera (Portland), 6, 119
Hotel Monaco (Portland), 119
Hotel Monaco (Seattle), 5, 59
Hotel Vintage (Seattle), 59–60
Hotel Vintage Plaza (Portland),
  122
Inn at Arch Rock (Depoe Bay),
  208
Inn at Cape Kiwanda (Pacific City),
  201
The Inn at Manzanita, 199
Inn @ Northrup Station (Portland),
  6, 122
Inn at the Market (Seattle), 5, 60
The Inn at Virginia Mason & The
  Baroness Hotel (Seattle), 5, 63

Ireland's Rustic Lodges & Gold
  Beach Inn (Gold Beach), 232–
  233
Jot's Resort (Gold Beach), 233
Jupiter Hotel (Portland), 125
Looking Glass Inn (Lincoln City),
  204
McMenamins Kennedy School
  (Portland), 6, 123
The Mark Spencer Hotel
  (Portland), 122–123
Newport Belle Bed & Breakfast,
  210–211
The Nines (Portland), 115, 118
Ocean Haven (Yachats), 218
The Ocean Lodge (Cannon
  Beach), 7, 194
Overleaf Lodge (Yachats), 7, 218
Pan Pacific Hotel Seattle, 57–58
Paradise Inn (Paradise), 103–104
Portland Mayor's Mansion, 6–7,
  123–124
RiverPlace Hotel (Portland), 120
Sentinel (Portland), 6–7, 120
Silver Cloud Inn Northwest
  Portland, 124
Starfish Manor Hotel (Lincoln
  City), 204
Stephanie Inn (Cannon Beach), 7,
  195
Sylvia Beach Hotel (Newport), 7,
  212
Timberline Lodge, 140, 170–171
Tu Tu' Tun Lodge (Gold Beach), 7,
  233–234
Warwick Seattle Hotel, 62
The Waves/The Argonauta Inn/
  White Heron Lodge (Cannon
  Beach), 195

Restaurants

Alloro Wine Bar (Bandon), 9, 228
Ancient Grounds (Seattle), 74
Andina (Portland), 8, 128
Anna's by the Sea (Gold Beach),
  234
April's at Nye Beach (Newport),
  212
Aqua (Seattle), 68–69
Astoria Coffeehouse & Bistro, 187
Ava Gene's (Portland), 8, 131
Baked Alaska (Astoria), 186
Bamboo Sushi (Portland), 134
Bandon Coffee Cafe, 227
Bandon Fish Market, 227–228
Bar Avignon (Portland), 131
Bastille (Seattle), 71
Bauhaus Books & Coffee (Seattle),
  74
Bay House (Lincoln City), 205
Bijou Café (Portland), 134
Blackfish Cafe (Lincoln City), 205
Bread and Ocean (Manzanita),
  199–200
BRIDGEwater Bistro (Astoria), 186
Bridgewater Fish House and
  Zebra Bar (Florence), 221
Café Campagne (Seattle), 71